DEDICATIONS

In the end, our personal achievements and professional successes are not just the result of our personal efforts but augmented by the earned (and unearned) privileges we enjoyed and the support we received from our family, friends and professional colleagues.

To my late parents Odo Claus and Simonne Léonard who sacrificed everything for the education of their children and my husband Bob Hector for his love, loyalty, and enduring support of my professional work.
LISBETH CLAUS

To my late father Lee Baker who first opened my eyes to a fulfilling career in Human Resources, who after a long and successful career in Finance transitioned to HR at Ford Motor Company, and for my immediate family who pretended to be interested in all my "HR Stories" over the years.
SCOTT BAKER

To my wonderful wife Martine and my three amazing kids: Lennart, Andreas and Astrid who are always there to support me.
PETER VERMEULEN

ACKNOWLEDGMENTS

Writing a book is a collective effort. Lisbeth, Scott and Peter draw much of their energy from the many learners they had the privilege to teach, coach and learn from during their professional careers. Inspiration and support also came from the following:

- The Willamette University MBA for Professionals, Salem cohort Class of 2020, for encouraging Lisbeth to turn her lectures, class notes, slides, and interactive exercises into a book and learning-in-a-box toolkit;
- Teaching and research assistants: Laurent Kounouho (Monterey Institute of International Studies), Simona Bucur, Kristy Cassell, Anna Sevastoyova, Himalaya Rao-Potlapally, Helen Phan-Lesti, Colin Rice and Eva Golubeva (Willamette University);
- Editor Ryan Tokeshi and graphic designer Jason Petz for their continued support of the Global Immersion Press publications.

TABLE OF CONTENTS

INTRO

LIFELONG LEARNING IS KEY TO EMPLOYABILITY

INTRO

LIFELONG LEARNING IS KEY TO EMPLOYABILITY

DESCRIPTION

The introduction describes the motivation for writing this book, the overall learning objectives and contents, and why this book is different. The introduction also guides the reader on different ways to use this book to become a more effective manager/leader.

LEARNING OBJECTIVES

Upon completion of the learning experience detailed in this book, you will be able to:

1. Diagnose and analyze individual, group, and organizational behavior from different perspectives (strategic, political, and cultural lenses) and prescribe evidence-based courses of action (**three lenses**);
2. Improve the experience of workers, drive diversity and inclusion to the next level, and nurture the organizational culture (**organizational culture, diversity, and employee experience**);
3. Identify the critical success factors of a high performing team and map, bridge, and integrate personal, cultural, and team role differences for team effectiveness (**teams and teamwork**);
4. Link motivation theories to the engagement and leadership development of individuals in organizations (**motivation & leadership**);
5. Identify opportunities to bring data, analytics, and technology to people, project, and process management (**data, analytics, and HR digitization**);
6. Identify the role of the manager in attracting, developing, and retaining talent for the global organization (**talent management**);
7. Identify and analyze the dynamics of managed change in organizations and design the steps for the successful execution of a global organizational change initiative (**innovating and managing change**);
8. Make sustainable managerial decisions that are ethical and legally compliant (**decision-making**);
9. Develop appropriate strategies for managing yourself, being managed, and managing others in traditional and progressive organizations (**management**).

GUIDING QUESTION

What are the essential capabilities (metacognitive skills) required for lifelong learning?

During her 25 years of continuous teaching at Willamette University in Salem, Oregon (2002-2020) and the Monterey Institute of International Studies in Monterey, California (1994-2001), Lisbeth has inspired and impacted more than 2000 graduate students from all corners of the earth to better navigate the global scope of management. Many of her students have stayed in contact with her and shared practical feedback on their challenges as managers and emerging leaders. Throughout the years, Lisbeth regularly updated her course content to reflect the changing world of work and the evolution of management. Alumni have shared ideas about her core teaching content and the specific skills, knowledge and tools that were most relevant and impactful as their careers blossomed and grew as part of the global workforce. While retirement is not really her 'thing', the time has come for her to prepare the customary 'last lecture' before leaving academia. Her students and alumni have urged her to share the vast knowledge and resources she has accumulated to current and future generations of emerging managers and leaders. With the help of two HR executives, trusted colleagues and friends, she has completed the daunting task of taking 25 years of course content and student/ alumni feedback and writing a book. She has worked closely with her co-authors throughout the years to ensure her university teaching reflects progressive management practices and her students are ahead of industry standards in terms of managing themselves, managing others, and being managed. In addition to a long and successful teaching career, Lisbeth leveraged her broad liberal arts education and 45-plus years of 'real work' experience as an manager, consultant and respected global HR expert. Scott is known for strategically aligning the People Team to achieve business objectives, to experiment with and implement innovative initiatives and programs, and to stretch and develop individual members of his team. Peter is a results-driven HR advisor and coach with global experience championing talent management, employee engagement, and transformational change with particular strengths in HR systems and innovation. He has held executive positions in companies such as Johnson & Johnson and Amazon. Together, the authors have a combined total of 100 years of experience in developing and coaching managers and emerging leaders and working with people of every generation—from baby boomers to millennial—in organizations. In their experience, they see three types of managers in the workplace. The first type is the emerging leader, or the person who aspires to be a genuine leader and is starting to develop their leadership style and skills. The second type is an experienced manager who has the confidence and ability to successfully manage a team and continuously aspires to improve his/ her effectiveness as a lifelong learner. The final type of manager may be a technical person who was promoted to the job of manager because the compensation was higher or they did not want to have a new boss, so they moved into the role themselves. They may have aspired to the role but now are burnt out, or they just don't care anymore and they don't have a 'way out' without taking a role with less pay and responsibility—these managers may have teams with high turnover and low employee engagement. The organization may keep them in the role for their technical, historical, or organization knowledge and connections. Our passion and dream is to support you to Be(come) an AWESOME Manager so you and the people around you may always enjoy work.

Welcome to *Be(come) an AWESOME Manager*, which will prepare you for the 'soft side' of management and managerial roles in organizations. Soft does not necessarily mean touchy-feely. On the contrary, our focus is on concepts, theories, and evidence-based knowledge as well as describing human behavior in organizations related to the broader context based on what really matters to people. We will explore human behavior with knowledge derived mainly from behavioral sciences such as psychology and sociology and try to identify patterns that are useful in managing and making decisions in organizations.[1] In his 2017 book, *The Fuzzy and the Techie*, Scott Harley argues that the humanities and social sciences (referred to as "the fuzzies") and engineering and the hard sciences (referred to as "the techies") are both required to find solutions to problems and that they are complementary set of skills that are equally necessary in today's technology-driven economy.[2]

Acquiring greater proficiency in the softer side of management to better understand human behavior will serve you well in your career and throughout your life. As your coaches, we will share with you both explicit and tacit management knowledge. In this learning journey, you will not only acquire abstract theoretical concepts (explicit book knowledge), but also learn by analyzing real-life cases and vignettes, engaging in skill practice exercises, and applying what you learn to real-life situations.

CONTENT

This book covers the expected learning outcomes required for baseline disciplinary MBA knowledge in organizational behavior. It explores the basic interpersonal dimensions of 'effective' managerial behavior and views people management from the perspective of the team, team leader, and manager. There is a long-standing debate on whether management is a 'craft'/ 'art' (in an Aristotelian sense) or a 'science' (in a Platonian sense). In fact, management is a lot about dualities and resolving them. It does not always look for the 'right' answer but for the 'best' one under the circumstances. After all, management is about human behavior that is contextual in time and place. Remember that we are dealing with a 'soft' area of human behavior that has a lot of uncertainty which we aim to avoid, eliminate, and manage appropriately! Managerial behavior can be revealed in individuals who operate as individuals and in groups mediated by managerial action within a larger organizational context leading to overall organizational performance.

This book focuses on individuals and teams in organizations, related HR management processes, organizational design, change processes, and the broader global context in which individuals, teams, and organizations operate. It emphasizes how to diagnose and analyze individual and group behavior from different perspectives (strategic, political, and cultural lenses) and various levels (micro, meso, and macro) of the organization. It contrasts the management practices of more traditional (post-modern) organizations with progressive start-ups in all sectors (for profit, non-profit, and public). The goal of this book is to enhance your knowledge of management concepts and theories one bite at a time so you can: increase organizational effectiveness in terms of better managing yourself, other individuals, and teams; understand the impact of organizational design, power and authority; improve decision-making, manage change processes, and potentially conflicting demands of various stakeholders in the organization. The outcome is to identify leading management practices and appropriate courses of managerial action in a legally compliant and ethical manner, making you a more effective manager regardless of your employment sector (private, public, or non-profit).

CENTRAL THEMES AND PERSPECTIVES

Employers want their talent not just to have a degree. They are interested in a broad range of competencies, or KSAOs (Knowledge, Skills, Abilities, and Other person-related factors). Managerial competencies often include the core knowledge base of an MBA degree. They also include intellectual agility (analytical and critical thinking skills), cultural sensitivity, ability to work on diverse teams, being engaged, innovative, and disciplined, and having a dose of emotional intelligence and resilience. This book uses an eclectic approach based on a number of interwoven central themes and perspectives:

Central themes

There are a few interconnected central themes in this book:

1. **Three levels of analysis**—namely looking at managerial issues from a micro (individual, team, and manager), meso (organization, industry) and macro (societal) point of view;
2. **Pattern recognition**—developing schemes, patterns, and heuristics to get to the underlying issues rather than surface manifestations of behavior;
3. **Managing self, managing others, and being managed**—being a good manager requires a holistic understanding of oneself;
4. **Three lenses**—viewing phenomena from three different perspectives of strategic, political, and cultural lenses.

Perspectives

We look at managerial situations from a variety of perspectives:

1. **Application to multiple sectors**—while the context may differ, management practices can be applied to for profit, non-profit, and public organizations;
2. **Integration of management disciplines**—each management discipline has something to offer;
3. **A global perspective**—we must look beyond the domestic and ethnocentric perspective in solving problems;
4. **An ethical perspective**—ethics and integrity are the foundation of sustainable management practice;
5. **Multiple thinking modes**—both data-driven and sense making driven, using deductive, inductive, and abductive thinking;
6. **Traditional and progressive organizations**—companies are somewhere on a continuum of old and new management practices.

MODULES

This book uses a modular format by focusing on interrelated Organizational Behavior (OB)/ Human Resource Management (HRM) topics.

MODULE ONE

Managing in the new world of work and the worker

This module reviews the trends (globalization, demographics, and information technology) impacting work and the worker and the ramifications of the 4th industrial revolution for work, employment, talent management, and the employee experience.

MODULE TWO

The strategic lens and organization design

This module introduces the concept of the three lenses. Then, it views management issues from the strategic lens perspective, contrasts the old and new organization, and identifies the building blocks of organizational design.

MODULE THREE

The political lens

This module looks at organizations from the perspective of political lens in terms of who defines the issues in organizations, what gives them the power and authority to define solutions, and how decision-making and negotiation outcomes can be achieved that serve both personal, stakeholder, and organizational interests.

MODULE FOUR

The cultural lens

This module analyzes organizations from the cultural lens, applying cultural concepts and theories to managerial action in organizations and analyzing how culture impacts behavior and shapes individual and group behavior. After defining culture, we review the major value dimensions that have been proposed by leading cultural theorists for national culture and how they can be used to increase one's cultural competency. The module also focuses on corporate/organizational cultures, the importance of creating organizational culture based on leadership principles, and having the ability to take the pulse of how the culture is experienced by workers.

MODULE FIVE

Equity and equality through diversity, inclusion, belonging, and support

This module explores the many dimensions of diversity, inclusion, belonging, and support (DIBs) beyond gender and race. It goes above and beyond traditional D&I initiatives by looking at its meaning in a more global context and introducing the notions of equity and intersectionality. Finally, it focuses on how to become more inclusive and the design of an organizational architecture needed to support the authenticity of the worker so that everyone can bring their 'whole' self to work.

MODULE SIX

Individuals, teams, and teamwork

After reviewing what constitutes a team, its purpose, different types of team configurations, team critical success factors, and components of team effectiveness and operation, this module explores the impact of cognitive style and cultural diversity on team effectiveness. Using the team role typology developed by Meredith Belbin, the nine team roles of a successful team are described each with their strengths and allowable weaknesses. Using the MBI-model (mapping, bridging, and integrating), predictions can be made as to the possible team dynamics issues that are likely to occur and ways to improve team effectiveness whether the team is co-located or virtual.

MODULE SEVEN

Motivation, engagement, and the employee experience

This module summarizes the various motivation theories and identifies how they contribute to either a motivating or demotivating work environment. We focus on the organizational context that affects engagement/disengagement as well as ways to improve the employee/worker experience.

MODULE EIGHT

Decision-making and behavioral economics

This module explores the way people make decisions based on bounded rationality, willpower, and self- interest (*homo sapiens*) rather than economic rationality (*homo economicus*). It further shows how unconscious biases, choice architecture, and behavioral nudging impact individuals and teams in organizations.

MODULE NINE

People analytics and HR digitization

This module focuses on the digitization of people management and evidence-based knowledge for decision making. We review the use of people analytics, data mining, sentiment analysis, and A/B testing in managerial decision making and apply design thinking to management solutions.

MODULE TEN

Managing people, projects, and processes

This module looks at value-added activities and professional skills in managing people, projects, and processes in traditional and progressive organizations with a special focus on agile management tools and techniques.

MODULE ELEVEN

Talent management reinvented

This module introduces the concept of dynamic open talent in contrast to the different HR approaches and processes that have traditionally been part of talent management. It reviews how different companies have managed the organization's physical, technological, and cultural touchpoints with workers.

MODULE TWELVE

Performance management

This module evaluates evidence-based knowledge about performance management, the new performance management paradigm adopted by high performing organizations and the managerial skills required to manage employee performance based on an employer's prevailing organizational performance culture.

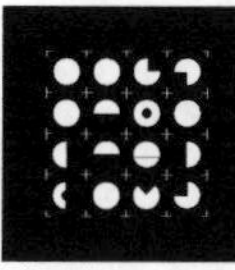

MODULE THIRTEEN

Day-to-day people management

This module spotlights developing managerial skills for traditional and progressive work environments including contingency management (based on A-B-C worker classification), crucial conversations, coaching, mentoring, teachable moments, and developing Objectives and Key Results (OKRs).

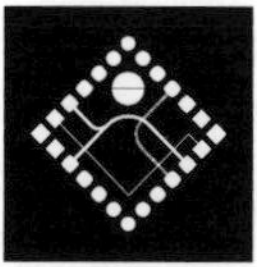

MODULE FOURTEEN

Managing change, innovating, and executing globally

This module focuses on managing change in organizations and implementing successful organization-wide global change initiatives.

MODULE FIFTEEN

Ethics, compliance, corporate social responsibility, and sustainability

This module explores ethics and compliance in decision-making and looks at corporate social responsibility and sustainability in terms of the human capital of an organization.

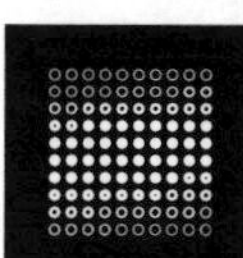

MODULE SIXTEEN

Self management, wellbeing, and preparing for career transitions

The basic premise of this module is that effectively managing others and being managed requires managing oneself and identifying one's own strengths. It explores the process of self-discovery of one's strengths and reviews ways to build a personal brand around these strengths while maintaining overall well-being and stress management. In addition, this module focuses on the development of tangible and intangible assets for career transitions.

WHY THIS BOOK IS DIFFERENT!

There are a few reasons why this book is different from other managerment books:

1. We are passionate about developing awesome managers;
2. Our content blends traditional and progressive management practices;
3. Our pedagogy is eclectic;
4. The modular approach allows for bite-size learning;
5. We provide 'learning-in-a-box' tools;
6. Our hybrid learning format is flexible;
7. We focus on developing lifelong learning skills;
8. We allow you to better understand your organization and your management style.

1. Our passion for developing AWESOME managers and organizations

Business disruption is not just a passing trend, it's the new normal. The major causes of disruption are the rapid advancement of technology and globalization allowing new or modified business models and innovations to be introduced or scaled at an ever-increasing rate and with rapidly declining costs. A company is most likely to either disrupt others or be disrupted. There is no greater reward for a manager than to develop and stretch his/her team members. Each employee is unique with their own strengths, interests, and development areas. The manager's role is to improve the effectiveness of individual employees and the team overall. Doing this provides the manager with an incredible intrinsic award that carries through the remainder of their life; not to mention that managing a high performing team of engaged employees allows the manager to accomplish more and be rewarded by compensation, responsibility, etc. Employees always remember the very good managers who developed and supported them. They also never forget the really poor managers who made their life miserable. Decide to be remembered as an AWESOME manager!

2. Blend of traditional and progressive management practices

Our role as authors is to bring you the traditional (read 'classic' management) thinking based on research, management experience, and leading practices. But throughout this book, we will also provoke you with newer and more progressive managerial practices that are being used in selected companies—many of them in the IT sector and in Silicon Valley and Pacific Northwest organizations. Throughout the book, we will *#ZigZag* between traditional and progressive managerial practices.[3]

3. Eclectic pedagogy

Our learning philosophy focuses on four specific elements:

i. Bridge the academic and practical gap by providing evidence-based knowledge as well as meaningful practical applications to diverse learners;
ii. Integrate the knowledge of different management disciplines as no preferred management discipline has the ultimate answer to complex workplace problems;
iii. Have learners gain self-knowledge to change themselves and facilitate change in teams and organizations; and
iv. Provide learners with the critical skills to acquire lifelong learning competencies.

4. Modular content for bite-size learning

Learning does not have to be overwhelming but happens best 'one bite at a time.' This book is not intended to be read as most business books—where the first chapter and last chapters tend to contain the the highlights of the book and the chapters in between dive deeper into the content. Although we connect the dots in the learning map with our central themes and perspectives, each module in this book can be seen as a stand alone subject matter. This allows you to focus on each module, take a deeper dive into the subject matter, and critically reflect upon the content and how you will apply it in your daily work life. While we recommend you follow the flow of modules in the learning map, you ultimately decide which modules are most applicable to you.

i-2. 'Learning in a box' supporting instructional materials

Preparation	Read the module	Book
	Answer the 4 critical reading questions	Book
f2f Learning	Lecturette with PowerPoint® slides	Contact Lisbeth Claus (LinkedIn)
	Interactive exercises from workbook	Contact Lisbeth Claus (LinkedIn)
Post-module activities	Answer guided reading questions	Book
	Define the key terms	Book
	Take an assessment	Book
	Answer multiple choice questions	Contact Lisbeth Claus (LinkedIn)
	Read more	Book

Lisbeth Claus LinkedIn

5. Learning-in-a-box tools

This book is designed as 'learning-in-a-box' product—a combination of everything you need to meaningfully learn the content or subject matter covered in this book. Besides the book, the box consists of a lecturette with PowerPoint® slides, interactive exercises, assessments, instructional vignettes, and a quiz for each module (see i-1). Because we believe in impacting as many managers as possible, these box components are available electronically free-of-charge by contacting Lisbeth Claus via LinkedIn. https://www.linkedin.com/in/lisbeth-claus/

6. Hybrid learning

You can use this book in a number of ways depending on your preferred learning situation and style:

i. **Self-study**—simply read a module, answer the guided reading questions, and journal answering the questions that are at the basis of lifelong learning.

ii. **Organize a weekly 'business book club' or 'lunch and learn' or 'learning' event with others**—you can do this at work or with other interested learners in your network. We suggest you plan a 15-week cycle for the entire book and debrief your self-study answers. Rotate the facilitation of the session among the members of the group.

iii. **Facilitate a 15-week class**—become a learning coach and teach/facilate a course using the book as a textbook supported with our learning-in-a-box materials.

iv. **Embed it in your company's management/ leadership development training**—Make it an integral part of the development of your managers. HRD can take the lead as initial instructors and develop people who went through the program as faciliators of future cohorts.

7. Lifelong learning

The content of this book—in other words the learning outcomes learners need to achieve—is the baseline knowledge that one must have when completing a graduate-level MBA course in management and organizational behavior. Yet the acquisition of lifelong learning skills—or the metacognitive strategies that lead to effective learning—are also of critical importance as the shelf-life of knowledge is getting shorter.

8. Understand self and organization

At the end of each module, we refer you to assessments that give you a better understanding of yourself and your organization.

LIFELONG LEARNING SKILLS

Before you delve deeper into the management content of this book, we strongly urge you to reflect on your own learning capabilities and the educational research that guides effective learning. Today, lifelong learning and development is the new currency for employability, job satisfaction, and perhaps even some form of retirement security as knowledge and skills as productive assets are a major part of your intangible assets. Therefore, we summarize key points to enhance your understanding of lifelong learning principles including levels of learning, metacognitive learning skills, learning agility, critical thinking, feedback, peak performance, and developing a growth mindset.

Levels of learning

Following Bloom's taxonomy, there are different levels of increasing learning from lower-level thinking to higher-level critical thinking (knowledge, comprehension, application, analysis, synthesis, and evaluation) of any subject matter.[4] In lifelong learning, you should aim at increasing your learning thresholds of learning based on their utility, your strengths, needs, and interests.

In their 1996 book, *The Career Architect Development Planner*, Michael M. Lombardo and Robert A. Eichinger developed the 70:20:10 model of when and where people learn best in the workplace.[5] They show that:

- 70% of the learning comes from experience typically acquired on the job;
- 20% of learning from various other forms;
- 10% from structured courses and programs.

Metacognitive learning skills

Surprisingly many people—even those with a college degree—have yet to develop metacognitive awareness or an awareness of one's own learning. Metacognitive learning skills depend on three factors:

1. Your preconceptions about how the world works;
2. Developing learning competencies—through a deep foundation of factual knowledge and understanding facts and ideas in the context of a conceptual framework;
3. Organizing knowledge in ways that facilitate retrieval and application.

You can take control of your own learning by defining learning goals and monitoring progress in terms of:

- Where am I going?
- Where am I now?
- How will I close the gap?

In their 2010 book, *How Learning Works*, Susan Ambrose et al. (2010) developed seven research-based principles of learning:[6]

1. Prior knowledge can help or hinder learnin;g
2. How you organize knowledge influences how you learn and apply what you know;
3. Your motivation determines, directs, and sustains what you learn;
4. To develop mastery, you must acquire component skills, practice integrating them, and know when to apply what you have learned;
5. Goal-directed practice coupled with targeted feedback enhances the quality of your learning;
6. Your current level of development interacts with the social, emotional, and intellectual climate of the course to impact learning;
7. To become a self-directed learner, you must learn to modify your approaches to learning.

Learning agility

Learning agility is the capacity to quickly develop effective behavior and to apply it. According to Boskma et al, as stated in their 2017 book *Agile HR*, learning agility has four components[7]:

1. **Result agility**—focusing on results, personal impact, and motivating others;
2. **People agility**—having interactions with others, open-mindedness and insight into client needs and specific context;
3. **Mental agility**—dealing with complexity, identifying patterns, and making connections; and

4. **Change agility**—embracing uncertainty, experiment, and understanding probability.

Besides that, learning agility also requires self-consciousness in terms of knowing your strengths and limitations, actively seeking feedback, and understanding your impact on others.

Critical thinking

Critical thinking often involves a series of stages and steps. The following process is fundamental to critical thinking:

1. Becoming aware that assumptions exist
2. Making assumptions explicit—that is naming what is implicit
3. Assessing the accuracy and validity of assumptions

A way to assess one's assumptions is by asking ourselves the following questions:

1. Do these assumptions make sense?
2. Do they fit reality as we have come to understand and experience it?
3. Under what conditions do they seem to hold true?
4. Under what conditions might they be false?

This is when face-to-face learning interaction comes in. While learning can effectively occur in a variety of multi-faceted and hybrid formats, ranging from ex-cathedra lectures to online resources, human interaction in the learning process adds another dimension to learning, especially in the understanding and practice of human behavior and the development of innovation.

Feedback

Feedback is vital to learning and development. Research on feedback shows it works best when it is individualized as no single approach works equally well for everyone.[8] Think about yourself and how you prefer to get feedback—directly or indirectly, right away or later on, in a social or private setting, in self-comparison manner, in person or via an app—and let others know your preferred mode of receiving feedback. But, as suggested by M. Tamra Chandler's in her 2019 book, *Feedback (and Other Dirty Words)*, we encourage you to be a feedback 'seeker' or *"an individual who proactively requests feedback from others with the intention of self-development or growth."*[9]

Peak performance

In their 2016 book, *Peak: Secrets from the Science of Expertise*, Anders Ericsson & Robert Pool discuss conditions for the development of expertise and achieving peak performance.[10] Peak performance is the result of several conditions:

- Requires a teacher who can provide specific activities;
- Involves well-defined and specific learning goals;
- Requires a person's full attention and conscious action;
- Involves feedback and modification of effort in response to that feedback;
- Produces and depends on mental representation;
- Systematically works to improve micro-aspect of each skill.

They assert that 'deliberate practice' trumps innate talent because it develops 'mental representation'—a brain schema or shortcut developed through deep experience and practices. Yet expertise takes hard and deep work (10,000 hours).

In his 2019 book, *Range: Why Generalists Triumph in a Specialized World*, David Epstein contradicts the generally accepted view presented above and argues that in most fields—especially those that are complex and unpredictable—generalists, not specialists, are primed to excel.[11] Walter Isaacson, the author of biographies of Steve Jobs and Leonardo Da Vinci, said in a 2017 interview that a genius develops by crossing disciplines, engaging in playful curiosity, finding patterns, showing continuous passion, and dealing with setbacks and failures.[12] Taking an eclectic view, both deliberate practices AND an ability to apply explicit and tacit knowledge from different disciplines and learning from failures are key ingredients to achieving excellence.

Growth mindset

When looking at why some people fail and others succeed, one of the determining factors is 'grit,' the passion and perseverance to reach long-term goals, to follow through on commitments, and sticking with it for the future. In other words, the road to success is more of a marathon than a sprint! It requires a growth mindset. In her 2007 book, *Mindset: The Psychology of Success*, Carol Dweck makes a distinction between a 'fixed mindset' (intelligence is fixed—a more deterministic view of the world) and a 'growth mindset' (intelligence can be developed—a greater trust in free will). People with a growth mindset are learnatics who have a tendency to accept challenges, consider setbacks and effort as a path to expertise, learn from feedback, and find inspiration in the success of others. These people reach increasingly higher levels of performance.[13]

This book will help you by developing your own meta-cognitive lifelong learning skills, making you rely on evidence-based knowledge, growing your learning agility, and—hopefully making you a learnatic for life! Learnatic is term that was coined by Sebastian Bailey, co-founder of Mindgym.[14] According to him, organizations must hire so-called learnatics or professionals with a strong desire for freedom, autonomy, flexibility, and an almost insatiable hunger for learning. As you read on, we welcome you to our learning ecosystem and request your feedback for continuous improvement of our product. ■

REFERENCES

1 Madsbjerg, C. (2017). Sensemaking: *The Power of the Humanities in the Age of Algorithm* (First Ed.). New York: Hachette Books.

2. Harley, S. (2013). *How to Say Anything to Anyone: A Guide to Building Business Relationships That Really Work*. Denver: Greenleaf Book Group Press.

3. Claus, L. & Arens, L. (2019). *#ZigZagHR: Why the Best HR is no Longer HR*. Silverton: Global Immersion Press.

4. Bloom, B., Krathwohl, David R., & Masia, Bertram B. (1956). *Taxonomy of educational objectives: The classification of educational goals* (First ed.). New York: David McKay Company.

5. Lombardo, M. M. & Eichinger, R. W. (1996). *The Career Architect Development Planner* (1st ed.). Minneapolis: Lominger.

6. Ambrose, S.A., Bridges, M. W., DiPietro, M., Lovett, M. C., & Norman, M.K. (2010). *How Learning Works: Seven Research-Based Principles for Smart Teaching*. San Francisco: Jossey-Bass.

7. Boskma, W., Buizer, M., van de Hoef, N, Peters, G. & Zelen, W. (2017). *Agile HR*. Amsterdam: Nubiz.

8. Torres, N. (2019). "Instant feedback hurts our performance," *Harvard Business Review*, 97(4): 32-33.

9. Chandler, M. T. & Grealish, L. D. (2019). *Feedback (and Other Dirty Words): Why We Fear It, How To Fix It*. San Francisco: Berrett-Koehler Publishers.

10. Ericsson, A. & Pool, R. (2016). *Peak: Secrets from the New Science of Expertise*. Boston: Houghton Mifflin Harcourt.

11. Epstein, D. (2019). *Range: Why Generalists Triumph in a Specialized World*. New York: Riverhead Books.

12. Isaacson, W. (2017). The Greatest Genius of Them All. October 26 (Accessed: January 5, 2018). https://www.52-insights.com/science-walter-isaacson-greatest-genius-of-them-all-innovation-interview-da-vinci-jobs/

13. Dweck, C. (2007). *Mindset: The New Psychology of Success*. New York: Ballantine Books.

14. Bailey, S. & Black, O. (2014). *Mind Gym: Achieve More by Thinking Differently*. New York: Harper Collins.

GUIDED READING QUESTIONS

1. What are the central themes of this course?

2. What different perspectives does this book take?

3. How does one develop meta-cognitive skills?

4. What is learning agility?

5. What is a growth mindset?

6. What does peak performance require?

FOLLOW-UP CRITICAL THINKING QUESTIONS

1. What is my major takeaway from this reading?

2. What do I already know about this subject?

3. What follow-up questions do I have about this?

4. How can I apply this in real life?

KEY TERMS

Abductive thinking
Bloom's taxonomy/levels of learning
Coaching
Critical thinking
Deductive thinking
Employment sector (private, public, or non-profit)
Explicit knowledge
Feedback
Fixed mindset
Fuzzies
Generalists
Grit
Growth mindset
Higher-level thinking
Human Resource Management (HRM)
Inductive thinking
Intellectual agility
Knowledge, Skills, Abilities, and Other person-related factors (KSAOs)
Leadership
Learnatic
Learning agility
Lower-level thinking
Managerial action
Mental agility
Mental representation
Mentoring
Metacognitive awareness
Metacognitive skills
Organizational Behavior (OB)
Pattern recognition
Peak performance
People agility
Progressive organizations
Rationality
Result agility
Self-directed/self-regulated learner
Self-management
Soft side of management
Specialists
Tacit knowledge
Techies
Thin data
Thick data
Traditional organizations
Unconscious biases
3 lenses (strategic, political, and cultural)
3 levels of analysis (micro, meso, and macro)
3 sectors (for profit, non-profit, and public sector)
70:20:10 model
7 principles of learning
4 components of learning agility

LEARNING ASSESSMENT

Critically reflect on the content and the different concepts in this module and rate your own competency using the assessment scale.

Competency	I never heard of it	I heard of it but have limited knowledge of it	I can reasonably explain it to others	I have used it, done it, applied it
Level of learning	0	1	2	3
Metacognitive learning skills	0	1	2	3
Learning ability	0	1	2	3
Critical thinking	0	1	2	3
Feedback	0	1	2	3
Peak performance	0	1	2	3
Growth mindset	0	1	2	3

VIGNETTE

SIEMENS EMPOWERS PEOPLE TO OWN THEIR CAREER[1]

Founded in Berlin, Germany in 1847, Siemens has evolved over time to become a global powerhouse in areas of electrification, automation, and digitization. The company is also a leading supplier of systems for power generation and transmission in to medical diagnosis equipment. With more than 351,000 employees worldwide, the company has five generations of people working together. The aspirations of this diverse group of workers are changing over their lifetime (whether they focus on career vs. work life balance) and the company understands that organizations need very flexible models and a range of options to meet the expectations of the workforce on their career journey. As a result, Siemens is focused on lifelong learning and development and introduced a number of initiatives to promote skills assessment, internal mobility, and job tagging so people are empowered to own their career. Since no one can exactly know how the world will look like in the future, Siemens believes they must empower the people to find all the digital learning solutions and scale it up to the organization to make it more visible.

The company provides, on a global basis, the opportunity for a self-assessment of one's strengths using a commercially available digital strength assessment instrument. Employees are asked whether they are interested in getting a digital version of their strengths. The assessment is private, and HR is not involved. The company urges its employees to own their career and empowers them with flexible career tools to match their skills and experience with internal job opportunities. In terms of skills assessment, employees can voluntarily create meaningful profiles of their skills and experiences through an in-house LinkedIn. They can update additional skills, wishes, questions, and projects they would not necessarily share externally on their profiles. There is full transparency on the job availabilities for all levels all over the world. Besides creating full transparency on jobs within their internal job market, Siemens introduces many other career innovations such as enabling employees to proactively show their interest in a certain job position through internal mobility opportunities and job tagging. An employee who sees a position they like and want to be considered as a candidate in the future can tag themselves to the person currently holding the job. While 50% of the taggers don't quite understand what the position entails, the other half does and are real succession material. HR is not involved as it is a personal channel between the manager and tagger. It is the employee's responsibility to treat the interaction professionally.

The company invests as much as 600 million Euros a year in learning and is centered on trying and exploring, continuous learning, and development owned by the employee. Empowering people to assess their own skills and matching individuals with internal jobs have many intended and unintended outcomes for Siemens. In addition to facilitating internal career mobility, the development tools help motivate the talent about the possibilities; make it easier to have careers between different divisions; have a positive impact on diversity (especially women); and make succession planning more fluid.

Robert Neuhauser, EVP and Global Head of People and Leadership at Siemens in Munich, Germany, is a firm proponent of "*taking HR out as the middle person between the employee and their career. Instead, give employees flexible career tools and remove the barriers that prevents them to own their career.*"

REFERENCES

1. This vignette was prepared by Professor Lisbeth Claus for the sole purpose of illustrating a global HR practice for instructional objectives. Global HR in Action © 2019, Global Immersion Press, All Rights Reserved.

GUIDED READING QUESTIONS

1. How does Siemens allow its employees to "own" their career?
2. What steps can (and should) you take to be in charge of your own career?

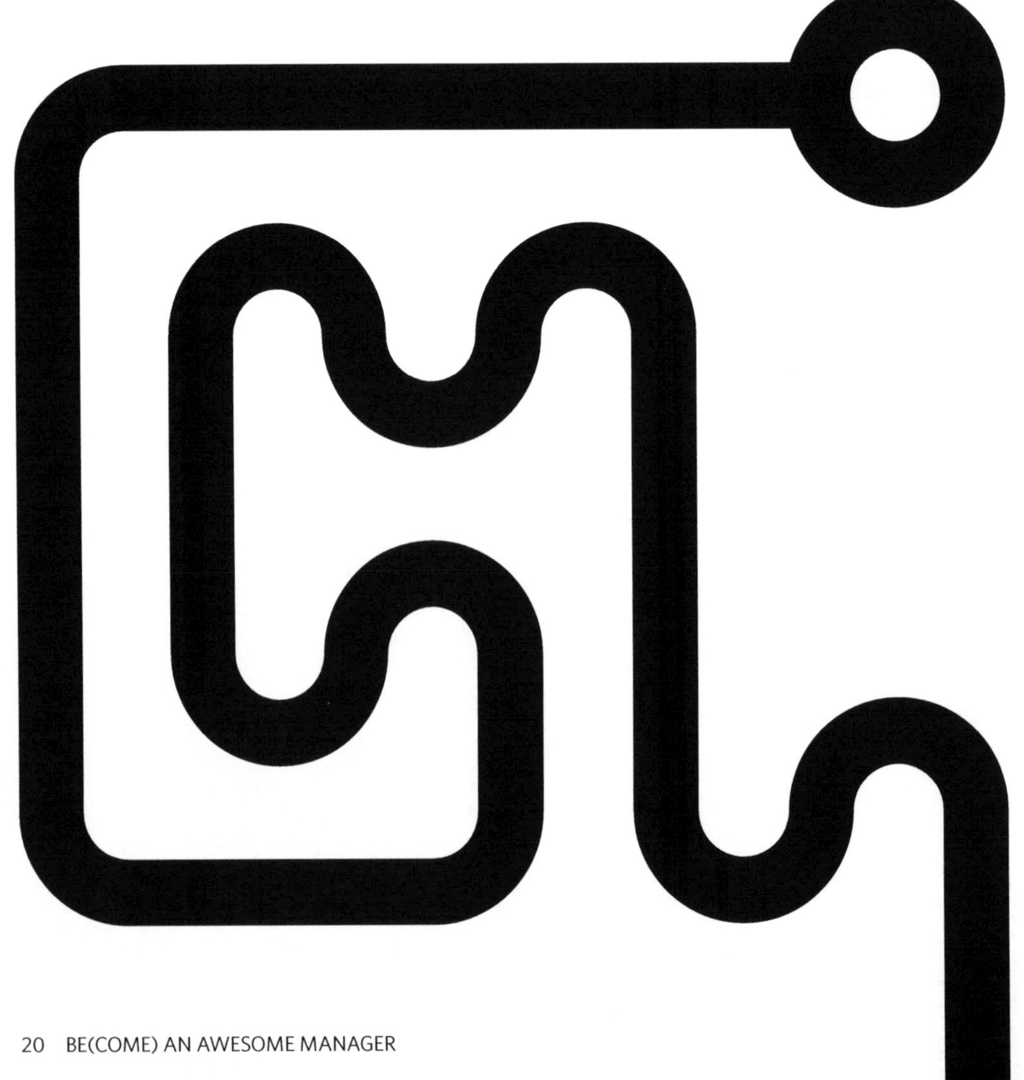

MODULE ONE

MANAGING IN THE NEW WORLD OF WORK AND THE WORKER

MODULE ONE

MANAGING IN THE NEW WORLD OF WORK AND THE WORKER

DESCRIPTION

This module reviews the trends (globalization, demographics, and information technology) impacting work and the worker and the ramifications for employment, talent management, and the talent experience. It introduces the notion of 'dynamic open talent' in the broader context of managing talent in the era of the 4th industrial revolution.[1]

LEARNING OBJECTIVES

Upon completing the learning experience, you will be able to:

- Describe the key drivers of the 4th industrial revolution
- Describe the dimensions of a dynamic open talent strategy
- Discuss the ramifications of the new world of work for the employer, the worker, and the society

GUIDING QUESTION

Will artificial intelligence eventually take away my job?

SENTHIL started as a junior HR professional in Hyderabad, India at Amazon. He is somewhat excited and worried at the same time about the launch of HR chatbots in India and the impact this might have on his job. Highly trained chatbots provide instant, accurate responses to common HR queries. Meanwhile, with chatbots handling rote, simplistic requests, HR professionals are asked to step up and provide more strategic HR support to their customers. Senthil is excited to work on more strategic projects but is also worried about the skillset needed to be successful.

GREGORY, a retail operator at Walmart enrolled himself in a corporate sponsored educational and reskilling program. The company allowed him to enroll in online degree programs for only $1 a day at three different universities. Alex hopes to complete his online degree in cybersecurity over the next 12 months.

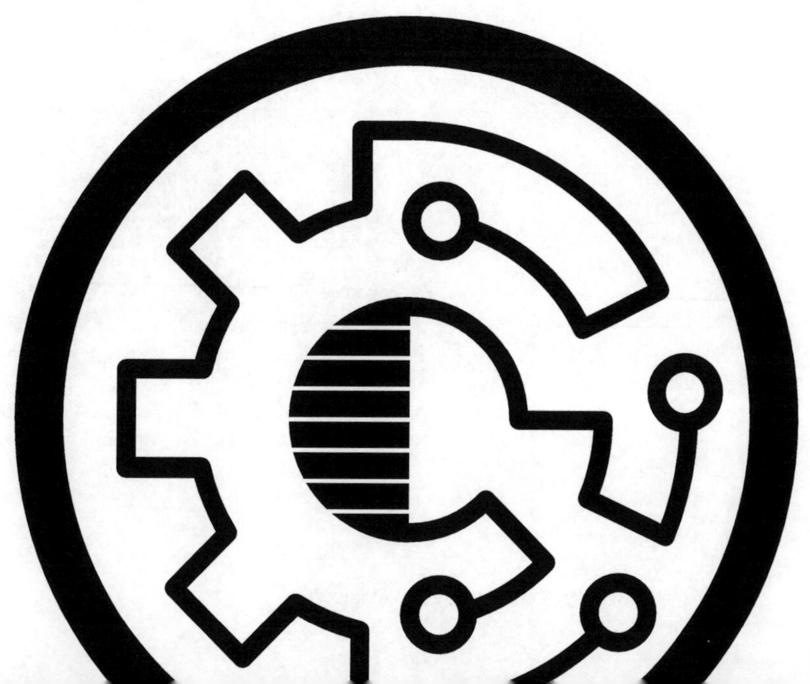

#Imagine... a future worker applies for a job without a resumé or curriculum vitae and being hired without having been prior interviewed by a person. Smart algorithms predict who is likely to leave your company and when; chatbots answer HR generalist questions; employees have unlimited paid time off and total flexibility as to when and where they work! No need for imagination—the future is already here for some progressive companies!

In the last 200 years, employers have shifted their focus a few times with regard to their employees. During the first industrial revolution, the focus was on utility: what do people need to do their job? During the second industrial revolution, the focus shifted to productivity: what do people need to do their work as efficiently as possible? During the third industrial revolution, the attention went to engagement: how can people become more engaged at work so productivity increases and employees gain? We have now landed in the fourth industrial revolution and everything is focused on the employee experience.[2]

Today, engagement is all about the employee experience, or in other words: how we create the ultimate experience for our employees (and workers) and how we set up the workplace and nurture the optimal work environment so employees want to show up and make an effective contribution. It is rather sobering that companies invest a lot of time, money, and energy in the creation of the ultimate (external) customer experience, but do not seem to translate that to the internal (customer) experience of their employees. That's not only unfortunate, but also has far reaching consequences for operating results: engagement and productivity are becoming relatively low and workers are disengaging and dropping out either mentally, physically, or both. In this module, we establish the current challenges in the modern employment landscape

1-1. Drivers of 4th Industrial Revolution

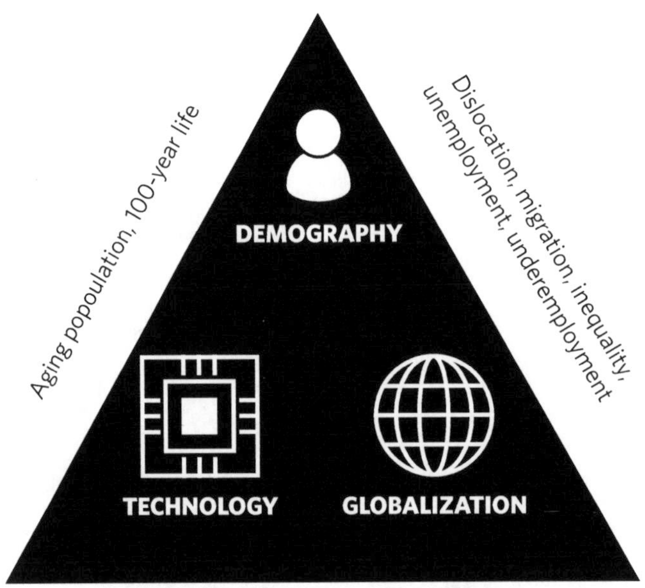

WORK AND THE WORKER IN THE 4TH INDUSTRIAL REVOLUTION

The driving forces of what has been labeled the 4th industrial revolution we're currently experiencing are demography, technology, and globalization. They are coming together and creating a perfect storm in the world of work and the worker (see 1-1).

Demography

The world's population is dramatically changing in terms of both life expectancy and its multicultural composition. A person born in 1960 could, on average, expect to live to the age of 52 (with a high of 84 years in Japan and a low of 49 in Swaziland). Today, life expectancy in the West is around 72 years of age.[3] This trend, driven mainly by declines in infant mortality and chronic diseases of middle and older ages, is expected not only to continue, but also to increase even more dramatically and to make the '100-year life' a reality for more than 50% of children born in the West today.[4] This upward trend in multigenerational workforce teams comes hand-in-hand with an increase in the diversity of the workforce.[5] Companies are increasingly recognizing the need for the workplace to meet the needs of people of all backgrounds to mirror their customer base.

People live longer and work longer, or that is at least the assumption. This does not seem to happen as much in European countries compared to the United States. The fact that Europeans want to leave the workforce as quickly as possible and still continue to leave in droves is in sharp contrast with the work ethic in the United States, where baby boomers who lose their jobs in their fifties and sixties simply start all over again, often in lower paying jobs. This is partially because American society and other countries do not have a social safety net compared to most European countries. Besides, among most baby boomers in the U.S., a *#YesWeCan* (or else *#WeHaveNoChoice*) mentality in work—especially knowledge work—is synonymous with having a meaningful life. Whereas in Europe, people and politicians engage in endless debates and negotiations about early retirement for a long list of heavy occupations. This also forces us to think differently about careers as being more non-linear with workers taking a gap year, changing careers, starting their own company, going back to school, etc.

Currently, there are four generations working together on the floor. This represents great challenges according to Lynda Gratton and Adam Scott's 2016 book, *The 100-Year Life: Living and Working in an Age of Longevity*, which points out that one needs more money when one lives longer. This means working longer, or living with less, or saving more and working longer than we really want or are able.[6]

> *DEMOGRAPHY = Diversity is needed, different generations working together, people working longer!*

Technology

Three key elements of technology, artificial intelligence (circa 1950s); machine learning (1980s to 2010); and deep learning (2016-today), have changed work dramatically.[7] Artificial intelligence will continue to replace work previously done by people with robots and computers. Jobs will increasingly concentrate at opposite ends of the high-low spectrum as routine cognitive and manual labor skills are supplanted with technology. By now, information technology has led to a 'gig economy,' where workers take freelance and short-term contracts in lieu of permanent jobs.

Big data and the Internet of Things (IoT) are the new gold, not just in companies, but also in daily life where digital developments succeed each other at a dizzying tempo. Technology, especially developments in artificial intelligence, machine learning, and deep learning, has an unmistakable impact on work and will have an increasing impact in the future. On one hand, many risky jobs are being replaced by robots and computers; it is an economic reality that employers want to get work done in the most cost efficient manner. Computers, robots, and machines don't get tired, don't get sick, don't get pregnant, and don't take vacations. They make rational decisions based on algorithms and are, therefore, less susceptible to the unconscious biases of people. On the other hand, many tasks will still need to be done by people. Think about anything that has to do with empathy, creativity, and innovation. The fact that people will be free from certain tasks suggests HR will get more time to focus on the bridge function between employee expectations and organizational objectives. This function is a lot more strategic than the transactional HR functions absorb time every day.

TECHNOLOGY = Brave new digital world, robots on the rise

Globalization

In the wake of Brexit, recent election results worldwide, and trade wars, it can be argued that the tensions surrounding globalization are more acute than ever. While the turn of the 21st century brought a unified global focus on working together across nations, the current world context is one of autocratic leaders and a culture of individualization that has only served to highlight the dark side of globalism. The threat of terrorism, forced migration, unemployment, underemployment, and growing inequality are all redefining globalism itself. Because of globalization, labor has become more accessible and cheaper across borders; employers must now compete with companies in countries where taxation and social security are completely different. In Europe and the U.S., the pendulum has swung completely in the other direction toward protectionism and anti-globalization (Brexit, U.S. trade negotiations). Work may have become more accessible and cheaper, but it is unfortunately coupled with growing inequality, increasing gap between the haves and have nots, and growing un(der)employment, especially among younger workers. This creates big challenges for HR in terms of legal regulations in different countries, localization of HR practices, and growing diversity of teams in the workplace. Employers have difficulty finding employees with the right competencies and engagement. In the U.S. for example, Amazon is looking for 500,000(!) extra workers to support its expansion over the next five years. For HR, this means talent management must cross the borders and use different recruiting and selection methods to fill its vacancies.

GLOBALIZATION = Think global, act local

THE TALENT DISRUPTION CHALLENGES

The impact of the 4th industrial revolution is dramatic for workers. Demographic pressures from the marked increases in life expectancy and growing demands for diversity and inclusion, coupled with mass migration, the disconnect of work from a physical site, and the supplanting of human work by artificial intelligence—all within the context of a global economic downturn and failing social support systems—has created an increasingly fearful, overwhelmed, and disengaged worker terrified of "having to work forever" in less secure independent contract gigs.[8] The constant need to reinvent themselves and remain resilient as they face career changes from disruptions and setbacks leaves many of today's global workers unprepared to survive the new world of work[9] and increasingly seeking freedom from the stifling corporate job.

As globalization, technology, and demographic change brought forth by the 4th industrial revolution dramatically shifts the worker and the workplace, the talent management role of global HR must also rapidly evolve. Since the beginning of modern management practices, HR, as we know it, has changed alongside its external context, evolving first from personnel management to strategic talent management with *The War for Talent'* as its roadmap.[10] HR's talent management focus during this incarnation was one of global-local strategies designed to leverage people to the advantage of the organization. Through these strategic choices and operational HR activities focused on putting the right people in the right job at the right time, and at the right cost,[11] talent management was built on a foundation of tools from other management disciplines including marketing (i.e., employee value proposition and employer branding),[12] management science (i.e., identifying pivotal talent and efficiency, effectiveness, and impact of HR),[13] and operations management (i.e., reducing the talent uncertainties on the demand and supply side of labor).[14] These dramatic changes in the nature of work and the worker are forcing HR to become strategic since they can no longer hide behind transactional HR. Will HR embrace or resist this challenge? What is the implication for HR and the business? Most certainly, other functions may force HR to change, but what will the impact be?

DISRUPTION

According to Clayton Christensen, disruption is "a process by which a product or service takes root initially in simple applications at the bottom of the market and then relentlessly moves up market, eventually displacing established competitors."[15] Christensen talks about *disruptive innovation* because business models enabled by technology can create disruptive impact. Can you think of business models that have been disrupted by innovation beyond Uber and AirBnB?

There are many questions today that are a part of the disruption debate: Who is most likely to be affected? How will we put humans 'back to work'? Does AI increase (human) productivity? How open and competitive are the key players (winner-takes-all IT companies)? What is the role of government? Are social media improving our social interactions? Is the privacy loss warranted? What can people do to deal with the threat of disruption of their job? What does this new world of work and the worker—that is becoming the new normal—mean for the talent, the employer, and the society? In this book, we look at the implications of the changing environment on management practices and the different stakeholders of the enterprise.

Thomas H. Davenport and Julia Kirby, in a 2015 *Harvard Business Review* article, talk about the 'augmentation' and suggest different strategies people can take in view of automation.[16]

The strategies to augment are:

1. **Step up**—to higher intellectual grounds, which requires more big-picture thinking and a higher level of abstraction compared to computers;
2. **Step aside**—using mental strengths that aren't purely cognitive but draw on multiple disciplines (interpersonal and intrapersonal intelligences);
3. **Step in**—modify and monitor the work of computers, make it better and ensure computers are doing a good job;
4. **Step narrowly**—find a specialty within your profession that would not be economical to automate;
5. **Step forward**—bring about the next level of encroachment of machines and find an opportunity for automation.

While the external environment impacts organizations and can disrupt them, the 'inside' story is just as important. "*It's the story of building the business, expanding and retaining a quality workforce, strengthening the culture, upgrading the systems, learning from experience, adapting the business model, holding down costs, and mobilizing the people to carry it out perfectly, again and again.*" This is the central theme of a 2016 book, The Founder's Mentality, by Chris Zook and James Allen.[17] They describe the need to maintain a founder's mentality consisting of three main traits: an insurgent's mission, an owner's mindset, and an obsession with the front line. They argue that companies, as they grow larger, lose the founder's mentality and must eventually overcome three internal yet predictable crises of growth during their life cycle:

Overload—the crisis of high growth;
Stallout—the crisis of low or slowing growth;
Freefall—the crisis of obsolescence and decline.

While external disruption may trigger a freefall, the root cause is often internal as the company did not adapt fast enough and "*did not have a second-generation engine for its business ready to go when the first-generation engine became obsolete*" through external turbulence.[18]

TOWARD A NEW DYNAMIC OPEN TALENT MARKET APPROACH

Despite the increased use of robotization and artificial intelligence in the production of work, having the requisite talent remains the driver of growth and innovation for global companies. For an organization to get a comparative advantage through talent today, it requires a different strategic and operational approach which radically changes how talent is viewed, attracted, and retained. Current talent management must move beyond the war for talent. The current battle is about how to engage and retain valuable employees by offering them compelling experiences at work.[19] All signs for the future of talent management point to the development of a dynamic open talent market and a re-imagination of the talent strategy for both the organization and the talent.

According to a 2019 White Paper by Lisbeth Claus and Danielle Monaghan, *Dynamic Open Talent* (DOT) has various dimensions—a portfolio of talent, flexibility, work agility, and boundaryless talent fluidity enabled by technology and data. In a reinvented HR, a closed talent system is replaced by a more dynamic and open market approach.[20] For example, Amazon invests heavily in apps and technology to support this more dynamic and open market approach with an aim to recruit the talent wherever the talent resides and whenever the business need is there. Such a new strategic talent management approach—embraced today by only handful of companies—is imperative because of the 4th industrial revolution and the short and long-term changes to the economic outlook of the global workforce. The digital age has created a 'new normal,' affecting the pool of talent markets across the globe. Longer living, technology, and globalization allows employers to choose from a vast variety of talent wherever the talent resides, whenever they are available, and whenever employers need them. The global workforce supply and demand of labor is projected to be at crisis levels by 2030, meaning 'top' talent is becoming scarce and is being employed at multiple companies at once. Digitization has fundamentally changed the structure of work and the worker. Uberization of talent and the workforce is driven by three converging factors of the digital age: companies need more agility and flexibility, the younger generation thinks entrepreneurially, and digital tools facilitate the connection between companies and talents. The fundamental forces driving change in the future of work requires different organizations and approaches to strategy, talent, and work.

Two individual worker characteristics impact talent management, the skill level of the worker and the new expectations of the workforce. High-skilled labor usually enjoys a skill premium with either deep (T-shaped) or broad (M-shaped) knowledge and is poised for greater employability able to augment artificial intelligence. However, the rest of the labor continuum faces big problems. Low-skilled labor is bound by minimum wage requirements and is likely to be eliminated and disrupted by new technologies. Medium-skilled talent is vulnerable to becoming irrelevant unless they continue upgrading their skills through lifelong learning. The changing expectations of the workforce are largely attributed to millennials and is defined by culture, passion, meaning, and collaboration. Millennials also have a different value system, mainly seeking autonomy, technology, and flexibility.

An open talent economy, based on the concept of an 'open economy,' is a contender to be a new talent management paradigm that will lay the groundwork for the dynamic open talent market concept. Dynamic open talent should be viewed as an ecosystem with five interrelated dimensions (portfolio of talent, flexibility, work agility, talent fluidity, and technology/data-enabled).

1. **Portfolio of talent**—hiring talent on the talent continuum;
2. **Flexibility**—letting people work anytime from anywhere;
3. **Work agility**—focusing on assignments and roles rather than job descriptions;
4. **Talent fluidity**—letting employees cross both internal and external boundaries;

5. **Technology and data-enabled**—utilizing data, tools, and integrated platforms for people management.

Talent expects a new social contract in response to the changing socio-political and legal environments facilitating the dynamic open talent market. The old social contract of the 3rd industrial revolution focused on commitment and stability. However, this contract has slowly become irrelevant. Employees expect employers to act as a social enterprise, which leads to a dynamic open talent market that needs to be managed and reconciled by various stakeholders.

How Do You Shape Your Future?

If you have talent, you 'own your career' and are responsible for creating current, future, and long-term value for yourself (the fire person) and others ('not unto ourselves are we born').

In his 2017 book, *The Day after Tomorrow*, Peter Hinssen looks at the time and effort we put in to create value and the return we get from it. We tend to spend 93% of our energy on today, 7% on tomorrow and 0% on the day after tomorrow. Yet, the current value, future value, and long-term value of these investments in terms of value creation is exactly the opposite.[21] In a 2019 blog with a provocative title, Learning Is The New Pension, Heather E. McGowan states that we need to shift "*from learning in order to work, to working in order to learn continuously*" and that "*learning is the new future value that we all—individual and organizations—need to create today for tomorrow.*" She suggests that to stay current, we should spend an hour a day learning.[22] Think about the following: how much time and effort will you put in your learning to create short-term current value (enhance your current skills or upskilling), how much for future value (i.e., reskilling), and for long-term value (the next 50 years of your work/life)? What activities can you undertake today to build value for the future? ▮

REFERENCES

1 This module is based on previous publications: Claus, L. & Baker, S. (2018). The Global HR Stack: External and Internal Tools and Methodologies Impacting HR. Pp. 35-63 in Claus. L. (ed.), *Global HR Practitioner Handbook*, volume 4. Silverton: Global Immersion Press; Claus, L. & Arens, L. (2019). *#ZigZagHR: Why the Best HR is no Longer HR*. Silverton: Global Immersion Press; Claus, L. & Monaghan, D. (2019) Dynamic Open Talent. Global HR Consortium/HR Roundtable.

2 Morgan, J. (2014). *The Future of Work: Attract New Talent, Build Better Leaders, and Create a Competitive Organization*. New York: John Wiley & Sons.

3 Life Expectancy at Birth, Total (Years), Worldbank 2010. (Accessed: July 11, 2019). http://data.worldbank.org/indicator/SP.DYN.LE00.IN

4 Gratton, L. & Scott, A. (2016). *The 100-Year Life: Living and Working in an Age of Longevity*. London: Bloomsbury Publishing.

5 Grubb, V. (2017). *Clash of the Generations: Managing the New Workplace Reality*. Hoboken, New Jersey: John Wiley & Sons.

6 Gratton, L. & Scott, A. (2016). *The 100-Year Life: Living and Working in an Age of Longevity*. London: Bloomsbury Publishing.

7 Copeland, M. (2016). *What is the difference between artificial intelligence, machine learning and deep learning?* July 29 (Accessed: January, 2019). https://blogs.nvidia.com/blog/2016/07/29/whats-difference-artificial-intelligence-machine-learning-deep-learning-ai/

8 P.N. Unankar, S. Paul & W. Yasmeen (2014). *The overwhelmed employee – Simplify the work environment*. Global Human Capital Trends 2014 – Engaging the 21st-century workforce pp. 97-102. Accessed June 15, 2017. https://www2.deloitte.com/au/en/pages/human-capital/articles/overwhelmed-employee-simplifyenvironment. html

9 Gratton, L. & Scott, A. (2016). *The 100-Year Life: Living and Working in an Age of Longevity*. London: Bloomsbury Publishing.

10 Michaels, E., Handfield-Jones, H., & Axelrod, B. (2001). *The War for Talent*. Boston: Harvard Business Press.

11 Claus, L. (2013). Global Talent Management: An Overview. Pp.117-137 in L. Claus (ed.), *Global HR Practitioner Handbook*, volume 1. Silverton: Global Immersion Press.

12 Michaels, E., Handfield-Jones, H., & Axelrod, B. (2001). *The War for Talent*. Boston: Harvard Business Press.

13 Boudreau, J., & Ramstad, P. (2007). *Beyond HR: The New Science of Human Capital*. Boston: Harvard Business School Press.

14 Cappelli, P. (2007). "Talent Management for the Twenty-First Century," *Harvard Business Review*, 86(3), 74-38.

15 Christensen, C (2017). *Disruptive Innovation*. (Accessed: June 15, 2017). http://claytonchristensen.com/key-concepts/

16 Davenport, T. & Kirby, J. (2015). "Beyond Automation," *Harvard Business Review*, 93(6): 59-65.

17 Zook, C. & Allen, J. (2016). *The Founder's Mentality: How to Overcome the Predictable Crises of Growth*. Boston: Harvard Business Review Press, p. 2.

18 Ibid. p. 56.

19 Morgan, J. (2017) *The Employee Experience Advantage: How to Win the War for Talent by Giving Employees the Workspaces they Want, the Tools they Need, and a Culture they Can Celebrate*. New York: John Wiley & Sons.

20 Claus, L. & Monaghan, D. (2019) *Dynamic Open Talent*. Global HR Consortium/IT Roundtable.

21 Hinssen, P. (2017). *The Day After Tomorrow*: Hoe Overleven in Tijden van Radicale Innovatie. Leuven: Van Duuren Management.

22 Mc Gowan, H.E. (2019). *Learning Is The New Pension*. October 29. (Accessed: October 29, 2019). https://www.linkedin.com/posts/heathermcgowan_learning-is-the-new-pension-activity-6595023809307308032-qOBK

GUIDED READING QUESTIONS

1. What are the drivers of the 4th industrial revolution?

2. How is the 4th industrial revolution impacting work and the worker?

3. How can automation be augmented by people?

4. What is a founder's mentality?

5. Discuss the "talent continuum" dimension of the DOT approach and what it means for the talent, the employer, and the society.

6. Discuss the "talent flexibility" dimension of the DOT approach and what it means for the talent, the employer, and the society.

7. Discuss the "talent fluidity" dimension of the DOT approach and what it means for the talent, the employer, and the society.

8. Discuss the "work agility" dimension of the DOT approach and what it means for the talent, the employer, and the society.

9. How is the DOT approach enabled by technology and data?

10. How do I prepare myself to own my career in this new context of work and the worker?

FOLLOW-UP CRITICAL THINKING QUESTIONS

1. What is my major takeaway from this reading?

2. What do I already know about this subject?

3. What follow-up questions do I have about this?

4. How can I apply this in real life?

KEY TERMS

Artificial intelligence
Automation
Chatbot
Demography
Digitization
Disruption
Dynamic open talent
Founder's mindset
Freefall crisis
Globalization
Machine learning
M-shaped knowledge
Overload crisis
Robotization
Stallout crisis
Step aside
Step forward
Step in
Step narrowly
Step up
Talent continuum
Talent fluidity
Talent portfolio
Technology
T-shaped knowledge
Uberization
Work agility

LEARNING ASSESSMENT

Critically reflect on the content and the different concepts in this module and rate your own competency using the assessment scale.

Competency	I never heard of it	I heard of it but have limited knowledge of it	I can reasonably explain it to others	I have used it, done it, applied it
Artificial intelligence	0	1	2	3
Augmentations	0	1	2	3
Digitization of HR	0	1	2	3
Dynamic open talent	0	1	2	3
Founder's mentality	0	1	2	3

MODULAR-SPECIFIC ASSESSMENT

The Founder's Mentality® Diagnostic Survey

This two-page assessment gauges whether your organization has a Founder's Mentality in terms of insurgency, front-line obsession, and owner's mindset.

Source: Zook, C. and Allen, J. (2016). *The Founder's Mentality. How to Overcome Predictable Crises of Growth.* Boston, MA: Harvard Business Review Press, pp. 35-36.https://media.bain.com/founders-mentality/

VIGNETTE

MBA DISRUPTION — EXTERNAL AND INTERNAL FACTORS OF A FREEFALL[1]

The brick-and-mortar U.S. MBA degree is experiencing a freefall with double digit declines in applications and enrollments. The decline is across the board and it is predicted that 10% to 20% of the top 100 MBA. programs in the U.S. will likely close in the next few years, with even greater fallout among second and third-tier schools.[2] Business school administrators attribute a combination of external factors to this decline and crisis in business education: a strong U.S. economy keeping people on the job, U.S. anti-immigration and visa policies, the high price of the degree, opportunity cost of returning to school, overseas competition, and the proliferation on online degrees and newer technology platforms delivering quality education at a lower cost.

Traditional full-time, brick-and-mortar MBA programs have been shutting down at an alarming rate. As Chris Zook and James Allen argue in their 2016 book, *The Founder's Mentality*, the free fall crisis is the most existentially threatening for a company as it has stopped growing in its core and its business model that used to work so well in the past, suddenly seems no longer viable in a changing market. While at first the causes of the freefall appear to be external, the root cause is internal and the company did not adapt fast enough when its core business became obsolete.[3] One would expect that a management faculty preparing future leaders has the internal knowledge to turnaround its own disrupted business model.

Critics of management education have argued that business schools have failed to grapple with technological disruption and relevance of the traditional management education curriculum (often a few years behind industry standards) is being challenged. Priorities must focus on getting the costs of the MBA under control (resulting in a reduction of student loan amounts); embrace technology, and provide hybrid degrees that mix face-to-face classroom soft-skill experience with digital delivery; and get better at teaching technology and the technical skills to deal with artificial intelligence and data analytics.[4]

How are the surviving business schools responding to this disruption? How can business schools rescue themselves and deal with the paradox that while learning is the new currency for employability, the knowledge they sell is for the most part available and accessible for free on the Internet. Rescuing the MBA program from free fall requires a real reinvention at multiple levels.

New leadership team—business school leaders must rebuild the future rather than resurrecting the past. The new leader is someone who can promote a founder's mentality among faculty, administration and staff. Such a Dean may likely have to come from outside of academia!

New business model—business schools must reengineer their operations through digitization; initiate drastic cost reductions, find new sources of revenue and financing methods, collaborate with 3rd party partners, and divest some of its business lines.

New purpose—business schools must evolve toward critically including the role of business in society, its purpose and value, and new forms of social capitalism including all stakeholders and sustainability in a global environment. This requires redefining the mission and vision of management education.

New learner experiences—business schools must reevaluate the student experience from prospective student to alumni and focusing efforts on improving the user experience resulting in increased flexibility, customizable curricular paths, learner agility, and loyalty.

New teaching methods—faculty must move away from traditional 'slide and text' lectures—even abandon the traditional PPT lectures—and be more interactive in their pedagogy and focus on teaching more effectively using a combination of online and hybrid teaching methods.

New content—in line with a new purpose of business, faculty must expand what they teach from traditional to progressive practices; stockholder to stakeholder, critical thinking, analytical and professional skills with longer shelf-life, and close the academic-practice knowledge gap.

New learning experiences—business schools must be agile and experiment with new learning experiences in a variety of forms (degree and non-degree learning combinations) and timeframes (from batches to full degrees), test their viability, and then be able to scale rapidly. This will require agile academics where learning (and teaching) is not necessarily coinciding with current academic trimester or semester calendars.

New customers—as learning becomes a life-long endeavor, the university student must span over different generations and include diverse groups of customers. Business schools must be able to provide customized user experiences to a mosaic of learning needs and diverse backgrounds of talent.

New capability—while dealing with freefall, business school must still innovate and devote enough energy investing in a new capability to grow over the long term.

REFERENCES

1. This vignette was prepared by Professor Lisbeth Claus for the sole purpose of illustrating a global HR practice for instructional objectives. Global HR in Action © 2019, Global Immersion Press, All Rights Reserved.
2. Byrne, J. (2019). "It's official: the M.B.A. Degree is in Crisis. August 20. (Accessed: December 5, 2019). https://www.forbes.com/sites/poetsandquants/2019/08/20/its-official-the-mba-degree-is-in-crisis/#4e4e4a0d52df;
3. Zook, C. & Allen, J. (2016). *The Founder's Mentality. How to Overcome Predictable Crises of Growth*. Boston, MA: Harvard Business Review Press.
4. The MBA disrupted. *The Economist*, November 2, 2019, p. 14.

GUIDED READING QUESTIONS

1. For working professionals: What are your management learning goals and how can business schools support them?
2. For MBA students: What can business schools do to improve your student experience?

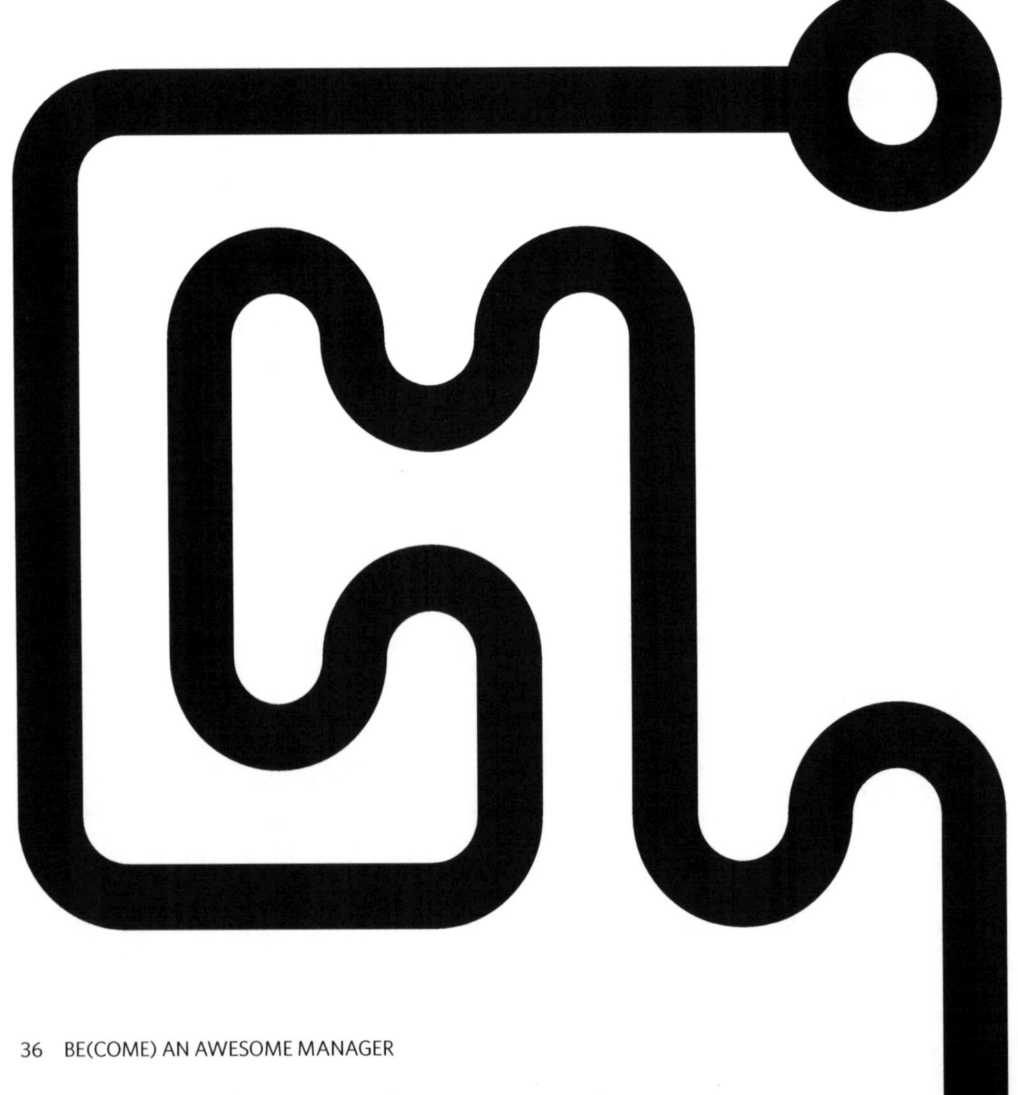

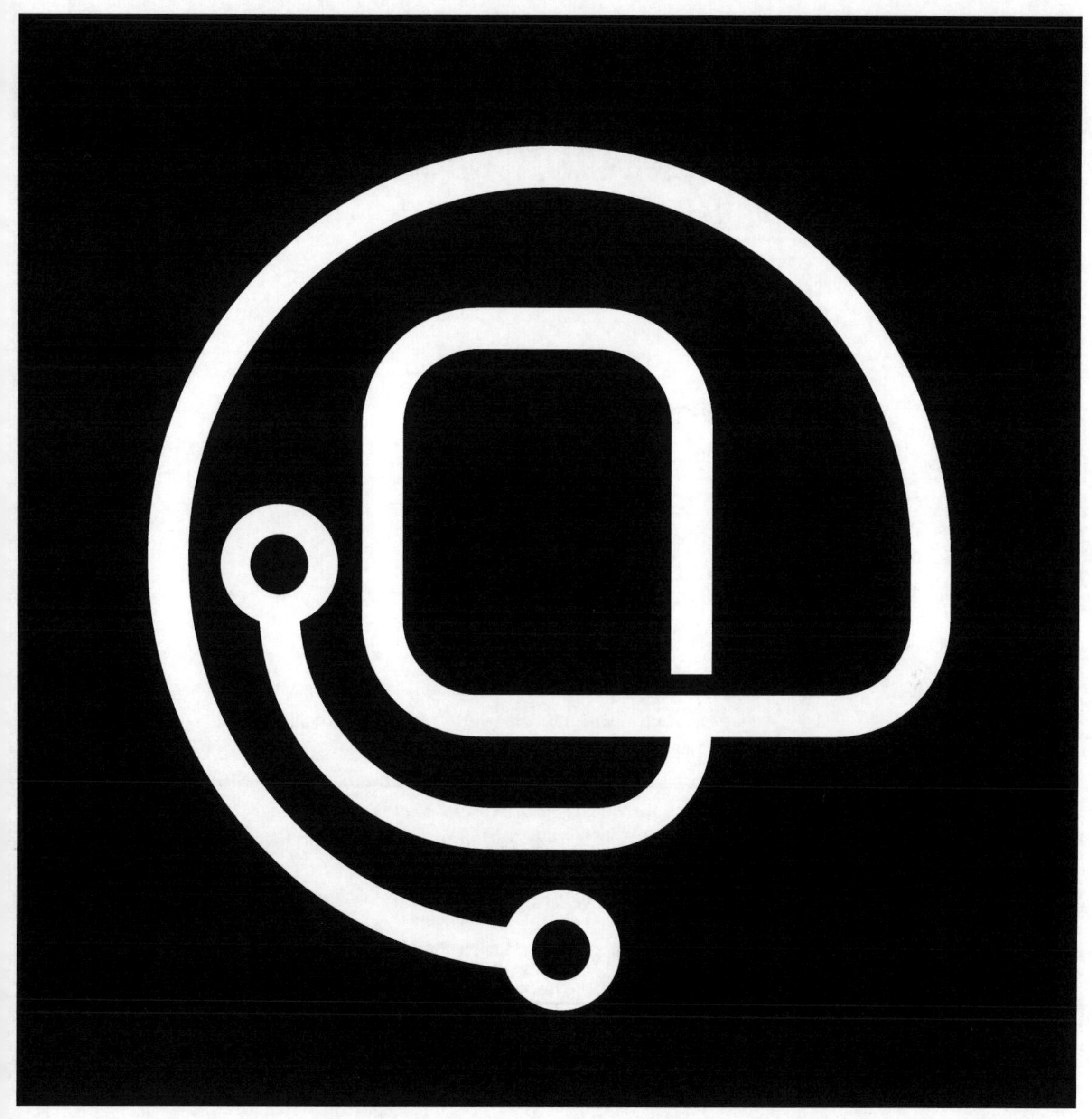

MODULE TWO

THE STRATEGIC LENS AND ORGANIZATIONAL DESIGN

MODULE TWO

THE STRATEGIC LENS AND ORGANIZATIONAL DESIGN

DESCRIPTION

This module introduces the concept of the three lenses. Then, it views management issues from the strategic lens perspective, contrasts the old and new organization, and identifies the building blocks of organizational design.

LEARNING OBJECTIVES

Upon completing the learning experience, you will be able to:

- Compare the formal object of the three lenses
- Compare the three levels of managerial analysis
- Identify the structural features of the 'new' organization
- Describe the shift in organizational paradigms over time
- Map the formal structure of an organization
- Identify different organizational structures and their advantages and disadvantages
- Distinguish between a 'traditional' and 'progressive' organization

GUIDING QUESTION

Are flat organizations better than hierarchical ones?
Is there a 'structural' difference between the 'traditional' and 'progressive' organization?

Walnut River Enterprises was almost doubling in size every year since it was founded five years ago. The company's main products were protective and decorative cases for mobile phones and tablets (iPads). Although the company was based in Amsterdam, most of the manufacturing was done in China while the most popular market for the products was in the U.S., Walnut River was excited about introducing a new rugged, protective product for laptops targeting customers who used laptops in outdoor environments and the military. As the company grew in size, the complexity of decision-making and difficulty in collaborating across teams became more disruptive to the organization. Customer expectations and preferences for the products created by Walnut River were changing every 30 days. Efficient decision-making and timely execution were critical to the continued success of the company. There were already signs of infighting between engineering, sales, and manufacturing that resulted in lost time in executing new innovative designs and products. It was time to design and implement a new organizational structure.

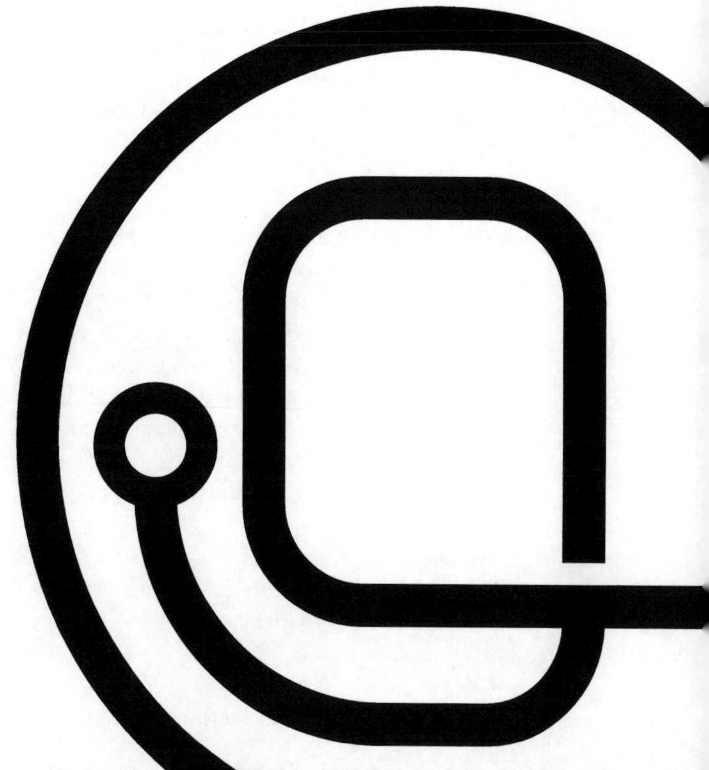

According to the philosophy of science, scientific discovery has a 'material' object (what you study), a 'formal' object (the angle from which you study it), and a 'method' (a way in which these objects are observed and analyzed). Management draws especially on knowledge of the behavior sciences such as sociology, anthropology, psychology, and social psychology. Behavioral sciences have human behavior as their material object but different formal objects. Psychology studies human behavior from the individual perspective; sociology studies human interaction in groups and societies; social psychology studies how personality and individual behavior are influenced by others such as groups and social circumstances; and, anthropology focuses on the impact of culture on human behavior. There are different types of methods from qualitative to quantitative ways to analyze the objects.

Being able to view human behavior from different perspectives—whether in a managerial situation or in an organizational context—provides alternative explanations of not only 'how' people behave but also 'why' they behave in a certain way. Applied to managerial behavior (managing and being managed), Organizational Behavior (OB) is commonly viewed from the perspective of three lenses—strategic, political, and cultural—and three different levels of analysis—micro, meso, and macro. The conceptual framework of management also requires a historical perspective as managerial behavior evolves over time and place.

THE THREE LENSES

The three lenses[1] provide us with three different ways of viewing the same thing or situation. The strategic lens looks at the strategic intent of the organization (strategy) and how it organizes itself (structure) to achieve these objectives. The strategic lens examines the flow of tasks and information, or how things get done. Using this lens, organizations look at optimizing workflows to meet the goals and objectives of the company. The strategic lens focuses on grouping, linking, alignment, and fit. This approach stems mainly from the structural-functionalism theory in sociology.

The political lens looks at how power and influence are distributed and wielded in an organization as well as the preferences of the individuals and groups who lay claim to power. Remember, executives and managers are not the only ones with power. Stakeholders such as internal (employees and Employee Resource Groups) and external (clients) unions, customers, suppliers, and government regulators all have different degrees of power. These stakeholders also have different interests and requirements that need to be balanced. If you understand who has power and what their motives are, you can begin to predict what type of decisions are likely to be made. This knowledge can then begin to guide your own decisions as well. As the political lens is focused on stakeholders and issues related to power, interests, and potential conflict, the tools of the political lens are stakeholder analysis, negotiation, and conflict resolution. This approach stems from conflict and duality theory in sociology and political science.

The cultural lens is used to observe how a company's history and past actions have shaped employee assumptions and have affected the organization's future actions. The cultural lens focuses on the 'meaning' of things using basic assumptions, values, mental models, schemas, and emotions. We've all heard the popular phrase about organizational culture, "But that's how we've always done things around here." While the culture of an organization typically unfolds over time, it can be shaped and developed to provide direction and leadership. This approach stems mainly from anthropology but also from the theory of symbolic interactionism in sociology.

> *The use of different lenses makes human behavior of individual, groups, and organizations more insightful. The strategic lens is about structured social interactions and focuses on groupings, linkages, alignment, and fit; the political lens is about power, interests, and conflicts; and the cultural lens is about basic assumptions, mental schemas, and meaning.*

THREE LEVELS OF ANALYSIS

Being able to analyze human behavior in micro, meso, and macro groupings is also extremely valuable because human behavior can only be fully understood in its broader social 'umwelt' (the environment) as it is experienced by each individual. The different levels of analysis provide us information about human behavior in its structural, political, and cultural context. When analyzing something from the 'micro' level, the emphasis is on individual behavior—the how and the why —and focuses on personality, socio-graphics, aptitudes, and competencies. This level of analysis relies heavily on people's innate characteristics and personalities—not something that is easily changed—that influence their behavior. At the 'meso' or middle level of analysis, the emphasis is on behavior of the individual in the context of the team and the managerial lines of reporting (supervisor vs supervisee). At the broader 'macro' level, the focus is on analyzing the firm and those interacting with the organization (board of directors, executives, managers, employees, unions, suppliers, customers), the industry (competitors, regulators, strategic partners, alliances/joint ventures), and the broader PESTLE (political, economic, social, technological, legal, and environmental factors) framework (see 2-1).

> ***Micro level****–focuses on individual behavior*
> ***Meso level****–focuses on internal organizational behavior*
> ***Macro level****–focuses on the external context of the firm*

THE STRATEGIC LENS

The main question when using the strategic lens is: "What is is the strategic intent of the organization and how do they organize to achieve that intent?" Strategy and structure are the two main elements of analyzing a managerial situation from the perspective of the strategic lens. Organizations have a strategic intent (called strategy). Most companies have a revolving three-to-five year strategic plan in place that becomes the cornerstone of all processes within the company. Ideally, they organize (structure)

2-1. Understanding Managerial Situations

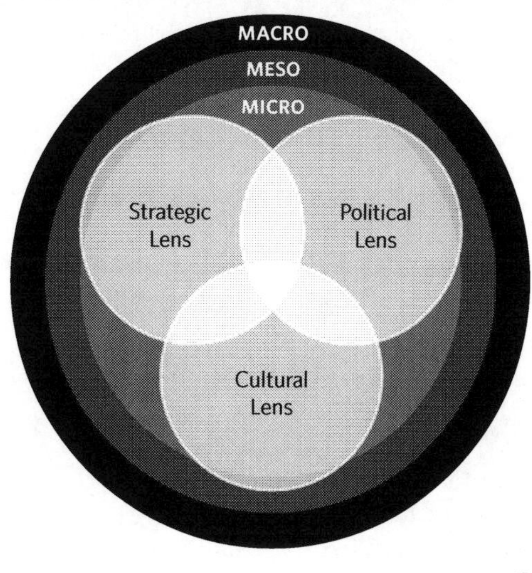

themselves to meet these strategic goals. Two specific management disciplines—strategic management and organization design—provide the backbone of the strategic lens.

STRATEGY + STRUCTURE

> *The strategic lens is about strategy and structure!*

Strategy

Organizations have a strategic intent in terms of what they were set up to do. Strategy is about the choices one makes as an organization—and to the same extent as a person. As the French author Andre Gide stated eloquently, '*Choisir c'est renoncer*' (to choose is to renounce). Organizations must make choices about what they will do or pursue (as well as what they will not do) and how they will create value. Strategy is about having an attractive value proposition.

Johnson and Johnson (J&J) is a company famous for using a set of values known as CREDO for guiding its actions. Managers are trained on how to use the CREDO in the decision-making process. The company values putting patients and people before profits. J&J's

actions in the 1982 Tylenol contamination case set the company up as the gold standard for crisis management, showing that management matters. If organizations accomplish their strategic intent (think of the March of Dimes!) or they are disrupted (think about the Encyclopedia Britannica!), they need to set a 'new' intent and reinvent themselves by pursuing new and other value-added choices.

Structure

In sociology, structure is defined as the distinctive and stable arrangement of institutions, whereby human beings in a society interact and live together. A structure is a pattern of interactions. Once organizations have made their choice (identified their strategy), they must organize to meet that intent, i.e., develop a structure that will allow them to meet their strategic goals. The organizational structure represents a network of postions that are in a certain fixed relationship with one another. Today, the focus is much more on the organizational culture (many progressive agile companies even proclaim "it's all about the culture"). Understanding the importance of structure tends to be neglected.

> *Both structure AND culture are equally important to understanding human behavior.*

In his 1977 book, *The Visible Hand: The Managerial Revolution in American Business*, Alfred Chandler proclaimed "*structure follows strategy*."[2] The need to organize, reorganize, or restructure is triggered by an intended strategy or strategic shift driven by new technologies or market changes. Organizations should not restructure for the sake of reorganization itself, but rather, because the existing structure no longer allows the organization to meet its strategic intent, the environment in which they operate has changed, or the organization has made new and different strategic choices. Yet, often when new managers or executives take over, they not only have an urge to reorganize but choose do so.

The sociological view of structure has evolved over time in accordance with espoused theories. Among others, structure has been viewed as a social fact, a bureaucracy, a function, and a symbol (for details see textboxes 2-2 to 2-5). Delving into textboxes and reading about these rather academic and theoretical views of stucture, as a management practitioner you may ask yourself, "So what?" or "What do I do with this information?" In management, the pendulum tends to swing back and forth from structure to culture based on the *Zeitgeist*. While the focus during the 3rd industrial revolution was more on structure than today, with the 4th industrial revolution, the notion of culture is more prevalent. Yet, misunderstanding and underestimating the impact of structure on management leads to a failure of fully understanding the complexity of managerial situations.

2-2. Structure as a Social Fact

In his 1895 book, *The Rules of the Sociological Method*, sociologist Emile Durkheim described structures as social facts that are "*independent of individual manifestations.*"[3] In other words, social structures transcend individuals and exert social control over them. Applied to management, the way we structure an organization influences the type of social control that will be exerted over individuals.

2-3. Structure as a Bureaucracy

Max Weber viewed the structure as 'bureaucracy' or the way of administratively organizing large numbers of people who need to work together.[4] He saw bureaucracy as an efficient and rational way to organize the activities of people, groups, and organizations. Many formal organizations in the public and private sector, including universities and governments, still rely on bureaucracy to function. Weber noted six major principles of the formal organizations or bureaucracy:

1. **Specialization and division of labor**—work is to be done by functional specialists and people are organized into units based on the type of work they do or skills they have;
2. **A formal hierarchical authority structure**—each level controls the level below and is controlled by the level above. The formal hierarchy is the basis of central planning and centralized decision-making;
3. **Management by a standard of formal written rules and regulations**—controlling rules allow decisions made at highest levels to be executed consistently at all lower levels;
4. **An 'up-focused' or 'in-focused' mission**—the organization's purpose is to serve the stockholders, the board, or whatever agency empowered it (up-focused) or the organization's purpose is to serve the organization itself and those within it (in-focused);
5. **Purposely impersonal**—the idea is to treat all employees and customers equally, and not be influenced by individual differences;
6. **Employment based on technical competencies and qualifications**—functional specialties are key to personal and organizational status.

In 1955, Cyril Nortcote Parkinson added a seventh principle of bureacracy, namely the predisposition of staff to grow 'above the line.' It is the basis of his humorous 'Parkinson's Law.' He demonstrated that management and professional staff tends to grow at predictable rates, almost without regard to what the line organization is doing.[5]

Key features of the formal organizations are predictability, reliability, impartiality, expertise, and clear lines of control.[6] The bureaucratic form is so common that most people accept it as a normal way of organizing almost any endeavor. People in bureaucratic organizations generally blame management, the founders, or the owners for the ugly side effects of bureaucracy without knowing that the real cause is the organizational form or structure itself.

2-4. Structure as a Function

Structural functionalism combines structure with function. In functionalism, each part of the structure has a function. The different parts of the system all work together—similar to the different parts of a clock—and constantly strive to be in homeostasis or equilibrium. Looking at structure this way helps us understand 'how' things work but provides little insight into 'why' they work (or don't). This way of looking at organizations as a social system was popularized in the U.S. in the 1960s through the work of sociologist Talcott Parsons.[7]

2-5. Structure as a Symbol

Symbolic interactionism focuses on the 'why' and explains human behavior in terms of social interactions and the use of meaningful symbols. Individuals derive meaning from their social interactions with others and the larger organizational context. In this perspective, symbols of everyday life, what they mean, and how people interact with each other shape the organizational culture. As individuals shape and are shaped by their social interactions, how the organization is structured impacts these social interactions, which gives meaning to the people interacting and influences their behavior.[8] Ideology—or the sum total of a person's values, beliefs, assumptions, and expectations—also colors our ways of thinking about organizations as structures and can foster an ideology that rationalizes human behavior. In his 1986 book, *Images of Organization*, Gareth Morgan[9] viewed organizations from a post-modern perspective using different metaphors for organizations:

Organization as machine—a metaphor that uses concepts such as efficiency, waste, maintenance, order, clockwork, cogs, programs, inputs, outputs, standardization, production, and re-engineering;

Organization as organism—a metaphor that uses concepts such as living systems, environmental conditions, adaptation, life cycles, recycling, needs, homeostasis, evolution, survival of the fittest, health, and illness;

Organization as brain—a metaphor that uses concepts such as learning, parallel processing, distributed control, mind-sets, intelligence, feedback, requisite variety, knowledge, and networks;

Organization as culture—a metaphor that uses concepts such as society, values, beliefs, laws, ideology, rituals, diversity, traditions, history, service, shared vision, mission, understanding, and families;

Organization as political system—a metaphor that uses concepts such as interests, rights, power, hidden agendas, back room deals, authority, alliances, party-lines, censorship, gatekeepers, and leaders;

Organization as psychic prison—a metaphor that uses concepts such as conscious and unconscious processes, repression, regression, ego, denial, projection, coping, defense mechanisms, pain, and dysfunction;

Organization as flux and transformation—a metaphor that uses concepts such as constant change, dynamic equilibrium, flow, self-organization, systemic interactions, attractors, chaos, complexity, butterfly effect, emergent properties, dialectics, and paradox;

Organization as instrument of domination—a metaphor that uses concepts such as alienation, repression, imposing values, compliance, charisma, maintenance of power, force, exploitation, discrimination, and corporate interest.

OLD VERSUS NEW ORGANIZATION

Although organizations and their structures have evolved over time to meet the changing context, the formal 'command and control' maintstream organization has lost some of its usefulness when dealing with the new world of work and the worker. The traditional focus of management focused on planning and control, continuous improvement, process optimiziation, and controlling people is no longer sufficient as organizations are now dealing with rapid change and disruption. They need people who are innovative, creative, and agile.

The 'New' Organization

At the height of the 3rd industrial revolution (1980s-1990s), certain features of the formal (old) organization (read bureaucracy) were replaced with new features leading to a 'new' form of organization. Today, we talk about structural characteristics of organization on a continuum from 'old' to 'new'.

In their classic organizational behavior textbook, *Managing for the Future: Organizational Behavior & Processes*, Debora Ancona et al. describes five characteristics of the new (vs old) organization: flat, flexible, diverse, networked, and global.[10] They also identify the managerial implications and challenges of each dimension—and the impact they have on mananaging. Let's explore how they describe what each characteristic means to an organization and the people working in it.

What does it mean to be **flat** (vs tall)?

- Fewer layers of management (structural lens, organizational design);
- Empowerment of lower organizational levels: rights and responsibilities (political lens);
- Reduction of perceived differences in status across organizational members (cultural lens, power distance).

What does is mean to be **flexible** (vs inflexible)?

- Ability to respond quickly to different situations (external environment);
- Fewer rules and procedures;
- Greater encouragement of initiatives;
- Innovation;
- Agility.

What does it mean to be **diverse** (vs homogeneous)?

- Various ascribed and achieved backgrounds of people;
- Variety of different perspectives and viewpoints;
- Variety in terms of people and their communities of interests;
- Organizational support for belonging.

What does it mean to be **networked** (vs isolated)?

- Heavy reliance on links and networks between individuals or subunits (inside and outside of the organization);
- Internally: individual vs team as a key unit;
- Externally: very limited external links vs very extensive external links;
- Growing importance of teams, task forces, swarms, etc. (lateral relationships);
- Creation of ecosystems.

What does it mean to be **global** (vs domestic)?

- Interdependent yet connected;
- Glocal: global and local;
- A lot of global mobility;
- Being an integrated enterprise;
- Networks with suppliers and customers across borders.

These characteristics distinguish the traditional organization (tall, inflexible, homogeneous, isolated, and domestic) from the progressive organization (flat, flexible, diverse, and global). As we are currently experiencing the 4th industrial revolution, as a result of demography, technology, and globalization, we prefer using the terms 'traditional' (old) vs 'progressive' (new) organization in this book. How progressive is your organization in terms of these structural elements?

Organizational Shifts over Time

Several authors have described the paradigm shift of organizations due to the changing external context. In his 2017 book, The Day After Tomorrow, Peter Hinssen described organizational shifts in terms of the 3rd (20th century) vs 4th (21st century) industrial revolutions (see 2-6).[11]

2-6. Organizational Shifts from 20th to 21st Century

20th Century	21st Century
Large	Scale
Slow	Fast
Stable	Agile
Enclosed	Porous
Dative (to/for)	Ablative (by, with)
Standalone	Networked

To what extent is your employer operating in the 20th or 21st century?

In their 2012 book, The Rainforest: The Secret to Building the Next Silicon Valley, Victor Hwang and Greg Horowitt argue that there are old rules for production (plantation) and new rules for innovation (rainforest). The rules of the plantation for production are efficiency, productivity, profitability, and scalability while the rules of the rainforest for innovation are radical, serendipitous, fall forward, and non-linear. Is your employer operating according to the rules of the plantation for production or those of the rain forest for innovation? According to Hwang and Horowitt, not only are the rules different for these two types of organizations, but so is the style of their workers.12

In the rules of plantation of production, workers:

1. Excel at their job;
2. Are loyal to the team;
3. Work with those they can depend on;
4. Seek a competitive advantage;
5. Do the job right the first time;
6. Strive for perfection;
7. Return favors.

In the rules of the rainforest for innovation, workers:

1. Break rules and dream;
2. Open doors and listen;
3. Trust and are trusted;
4. Seek fairness, not advantage;
5. Experiment and iterate together;
6. Err, fail, and persist;
7. Pay it forward.

Does your personal style as a worker align with the rules of the plantation or those of the rainforest for innovation?

Tanmay Vora expressed graphically for the World Economic Forum how the pillars of the traditional organization are in flux for (see 2-7).13 While the infographic describes the organization's transformation as a mindset from structure to culture, the importance of organizational design of the organization cannot be ignored.

What is the mindset of your organization?

2-7. Mindset Shifts for Organization Transformation

Source: Tanmay Vora, *Mindset Shifts for Organization Transformation*, World Economic Forum, 2017.

ORGANIZATIONAL DESIGN

Organizational design basically has to do with shaping the social instrument called 'structure.' Strategic design is about building an organizational structure (divide and link) and making all the parts work together internally and externally (alignment and fit).

Differentiation and Integration

Two interrelated concepts of structure are 'differentiation' (grouping) and 'integration' (linking).[14] Organizational design is foremost differentiation. Organizations are complex. Therefore, they need to be organized to get the work done. While organizing, they divide and differentiate (into silos) based on their strategic intent (i.e., what they want to accomplish). This is called 'groupings' in organizational design. Integration is a direct result of grouping. As soon as differentiating and organizing are complete, the need to re-integrate what has been grouped or divided up. This is what we call 'linkages' in organizational design. Integration is done through formal and informal mechanisms.

Organizational design answers the basic questions of how to best organize the organization to achieve the strategic intent. Subsequently, the constraints and assumptions shaping the design of the organization and the common design formats of organizations come into play. Designing organizations means answering the question, 'How to best organize human activity?' The right answer in management is usually, 'It depends.' Your task as a manager is to identify, 'on what does it depend?' The correct answer is evasive, namely 'the situation.' Human activity is structured according to the constraints of the situation (design shapers), the choices the organization makes (design choices), and the various patterns of design formats or structures that organizations commonly use.

1. Design Shapers

Common organizational design shapers are goals, environment, complexity, people, and size.

GOALS—an organization is a consciously constructed system having parts that are interrelated to achieve certain goals and ends. A goal is an intention coupled with an action. Goals are derived from the organizational strategy (which direction the organization wants to go and what it wants to accomplish) and embedded in the organization's mission, vision, and values. Organizations cannot pursue everything and must be selective. Is the goal of the organization clear or unclear to its members? Is the goal simple or complex or a mix of both? All organizations, even small ones, engage on purpose in activities not aimed directly at the task to perform (or output goal). Yet these other (support) goals are vital for organizational success. Think of goals as a goal basket of output vs support goals. Output goals are those that pertain to the organization's output or productivity. Support goals indirectly support the eventual accomplishment of the output goal. Major support goals are adaptation, management, motivation, and position.

> *Adaptation goals*—having to do with the organization's need to adapt to the environment;
>
> *Management goals*—having to do with running the enterprise;
>
> *Motivation goals*—having to do with maintaining or improving the organization and its results;
>
> *Position goals*—having to do with maintaining or improving the organization's position in the industry or community.

With regard to the goals, these design questions come up. 'What is the mix of organization commitment to these goals? What proportion of resources does management put in the various goal baskets?'

ENVIRONMENT—the environment can be static or dynamic and some organizational environments are mechanic while others are more organic. A dynamic environment will require greater structural agility than a more static environment. Mechanic organizations tend to have highly centralized authority, specialized functions, and formalized policies, procedures, and processes leading to a structure of tight controls. Organic organizations tend to be flatter, decentralized, and have a great deal of communication and participation in decision-making, leading to greater empowerment.

COMPLEXITY—tasks can range from being routine (with low role discretion) to highly complex (requiring high role discretion and autonomy).

PEOPLE—the people in the organization can be classified according to quite a number of characteristics such as local vs cosmopolitan, authoritarian vs democratic, and professions vs occupations.

SIZE—finally, the size of the organization (large vs small) matters in terms of the most appropriate structure. Larger organizations will have greater need for differentiation (as well as for integration). The smaller the organization, the more agile it can be.

2. Design Choices

Structure is a multi-dimensional concept that includes a set of choices related to specialization, formalization, centralization, differentiation, and coordination.

> *Specialization*—relates to tasks, expertise, division of labor, and efficiency. Is the task simple routine or highly complex?
>
> *Formalization*—the degree to which rules and regulation govern people's behavior and discipline. Are things done formally (i.e., control) vs informally (i.e., letting go)?
>
> *Centralization*—the degree to which decision-making is concentrated. Is decision-making centralized or decentralized?
>
> *Differentiation*—the extent to which labor is divided horizontally vs vertically; by staff vs line. Does hierarchy impact the way the work is done?
>
> *Coordination*—the extent to which work labor is coordinated and integrated. Is coordination done in a formal or informal manner and in an authoritarian or democratic manner?

The notion of span of control—or the number of subordinate people who report to a manager— and layers—or the number of different levels of reporting in the organization from the CEO to the bottom floor—are also evolving with organizations favoring a larger span of control resulting in fewer levels in the organization. Companies like Amazon measure span of control as a Key Performance Indicator (KPI) where 80% of all managers must have six direct reports.

In addition, in many progressive workplaces, the focus is shifting away from control to a more people-oriented trust role by moving from the 'trust and verify' (a somewhat untrustworthy political phrase) to 'trust and let go' (assume your employees will do the right thing). The rule book is slowly being replaced by a manifesto or a set of principles on how to treat people we work with and what we expect from them. The choice of control versus let go also depends on the nature of the work and the structure of the organization. The pendulum is definitely swinging toward trusting that people will do the right thing rather than controlling for the few 'bad apples' that may force the policing of work practices.

> *The challenge for organizations is to create structures of employee and labor relations that use the best traditional methods of compliance with innovative methods of building a culture of real trust, teamwork, and leadership.*

3. Design Formats

Design formats are the dimensions that differentiate the organization. There are different patterns of organizational structures each with advantages and disadvantages (see 2-8):

Functional structure—grouping by expertise or function;

Business or product structure—grouping by service or product;

Marketing group structure—grouping by geography (region) or customer (market segment);

Hybrid structure—grouping by more than one dimension whether a matrix structure (two different groupings of equal weight) or front back structure (front is organized by market and its functions; back is organized by product or business unit).

Each organization design format has its own advantages and disadvantages.

In the current 4th industrial revolution work configuration, where the strategic focus is to actively grow virtual groups and stop investing in brick and mortar site, the notion of organization structure is being reevaluated and new design concepts are constantly emerging.

2-8. Advantages and Disadvantages of Design Formats

Type	Advantages	Disadvantages
Functional structure (Functional organization)	Allows development of deep functional expertise and a high degree of specialization of knowledge within each function. Economies of scope (easy to transfer resources across activities within the function). Allows each group to create, separate, incentivize, and control systems to reinforce its needs and strengths.	Cost of integration across functions Sequential interdependence across functions Not responsive to changes (market/ customers) Specialization leads to narrow perspectives Difficult to solve problems that require joint effort Difficult to assess cost on a product line basis Difficult to assess accountability for total performance Tall hierarchies inhibit information flow Promotes functional silos Does not develop general managers
Product division structure (Business or product structure)	Transparency of performance Clear strategic focus for the product/service division or business unit	Business units and their P&L (profit and loss) makes it difficult for units to share resources Duplication of activities (staff functions) May inhibit new business creation (in favor of expansion) Expertise is spread across experts Missed learning opportunities in core functions Promotes business unit silos
Customer division structure (Marketing group structure - geography or customer)	Capacity for developing deep customer/ market knowledge Tailor products/services to differentiated market needs	Duplication of activities and resources Erosion of deep technical expertise Missed opportunities for synergies and learning
Function/product matrix (Hybrid structure)	Can focus on two dimensions	Complicated (2 bosses) Dual systems (rules and controls)
Front-back structure (Hybrid structure)	Advantages of product, market Functional organizations without disadvantages of matrix	Fragmentation of technical expertise (back) Poor integration of market needs and R&D

Source: Ancona, D., Kochan, T., Scully, M., Van Maanen, J., & Westney, D. E. (2005). *Managing for the Future: Organizational Behavior & Processes* (3rd Ed.). Cincinnati: South-Western College Publishing. M1-11- M2-13

INTEGRATION

Differentiating and organizing creates the need to re-integrate what has been divided up! The simple fact of organizing creates divisions and silos that must be re-integrated. How to best organize means balancing the need to organize (i.e., differentiate) vs the need to integrate. Organizations integrate through formal and informal mechanisms called 'linkages.' Formal linking mechanisms consist of rules, central procedures, policies, schedules, taskforces, committees, project management, and the coordination of these activities. Informal linking mechanisms are shared frameworks, lateral relationships, corporate culture, best practice, leadership development, socialization of new recruits, and glue technology.

Glue technology—a term coined by Paul Evans et al. in their 2011 book, *The Global Challenge*,[15] is a good term for what management does, especially in organizations that are divided by more than the organizational structure, such as global companies operating in different geographic areas and the need for integration as a result of mergers and acquisitions. The vertical pillars of glue technology are the coordination tools such as cross-boundary teams, cross-boundary steering groups, know-how sharing, and regional or global process management. The horizontal bars are enabling mechanisms or lateral relationships and coordination between people increasingly facilitated by electronic communication technology.

FIT AND ALIGNMENT

The fundamental building blocks of the strategic lens are differentiation (groupings) and integration (linkages). Two complementary notions in the strategic lens are fit and alignment. When the external environment changes and the strategy changes meet the emerging challenges, the organization is faced with a need to make design changes 'fit' the changed external context. In addition, the organization needs to internally align the different pieces of its operation to fit together.

> *The strategy has to 'fit' to the external environment and the differentiated groupings and systems have to be internally 'aligned' within the organization.*

In progressive organizations, strategy and structure are intricately linked to a new mindset (read culture) where people can be trusted, meaningfully engage, and contribute to the purpose of the organization.

Robert H. Waterman, Thomas J. Peters and Julien R. Phillips of the consulting firm McKinsey argued there is more to organizations than structure and refer to successful strategy execution as an alignment of the seven S's: three hard S's (strategy, structure, and systems) and four soft S's (shared values, skills, staff, and style).[16]

1. **Strategy**—a coherent set of actions that supports the vision and direction of the organization and assures organizational success;
2. **Structure**—the organizational design itself affecting decision-making, hierarchy, formalization, roles, and responsibilities that define the lines of reporting and division of responsibilities;
3. **Systems**—the processes and flows that enable the organization to operate effectively and the various operational systems (ERP, HRIS, IS, etc.) around which the organization operates;
4. **Shared values**—the shared understanding of what is important, mission, goals, and the values that go beyond the formal output goals of the organization;
5. **Skills**—the competencies required to carry out the strategy and the capabilities that are possessed by the organization as a whole rather than by the individuals within it;
6. **Staff**—the people in the organization or the competent, well-trained, motivated, rewarded (compensated) individuals who carry out the strategy;
7. **Style**—the leadership and organizational culture or the way management collectively allocates time and attention and uses symbolic behavior indicating what is important.

> *The fundamental building blocks of the strategic lens are 'differentiation' (groupings) and 'integration' (linkages). Strategy is important to guide people in the choices that organizations have made. Structure is important because it impacts the way people interact with one another—especially in terms of communication and collaboration.*

THE STRATEGIC LENS AND OTHER WORKFORCE ISSUES

A number of other organizational patterns, such as line vs staff, the existence of dual lines of authority, and dual types of workers also influence how we examine human behavior from the perspective of the strategic lens.

Line vs Staff

Authority is the right to make decisions, to direct work of others, and to give orders. That is where the distinction of line vs staff comes in.

> *The line supports the external customer through their products and services. Staff managers (the managers of the functions) assist and advise the line managers in accomplishing these goals—usually because of their functional professional authority resulting from expertise.*

Line managers (the managers of people) are in charge of accomplishing the organizational objectives. They have the authority to direct work of subordinates as their direct supervisor or manager. Staff supports the front-line managers who are their internal customers. In management today, there is a great deal of devolvement going on where responsibilities are shifted from the staff to the line in a customer-agent relationship; and switches the staff's work from being part of overhead costs to being part of an internal cost center.

Dual Lines of Authority

Due to the increased professionalization of work, organizations often have dual lines of authority. These organizations are more difficult to manage.

> *The administrative line reflects the 'structure' of the organization (the line of command) while the professional line is independent with regard to the professional aspects of their work (discretionary professional autonomy).*

The administrative line usually serves at the pleasure of the professional line. As work becomes more and more professionalized (by legal mandate), these types of dual lines of authority are likely to grow. Examples of organizations with dual lines of authority are:

- Hospitals (medical staff and hospital administrators)
- Academic institutions (faculty and deans/staff)
- Pharmacist and veterinarians in retail stores (professionals vs department and store managers)
- Internal audits (auditing accountants vs management)

The so-called separation of church and state in an organization's line of authority, intended for quality assurance and as a mechanism for check and balances, is the result of the professionalization of many occupations where workers gain control and discretionary autonomy through the nature of their work (based on a body of knowledge acquired through higher education, licensing and certification, and professional code ethics) in contrast with the traditional unionization of workers which is more focused on working conditions and bread and butter issues.

Although not a new concept, the helix organization is trying to remedy the difficulties encountered by matrix organizations and the dual reporting structure by separating people-leadership tasks from day-to-day business leadership. The helix design disaggregates the traditional management hierarchy into two separate, parallel lines of accountability that are roughly equal in power and authority. One line of authority is focused on developing people and capabilities, sets work standards, and drives functional excellence. The other line of authority focuses people and capabilities on business priorities, creating value, and customer experience satisfaction. This organizational design is not yet widespread and requires an agile mindset and talent infrastructure.[17]

Duals Types of Workers

Increasingly as employers are hiring on the talent continuum, organizations also have dual types of workers based on whether they are employees or contingent workers (contract, freelance, gig economy workers, etc.) and paid staff or volunteers. These workers are working side-by-side in blended teams with uneven social contracts.

The Strategic Lens Applied to Sectors

Is managing different in the three sectors (for-profit, non-profit, and public sector)? To what extent are the three sectorial worlds similar (or different) in both strategic intent and structure? The root of the answer to these questions is in the values and norms or ideology at the basis of those different sectors.

For-profit management:

- Serving customers;
- Making profit;
- Making investments that have a return;
- Traditional vs agile management values;
- Legacy organizations vs start-ups.

Non-profit management:

- Emphasis on disciplined performance and organizational capacity;
- Focus on contribution to reserves and outcomes;
- Focus on self-sufficiency;
- Assessment of use of resources and budgets;
- Governance and transparency.

Public sector management:

- Customer is much broader than the taxpayer;
- Emphasis on disciplined performance and organizational capacity;
- Reinvention of government (setting policy, contracting others to deliver the services);
- Outsourcing the provision of public service by for-profit organizations;
- New culture of performance among public managers;
- Assessment of use of resources and budgets;
- Accountability, governance and transparency;
- Public sector sees business not as a pariah but as a role model.

Old vs New Social Contract

The changing context of work has engendered a larger societal debate about the role of the organization and the evolving social contract between the employer and the workers. From a talent perspective, two major forces are impacting talent management in the context of a changing social contract: the skill level of the worker (skilled vs non-skilled) and the expectations of the workforce (mainly millennials).

The work output of an organization is assembled from a continuum of tasks (traditionally bundled into roles and jobs) that differ in complexity. In order to perform these tasks, firms hire on a continuum from low to high-skilled workers. Businesses know workers are no longer 'permanent' and cannot ensure their skillset will be needed in the future. Average workers are vulnerable and easily become irrelevant unless they can continuously upgrade their skills through learning and development. Millennials have different work expectations and expect employers to act more as a social enterprise.

The old social contract of the 3rd industrial revolution focused on stability, long-term mutual commitment, and certainty between the employer and the employee. A job provided health, unemployment and pension benefits, and a great deal of security in return for individual performance, commitment, and loyalty to the organization. However, this contract has slowly become irrelevant. Declining union membership, corporate restructuring, downsizing, and unemployment fluctuations disrupted the employer-employee relationship and now a new social contract is starting to emerge. Today, there is a great deal of uncertainty and the mutual commitments between employers and the workforce are quite different. The expectation to act as a social enterprise is a feature of the current 4th industrial revolution. The varying needs of the stakeholders involved in the economic production of work need to be managed and reconciled.[18] ▮

REFERENCES

1 The discussion of the three lenses is based on the work of: Ancona, D., Kochan, T., Scully, M., Van Maanen, J., & Westney, D. E. (2005). *Managing for the Future: Organizational Behavior & Processes* (3rd Ed.). Cincinnati: South-Western College Publishing.

2 Chandler, A. (1977). *The Visible Hand: The Managerial Revolution in American Business*. Cambridge: Belknap Press.

3 Durkheim, E. (2009). *Les Règles de la Méthode Sociologique* (1894), Paris, Payot, Collection Petite Bibliothèque Payot.

4 Waters, T & Waters, D. (2015). *Weber's Rationalism and Modern Society*. New York: Palgrave Macmillan.

5 Parkinson, C. N. (1955). Parkinson's Law. *The Economist*, November 19.

6 Ancona, D., Kochan, T., Scully, M., Van Maanen, J., & Westney, D. E. (2005). *Managing for the Future: Organizational Behavior & Processes* (3rd Ed.). Cincinnati: South-Western College Publishing.

7 Parsons, C. (1951). *The Social System*. England: Routledge & Kegan.

8 Blumer, H. (1986). *Symbolic Interactionism: Perspectives and Methods*. University of California Press.

9 Morgan, G. (1986). *Images of Organization*. Beverly Hills: Sage Publications.

10 Ancona, D., Kochan, T., Scully, M., Van Maanen, J., & Westney, D. E. (2005). *Managing for the Future: Organizational Behavior & Processes* (3rd Ed.). Cincinnati: South-Western College Publishing.

11 Hinssen, P. (2017). *The Day After Tomorrow: Hoe Overleven in Tijden van Radicale Innovatie*. Leuven: Van Duuren Management.

12 Hwang, V. & Horowitt, G. (2012). *The Rainforest: The Secret to Building the Next Silicon Valley*. Los Altos Hills: Regenwald.

13 Vora, T. (2017). *Mindset Shifts for Organization Transformation*, World Economic Forum.

14 Ancona, D., Kochan, T., Scully, M., Van Maanen, J., & Westney, D. E. (2005). *Managing for the Future: Organizational Behavior & Processes* (3rd Ed.). Cincinnati: South-Western College Publishing.

15 Evans, P., Pucik, V., & Björkman, I. (2011). *The Global Challenge: International Human Resource Management* (2nd ed.). New York: Mc Graw-Hill.

16 Waterman, R.H., Peters, T., & Phillips, J. R. (1980). "Structure is not organization," *Business Horizons*, 23(3), 14-26.

17 De Smet, A., Kleinman, S., & Weerda, K. (2019). "The helix organization," *McKinsey Quarterly*, October 2019. (Accessed: November 20, 2019). https://www.mckinsey.com/business-functions/organization/our-insights/the-helix-organization.

18 Claus, L. & Monaghan, D. (2019) *Dynamic Open Talent*. Global HR Consortium/IT Roundtable.

GUIDED READING QUESTIONS

1. What are the characteristics of the new organization?

2. What is the best way to organize?

3. What do differentiation, integration, alignment, and fit mean for organizational design?

4. What are formal and informal integration mechanisms?

5. What are organizational design choices and shapers?

6. What are common design formats?

7. What are the advantages and disadvantages of different types of organizational structures?

8. What is the difference between line and staff?

9. What are examples of organizations with dual lines of authority?

10. What are blended teams?

11. How do management values differ by sector?

FOLLOW-UP CRITICAL THINKING QUESTIONS

1. What is my major takeaway from this reading?

2. What do I already know about this subject?

3. What follow-up questions do I have about this?

4. How can I apply this in real life?

KEY TERMS

Alignment
Blended teams
Bureaucracy
Design choices
Design formats
Design shapers
Differentiation
Fit
Formal object
Glue technology
Groupings
Helix organization
Homeostasis
Ideology
Integration
Layers
Linkages
Material object
Non-profit sector
Organizational design
Parkinson's law
PESTLE
Private sector
Professionalization
Public sector
Social fact
Span of control
Symbol
Unionization

LEARNING ASSESSMENT

Critically reflect on the content and the different concepts in this module and rate your own competency using the assessment scale.

Competency	I never heard of it	I heard of it but have limited knowledge of it	I can reasonably explain it to others	I have used it, done it, applied it
Three lenses	0	1	2	3
Three levels of analysis	0	1	2	3
Strategy	0	1	2	3
Formal organization	0	1	2	3
New organization	0	1	2	3
The seven S's	0	1	2	3
New social contract	0	1	2	3

MODULAR-SPECIFIC ASSESSMENT

Mapping your organization

This assessment allows you to map how your organization meets the characteristics of the 'old' versus the 'new' organization.

Source: Ancona, D., Kochan, T., Scully, M., Van Maanen, J., & Westney, D. E. (2005). *Managing for the Future: Organizational Behavior & Processes* (3rd Ed.). Cincinnati: South-Western College Publishing. M1-27.

VIGNETTE

WHAT IT'S REALLY LIKE TO WORK FOR THE $70K COMPANY

By Bobby Powers, Published October 4, 2019

https://medium.com/swlh/what-its-really-like-to-work-for-the-70k-company-9311299ddabf
Reprinted with permission.

***DISCLOSURE:** I am a current employee of Gravity Payments. My company did not ask me to post this, nor did I ask permission. My goal with this article is to offer an insider's view into a company that has been in the news a lot this past week. The thoughts expressed in this article are mine alone and are not intended to reflect the opinions of Gravity Payments.*

Employees come for the money but stay for the autonomy. If you've been paying attention to the news, you've likely heard about Gravity Payments. CNN, ABC, CBS, and others have chronicled our company's decision to pay every employee a "living wage" of at least $70,000 per year, including employees in lower cost of living cities like Boise, Idaho, where we recently opened a new office. Numerous friends have reached out to me to ask for a job at my company or ask what it's really like to work at Gravity. I guess that makes sense. There is a certain allure around Gravity which is fueled by the fact that we have a company founder who reduced his own salary so everyone else can get paid more. In today's money-grubbing economy, that sort of behavior draws a lot of attention.

I wanted to write this article to explain what it's really like to work at Gravity. If you've clicked into this story because you're craving some juicy "tell-all" of corporate deception, malfeasance, and inauthenticity, you're going to be disappointed. No, the company's not perfect. Yes, we have problems — just like any business. But it's a pretty damn good place to work...just not for the reasons that everyone thinks from the outside.

Outsiders think that the main appeal of Gravity is the salary, but internally, employees rarely talk about that aspect of the company. That's not what keeps people at the company. Although people may initially hear about Gravity because of the company's economic stance, they often decide to join the company because of Gravity's heart for small businesses, and they stay because of the autonomy they're afforded as employees.

It's a business culture unlike any I've experienced. In many ways, it's quite weird, but it works. Beginning with their very first morning at Gravity, every new hire is instructed: "Be your own CEO." The company expects every employee to think like an owner of the business and make decisions with the type of autonomy that is often only afforded to senior executives. Employees on the front lines are encouraged to make decisions that could impact thousands of dollars of revenue or expenses. I realized this in my first few months with the company when I received a company credit card without going through a corporate expense training. When I asked to see the company expense policy, I was met with blank stares. The lead accountant told me, "We trust you to make wise decisions. Be smart and let me know if you run into any questions." "Hmmm, that's strange," I thought. That definitely would not have flown at any of my past employers.

But that's just the way things are here. When I first asked for budgetary approval for bringing in a guest speaker, my manager told me we didn't have budgets. Questions like "What do we expect to gain from this event?" and "How can we quantify the ROI from this investment?" replace P&L reports and budgetary constraints.

Employees are given relentless autonomy to make decisions and find new ways to expand the business. As an example of that, I was even given the chance to build my own role within the company. I started at the company on the finance team, but after working in that role for six months and dabbling in a few projects along the way, I realized that I had a passion for learning and development (L&D). The company didn't have an L&D function, so I was told that I could create one if I could prove its value. I wrote a job description, began developing a new hire training schedule and leadership development materials to prove my training abilities, then pitched the creation of an L&D position to a few company leaders. After meeting with them two or three times, I was told that I could formally move into the new role that I had built — handling L&D for the entire company. But, I am by no means the first person to have done something like this at Gravity. Colleagues of mine have built entire departments from scratch based upon ideas they've had to expand the business. One of our sales reps recently developed a business idea that has blossomed into a new revenue stream for the company. Customer service reps have taught themselves how to code and transitioned into software development roles. Technical equipment reps have taught themselves marketing, then transitioned into management positions within the marketing team. The number of career shifts I've seen within the company is staggering.

As I've been with the company longer, I've realized that the job autonomy is even broader than I previously thought. After telling my manager about my career goal to write a book someday, he asked me why I couldn't write one on company time. I wish I could have seen my facial expression at the time. We had been looking for a way to teach leadership skills to new managers, and my manager said a leadership book could be a good teaching mechanism. So I literally wrote a book on company time — a book that we now give out to every person who moves into a management role at the company.
It's opportunities like that which keep me at the company— not the living wage philosophy. That's what outsiders may never understand: what makes a company famous or infamous may simply be the aspect of the firm that is easiest or sexiest to write about in the popular press.

It's easy to write about $70,000. It's much harder to write about job autonomy and company culture.
For every article you read online about dynamic work cultures (Google, Amazon, Facebook, Gravity, etc.) there is a hidden backstory that likely differs from the sensationalized story in the press. Is $70K sustainable? Publications have written countless articles about Gravity's original decision back in 2015 to pay every employee at least $70,000 per year.

Rush Limbaugh said the decision was "pure, unadulterated socialism" and that it was a "disaster" for the company. The NY Times reported that a Gravity client said the pay bump "makes it harder for the rest of us," by which he presumably meant companies who are trying to pay employees equitably but only have so much cash. And, of course, everyone wonders how the company can sustain paying every employee such a high salary — including roles whose "market value" is nowhere near that figure. But as I see it, a company that expects every person to act like a CEO does not have "entry-level positions." Many of the individuals who staff Gravity's front-line teams have worked in management positions elsewhere. They are not your run-of-the-mill employees who just show up to punch the clock, answer a few phone calls, and leave at 5 o'clock.

Two-time Pulitzer Prize winner Nicholas Kristof wrote a follow-up article on the Gravity $70K decision earlier this year. His conclusion? Taking care of employees by offering equitable pay is "not the death of capitalism but perhaps part of its rebirth." I hope Kristof is right. The numbers suggest that he is. After all, Gravity's business has swelled since the $70K decision in 2015. The volume of credit card payments processed by the business has nearly tripled. The company has been selected as one of the 100 Best Companies to Work For in Washington for three years. Executives from other firms, motivated by Gravity's people-first mission, have taken pay cuts to come work for the company. Employee attrition dropped 19 percent. Profits have increased. The company's growth has led to the company moving into newer, bigger, and nicer offices in both Seattle and Boise.

I hope that other companies will follow Gravity in the foray to pay living wages. But beyond that, I hope that companies will continue to find innovative ways to trust their employees, treat them like valuable participants in the business, and give them projects that align with their deepest passions and career goals.

GUIDED READING QUESTIONS

1. What is thee value proposition of the Gravity Payments rewards strategy?
2. What are the 'strategy and structure' components at Gravity Payments?
3. What is the nature of the social contract between Gravity Payments and its employees?

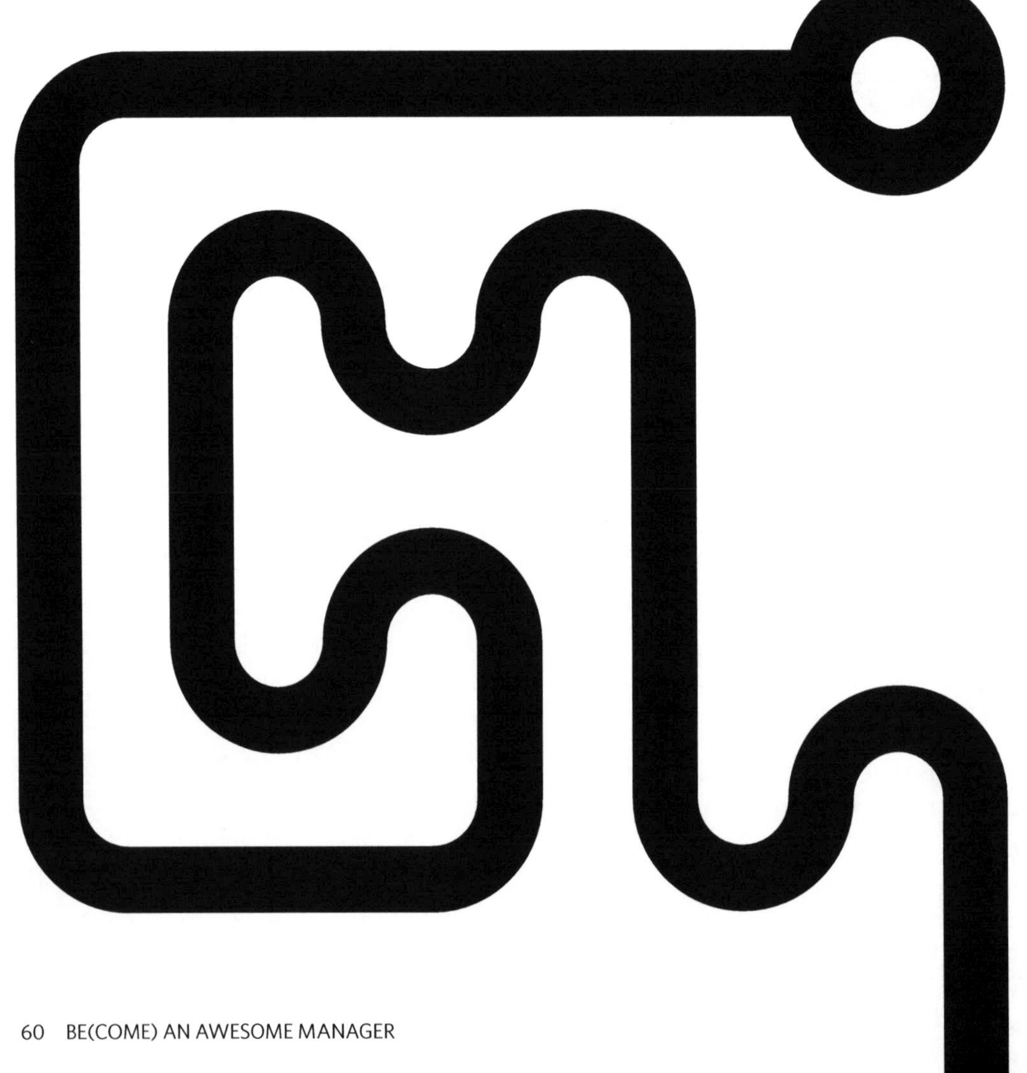

MODULE THREE

THE POLITICAL LENS

MODULE THREE

THE POLITICAL LENS

DESCRIPTION

This module looks at organizations from the perspective of political lens in terms of who defines the issues in organizations, what gives them the power and authority to define solutions, and how decision-making and negotiation outcomes can be achieved that serve both personal, stakeholder, and organizational interests.

LEARNING OBJECTIVES

Upon completing the learning experience, you will be able to:

- Describe the focus of the political lens
- Distinguish between power and authority
- Distinguish between 'old' and 'new' power
- Identify stakeholders and their requirements
- Practice negotiation as a political lens tool

GUIDING QUESTION

How do I develop and use 'new' power?

GEORGE relocated his family to another part of the country to start a job with another company. He accepted the job offer because he felt his experience and skills would make an immediate impact on the company. His new boss was very complimentary of his background during the interview process and he felt that he would enjoy working for her. After three months on the job, he realized some of his peers had more influence with his boss than he did. In fact, he had to learn to 'pre-sell' an idea with his peers to get their support prior to proposing it to his boss even though he was considered 'the expert' in the specific area. He quickly learned that his specific responsibilities and authority were overshadowed by the opinion of others in the organization who had a stronger influence on his boss. He learned that he would have to spend more time and energy working to build his own influence with the boss. He sighed as he thought it might take him two to three years to make the same impact as his peers.

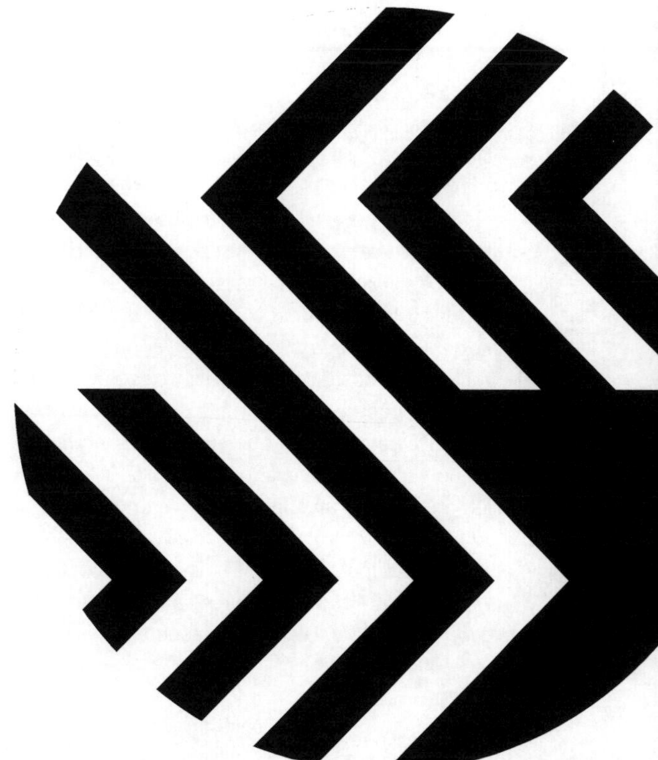

The political lens looks at how power and authority are distributed and wielded in organizations as well as the preferences of the individuals and groups who lay claim to power. Two fundamental elements of the political lens are power and authority, and their sources of legitimation. Individuals, groups, and departments compete with each other over the many kinds of (scarce) resources. Using the political lens, one looks at who gets how many resources, what kinds of resources, and how they are allocated.

The political lens is closely linked to the notion of stakeholders or people who have a stake in the organization. Stakeholders of an organization, whether internal or external customers, have different interests and these requirements are often in conflict with one another. Stakeholders not only have different interests and requirements, but they also have different degrees of power. Managing using the political lens means being able to balance these various elements. The need to build coalitions, form networks for the exchange of information and resources, and the 'give and take' opportunities that networks offer come from managing using the perspective of the political lens. As a result, negotiation and conflict resolution are the '*par excellence*' tools of the politcal lens.

POWER

Power is the 'ability' to elicit behavior from others that may not be evoked otherwise. According to Bertrand Russell, power is the ability to get people to do what you want them to do that they may not be willing to do otherwise. It is one's ability to reach goals and produce intended effects.[1] All effective actions in organization are political. They require mobilization of support and resources and attracting people possessing the resources to provide to others. Being able to mobilize interests and power to get things done is an important element of being an effective manager. Power is rooted in the control of resources. Traditionally, the degree of one's power is linked to the control of valuable and scarce resources and depends on how much people value these resources.

AUTHORITY

While power is the 'ability' to command, authority is the 'right' to command! According to Max Weber, there are different sources of authority, each with their own legitimacy:[2]

- **Rational-legal**— legitimized by legally enacted rules and regulations; bureaucratic nature, control over valued resources; control over people.
- **Traditional**—legitimized by long-established cultural traditions; influence on decisions and choices; capability to exact change.
- **Charismatic**—legitimized by personal abilities to inspire people; respect; ability to make choices; fear; money; freedom.

However, for authority to be legitimate, the 'command has to be accepted' by the person over whom one is trying to exert authority. According to Chester Barnard's acceptance theory of authority, there are four conditions necessary for the acceptance of a command:[3]

1. The person can and does understand it
2. The person believes the decision to accept the command is in the best interest of the organization
3. The command is in their best interest
4. The person is able to carry out the command

When people join an organization, they anticipate a 'zone of acceptance' or an '*a priori*' notion that the command is only acceptable if it is in the range of acceptance. People question commands that fall outside of the Zone Of Possible Acceptance (ZOPA).[4] This principle also holds for the outcomes of negotiation.

LEGITIMACY OF POWER AND AUTHORITY

Think about an individual who has power in your organization:

- How would you categorize the power of that individual?
- Did the use of their power have a positive or negative impact (or no impact) on you, the team, or the organization?
- Are power and authority used effectively by that person?
- What are legal and ethical considerations of (mis)using power?

As individuals, we have a tendency to rely and use certain sources of power and authority based on our personal preferences and past experience of using that power (un)successfully. Several inventories have been developed to ascertain the source of your power. Using these personality inventories, you can identify the source you rely on most when using power and authority as well as how much personal power you have developed. The source of power is either based on the person or the organization.[5]

Sources of power developed by the person:

- **Informational power**—based on facts or reasoning the person possesses and is able to share convincingly;
- **Expert power**—based on superior judgment or knowledge in a specific area;
- **Referent power**—based on being a role model for a person and generating feelings of support, respect, and goodwill.

Sources of power developed by the organization:

- **Legitimate power**—based on position and role, on formal right to direct others in certain matters, and on the obligations of others to follow those directions (positional authority);
- **Reward power**— ability to give rewards when others comply with your wishes based on the leader's control over things that team members desire;
- **Coercive power**—based on the leader's formal rights to discipline or punish.

Personal power is composed of the sum of three forms of power: knowledge power, relationship power, and inner power.[6]

- **Knowledge Power** (KP)—is the explicit and tacit knowledge acquired through education, experience, and continuous learning;
- **Relationship Power** (RP)—includes the network ties and the strong relationships that we have built with various communities;
- **Inner Power** (IP)—is the deep strength, courage, and commitment to stand up for one's beliefs and love of life.

But as Jeffrey Pfeffer observed, in today's context of work: "*Anyone who has to shepherd a cross-functional project through a large organization has lots of responsibility but virtually no line authority to compel anyone to do anything.*"[7]

'OLD' VS 'NEW' POWER

The traditional model used to accumulate power described above is more reflective of the characteristics of the old organization. In the new organization (flat, flexible, diverse, networked, and global), power is used differently.

In their 2018 book, *New Power: How It's Changing The 21st Century - And Why You Need To Know*, Jeremy Heimans and Henry Timms talk about how power is shifting from 'old' vs 'new' power and how they produce different effects.[8] Old power is enabled by what people and organizations own, know, or control that nobody else does, and is based on professionalism and specialization. New power is enabled by peer coordination and crowds. Old power requires mere consumption, while new power requires participation. Heimans and Timms juxtapose the characteristics of old and new power models (see 3-1).[9]

3-1 Old vs New Power

Old power	New power
Works like a currency	Works like a current
Held by few	Held by many
Jealously guarded when gained	Purposely distributed
Closed	Open
Inaccessible	Participatory
Leader driven	Peer driven
Downloads	Uploads
Captures	Distributes

Source: Heimans, J. and Timms, H. (2014). "Understanding 'new power'." *Harvard Business Review*, December, 92(12):48-56.

The shift from old to new power can be viewed on a participation scale with increasing levels of commitment:

- **Consuming**—traditional consumption;
- **Sharing**—sharing other people's content or ideas;
- **Shaping**—remixing or adapting content or ideas;
- **Funding**—crowdfunding or endorsing with money;
- **Producing**—creating or delivering content or assets with a peer community;
- **Co-owning**—having partial or complete ownership in content or assets.

Heimans and Timms argue that the battle and balancing between old and new power will be a defining feature of society, organizations, and businesses in the coming years.[10] In order to effectively balance power, it is essential to be able to manage different stakeholders.

STAKEHOLDERS

Stakeholders are those who have a 'stake' in the organization. All organizations have 'internal' and 'external' stakeholders or customers. Stakeholders can be at the individual or collective level (groups or organizations). These stakeholders have diverse 'interests' or requirements, varying degrees of power and authority, as well as different types of power- from old to new. The interests of stakeholders not only vary, they may also be conflicting with one another. Although stakeholders have different degrees of power and authority, all the stakeholders vie for control and influence based on their interests. Tools of the political lens, among others, include stakeholder management, negotiation, and conflict resolution.

Stakeholder Management

Managers must understand the stakeholders by looking beyond individuals. Managing stakeholders involves paying attention to individuals, groups, and organizations who can affect, be affected, or perceived to be affected by your actions. Stakeholder management requires engagement, communication, and consultation with stakeholders preferably before, during, and after specific actions are taken that affect them and their interests. Stakeholder management is one of the 10 critical functions of project management.[11] Managing stakeholders is also vital in change management. Stakeholder management, negotiation, and conflict resolution are managerial skills that managers can develop through professional continuing education workshops and deliberate practice.

Negotiation

The adage 'managing is negotiating,' is a typical way to look at managing from the point of view of the political lens. It is unavoidable that people will have differences. Settling these differences involves compromise. The role of the manager is to facilitate, align, negotiate, and find compromise with different stakeholders as well as solve conflicts before they get out of hand.

Conflict Resolution

Poor communication is one of the main sources of conflict in the workplace. Conflict resolution is finding solutions to disagreements that affect the individual, the team, and/or the organization.

LETTING GO OF CONTROL

In today's dynamic open talent environment, there is a great deal of discussion about letting go of control and building trust. In his 2015 book, *Work Rules*, Laszlo Bock asserts that managers have a tendency to accumulate and exert power, whereas employees have a tendency to follow orders. To counteract the (mis)use of power, he suggests eliminating status symbols, making decisions based on data rather than on manager's opinion, finding ways for people to shape their own world and the company, and expecting a lot from people. He further states that, "*you just need to fight the petty seductions of management and the command and control impulses that accompany seniority.*" [12] Ron Robert talks about the paradox of control: "*To gain control, you must often relinquish control (delegate and trust)*"; and "*There is no greater way to lose control than to try to control everything.*"[13] He further asserts that to obtain sustainable success, managers must balance exerting and relinquishing control. ▌

REFERENCES

1 Russell, B. (1938). *Power: A New Social Analysis* (1st ed). New York: Routledge.
2 Weber, M, Henderson, A., & Parsons, T. (1947). *The Theory of Social and Economic Organization.* New York: Oxford University Press.
3 Barnard, C. (1968). *The Functions of the Executive.* Cambridge: Harvard University Press.
4 Herbert, S.A. (1947). *Administrative Behavior: A Study of Decision-Making Processes in Administrative Organization.* New York: Macmillan.
5 French, J. R. P. & Raven, B. (1959). *The Bases of Social Power.* New York: Harper & Row.
6 Personal Power Inventory. (Accessed: January 31, 2020). https://outsmartyourbrain.com/personal-power-inventory/
7 Pfeffer, J (2010). "Power Play," *Harvard Business Review*, 88(7/8):84-92
8 Heimans, J. and Timms, H. (2018). *New Power: How It's Changing The 21st Century - And Why You Need To Know.* New York: Doubleday.
9 Heimans, J. and Timms, H. (2014). "Understanding 'new power'," *Harvard Business Review*, 92(12):48-56.
10 Ibid.
11 Project Management Institute. (2017). *A Guide to the Project Management Body of Knowledge* (6th ed.). Newton Square: Project Management Institute.
12 Bock, L. (2015). *Work Rules: Insights from Inside Google That Will Transform How You Live and Live* (1st ed.). New York: Twelve, p. 148.
13 Robert, R. (2102). "How to gain control by letting go," Fast Company July 9. (Accessed: January 30, 2020). https://www.fastcompany.com/1841995/how-gain-control-letting-go

GUIDED READING QUESTIONS

1. What is the difference between power and authority?

2. How is power legitimatized?

3. How is authority legitimatized?

4. What are the characteristics of old vs new power?

5. What are the participation activities that occur when power shifts from old to new?

6. What are the different sources of power?

7. What are common tools of the political lens?

FOLLOW-UP CRITICAL THINKING QUESTIONS

1. What is my major takeaway from this reading?

2. What do I already know about this subject?

3. What follow-up questions do I have about this?

4. How can I apply this in real life?

KEY TERMS

Authority
Conflict resolution
Interests
Legitimation
Negotiation
New power
Old power
Power
Stakeholder
Stakeholder management
Zone of acceptance

LEARNING ASSESSMENT

Critically reflect on the content and the different concepts in this module and rate your own competency using the assessment scale.

Competency	I never heard of it	I heard of it but have limited knowledge of it	I can reasonably explain it to others	I have used it, done it, applied it
Power	0	1	2	3
Authority	0	1	2	3
New power	0	1	2	3
Stakeholder management	0	1	2	3
Negotiation	0	1	2	3
Conflict resolution	0	1	2	3

MODULAR-SPECIFIC ASSESSMENT

Personal Power Inventory

This assessment allows you to determine the source of power you are more likely to rely on.

Source: https://outsmartyourbrain.com/personal-power-inventory/

VIGNETTE

HOW NEW POWER IS GIVING WORKERS A VOICE IN ORGANIZATIONS[1]

Workers are mobilizing the community by building authentic relationships with others (internal and external customers), linking to a higher purpose and mobilizing people into action—all with greater transparency and urgency. We see many examples of this in social movements related to the MeToo movement, BlackLivesMatter, the re-mobilization for gender pay equity, climate change initiatives, and even employers becoming engaged in a variety of civic issues.

- **#MeToo**—sexual harassment survivor and activist Tarana Burke created the phrase 'Me Too' more than a decade ago. In October 2017, #MeToo spread virally on social media following the widespread sexual-abuse allegations against media and film producer and Hollywood mogul Harvey Weinstein.
- **BlackLivesMatter** (BLM)—an international activist movement originating in the African-American community and campaigns against violence and systemic racism towards black people. Since February 2012, the hashtag is used on social media after the acquittal of George Zimmerman in the shooting death of African-American teen Trayvon Martin.
- **Gender pay equity**—in spite of a long history of trying to close the gender gap through social and legal means, the lack of parity persists and would, at this pace, take many years to close. To expedite closing of the gap, Melinda Gates pledged $1 billion to promote gender equality.
- **Climate change**—considered to be one of the world's greatest future challenges for humanity, environmental concerns and sustainability are a top priority especially among the younger generation of workers. The campaign of teenage climate activist Greta Thunberg has gained international recognition and urges politicians and corporations to act now.
- **Corporate civic engagement**—is increasingly considered an important branding element of a business, not just for consumers but also for employees. Both consumers and employees want to work with companies that support their ideals and make a difference in the civic communities in which they operate.

What these movements have in common is that they all use 'new' power. But what exactly is new power? In a summary and review of a 2018 book New Power, by Jeremy Heimans and Henry Timms, the central theme is summarized as follows: "*Digital connectivity has changed our era's power dynamics. Old power, with its centralized top-down hierarchy, is being replaced with a bottom-up new-power system that prizes decentralization, collaboration, and transparent execution. These systems have different models and values, but it's not simply a case of 'new power = good; old power = bad.' Both have merits and disadvantages. And although they can be blended, new power offers a fresh set of tools for building crowds, spreading ideas, and leading organizations.*"[2]

According to Heimans and Timms, new power uses three distinct leadership tools: *signaling, structuring*, and *shaping*.

- **Signaling**—through their actions, they signal desirable behaviors to adherents;
- **Structuring**—they flip the old-power hierarchical pyramid and build a more inverted pyramid, where power flows from the bottom up;
- **Shaping**—they influence the general direction of an organization, subtly mold the beliefs and attitudes of their followers, and subconsciously change the rules of the game.

Why do these recent social movements matter to employers and the workplace? How are employers signaling, structuring, and shaping their response?

The #MeToo movement has changed the American workplace and has a significant impact on workplace culture with new (and improved) training on harassment in the workplace and how managers interact with employees. The #BlackLivesMatter movement has not only polarized America but also the workplace as a microcosm of society often dividing workers over these issues.
The gender pay gap has shown to be slow and difficult to close, making it critical for employers to continue the push toward equal pay for equal work. Companies are being pressured to address pay and equity issues and make wage gap audits and report transparent. Employers like Intel and Starbucks who have reached pay parity for genders are using it as a value proposition to attract talent. With regard to climate change, employers are being urged by their workers (especially the millennial generation) to take immediate action to address climate change issues and shift their policies by reducing their carbon footprint and promoting environmentally conscious behavior among employees. Civic engagement of employers is changing at the request of the millennial worker. New generations of workers push their employers to go beyond community engagement and take political stands on important issues facing the world.

While the impact of these social movements are creating outcomes that produce greater equality, diversity, inclusion, and creating momentum for employers, there can also be negative residual impacts. Employee Resource Groups (ERGs) are another mechanism to give employees a voice in organizations.

Rapid expansion of new power leaves people uncertain as to what the proper behavior is for employees, managers and the organization and what risks these behaviors—or the lack thereof—entail. The new generation of talent demands having a voice in these matters—without ignoring these rights also come with mutual responsibilities.

REFERENCES

1. This vignette was prepared by Professor Lisbeth Claus for the sole purpose of illustrating a global HR practice for instructional objectives. Global HR in Action © 2020, Global Immersion Press, All Rights Reserved.
2. Heimans, J. & Timms, H. (Accessed: January 5, 2020). https://lifeclub.org/books/new-power-jeremy-heimans-and-henry-timms-review-summary.

GUIDED READING QUESTIONS

1. How are these social movements impacting the workplace?
2. How does an organization signal, structure, and shape new power in response to these social movements?
3. What rights and responsibilities come with employees having a voice?

MODULE FOUR

THE CULTURAL LENS

MODULE FOUR

THE CULTURAL LENS

DESCRIPTION

This module analyzes organizations from the cultural lens, applies cultural concepts and theories to managerial action in organizations, analyzes how culture impacts and shapes individual and group behavior. After defining culture, we review the major value dimensions that have been proposed by leading cultural theorists for national culture and how they can be used to increase one's cultural competency. The module also focuses on corporate/organizational cultures, the importance of creating organizational culture based on leadership principles, and having the ability to take the pulse of how the culture is experienced by workers.

LEARNING OBJECTIVES

Upon completing the learning experience, you will be able to:

- Describe the focus of the cultural lens
- Define culture
- Identify how culture is learned
- Summarize the sociological culture-structure concept
- List the different types of culture
- Describe the cultural value dimensions distinguishing societies
- Relate the value dimensions (Hofstede, Trompenaars, Hall, Meyer) to cross-cultural understanding
- Distinguish between core, flex, and shared zone in cultural intelligence
- Identify means of acquiring cultural competency
- Apply dilemma reconciliation to common cultural management situations
- Map organizational cultures and describe advantages and disadvantages of different types
- Describe the impact of culture on management practices

GUIDING QUESTION

Are you culturally savvy?

At a recent Townhall meeting, MRS. ICHIKAWA, a financial analyst at Johnson & Johnson in Tokyo, Japan, was publicly awarded a KUDOS award by her boss in New Jersey, U.S. for her contributions. Mrs. Ichikawa was terrified. She strongly felt that the recognition did not belong to her alone, but to her entire team. One month later, Mrs. Ichikawa resigned from Johnson & Johnson.

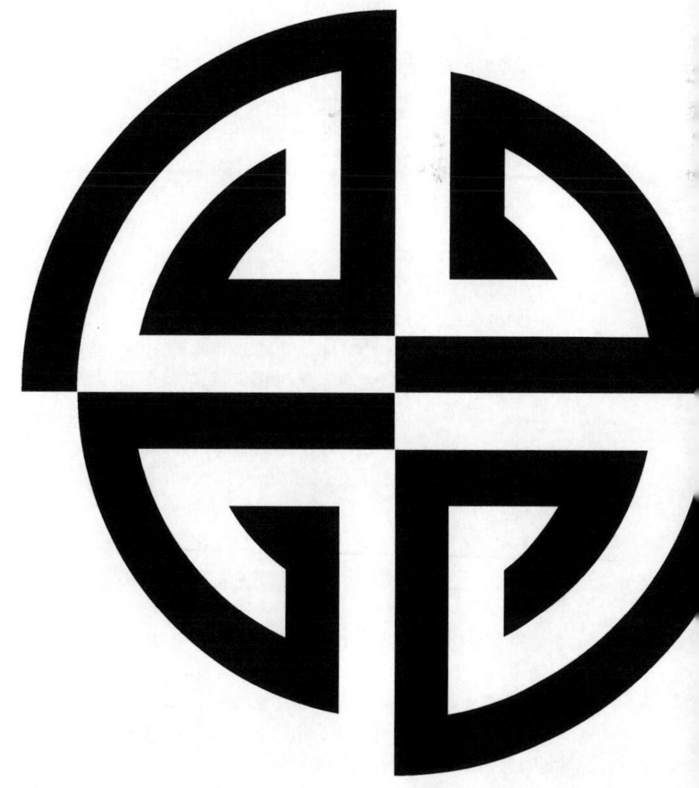

CULTURE[1]

Managing global organizations differs in at least four different ways from working domestically. As the scope of organizational activities extends beyond domestic borders to different geographic areas around the world, the most obvious outcome is that—*geographic distance*—becomes greater and time zone differences take effect. When the workday starts in San Francisco, it has ended in London and the Middle East, and it's already the next day in Australia. Global teams must operate 24 hours a day, 7 days a week, 365 days a year, yet people working on the same team may be dispersed across the globe. Second, as organizations cross borders, they must deal with the greater *cultural diversity* of the people involved. The workforce is becoming more and more diverse, and organizations must use the multiculturalism of the people working together to their advantage. In some countries, diversity is widely viewed as advantageous to organizational success. In others, diversity is viewed as a threat and thus resisted. In either case, the social systems and work expectations unique to each country are based on institutionalized norms of behavior and mores. Third, when working across borders, one must take into account different *legal and social systems* in the various countries of operations. Organizations must follow the laws and regulations of the nations in which they operate. These laws are not only different, but may also be in direct conflict with one another. Finally, global organizations deal with the *cross-border movement* of capital, goods, services, and people. It is far more complex to move people across borders than to work out the logistics of moving goods, services, and money.

Although all these differences between the domestic and global operations of organizations account for the greater complexity of global management, effective cross-cultural management is key. By not understanding and/or ignoring cultural differences, there is a danger that viewing the world from one's own assumptions and perspectives will lead to misunderstanding the actions and behaviors of people working together in organizations.

Cultural understanding is of vital importance for global organizations because culture influences a variety of behaviors of people in the workplace. Culture impacts management practices in terms of how:

- Decisions are made;
- Problems are solved;
- People communicate;
- Negotiations are held;
- Conflict is dealt with;
- Work and its meaning are viewed;
- Time is perceived;
- People perform;
- Planning is done;
- People participate;
- Employees engage;
- The role of men and women is defined;
- Diversity is viewed;
- Ethical dilemmas are defined and solved;
- People manage other people;
- People experience being managed by others.

The purpose of this module is to get a better understanding of the impact of the cultural context on management. First, the notion of culture as studied by anthropologists and sociologists is explored. Second, the learning of culture is discussed. Third, common value dimensions developed by cultural theorists are reviewed as they apply to global management. Fourth, organizational culture is explored.

THE NOTION OF CULTURE

Culture is usually defined as a commonly held and shared set of beliefs and values as to how one is expected to behave in a particular group or society. Culture has also been defined "*as the collective mental programming of the human mind which distinguishes one group of people from another,*"[2] and described as "*the way in which a group of people solves problems.*"[3] Culture is not uniform or a monolithic concept but consists of different types of culture. The relationship between culture and structure in a particular society enables the socialization of its members and the exercise of social control. Due to the complexity of culture, metaphors are commonly used to illustrate what it entails.

Cultural Metaphors

In order to explain the notion of a culture, an implicit comparison is often made to other things that are quite unlike but have something in common with it. Popular cultural metaphors are: culture as an iceberg; culture as peeling an onion; and culture as a mirror image. The *iceberg* analogy of culture views the culture of a society as an iceberg where some aspects of the culture—above the water—are visible but the larger part of the culture is invisible and hidden below the surface. The tip of the iceberg is the visible conscious culture and its behavioral manifestations. On the explicit or surface culture are things like language, food, architecture, arts, literature, music, dress, pace of life, space and physical distance, climate, public emotions, and work ethics. Below the surface are the values and beliefs, or unconscious culture (driving the behaviors) that are invisible.[4] Those elements which are not as obvious, such as why someone eats or dresses the way they do, are represented by the much larger portion of the iceberg underwater (see 4.1).

Another analogy of culture, peeling an onion, is also based on the complexity of culture. By removing the multiple layers of culture—layer by layer—one gets to underlying core issues driving the culture. The outer layer at the surface is the explicit culture (i.e., the cultural artifacts), the inner core is composed of values and norms, and at a deeper implicit level are the core assumptions.[5] The analogy of culture as a *mirror image* implies other cultures are not randomly different but represent mirror cultures of each other. "*Everyone in the world is alike in certain key respects, but are almost opposite and mirror images in other respects (...) It is as if we held a mirror up to our culture and saw a looking glass world beyond.*"[6] Culture as a mirror image, the basis of their dilemma reconciliation theory, requires prerequisite knowledge of one's own culture before understanding others.

Different Types of Cultures

When referring to culture in global management, one must consider various cultural types: the culture of a society (often

4-1. Iceberg Metaphor of Culture

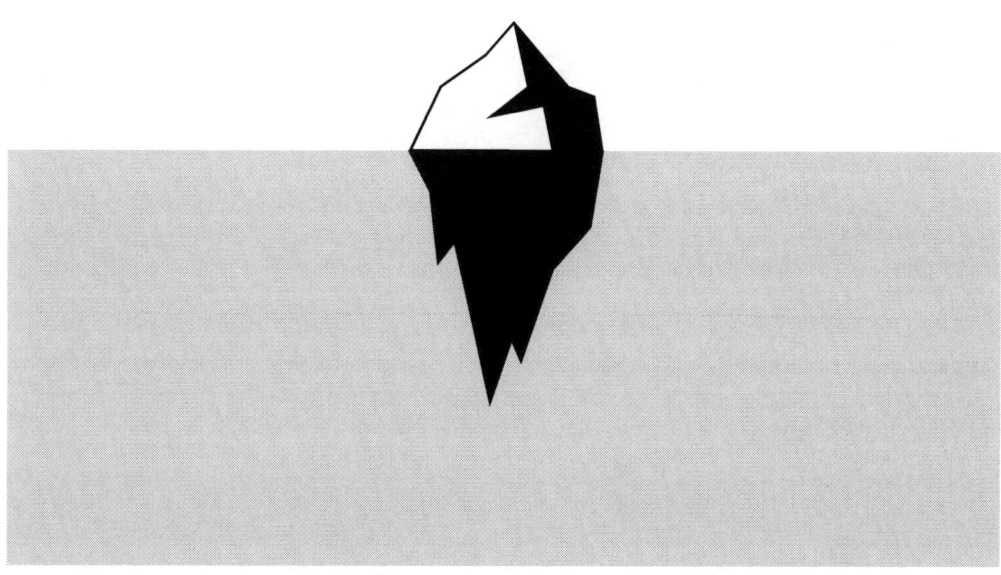

called national culture); the influence of subgroups and individuals (within societies or organizations); the culture of organizations (organizational or corporate culture); the culture of particular industries (industry culture); and the culture of professions (professional culture). Each of these different cultures has an impact on the way people manage others and are managed in a particular situation.

National culture—is referred to as the values, norms, and behaviors of the people in a sovereign nation or country. It is deeply rooted in its national heritage and outwardly visible by the artifacts and symbols that represent a particular nation. Yet, below the surface, people in that culture are likely to adhere to core assumptions and value orientations that are unique to that country. A few favorite proverbs illustrate the reality—and often myth—of popular culture. For example, in Japan, '*the nail that sticks out gets hammered down*.' In the U.S., one can go '*from rags to riches*,' while in Scandinavia, the Janteloven concept is engrained in the society and one of the Jante laws states, '*don't think of yourself as being better than us*.'[7] In Saudi Arabia, having *Wasta*, or knowing someone to get you what you want through connections, can be very instrumental to getting things done.

Subcultures—is a group of people within a culture who differentiate themselves from the larger culture. Subcultures may be driven by ethnic, gender, and linguistic diversity, or simply communities of interest. For example, the social, cultural, and structural differences between Wallonia and Flanders and the growing federalization of the political institutions often make it difficult to speak of Belgium as one nation.[8]

Organizational culture—refers to the values and behaviors common to an organization and is best expressed by the saying, '*this is how things are done around here*.' Organizational culture dictates how an organization conducts its business or accomplishes its mission, how people are treated (e.g., employees, customers, suppliers, and the community), how decisions are made, and what the general commitment and loyalty to the brand in terms of both customer and employee value proposition. Some organizations with strong organizational culture even label their way of doing as 'the—HP, Toyota, and Teva—way.' The importance and impact of organizational culture on organizations has been studied widely.[9]

Industry culture—is the type of work done by organizations in their industry and/or sector; comes with a specific set of values, norms, and behaviors regarding a particular way of thinking, behaving, and interacting with others and the environment. Industry culture impacts the level of internationalization of an industry/sector, the way technology and tools are used, the prevalent quality standards, the degree of competition, and the prevailing ethics. Industry culture is also influenced by the dominant professional groups that it employs. For example, the retail industry behaves differently than the financial industry, and not-for-profit organizations have different employment practices than the public sector.

Professional culture—relates to the behaviors appropriate to members of an occupational/professional group as a result of acquired competency in a particular body of knowledge, credentialing through university education, licensing by the appropriate professional group, and being held accountable for compliance with a professional code of ethics. Professionals in their practice have a great deal of autonomy and discretionary decision-making authority.[10] As a result, an accountant in an Indian firm is likely to have much more in common with a German accountant than both have with the HR practitioner in their firms, allowing professional culture to prevail over national culture. This could be due to selection (why individuals choose a particular profession) and/or causation (exposure to the profession and a result of both anticipatory and professional socialization). With today's global environment and the increased professionalization of work, the impact of professional culture on organizations should not be underestimated.

> *CULTURE TAKEAWAY CONCEPT # 1: Culture is not a monolithic concept but comprises national, organizational, industry, professional/functional, and many sub-cultures.*

Culture and Structure

Regardless of the definition adopted, culture deals with values, beliefs, needs, and attitudes that are socially preferable and expected in communities of people—whether they are nations, communities, organizations, industries, or professions. The preferences expressed in values (i.e., *what people value and like*) are then translated into expectations and become mores, modes of conduct, norms of behavior, regulations, and laws (i.e., *what people are expected to do*). Socialization is required to ensure the learning of and adherence to the culture of its groups. Thus, societies establish social systems and institutions as socialization and social control mechanisms. This sociological culture-structure relationship is expressed in 4-2. This is where the cultural meets the structural lens!

> *CULTURE TAKEAWAY CONCEPT # 2: All societies have basic assumptions made up of values (what we like to do) and norms (what we should do) that are eventually institutionalized into laws.*

The learning of culture

Socialization is the process by which people culturally integrate into a group and learn its values and norms. Societies create fundamental institutions (family, education, economics, religion, and politics) in order to shape the values, norms, and behaviors of their members. This is the way values and norms are institutionalized into the structure of a society, giving culture its enduring character and making it difficult to change.

> *CULTURE TAKEAWAY CONCEPT # 3: Culture is shared by the members of a group, organization, or society, learned through its socialization process, transmitted from generation to generation, and relatively stable over time.*

An emic view of culture is perceived by a person from within, while an etic view is viewed from an observer's perspective. An emic view of the culture explains human behavior from the point of view of the insider (native interpretation), while an etic view provides an outsider interpretation of behavior. Emic explanations usually focus on the impact of culture on the behavior of an individual (e.g., how risk is perceived in a certain culture). Etic explanations usually focus on how a certain phenomenon varies across cultures (e.g., the meaning of trust, the value of diversity, etc.). Emic explanations of culture can clash with etic views but both views can be integrated to guide managers in coping with cultural differences by anticipating sensitivities of employees in other cultures, identifying and choosing appropriate options, and implementing policy options.[11]

4-2. The Culture-Structure Context

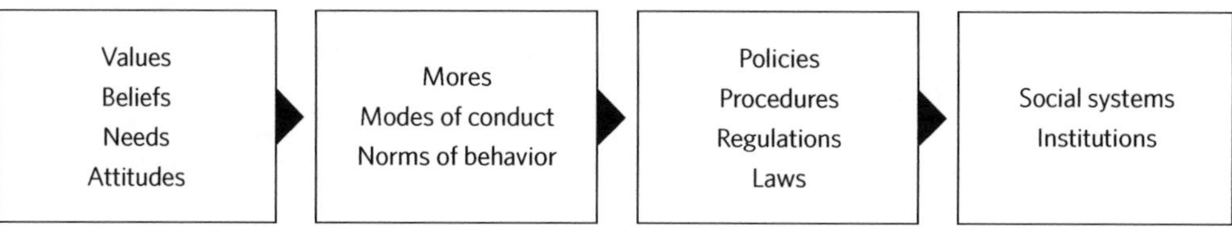

CULTURE TAKEAWAY CONCEPT # 4: Culture can be emic or etic.

The Role of Institutions

Reflecting its culture, each society is organized in a certain way and develops institutions by which it governs and controls itself. Institutions play a major role in culture as socialization and control mechanisms. Therefore, to better understand and function in a society that has a different culture, it is useful to have knowledge of the structural elements of that society, including the demographic, economic, legal, political, education, family, language, and religious institutions.

Demographic composition—Gender, age, race, and ethnic groups are ascribed dimensions that produce cultural variations within countries and lead to common subcultures within a society.

Economic systems—While there is controversy about the relationship between economic systems and culture, the way markets operate is intertwined with the formal institutions that support a society. Economists tend to view the rational utility-maximizing behavior of people while sociologists emphasize the role of cultural values and norms in economic life.[12]

Legal environment—The type of legal system, and particularly the existence of the rule of law, indicates the extent of formal mechanisms of social control and how norms and laws are handled and enforced.

Political system—Political institutions such as political parties, governments, and trade unions play various roles from making and enforcing laws, mediating conflicts, making policy, and holding individuals and organizations accountable.

Family structure—The importance of family is deeply embedded in cultures (Chinese, Hispanic, Italian, Spanish, Iranian, Japanese, etc.). The family is where cultural values are initially learned and the connection to other vital socialization institutions is anchored (especially educational opportunities and religious affiliation). It is also where gender differences related to family and work roles are first modeled.

Educational system—What and how things are taught and the way the educational system is organized are critical ways in which a society socializes the next generation (also called cultural reproduction) and prepares it for the workplace. For example, in Japan, the educational system reinforces in children the values of hard work and self-discipline. These values are then reflected in the workplace and reinforce the long-term orientation employers have in developing their employees.

Language—The different languages spoken around the world (as well as and the nonverbal component of communication) greatly complicate communication in the workplace and can create language barriers among people. How language barriers actually work is the domain of socio-linguists, but the impact of language on management practices has received limited attention. The reasons for this are likely twofold: the pre-eminence of English as the language of business and the fact that the leading cultural management theorists developed value dimensions that make no reference to language. Yet, the importance of language in terms of communication, knowledge sharing, and transfer as well as the development of trust cannot be negated. Substantial differences have been found in terms of language competencies, policies, and practices in Anglophone, Asian, Continental European, and Nordic multinational companies.[13]

Religion—Analogous to culture, religion is made up of a set of values, beliefs, and expected behaviors shared by the members of the group. However, each world religion has different principles and interpretations of their meaning. As with all institutions, adherents of a religion are socialized and taught its rites and rituals. Religions organize and influence the behavior of their members and exert social control. The impact of religion on work ethic and the workplace (such as leadership, ethics, diversity, cultural competence, and human rights) has been documented.[14]

> *CULTURE TAKEAWAY CONCEPT # 5: Culture is learned through the socialization process in the society's major institutions.*

Culture is a collective rather than an individual dimension. The cultural determinism view is that people are highly influenced by socialization in their cultural environment. Yet, there are individual differences in behavior with people from the same culture. Individual variations within a given culture may be as big as differences between cultures. This may be due to strong individual differences (i.e., personally traits) and people who do not fit the norm in their culture (i.e., having deviant behavior), but it can also be due to factors related to socialization into other types of cultures. For example, strong organizational and professional cultures may attenuate the impact of other types of national cultures. In this respect, the behavior of an employee in a global company with a highly globally integrated culture (such as IBM) may reduce the impact of national cultural differences between employees. When people behave as IBM employees, the values and the norms—acquired through strong onboarding—that underlie their behaviors are similar around the world. Similarly, the differences between two members of the same profession may be smaller than the cross-cultural differences between the countries. Finally, the exposure that one has with people from other cultures may not be akin to exposure to the 'average' person in that culture. These people are likely not random samples of their respective cultures as a result of the ways in which we are exposed to them (i.e., people who left their country, people who could communicate in another language, etc.). In each of these cases, we may attribute their behavior to the national culture while in fact it may be the result of other individual or socialization factors.

> *CULTURE TAKEAWAY CONCEPT #6: Differentiate between the behavior of individuals based on personality traits and the behavior learned through their cultural background. Differences within cultures should not be ignored and may be as large as the differences between cultures.*

CULTURAL VALUE DIMENSIONS

Culture can be best understood by looking at the cultural value orientations of what a particular group of people values. A value orientation is a preference developed by a cultural group. Research on how cultures differ on various value dimensions has been developed by anthropologists, sociologists, and management researchers. These value dimensions focus on national culture and are presented as ideal-type dimensions (usually on a high-low continuum or as opposing dimensions) that a particular culture is most likely to resemble. The value dimensions highlight how the people from a particular culture generally view power and authority, risk and ambiguity, human interactions and relations, status, activity orientation, time, communication, human nature, and the environment. Countries are low or high on these dimensions, or can be situated somewhere on a continuum of opposing views. The value dimensions developed by some authors (Kluckhohn & Strodtbeck, Hall, Hofstede, Trompenaars, and Meyer) are reviewed below and illustrated with some specific examples on how they affect cross-cultural management situations.

Florence Kluckhohn & Fred Strodtbeck

In their 1961 book, *Variations in Value Orientations*, Florence Kluckhohn & Fred Strodtbeck proposed the value orientation theory. They suggested that all human societies face a limited number of universal problems and need to answer five fundamental questions:[15]

1. On what aspect of time should we primarily focus?
2. What is the relationship between humanity and its natural environment?
3. How should individuals relate with others?
4. What is the prime motivation for behavior?
5. What is the nature of human nature?

Based on the answers to these questions, different cultures have unique preferences in terms of their relationships with others, basic human nature, activity orientation, relationship to the environment, and their view of time and space. While the work of anthropologists Kluckhohn & Strodtbeck is rarely applied to management today, it important for two reasons: (1) rather than focusing on cultural differences between two countries, for example Japan and the United States, it allows to use a standard value dimensions to compare multiple countries; (2) it has become the foundation of several of the more popular cultural value dimensions developed later and used today in cross-cultural management.[16]

Edward Hall

As an anthropologist, Hall focused on differences in cultural attitudes toward space (proxemics), time (monolithic versus polychronic) and low and high context human communication (see figure 4-3).[17]

Geert Hofstede

Collecting data in the 1960s and 70s with IBM employees worldwide, Hofstede developed four original dimensions (power distance, uncertainty avoidance, individualism, and masculinity).[18] Two additional dimensions were added later—long-term orientation or Confucian Dynamism and indulgence versus restraint (see 4-4). Scores are currently available for more than 70 countries.

Hofstede provides numerous examples of how his value dimensions affect management situations.[19]

Power distance—Countries with high power distance (such as Malaysia, Guatemala, Panama, Philippines, Mexico, and Venezuela) versus countries with small power distance (such as Austria, Israel, Denmark, New Zealand, and Ireland) may differ in terms of training, the views on subordinates, corruption, and compensation. In training, small power distance cultures value student-centered education in contrast to high power distance cultures that value teacher-centered education. In small power distance cultures, subordinates expect to be consulted, while in high power distance cultures they expect to be told what to do. In small power distance cultures, corruption is rare and scandals end political careers; in high power distance cultures, corruption is frequent and scandals are covered up. Cultures that are low on power distance have a strong belief in equality of compensation (equal pay for equal work) while in high power distance cultures there is greater disparity in income distribution.

4-3. Cultural Value Dimensions of Hall

Area	Value Dimension	Description
Communication	High Context	Information vested in the person and the relationship; informal, subtle ambiguity, face-to-face communication.
	Low Context	Clear and unambiguous messages, emphasis on time management, deadlines, punctuality, and contracts.
Time	Monolithic	Paying attention to doing only one thing at a time.
	Polychronic	Being involved with many things at once.

Source: Edward T. Hall, *Beyond Culture* (New York, NY: Doubleday, 1976).

4-4. Cultural Value Dimensions of Hofstede

Value Dimension	Description
Power distance (PDI)	The degree to which the less powerful members of a society accept the power and expect power is distributed unequally.
Individualism (IDV) versus collectivism	Individualism: a preference for a loosely-knit social framework in which individuals are expected to take care of themselves and their immediate families only. Collectivism: a preference for a tightly-knit framework in which individuals can expect their relatives or members of a particular in-group to look after them in exchange for unquestioning loyalty.
Masculinity (MAS) versus femininity	Masculinity: a preference in society for achievement, heroism, assertiveness, and material reward for success. Society at large is more competitive. Femininity: a preference for cooperation, modesty, caring for the weak, and quality of life. Society at large is more consensus-oriented.
Uncertainty avoidance (UAI)	The degree to which the members of a society feel uncomfortable with uncertainty and ambiguity.
Long-term orientation (LTO) versus short-term orientation	Long-term orientation: in societies with a long-term orientation, people believe that truth depends very much on situation, context, and time. They show an ability to adapt traditions to changed conditions, a strong propensity to save and invest, thriftiness, and perseverance in achieving results. Short-term orientation: societies with a short-term orientation generally have a strong concern with establishing the absolute truth. They are normative in their thinking. They exhibit great respect for traditions, a relatively small propensity to save for the future, and a focus on achieving quick results.
Indulgence versus restraint (IVR)	Indulgence: a society that allows relatively free gratification of basic and natural human drives related to enjoying life and having fun. Restraint: a society that suppresses gratification of needs and regulates it by means of strict social norms.

Source: "National culture dimensions," accessed December 15, 2012, http://geert-hofstede.com/dimensions.html

Uncertainty avoidance—Countries high on uncertainty avoidance (such as Greece, Portugal, Guatemala, Uruguay, Belgium, and El Salvador) versus countries low on uncertainty avoidance (such as Singapore, Jamaica, Denmark, Sweden, and Hong Kong) may differ in terms of empowerment, wellbeing turnover, rules, and planning. Managing in a low/weak uncertainty avoidance culture requires that the manager give subordinates a lot of latitude and empowerment versus managing someone in a high/strong uncertainty culture, which may require more direct guidance. In a low/weak uncertainty avoidance culture, employees may demand a greater focus on lowering stress and focus on subjective health and well-being versus a high/strong uncertainty culture wherein they are willing to tolerate high stress and focus less on subjective health and wellbeing. In a low/weak uncertainty avoidance culture, changing jobs is no problem versus a high/strong uncertainty culture, where people may stay in jobs even when disliked. In a low/weak uncertainty avoidance culture, there is a dislike of written and unwritten rules, policies and procedures versus a high/strong uncertainty culture, where there is an emotional need for rules even if they are not obeyed. Cultures that are high on uncertainty avoidance prefer careful planning to reduce risk and prefer step-by-step incremental, rather than sweeping changes. Cultures that are low on uncertainty avoidance can deal with greater amounts of unpredictability.

Masculinity—Masculine societies (such as Japan, Hungary, and Austria) versus feminine societies (such as Sweden, Norway, Netherlands, and Denmark) may differ in gender roles and work-life balance. In masculine societies, gender roles are highly differentiated versus in feminine societies, there is minimal differentiation between what men and women are expected to do. In masculine societies, work prevails over family versus in feminine societies, there is a greater balance between family and work.

Individualism—Individualist societies (such as the United States, Australia, Great Britain, and the Netherlands) versus collectivistic societies (such as China, Japan, Guatemala, Ecuador, Panama, Venezuela, Colombia, Pakistan, and Indonesia) may differ in rewards, pay for philosophy, task orientation, language use, and privacy. In individualist cultures, everyone is expected to take care of themselves and immediate family only. In collectivist cultures, people are born in extended families and clans which protect them in exchange for loyalty. In individualist cultures, there is an emphasis on personal achievement and pay for performance versus collectivistic cultures, in which the focus is on large extended family and groups and on entitlement and acquired rights. In individualist cultures, tasks prevail over relationships, versus collectivist cultures, in which relationships prevail over tasks. In individualist cultures, there is an 'I' consciousness and the word 'I' is indispensable, versus collectivist cultures which are 'we' consciousness. In individualist cultures, there is a right of privacy versus collectivist cultures, where the focus is on belonging.

Long-term orientation—Long-term orientation cultures, often referred to as Confucian Dynamism cultures (such as China, Hong Kong, Taiwan, and Japan) and short-term orientation cultures (such as Sierra Leone, Nigeria, Ghana, Philippines, and Norway) may differ in gratification, incentives provided, and the developmental opportunities given to employees. In short-term orientation cultures, there is a desire for employees to receive immediate gratification and incentives, while in long-term cultures personal gratification can be postponed if the long-term value is understood. Long-term oriented cultures may be willing to experience personal sacrifices (prolonged education, absence from family, and temporal inconveniences) as an investment in their future careers. Organizations with a long-term orientation (as is customary in Japan, for example) are more willing to invest in long-term developmental opportunities for their workforce in return for employee loyalty. Long-term oriented cultures focus more on thrift, having a sense of shame, protection of 'face', respect for tradition, and reciprocation of greetings, favors, and gifts.[20]

Indulgence versus restraint—In cultures where indulgence prevails (such as South and North America, Western Europe, and parts of Sub-Saharan Africa) versus cultures where restraint prevails (Eastern Europe, Asia, Muslim world) the importance of freedom of speech and leisure is affected, amongst other things.[21]

Fons Trompenaars

Based on research among employees of the Royal Dutch Shell Group, Trompenaars studied the effect of culture of management.[22] He questioned the well-intended 'universal' applications of management theories and set out to understand what common management terms mean to people in different cultures. Trompenaars developed seven fundamental dimensions of cultures arising from relationship with people,[23] the passage of time,[24] and relationship to the environment[25] (see 4-5).

Here are a few examples of how these dimensions affect management:

Universalism versus particularism—in universalistic or rule-based cultures (Canada, USA, Switzerland, Australia, Sweden, Norway, Germany Ireland, and United Kingdom) there is a preference for written contracts,

4-5. Cultural Value Dimensions of Trompenaars

Category	Value Dimension	Description
Relationship with people (rules versus relationships)	Universalism versus particularism	Universalism: adhere to standards which are universally agreed upon by the culture in which we lived; abstract; rule-based. Particularism: judgments focus on the exceptional nature of the present circumstances; relationship-based.
Relationship with people (the group versus the individual)	Collectivism versus individualism	Collectivism: orientation to the common goals and objectives of the group versus those of an individual. Individualism: prime orientation to the self.
Relationship with people (the range of feelings expressed)	Affective versus neutral	Affective: show their feelings plainly. Affectively neutral: keep their feelings carefully controlled and subdued.
Relationship with people (the range of involvement)	Diffuse versus specific	Specific: segregates the task relationships with co-workers and insulates them from other dealings—from specific to general Diffuse: every life space permeates all others— from general to specific.
Relationship with people (how status is accorded)	Achievement versus ascription	Achievement: status is accorded based on activities and achievements. Ascription: status is accorded by virtue of age, class, gender, education, etc.
Passage of time (how we manage time)	Past, present, and future orientation Sequential versus synchronous	Past time orientation: look for solutions in the past. Present time orientation: look for immediate effects. Future time orientation: long-term results of events. Sequential: time is viewed as a line of sequential events passing at regular time intervals Synchronous: time is viewed as cyclical and repetitive, compressing past, present, and future in common seasons and rhythms.
Relationship to nature (how we relate to nature)	Inner-directed versus outer-directed	Inner-directed: it is believed they can or should control nature by imposing their will upon it. They have an internal locus of control. Outer-directed: it is believed that man is part of nature and must go along with its laws, directions, and forces. They have an external locus of control.

Source: Fons Trompenaars, *Riding the Waves of Culture: Understanding Cultural Diversity in Business* (London: Nicholas Brealey Publishing, 1993).

headquarters shaping standardized operations, managers behaving with consistency, and a greater reliance on the courts to mediate conflict. In particularistic or relationship-based cultures (South Korea, Venezuela, Russia, Indonesia, China, Malaysia, Bulgaria, Greece, and India)[26] personal relationships with colleagues are important, flexible, unhurried, and based on personal trust and loyalty. Formal contracts are not perceived as important and easily modified or broken if circumstances change.

Specific versus diffuse—in specific cultures (such as the U.S. and Canada), relationships among people focus on the specificity of the task and managers and employees may not have a lot of interaction beyond work. In diffuse cultures (such as South America, Arab countries, SE Asia, and East Africa), home and work may be more intertwined.[27] In specific cultures, people tend to be task-oriented, versus diffuse cultures in which interactions are relationship-based.

Erin Meyer

Erin Meyer uses a cultural map for comparing cultures.[28] She identified cultural differences in various management situations on a continuum related to communicating (low context vs high context), evaluating (direct negative feedback vs indirect negative feedback), persuading (principle first vs application first), leading (egalitarian vs hierarchical), deciding (consensual vs top down), trusting (task-based vs relationship-based), disagreeing (confrontational vs avoids confrontation), scheduling (linear vs flexible time). She contributes to the cultural differences debate by showing how within a culture, individuals may deviate from the norm of their culture along the continuum.

> *CULTURE TAKEAWAY CONCEPT #7: Leading cultural theorists have identified value dimensions by which national cultures differ. These dimensions are useful as a starting point and help us understand the implications of cultural differences for managing and being managed.*

The above cultural value dimensions constitute the building blocks of cross-cultural understanding. Two particular caveats must be kept in mind when considering these cultural value dimensions. First, several of these value dimensions are interrelated and intertwined. Second, culture is a collective rather than individual dimension. Hence, individual variations within a given culture may be as big as differences between cultures.

CULTURAL DISTANCE

Cultural distance is the degree to which national cultural characteristics between countries differ based on their value dimensions. Kogut and Sing (1988) derived a measure of cultural distance between two countries by establishing a composite index based on the deviations of the four basic original Hofstede dimensions (power distance, masculinity, individualism, and uncertainty avoidance) of each country. The formula is as follows:

$$CDj = \Sigma 4\ i{=}1\ \{(Iij - Iiu)\ 2\ /Vi\}/4$$

- Iij = the index for the ith cultural dimension and j^{th} country
- Vi = variance of the index of the ith dimension
- u (e.g., the U.S.) = the other country
- CDj = the cultural difference of the jth country (e.g., the U.S.) from the other country.

Corrections for variances of each dimension were made, and the results were averaged.[29]

Note the Kogut and Singh measure is a mean-based index of cultural distance or a nation-to-nation comparison on cultural values that ignores the cultural variations that exist within a country. A greater cultural understanding can be derived from using both mean-based (such as the Kogut and Singh index) and variance-based measures of cultural distance taking the cultural variation within countries into account.[30]

> *CULTURE TAKEAWAY CONCEPT #8: Cultural differences within countries may be as great as cultural differences between countries.*

CULTURAL ADJUSTMENT

Cultural competence is important for global organizations, especially when they put diverse people on teams or send people on an international assignment. For both short- and long-term international assignments, global mobility confronts employees with the process of adjusting to the host country culture. Cross-cultural adjustment is the extent to which individuals are psychologically comfortable living outside of their home country.[31] It is different from assimilation, which is the process by which people fully take on the cultural characteristics of the host country and lose their own. Assimilation is not necessarily desirable for international assignees as it is equated to a 'go native' allegiance.[32] Cultural adjustment does not happen all at once, as it is a process that evolves over time. The flow of that process has a U-shaped curve.[33]

After a very short period of time in the country, the original 'honeymoon' phase is over and the international assignee's adjustment dips dramatically (called 'culture shock'). Culture shock is the anxiety and depression experienced by people when they move to a new social and cultural environment. It is *"precipitated by anxiety that results from losing all our familiar signs and symbols of social intercourse."*[34] It takes approximately nine months before the slope of the curve changes and the assignee develops some coping mechanisms, which eventually lead to 'adjustment,' but it takes one year before the international assignee reaches the same adjustment level as when they entered the country. 'Mastery' of the culture takes even longer and may require two years. When the international assignee is repatriated home upon completion of the assignment, a similar adjustment process ensues even to their former home country. A similar U-shaped curve reflects adjustment upon re-entry and reintegration, and reverse culture shock takes place upon return to the home country. The entry and re-entry curves combined form a W-curve.

> *CULTURE TAKEAWAY CONCEPT #9: Cultural adjustment usually involves the process of cultural shock. Re-entry involves reverse culture shock.*

ACQUIRING CROSS-CULTURAL COMPETENCIES

People working in multi-cultural environments, on global teams, and working and managing across borders need to acquire cross-cultural savvy. In order to successfully operate in a culturally diverse marketplace—whether internationally or domestically, organizations must reflect what the customer wants.

Cultural Competence

Organizations understand the advantages of having talent with a global mindset and consider the development of cross-cultural competencies in their employees desirable. Yet, there are common misunderstandings of what this entails and whether the efforts deployed to increase cross-cultural savvy do pay off. There are four foundational principles of cultural competence: The first principle is that cultural knowledge does not necessarily equate with cultural competence. The second states that cultural contact does not necessarily lead to competence. The third principle is that cultural contact may lead to a reduction of stereotype. Finally, the fourth principle posits that although extremely valuable in international business, language learning may not be sufficient for culture learning.[35] Cross-cultural competency in employees requires more than merely training. Acquiring cross-cultural competency is a process of learning, experiencing, and evaluating intercultural situations. Key elements of cultural intelligence are knowledge, mindfulness, and behavior.[36] Cultural learning follows the S-curve (a slow beginning, a steep acceleration, and plateauing), typical of complex skill acquisition, and becomes a lengthy process of understanding, experiencing, and evaluating cultural differences.

Understanding cultural differences—Understanding corresponds to the ability to 'recognize' and 'respect'' differences in value dimensions. An essential principle is the concept of 'core' and 'flex' developed by Julia Middleton as part of her 'cultural intelligence' model.[37] Julia Middleton describes cultural intelligence as an ability to communicate, relate, and succeed while working and/or being in another cultural environment. This ability is supported by the concepts of emotional intelligence (EQ) and intelligence quotient (IQ). However, cultural competence requires experience with people from other cultures and exposure to globally diverse locales in order to become culturally intelligent. An individual's 'core' contains the personal values, beliefs, morals, and philosophies. It also houses a person's biases, which helps to process information needed to survive, to make sound judgments and to distinguish between known and unknown situations. If left unchecked and hidden, such biases create blind spots that lead to 'stuckness' that may perpetuate ignorant behavior. 'Flex' describes the variety of behaviors, statements, actions, feelings, and thoughts that one applies and demonstrates based on the situation at hand. The shared zone is the area people from different cultures have in common, where each is able to understand and empathize with the other in the conversation or relationship. Being 'in the zone' together can open dialogue where both parties are engaged by listening, thinking, and responding with positive intent, and all of that leads to building relationship trust. Understanding culture is a gradual process of shedding one's ethnocentrism or the belief that "*our way is the best way,*"[38] which implies that our culture is superior over other cultures.

Experiencing cultural differences—experiencing occurs in person-to-person situations when we meet people from other cultural backgrounds or immerse ourselves in another culture.

Evaluating cultural differences—evaluating refers to the ability to contrast our understanding with our experience and to reconcile the cultural differences. But embracing other cultures does not necessarily happen at the expense of our own. Being rooted in one's culture is a pre-requisite for belonging.

> *CULTURE TAKEAWAY CONCEPT #10: Acquiring cross cultural competencies involves the interrelated processes of understanding, experiencing, and evaluating cultural differences.*

Acquiring Cultural Savvy

One of the challenges in working cross-culturally is to be able to follow the golden rule (treating others as WE would like to be treated) and the global rule (treating others like THEY would like to be treated) simultaneously. Because the development of cross-cultural management skills requires the processes of understanding, experiencing, and evaluating culture, managers may have very different starting points and learning trajectories due to their very different work and non-work backgrounds. Still, there are basic practices in acquiring cultural savvy.

Understand your own culture—The most important skill that a multicultural manager needs to acquire cultural savvy is a profound understanding of one's own culture.[39] This self-reflection is crucial to the process of learning about other cultures. It also requires an understanding of which personal behaviors (self and others) are preferred because of personal preferences and affinities and/or which ones are learned as a result of socialization in the culture. To gain a full understanding of one's culture often requires stepping out of one's culture to become aware that what we do is based on what we have learned as part of our culture.

> *CULTURE TAKEAWAY CONCEPT #11: The most important skills for the multicultural manager is 'to be aware of one's own culture.'*

Use stereotypes to your advantage—Stereotypes are often frowned upon and seen as negative, overly simplified, widely-held conceptions about a particular group (i.e., the behavioral norm) and everyone belonging to that group who are then assumed to possess those characteristics. Yet, stereotypes can be harmful or useful depending on how they are used. Stereotyping becomes helpful when it is consciously held, descriptive rather than evaluative, accurate, the first 'best guess', and modified based on observations. Effective stereotyping allows for better understanding and taking appropriate action in new situations.[40]

> *CULTURE TAKEAWAY CONCEPT #12: Develop cultural sensitivity by being aware of stereotypes that people have about your own culture and you about them.*

Contrast cultural value dimensions—when dealing with someone from another culture, a good starting point is to contrast the value dimensions of that culture with one's own. Once the cultural difference has been identified, explore the recommended tips for doing business based on the identified cultural distance. Then, explore the implications of managing someone or being managed by someone from that culture.[41] This preliminary exercise is an ideal starting point for doing business in a particular culture that goes beyond superficial business etiquette.

CULTURE TAKEAWAY CONCEPT #13: Map out differences in value dimensions between cultures and explore the implications of managing and being managed by someone from that culture.

Practice dilemma reconciliation—in his various international management publications, Trompenaars proposes a more complex process of dilemma reconciliation. The ability to reconcile dilemmas in organizations is viewed as the core of global leadership.[42] In this approach, opposing views are viewed not in a linear thinking mode but as a result of cultural differences, which are fused and blended. This requires a process of recognizing, respecting, and reconciling cultural differences. In this circular thinking approach, the strength of one extreme is extended by considering and accommodating the other. Hence the importance to practice an inclusive leadership style.

CULTURE TAKEAWAY CONCEPT #14: The process of dilemma reconciliation requires you to recognize, respect, and reconcile cultural differences.

Analyze the institutional framework—operating effectively within a country requires an understanding of the institutional framework at two broad levels: (1) the organizational, industrial, and professional practices; and (2) the major social institutions of the country. Because culture is institutionalized in the structure of the society, cultural understanding goes beyond the values and the norms and includes the functioning of the society. Therefore, it is often not a good idea to manage a foreign country's operations with an expatriate who lacks understanding of the culture and structure of that society, but to utilize local talent who are savvy about the institutional framework of how to get things done in that society.

CULTURE TAKEAWAY CONCEPT #15: The institutional framework of the organization, profession, industry, and society are an extension of the culture.

Test the depth of your understanding of culture through cross-cultural experiences—There is only so much learning that can be acquired through cultural training. Beyond the explicit learning of culture, a tacit understanding requires experiencing the culture. The most effective experiences for the development of successful global professionals are four primary development options, referred to as the 4 T's: Travels, Teams, Training, and Transfer. By far the single most powerful is 'Transfer', or living and working in a foreign country. However, taking advantage of all four experiences during one's career is the most effective way to acquire the complete set of global leadership competencies.[43]

CULTURE TAKEAWAY CONCEPT #16: Global leadership development is best acquired through a combination of Travels, Teams, Training, and Transfer during one's career span.

ORGANIZATIONAL CULTURE

As mentioned above, organizational culture—often equated with corporate culture and ignoring that the non-profit and public sector organizations also have cultures—is the set of values and beliefs that guides the behavior of people in an organization. Edgar Schein developed an organizational culture diagram that comprises the basic assumptions—what people take for granted in the company, or the espoused values; what people are told, and the artifacts; what people see.[44]

In a 2018 *Harvard Business Review* article, Groysberg et al.[45] calls culture the 'tacit order of the organization' shaping the attitudes and behavior of the people by specifying norms of what is encouraged, discouraged, accepted, or rejected within a group. They show that culture is shared, pervasive, enduring, and implicit. They map organizational cultures along two dimensions: (1) how people interact (independence to interdependence); and (2) their response to change (flexibility to stability) leading to eight different styles across organizations strongly characterized by 'results' vs. 'caring.' Each organizational culture has its own advantages and disadvantages. Their typology is summarized in 4-6.

> *CULTURE TAKEAWAY CONCEPT #17: Organizations should pay attention to shaping their culture.*

Culture is an important, yet often neglected, area of global management. As the soft side of global management, it is easily assumed that people simply learn this competency by doing. As a manager using the culture lens, you need to know now the meaning of culture, understand how culture impacts behavior in the workplace, acquire cultural competence, and be able to reconcile cultural differences. The organizational culture defines to a large extent how employees experience their company, their managers, and HR. The degree to which everyone feels appreciated in the workplace and can be fully engaged and the importance the company puts on wellbeing at work have an enormous impact on how employees experience their employer. ■

4-6. Tacit Order of Organizational Culture

Type of organizational culture	Description	Advantages	Disadvantages
Caring Warm, sincere, relational (63%)	Focuses on relationships and mutual trust	Improved teamwork, engagement, communication, trust, and sense of belonging	Overemphasis on consensus building may reduce exploration of options, stifle competitiveness, and slow decision-making
Purpose Purpose-driven, idealistic, tolerant (9%)	Exemplified by idealism and altruism	Improved appreciation for diversity, sustainability, and social responsibility	Overemphasis on a long-term purpose and ideals may get in the way of practical and immediate concerns
Learning Open, inventive, exploring (7%)	Characterized by exploration, expansiveness, and creativity	Improved innovation, agility, and organizational learning	Overemphasis on exploration may lead to lack of focus and inability to exploit existing advantages.
Enjoyment Playful, instinctive, fun-loving (2%)	Expressed through fun and excitement	Improved employee morale, engagement, and creativity	Overemphasis on autonomy and engagement may lead to a lack of discipline and create possible compliance or governance issues
Results Achievement, driven, goal-focused (89%)	Characterized by achievement and winning	Improved execution, external focus, capability building, and goal achievement	Overemphasis on strong authority and bold decision-making may lead to politics, conflicts, and a psychologically unsafe work environment
Authority Bold, decisive, dominant (4%)	Defined by strength, decisiveness, and boldness	Improved speed of decision-making and responsiveness to threats and crises	Overemphasis on strong authority and bold decision-making may lead to politics, conflicts, and a psychologically unsafe work environment
Safety Realistic, careful, prepared (8%)	Defined by planning, caution, and preparedness	Improved risk management, stability, and business continuity	Overemphasis on standardization and formalization may lead to bureaucracy, inflexibility, and dehumanization of the work environment
Order Rule abiding, respectful, cooperative (15%)	Focused on respect, structure, and shared norms	Improved operational efficiency, reduced conflict, and greater civic-mindedness	Overemphasis on rules and traditions may reduce individualism, stifle creativity, and limit organizational agility

Source: Boris Groysberg, Jeremiah Lee, Jesse Price and J. Yo-Hud Cheng (2018). The Leader's Guide to Corporate Culture. *Harvard Business Review*, 96(1):44-57.

REFERENCES

1. This module is an update of: Claus, L. (2013). The Cultural Context: A Template For Cross-Cultural Management. Pp. 51-79 in Claus. L. (ed.), *Global HR Practitioner Handbook*, volume 1. Silverton: Global Immersion Press.
2. Hofstede, G. (1991). *Culture and Organizations. Software of the Mind.* New York: McGraw-Hill.
3. Schein, E. (1985). *Organizational Culture and Leadership* (1st ed.). San Francisco: Jossey Bass.
4. Hall, E. T. (1989). *Beyond Culture.* New York: Anchor Books.
5. Trompenaars, F. (1994). *Riding the Waves of Culture: Understanding Cultural Diversity in Business.* Burr Ridge: Irwin Professional Pub.
6. Hampden-Turner, C. & Trompenaars, F. (2002). *A mirror-imaged world: doing business in Asia.* Pp. 144-167 in Joynt, P. & Warner, M., Managing Across Cultures: Issues and Perspectives (2nd ed.). London: Thomson.
7. What is Janteloven? (Accessed: December 27, 2019). https://www.scandinaviastandard.com/what-is-janteloven-the-law-of-jante/
8. Claus, L., Vloeberghs, D., & Pichault, F. (2002). "Belgian-style Human Resource Management: A Case of Mistaken Identity," *European Journal of Management*, 20(4):438.
9. Schein, E. (1985). *Organizational Culture and Leadership* (1st ed.). San Francisco: Jossey Bass.
10. Freidson, E. (1970). *Professional Dominance: The Social Structure of Medical Care.* New Brunswick: Transaction Publishers.
11. Morris, M., Leung, K., Ames, D., & Lickel, B. (1999). "Views From Inside and Outside: Integrating Emic and Etic Insights About Culture and Justice Judgments," *Academy of Management Review*, 24(4):781-796.
12. Weber, M., Parsons, Talcott, & Tawney, R. H. (1930). *The Protestant Ethic and the Spirit of Capitalism.* London: Allen and Unwin. For a summary discussion, see: Fukuyama, F. (2001). "Culture and Economic Development: Cultural Concerns," *International Encyclopedia of the Social and Behavioral Sciences* (Elsevier Science Ltd), 3130-3134.
13. Harzing, A. & Pudelko, M. (2013). "Language Compe–tencies, Policies and Practices in Multinational Corporations: A Comprehensive Review and Comparison of Anglophone, Asian, Continental European and Nordic MNCs," *Journal of World Business*, 48(1):87-97.
14. Weber, M., Parsons, Talcott, & Tawney, R. H. (1930). *The Protestant Ethic and the Spirit of Capitalism.* London: Allen and Unwin. For a summary discussion, see: Fukuyama, F. (2001). "Culture and Economic Development: Cultural Concerns," *International Encyclopedia of the Social and Behavioral Sciences* (Elsevier Science Ltd), 3130-3134.
15. Kluckhohn, F. & Strodtbeck, F. (1961). *Variations in Value Orientations.* Evanston: Row Peterson.
16. See, for example, their influence on Hall (time), Hofstede (power distance and individualism) and Trompenaars (passage of time and relationship to nature) as seen in: Gutterman, A. (2009). *Organizational Management and Administration: A Guide for Managers and Professionals.* Eagon: Thomson West.
17. Hall, E. T. (1989). *Beyond Culture.* New York: Anchor Books.
18. Hofstede, G. (1980). *Culture's Consequences: International Differences in Work-Related Values.* Beverly Hills: Sage; Hofstede, G. (1991). Culture and Organizations. Software of the Mind. New York: McGraw-Hill.
19. Hofstede, G. (2011). Dimensionalizing Cultures: The Hofstede Model in Context. *Online Readings in Psychology and Culture*, 2(1). (Accessed: July 1, 2015). http://scholarworks. gvsu.edu/orpc/vol2/iss1/8.
20. The 6 dimensions of national culture (Accessed: December 15, 2019). https://www.hofstede-insights.com/models/national-culture/
21. Hofstede, G. (2011). Dimensionalizing Cultures: The Hofstede Model in Context. *Online Readings in Psychology and Culture*, 2(1). (Accessed: December 15, 2019). http://scholarworks. gvsu.edu/orpc/vol2/iss1/8.
22. Trompenaars, F. (1994). *Riding the Waves of Culture: Understanding Cultural Diversity in Business.* Burr Ridge: Irwin Professional Pub.
23. Based on the work of: Parsons, T. (1951). *The Social System.* New York: Free Press.
24. Based on the work of: Hall, E. T. (1989). *Beyond Culture.* New York: Anchor Books.
25. Based in the work of: Kluckhohn, F. & Strodtbeck, F. (1961). *Variations in Value Orientations.* Evanston: Row Peterson.
26. Trompenaars, F. (1994). *Riding the Waves of Culture: Understanding Cultural Diversity in Business.* Burr Ridge: Irwin Professional Pub., p. 35.

27. Trompenaars, F. (1994). *Riding the Waves of Culture: Understanding Cultural Diversity in Business*. Burr Ridge: Irwin Professional Pub., p. 88.
28. Meyer, E. (2014). "Navigating the Cultural Minefield," *Harvard Business Review*, May, 92(5):119-123.
29. Kogut, B., & Singh, H. (1988). "The Effect of National Culture on the Choice of Entry Mode", *Journal of International Business Studies*, 19(3).
30. Beugelsdijk, S., Onrust, M., Maseland, R., & Van Hoorn, A. (2015). "Cultural Distance in International Business and Management: From Mean-based to Variance-based Measures," *The International Journal of Human Resource Management*, 26(2):165-191.
31. Black, J. (1990). "The relationship of personal characteristics with adjustment of Japanese expatriate managers," *Management International Review*, 30:119-134.
32. Black, J. & Gregersen, H. (1992). "Serving Two Masters: Managing the Dual Allegiance of Expatriate Employees," *Sloan Management Review*, 33(4):61-71.
33. Black, J., & Mendenhall, M. (1991). "The U-curve Adjustment Hypothesis Revisited: A Review and Theoretical Frame–work," *Journal of International Business Studies*, 22: 225-47.
34. Oberg, K. (1960). "Culture Shock: Adjustment to New Cultural Environments," *Practical Anthropologist*, 1:177.
35. Bennett, M. (1998). *Intercultural Communication: A Current Perspective*. Portland: Intercultural Press.
36. Clinton, D & Inkson, T.K. (2004). *Cultural Intelligence: People Skills for Global Business*, San Francisco: Berrett-Koehler Publishers.
37. Middleton, J. (2014). *Cultural Intelligence: The Competitive Edge for Leaders Crossing Borders*. London: Bloomsbury.
38. Adler, N. (2002). *International Dimensions of Organizational Behavior* (4th ed). Cincinnati: South-Western Thomson Learning.
39. Cass, P. (1998). *Training for the Multicultural Manager*. Washington D.C.: The Society for Intercultural Education, Training and Research.
40. Adler, N. (2002). *International Dimensions of Organizational Behavior* (4th ed). Cincinnati: South-Western Thomson Learning.
41. Trompenaars, F., & Hampden-Turner, C. (2011). *21 Leaders for the 21st Century*. New York: McGraw-Hill.
42. Both Geert Hofstede and Fons Trompenaars have provided multiple practical tips based on the differences in their value dimensions. In particular, see the website of Geert Hofstede "National culture dimensions," (Accessed December 15, 2012). http://geert-hofstede.com/dimensions.html and the end of each chapter of Trompenaars, *Riding the Wave of Culture*.
43. Black, J., Morrison, A., & Gregersen, H. (1999). *Global Explorers: The Next Generation of Leaders*. New York: Routledge.
44. Schein, E. (1985). *Organizational Culture and Leadership* (1st ed.). San Francisco: Jossey Bass.
45. Groysberg, B., Lee, J., Price, J., & Cheng, J. (2018). "The Leader's Guide to Corporate Culture," *Harvard Business Review*, 96(1):44-57.

GUIDED READING QUESTIONS

1. What is culture?

2. What is the relationship between the culture and the structure of a society?

3. What is the emic/etic difference in culture?

4. What are value dimensions and how are they used?

5. Provide a workplace example that is affected by differences in value dimensions related to: power distance; uncertainty avoidance; individualism versus collectivism; masculinity versus femininity; long-term versus short-term orientation; indulgence versus restraint; low and high context; monochronic and polychronic time.

FOLLOW-UP CRITICAL THINKING QUESTIONS

1. What is my major takeaway from this reading?

2. What do I already know about this subject?

3. What follow-up questions do I have about this?

4. How can I apply this in real life?

KEY TERMS

Assimilation
Achievement versus ascription
Affective versus affective neutrality
Confucian dynamism
Conscious and unconscious culture
Cultural adjustment
Cultural determinism
Cultural reproduction
Culture
Culture shock
DIBS
Dilemma reconciliation
Emic
Etic
Ethnocentrism and parochialism
Explicit and implicit culture
Face
Go native
High and low context
Iceberg metaphor of culture
Individualism versus collectivism
Indulgence versus restraint
Long-tern versus short-term orientation
Masculinity and femininity
Monochronic and polychromic cultures
Norms
Particularism versus universalism
Power distance
Proxemics
Reentry shock
Reverse culture shock
Stereotype
S-learning curve
Specific versus diffuse
Uncertainty avoidance
Values
Value dimensions

LEARNING ASSESSMENT

Critically reflect on the content and the different concepts in this module and rate your own competency using the assessment scale.

Competency	I never heard of it	I heard of it but have limited knowledge of it	I can reasonably explain it to others	I have used it, done it, applied it
Culture	0	1	2	3
Types of culture	0	1	2	3
Hall's value dimensions	0	1	2	3
Hofstede's value dimensions	0	1	2	3
Trompenaars' value dimensions	0	1	2	3
Meyer's value dimensions	0	1	2	3
Culture distance	0	1	2	3
U-curve of cultural adjustment	0	1	2	3
Cultural intelligence	0	1	2	3
Culture shock	0	1	2	3
Dilemma reconciliation	0	1	2	3

MODULAR-SPECIFIC ASSESSMENT

What's your cultural profile?

This assessment allows you to score your cultural profile on different continua and compare it to your country's norm.

Source: Meyer, E. (2014). "Navigating the cultural minefield. Learn how to work more effectively with people from other countries." *Harvard Business Review*, May, 92(5): 119-123. http://trib.al/zhXYzJC

VIGNETTE

POST-MERGER INTEGRATION AT TEVA PHARMACEUTICALS[1]

Teva, Israel's largest, and one of its oldest companies, operated as a domestic Israeli company for almost a century. In the 1990s, Teva undertook an internationalization strategy through acquisitions. As a result, Teva grew from less than 3,000 employees (1992) primarily located in Israel to more than 13,000 employees (2005) on three continents.[2] Post-merger implementation focuses mainly on cultural integration with Teva, talent management, retention, and adaptation to local cultures. Once the acquisition of a company has been approved, cultural and economic issues are key to integration. Cultural integration focuses on socialization into the Teva vision. Because HR people speak the same professional language, they are the first to make contact with the acquired organizations. HR economic issues revolve around developing a working plan budget (focusing on planning, controlling, and compensation), alignment of HR worldwide working plans (with an emphasis on cost differentials), and monthly tracking of labor costs and number of employees. Teva has a track record of a variance between HR planned number of employees and the actual number of less than 1%. This successful record has positioned HR as a strategic business partner with Teva's senior management in terms of supporting the acquisition strategy.

While there is a focus on HR metrics at the global level, Teva's corporate culture is strongly decentralized, focused on lateral services rather than functional silos and hierarchies, devoid of written policies, and embedded in a dynamic Israeli management style. Teva has 'policy guidelines,' not policies. Management in Teva's headquarters in Israel, Petach-Tikva, does not tell division management how to run its business. For example, HR has performance appraisal process guidelines, but there is no formal process, standard appraisal form, or performance review timetable for all units. Teva's informality is a core cultural aspect of the company and reflects the strategic orientation of the company, which emphasizes decentralization. Teva is a company that is built on relationships among people, not among roles.

In such a structure, Teva attributes an enormous importance to people. The focus is on constantly enriching the experience of people through brainstorming and participation. Everyone can say anything and is encouraged to contribute. There are no functional silos; people work laterally. In functional organizations, the culture is such that questions are directed to the person responsible for the function. At Teva, Israeli management asks the same question from everyone. Unlike in France or the U.S., where managers respect the domain of responsibility, Teva management crosses information from different sources in order to enrich the response. At first, working this way resulted in a lack of trust and miscommunication among the managers of the acquired companies. Now they attribute much of Teva's business success to the flexibility of the organizational structure. Another example of lateral services is the establishment of Shared Service Centers (SSC) as part of HR's organizational structure. According to Avi Robinson, Vice President HR International, "*The Shared Service Centers give lateral services to all sites in a particular geographic location. The two major parameters of success are service and efficiency*." These SSCs are focused on HR measurement in order to show results. In addition to SSC responsibilities, country HR managers play an active business partner role for all local Teva activities.

In addition to the formal post-integration mechanisms described above (such as lateral services and HR shared services), a number of initiatives are aimed at forging global workforce integration, both of general employees and of HR professionals. HR development projects such as the Teva Way, '*Shaar*' (or 'Gateway'), and Global Leadership operate at a global employee level. They are intended to integrate training and development activities, push strategy-derived issues, and provide some of the 'glue technology.' At the HR professional level, the global HR team (made up of country HR managers) meets face-to-face on a regular basis and works virtually on lateral projects. The Teva Way is very aspirational and informs every employee what kind of a company Teva wants to be. The Teva Way is about shared values and the alignment of local activities to global initiatives so that every Teva employee, regardless of location around the world, can share the trademark Teva culture. The focus is on accepting local cultural differences while still making a commitment and contribution to Teva and its success. It is not just a slogan, but a concerted effort to identify and disseminate Teva's core values.

Another development project is '*Shaar*' (called 'Gateway' in other countries). Designed to aid in the development of younger managers, Shaar has been running for nine years in Israel and has now expanded globally. Middle managers with various functional areas of expertise are selected early on in their careers and socialized into business development and leadership. This is an accelerated program where trainees are exposed to Teva's senior management and asked to work on lateral team projects, often in areas outside of their comfort zone. The objectives of Gateway are both lateral integration and employee development.

Finally, Global Leadership Development is one of the mechanisms for the development of senior managers. This program provides cross-border and lateral project opportunities and greater exposure to the senior management team.

Remaining an Israeli company in spite of its rapid growth is very important to Teva. There may be a sense of loss in Israel as the company grows from a domestic company to a major global company. As Teva grows through acquisition outside of its domestic market, the majority of its employees will reside outside of corporate HQ country. What it means to be a global Israeli company is much clearer in Teva Israel than in the company's operations around the world. From an Israeli perspective, Teva is the crown jewel of corporate success in a competitive global business environment. With regard to HR, they are the most advanced and a best practice to be emulated by other Israeli companies. Being a global Israel company is also part of the company's strategic vision with important HR implications.

REFERENCES

1. This vignette was prepared by Professor Lisbeth Claus for the sole purpose of illustrating a global HR practice for instructional objectives. Global HR in Action © 2006, Global Immersion Press, All Rights Reserved.
2. This vignette is based on the business case study on national and organization culture: Claus, L. (2006) Global HR at Teva Pharmaceuticals. Thunderbird International Business Review, 48(6): 891-905.

GUIDED READING QUESTIONS

1. What is HR's role in the pre- and post-merger phases of an acquisition by Teva?
2. What are the characteristics of the Israeli management style at Teva?
3. What does it mean for Teva to be an Israeli global company?

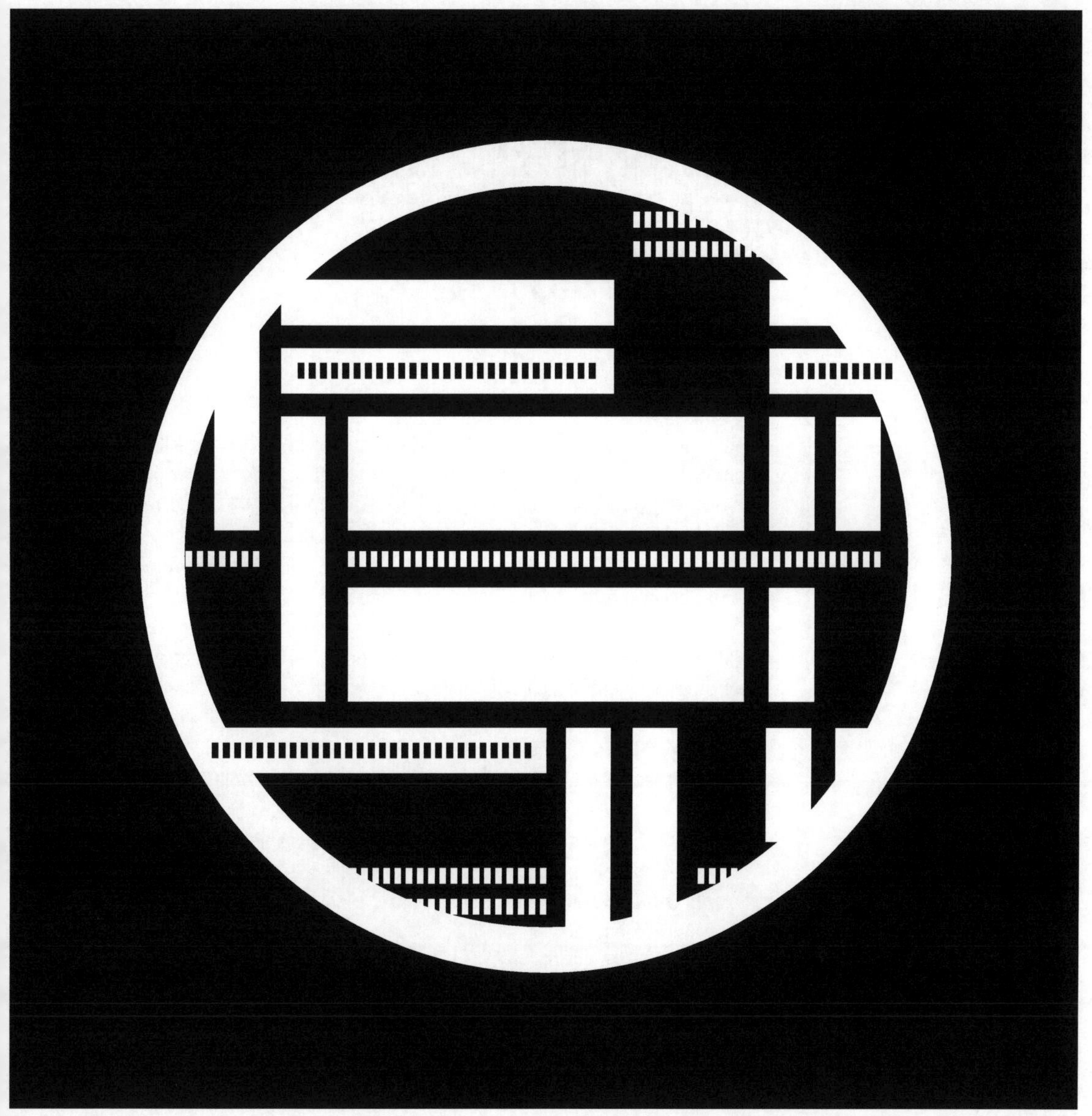

MODULE FIVE

EQUALITY AND EQUITY THROUGH DIVERSITY, INCLUSION, BELONGING, AND SUPPORT

MODULE FIVE

EQUALITY AND EQUITY THROUGH DIVERSITY, INCLUSION, BELONGING, AND SUPPORT

DESCRIPTION

This module explores how equity and equality can be furthered through diversity, inclusion, belonging, and support (DIBs). We look beyond the traditional race and gender D&I initiatives by exploring the meaning of DIBs in a more global context and introducing the notions of intersectionality, equality, and equity. Finally, this module focuses on how to become more inclusive and on the design of an organizational architecture needed to support the authenticity of the worker so everyone can bring their 'whole' and 'authentic' self to work and feel psychologically safe.[1]

LEARNING OBJECTIVES

Upon completing the learning experience, you will be able to:

- Describe different elements of the diversity mosaic
- Distinguish between equality and equity
- Apply the concept of intersectionality
- Define unconscious bias
- Integrate vertical and horizontal communities in the workplace
- Define psychological safety

GUIDING QUESTION

What is my 'authentic self' profile?

When MARIE speaks in a professional setting, she feels like she is walking on tightrope. She either feels barely heard or judged as too aggressive. As a result, Marie often decides that saying less is more. When her colleague Paul talks about virtually the same thing, heads nod in appreciation at his fine idea.

ELIZABETH is a nurse at the Cleveland Clinic. Over the years, she has learned that supporting African American patients at the Clinic requires a different approach. She understands many African Americans feel deep faith and may see illness as a natural consequence due to life choices. She is prepared to address issues in both a medical and spiritual realm and supports alternative methods of healing involving pastors, priests, or other religious figures while keeping the medical considerations in mind.

Diversity and inclusion (D&I) are now viewed as an imperative by (external) customers and (internal) employees alike. It is not only widely believed, but also shown through a growing body of research that D&I can have a critical impact on employee wellbeing and overall organizational performance in terms of brand, purpose, and team-based performance.[2] It is generally believed people can do their best work when there is a critical mass of people (some different and some similar to them) in the workplace to interact with. While diversity in the workplace is far from being achieved, HR departments now have functional activities directly related to promoting workplace D&I. Yet, in everyday HR operations, diversity still focuses on pigeonholing a person based on race and gender and a few usually observable characteristics.

In spite of all the D&I efforts, many organizations still have a long way to go. Current D&I management practices are simply not enough to create a well-balanced and diverse workforce. When looking at the diversity profile of the workforce—or the lack thereof—think of the different gaps and ceilings in employment opportunities, pay, and other equal opportunities by gender, race, and differentially-abled people who still exist in the workplace today. Despite the attention of companies and the allocation of many resources, technology companies, for example, have not been able to truly diversify their workforce. It could be argued that HR has basically not provided real return of value in this arena. One of the proofs that's often put forward is whether a random sample of a company's customers would match a random sample of their employees without one being able to distinguish between them. What companies really want is to reflect the availability of the diverse groups in the labor market in their workforce--let's say if 5% of the available talent in Germany are Turkish, a German company would like to hire at least 5% of its workforce to be Turkish.

DIBs

In progressive companies, D&I is being replaced by DIBs. While not perfect, HR has made more advancement with D&I in the past 10 years—simply powered by the naturally highly competitive environment for people and their expectations—than all the laws, D&I programs, and initiatives combined! Millennials are more alert to diversity and equal opportunities and, compared to other generations, are speaking up and do not tolerate exclusion, discrimination, and intolerance. Companies are desperate to hire and retain great employees and the competitive labor market and shortage of skilled workers is becoming the driving force for a smooth transition to an inclusive workplace. For those companies who do not, they will soon fail as the new generation of employees will vote with their feet and work for other companies. Compared to 10 years ago, the HR response today is more 'what can we do' versus 'here's what we can't do.'

One of the great impediments to DIBs is the lack of a precise definition of what the various elements mean (conceptualization) and their measurement (operationalization). Meg Bolger (2017) argues that when we can't hold diversity, equity, and inclusion as separate concepts—and understand how they interact—we can't set clear goals and strategies around them.[3]

Diversity

According to the Society of Human Resource Management (SHRM), diversity relates to who we bring into the organization while inclusion is how we make people feel welcome when they are here.[4] Diversity has finally moved from a focus on race and gender (its US historical roots in the civil rights and women's social movements) to a broader focus on global cultural diversity. It now encompasses many elements, including both person-based traits as well as a host of ascribed and achieved social characteristics. Diversity is the presence of difference of these person-based traits within a given setting.

Bolger makes an interesting observation that a person or candidate is not diverse but a unique, individual who may bring diversity to your team or your hiring pool. Diversity is about a collective or a group, a team or an organization and can only exist in relationship to others. To be a diverse organization simply means that you have the presence of differences of identity (e.g., gender and people of color, etc.) throughout your organization. However, an organization can be diverse without being inclusive. A company can be diverse without being equitable.[5]

When taking a broader global cultural diversity perspective, the issue of D&I in other countries around the world becomes even more complex than in the U.S., which has a longer legal and cultural tradition in this arena. Many countries have laws related to discrimination:

- Saudization, Emiritization, and Qatarization nationalization laws requiring employers to fill positions with quotas of local nationals
- Laws in various countries (Brazil, France) requiring disability quotas
- Countries (such as Singapore and others) where same sex marriages are forbidden by law and criminalized.

But having a diverse workforce or legal compliance with anti-discrimination laws does not necessarily make everyone feel welcome. How do the following diverse people feel in the workplace when they are in a minority position?

- A Caucasian Christian woman in the Middle East
- A Sudanese woman working in Europe
- A black person working in China
- A Sudanese worker in the Middle East
- A university-educated young man born in Belgium from Moroccan Muslim parents
- A single working mother
- An older worker with a millennial boss
- Someone with a strong 'foreign' accent
- A person covered in body tattoos
- A male working with an all-female team
- An LGBT international assignee and partner sent a country where the views on homosexuality are repressive
- A baby boomer who keeps working post retirement age

That's where the notion of inclusion comes in and how comfortable different people are and how well they are accepted by others in the workplace.

Inclusion

With a diverse workforce comes the need for inclusion, meaning making sure people are both comfortable and accepted by others in the workplace. Inclusion is about people with different identities feeling and being valued, their talent being leveraged and welcomed in the work setting. An organization can be diverse by the numbers of different people in its talent pool, but that doesn't mean everyone feels welcome or is valued. The simple fact of being diverse—although a great first step—does not make a company inclusive.

Etymologically, the notion of inclusion, being included within a group, has a connotation that the person who is different has to step up and become part of the dominant group and take on some of those expected behaviors. Even if 'diverse' people get into these organizations, they may not reveal their true self, thrive, or want to be there and feel included. A new and more empowered paradigm has emerged, driven largely by the millennial generation who grew up with more diverse and team-based education and exposure.

Bolger[6] argues that diversity and inclusion involve different types of management questions. Efforts to increase diversity involve questions like:

- How can we get more 'diverse' people into our pipeline?
- How can we incentivize recruiting 'diverse candidates?'
- Why aren't people of differing identities applying for our jobs?

Efforts to increase inclusion involves questions like:

- What is the experience for individuals who are the minority within the organization?
- What barriers stand in the way of people with marginalized identities feeling a sense of welcome and belonging?
- Why don't we realize what we are doing that is negatively impacting our new, more diverse teams?

The key question is not just how to hire people of diverse backgrounds, but often how to retain and develop them by nurturing an inclusive culture where minorities feel included, are respected, and feel they belong so they can thrive.

Belonging

Belonging, in relation to diversity management, means to have an environment where workers feel secure, supported, accepted, and included.[7] Belonging involves developing deeper connections with others by being able to share your authentic self and receiving acceptance in return.[8] Bringing one's authentic, whole-self to the workplace requires an environment with psychological safety.

The concept of psychological safety has extensively been explored in the research of Amy C. Edmonson. In her 2019 book, *The Fearless Organization*, she shows how creating psychological safety helps employees thrive and organizations succeed. Psychological safety is broadly defined as "a climate in which people are comfortable expressing and being themselves." In a psychologically safe environment, people can be their authentic self and not be hindered by interpersonal fear. They feel willing and able to take the inherent interpersonal risks of candor and can thrive.[9] While psychological safety benefits all employees, not just people who are not well represented in the organizations, feeling safe in speaking up, taking risks, and being one's authentic self can promote a sense of belonging, well-being, and engagement.

Support

The overarching goal of DIBs is to ensure that a company welcomes and celebrates all forms of diversity, all aspects of the company are inclusive, people feel like they belong, and workers are given the support they need to maximize their work-life potential. While support can come in many ways, an important source of support is the establishment of different affinity groups or an Employee Resource Group (ERG). An ERG is a group based on shared characteristics or life experiences that is set up to support employees in the work environment based on similar affinities. Diversity, inclusion, and belonging is not just an enlightened management philosophy but a strategy that must be supported with resources to make it happen through both cultural and structural change. Creating a workspace where everyone can thrive independent of their background is no easy task even with ample support.

INTERSECTIONALITY

How do marginalized and minority groups who are different from their dominant, advantaged, or privileged peers overcome intersectionality? The term intersectionality, coined as early as 1989 by legal scholar Kimberlé Crenshaw, refers to the multiple dimensions of a person's social identity and how they relate either to systems and structures of discrimination or forms of privilege. Its application in the workplace is more recent. Intersectionality is the idea that multiple group identities intersect to create a whole that is different from the component identities.[10] Laws and policies usually only address one form of marginalized identity. The 'intersectionality wheel' (see 5-1) is a commonly used graphic representation of these different social identities: a broad mosaic of different factors—as many as 50 personal and social characteristics—make up an identity. This approach allows people to bring their own authenticity into the workplace—some of which may not fit the mold of the observable, diverse characteristics.[11]

In line with the notion of intersectionality, Andrew Solomon, in *Far from the Tree* (2012), explores the concept of 'vertical' (or directly inherited) and 'horizontal' (or independently divergent) identities. Examples of horizontal identities are differently-abled people who do not share the values and preferences with their progenitors, such as deafness, blindness, dwarfism, Down Syndrome, autism, schizophrenia, multiple severe disabilities, prodigies, transgender individuals, etc.[12] How do they become fully-fledged contributors to society and secure gainful employment?

Many people who do not 'fit in' have a hard time getting their foot in the door through the interview and selection processes because we carry unconscious and conscious biases and stereotypes as to who fits in! How can employers tap into part of the skill set that we need and employ people who have the needed skills, but perhaps lack some other conventional skill? Neurodiverse people who have the knowledge, skills, and work ethic, but perhaps lack social skills;[13] tattooed people who don't have the acceptable 'look;' ethnically diverse people who belong to more than one minority group.[14] The U.S. Americans with Disabilities Act of 1990 makes it unlawful to discriminate in employment against a qualified individual with a disability and requires companies with more than 15 employees to provide reasonable accommodation (without undue hardship) in all employment-related decisions for people with disabilities.

5-1. Intersectionality Wheel

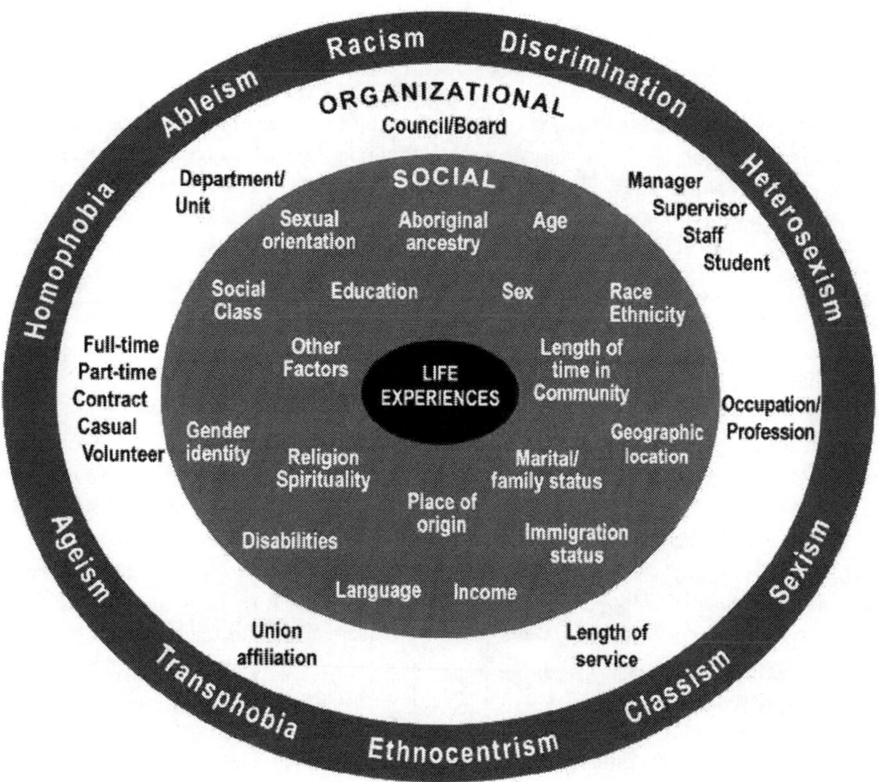

Source: Advancing Equity and Inclusion: A Guide for Municipalities (2015). City of all Women Initiative (CAWI), Ottawa. (Accessed December 5, 2019) https://www.cawi-ivtf.org/sites/default/files/publications/advancing-equity-inclusion-web_0.pdf

5-2. Equity vs Equality

Source: Advancing Equity and Inclusion: A Guide for Municipalities (2015). City of all Women Initiative (CAWI), Ottawa. (Accessed December 5, 2019) https://www.cawi-ivtf.org/sites/default/files/publications/advancing-equity-inclusion-web_0.pdf

EQUITY VS EQUALITY

The difference between equity, equality, and justice is often depicted by a tri-paned graphic of three people of different heights looking over a fence watching a game. In the first image (equality), each is given a crate to stand on (the tallest one does not need it, it helps the middle-height person, and is of no use to the shortest on); in the second image (equity), the tallest person does not get a crate (and does not need one), and the other two people get a different-sized crate adapted to their height; and in the third image (justice), the solid fence is replaced with a see-through one (i.e., the cause of the inequity or barrier is removed) and all three can see the game without any support (see 5-2).[15]

Lack of equity and justice are often related to historical and structural systems of inequality. The search for equity acknowledges there are inequalities and advantages (privileges) and barriers (discrimination) that exist. Different people experience different barriers (and in the case of intersectionality, often multiple barriers). Equity is a normative issue. It means no one is denied the possibility of advancement, benefits, or inclusion for belonging to a group that has been historically, economically, and socially disadvantaged. Equitable is about equality of opportunities and does not necessarily mean equal or treating everyone the same but treating them differently to ensure equality.

UNCONSCIOUS BIAS

An unconscious bias is an insidious bias that happens automatically (unaware) when making decisions. When making decisions fast and without data, we often fill in the gaps with the 'unconscious' bias. While this may help us to process information quickly and efficiently, it also leads us to make decisions that are not objective.[16]

MAKING DIBs HAPPEN IN AN ORGANIZATION

Implementing DIBS in an organization and ensuring the culture and the structure is conducive to the engagement and voice of different people is no easy task. Managers struggle with how to make the workplace more inclusive and equitable. In addition, it is difficult to understand the meaning of DIBs at a global level due to the different cultural meanings and laws around the world impacting diversity. At a very basic level, people in the workplace are grappling with do's (leading practices) and don'ts (things to avoid) when it comes to having every worker bring their authentic self to work.

In a 2016 White Paper entitled, *Turn Diversity and Inclusion into a Talent Strength*, Peter Vermeulen and Audra Jenkins argue that to strengthen its D&I position, companies must be able to quantify, measure, manage, and improve their initiatives just as any other business practice. They suggest a six-pack strategy for driving measurable D&I improvements with five components relating to the makeup of the workforce and one focusing on the workplace experience. Each element answers a key strategic question about the workforce and your organization:[17]

1. **Acquiring talent**—what is the mix of diverse talent you bring into your organization?
2. **Developing and advancing talent**—once you bring diverse talent through the door, how well do you support their abilities to develop skills and advance their careers?
3. **Retaining talent**—how well does your organization keep diverse talent?
4. **Representation**—how does the proportion of diverse groups in your organization compare to their availability in the market?
5. **Succession planning pipeline strength**—do you have diverse talent in your succession planning pipeline for critical roles? Are they ready now, or will they be ready in the future?
6. **Engagement**—what is the level of participation, commitment, and acceptance of diverse talent within your workforce?

Commonly Acknowledged Do's and Don'ts
DIBs requires a multidimensional and coordinated approach that deals both with the culture and the structure of the organization. Here are a few leading practices (Do) and pitfalls (Don't):

DO

Awareness and training
- Include diversity in the organization's mission statement
- Communicate DIBS goals and measure progress
- Increase awareness of DIBS through diversity trainings
- Educate leaders and managers on how to create and maintain an inclusive culture

Unconscious bias
- Reassess and improve practices in employment decisions
- Eliminate measurable bias from all talent processes
- Identify problem patterns in gender and racial biases
- Make people aware of their unconscious biases

Data and IT
- Increase reliance on data and analytics to reveal problems
- Measure organizational climate through sentiment analysis
- Anonymize résumés or candidates to reduce/eliminate bias
- Develop artificial intelligence practices to neutralize unconscious bias
- Conduct equity audits
- Use IT tools to nudge employees and managers

Culture
- Promote psychological safety for all
- Offer mentoring and coaching support
- Hold more effective and inclusive meetings

Structural support
- Set up Diversity Taskforce/Inclusion Council
- Establish Employee Resource Groups (ERGs) also known as affinity groups
- Consider search advocates in talent acquisition
- Eliminate salary disparities
- Promote the use of inclusive language
- Celebrate differences
- Give employees a voice about their needs
- Provide mechanisms for diverse employees to tell their stories and perspectives
- Recognize majority groups as part of organizational diversity (not just for minorities)
- Eliminate the root causes of inequities

One of the most important action items related to DIBs is to agree on some measurable outcomes, see them as part of deliverables objectives for the year, and hold leaders accountable. Be a disrupter and refuse to consider people for employment decisions if your slate is not diverse.

DON'T

While there are many don'ts when it comes to DIBs, here are some of the most important ones:

- Don't stereotype people based on their socio-biographics
- Don't assume that diversity is only about race and gender
- Don't shut out other points of view
- Don't continue the same old hiring practices, like disqualifying a candidate because they don't look or act like you
- Don't use 'culture fit' as a reason for rejecting a candidate
- Don't assume that you know what other people need and want

> *"When you are part of a place, growing that moment in its soil, there's never a need to say you're from there."*
>
> Tara Westover. Educated. New York: Random House, 2017, p. 206.

REFERENCES

1. We are grateful to the folllowing Willamette University students for exploring different aspects of DIBs in their MBA assignments: Alex Dass, Natasha Torres, Haley Roehrig, and Josh Fuentes.
2. Jackson, S.E. & Joshi, A. (2011). "Work Team Diversity." Pp. 651-686 in *APA Handbook of Industrial and Organizational Psychology*. American Psychological Association.
3. Bolger, M. (2017). What's the difference between diversity, inclusion and equity. October 24 (Accessed: December 20, 2019) https://generalassemb.ly/blog/diversity-inclusion-equity-differences-in-meaning/
4. *SHRM Learning System* (2016). Alexandria: Society for Human Resource Management.
5. Bolger, M. (2017) What's the Difference between Diversity, Inclusion and Equity? October 24 (Accessed: December 20, 2019). https://generalassemb.ly/blog/diversity-inclusion-equity-differences-in-meaning/
6. Ibid.
7. Creating a Sense of Belonging in the Workplace (2019). July 11 (Accessed: December 6, 2019). https://bigpicture-learning.com/sense -of-belonging/.
8. Bastion, R. (2019). The Business Case for Belonging, (2019), April 10 (Accessed: December 5, 2019) http://www.forbes.com/sites/rebekahbastan/2019/04/10/the-business-case-for-belonging/#2f6347b35f6d.
9. Edmonson, A.C. (2019). The Fearless Organization. Hoboken, NJ: John Wiley & Sons.
10. Crenshaw, K. (2016). *The Urgency of Intersectionality*. December 7 (Accessed: December 5, 2019). https://www.youtube.com/watch?v=akOe5-UsQ2o
11. Simpson, J. (2009). *Everyone Belongs: A Toolkit for Applying Intersectionality* (1st ed.). CRIAW/ICREF.
12. Solomon, A. (2012). *Far from the Tree: Parents, Children and the Search for Identity*. New York: Scribner.
13. Austin, R. & Pisano, G. (2017). "Neurodiversity as a Competitive Advantage: Why You Should Embrace It In Your Workforce," *Harvard Business Review*, 95(3),96-103.
14. Wadors, P. (2016). "Diversity Efforts Fall Short Unless Employees Feel That They Belong," August 10 (Accessed: December 2019). https://hbr.org/2016/08/diversity-efforts-fall-short-unless-employees-feel-that-they-belong
15. Advancing Equity and Inclusion: A Guide for Municipalities (2015). City of all Women Initiative (CAWI), Ottawa. (Accessed December 5, 2019). https://www.cawi-ivtf.org/sites/default/files/publications/advancing-equity-inclusion-web_0.pdf
16. https://www.gv.com/lib/unconscious-bias-at-work
17. Vermeulen, P. & Jenkins, A. (2016). *Turn Diversity and Inclusion into a Talent Strength*, The Linde Goup, Randstad Sourceright. May, (Accessed: January 5, 2020). https://insights.randstadsourceright.com/diversity-inclusion/turn-diversity-and-inclusion-into-a-talent-strength.

GUIDED READING QUESTIONS

1. What is the meaning of diversity, inclusion, and belonging?

2. What is the difference between equity and equality?

3. What is an unconscious bias?

4. What organizational support do diverse people need to be able to bring their authenticity to work and feel that they belong?

5. What is intersectionality?

FOLLOW-UP CRITICAL THINKING QUESTIONS

1. What is my major takeaway from this reading?

2. What do I already know about this subject?

3. What follow-up questions do I have about this?

4. How can I apply this in real life?

KEY TERMS

Authenticity
Belonging
DIBs
D&I
Diversity
Equality
Equity
Inclusion
Intersectionality
Intersectionality wheel
Pay equity
Psychological safety
Vertical and horizontal identities

LEARNING ASSESSMENT

Critically reflect on the content and the different concepts in this module and rate your own competency using the assessment scale.

Competency	I never heard of it	I heard of it but have limited knowledge of it	I can reasonably explain it to others	I have used it, done it, applied it
Diversity	0	1	2	3
Inclusion	0	1	2	3
Belonging	0	1	2	3
Support	0	1	2	3
Authenticity	0	1	2	3
Equity	0	1	2	3
Equality	0	1	2	3
Psychological safety	0	1	2	3
Unconscious bias	0	1	2	3

MODULAR-SPECIFIC ASSESSMENT

Psychological safety

A seven-question instrument that measures the psychological safety in an organization.

Source: Edmonson, A.C. (1999). Psychological safety and learning behavior in work teams. *Administrative Science Quarterly*, 44(2):350-383

VIGNETTE

SUPPORTING THE GLOBAL MOBILITY OPPORTUNITIES OF GAYS AND LESBIANS[1]

International assignments are a vital part of talent management in global companies. The global mobility of people supports the attainment of the strategic objectives of the company and develops the global skillset and leadership of its talent. Most companies have developed international assignment policies and procedures and work with their global mobility vendors to support the international assignment process of their employees worldwide. With a greater diversity of people now going on international assignment, some of the support requires customization to the needs of the assignees and their families. One area where the 'S' of 'DIBs' (Diversity, Inclusion, Belonging, and Support) needs attention is the global mobility of LGBTQ workers on international assignment as homosexuality is still illegal in 71 countries,[2] and the welfare of the employee as well as the employer's duty of care obligation come into play.

In their research of LGBTQ expatriates, Ruth McPhail, Yvonne McNulty, and Kate Hutchings have outlined the opportunities, barriers, and challenges for expatriation and the support gays and lesbians and their partners/spouses and children need from their company to successfully take part in an international assignment.[3] Besides the (il)legal LGBTQ status in more than a quarter of the world's countries, some of the other barriers include—but are not limited to—physical concerns of safety and security of the host country; lack and restrictions of rights and protection; criminalization; difficulties in obtaining visas and work permits; social norms, psychological and social fears; discrimination, lack of job security, limited career progression, safety concerns in 'coming out' to their employer, fear of stereotyping, and constant scanning for signs of acceptance.

What types of additional support—above and beyond the global mobility package of the mainstream traditional expat—do LGBTQ workers, their partners, and/or their children need when going on international assignment? Let's illustrate the exemplary support Benedikt Josef Wille received from his employers (Siemens) for relocating with his partner from Munich to Madrid for a planned (October 2018 to March 2020) assignment. The experience illustrates the difference that support means for the success of his international assignment and the engagement and retention of a valuable 'high potential' future leader.

At Siemens, the *HR International Assignment Program* (HIP) is a development program for HR professionals with great potential as well as high motivation and career aspirations. The development program contains an 18-month delegation where participants complete a demanding assignment in an HR role abroad and benefit from additional development measures. When applying for the program, Benedikt shared with his employer from the onset that he was gay, interested in the international assignment, and would want his partner, Dylan, to go with him on the assignment. Dylan, who has a Canadian nationality, left his job in Munich with Apple in order to accompany him. Their civil status—they are neither married nor legally partnered—is one of just boyfriends now more than three years. Since HIP is choosing any Siemens location worldwide for its high potential employees to go on the assignment, revealing to the company that he is gay and wants to take his partner along is necessary and useful information so that the company can send the couple to a gay-friendly country. Countries like Russia or Saudi-Arabia might have been more difficult. Siemens supported Benedikt as a candidate for international assignment by choosing Madrid, Spain as the host country location. Siemens supported (and paid for) the following services not just for Benedikt but also for his partner Dylan:

- An orientation trip to Spain;
- Intercultural training in Spain;
- Spanish language classes;
- Full-service relocation;
- Hired a lawyer in Spain who took care of the administrative work and residence;
- Hired a relocation manager who found an appropriate flat and also took care of other destination services;
- Trips back home to Germany;
- Lump sum settling-in allowance for expat private health insurance;

Because Benedikt was able to discuss his situation with his employer, Siemens customized elements of the expat package and took care of all the important global mobility issues for both of them. The global mobility support they received are in line with the diversity philosophy the company espouses. With regard to LGBTQ support, Siemens generally participates in Siemens Pride Parades and there are many LGBTQ Employee Resource Groups (ERGs) where the company operates around the world. As Human Resources Board Member (and ex-CHRO), Janina Kugel expressed: "*Siemens takes a stand for more openness: against homophobia and for mutually respectful interaction. At Siemens you don't have to leave your identity at the door. That's why many of our German sites fly the rainbow flag during Pride Week (...) It signals how much we value diversity.*"[4] Siemens not only supported the expatriation of a gay worker, but allowed Benedikt to bring his whole authentic self to the job—giving him a sense of belonging.[5]

REFERENCES

1. This vignette was prepared by Professor Lisbeth Claus for the sole purpose of illustrating a global HR practice for instructional objectives. Global HR in Action © 2019, Global Immersion Press, All Rights Reserved.
2. Avery, D. (2019). 71 Countries Where Homosexuality is Illegal. Newsweek, April 4 (Accessed: January 26, 2020). https://www.newsweek.com/73-countries-where-its-illegal-be-gay-1385974
3. McPhail, R., McNulty Y. & Hutchings, K. (2016). Lesbian and gay expatriation: opportunities, barriers and challenges for global mobility. *The International Journal of Human Resource Management*, 27(3): 382-406.
4. Diversity at Siemens: We don't hide diversity, we celebrate it. (Accessed: January 25, 2020). https://new.siemens.com/global/en/company/sustainability/diversity/siemens-takes-a-stand-for-more-openness.html
5. Special thanks to Benedikt Josef Wille, HR Business partner, Siemens, for sharing his story.

GUIDED READING QUESTIONS

1. How does Siemens Global Mobility support and impact the international assignment of LGBTQ workers?

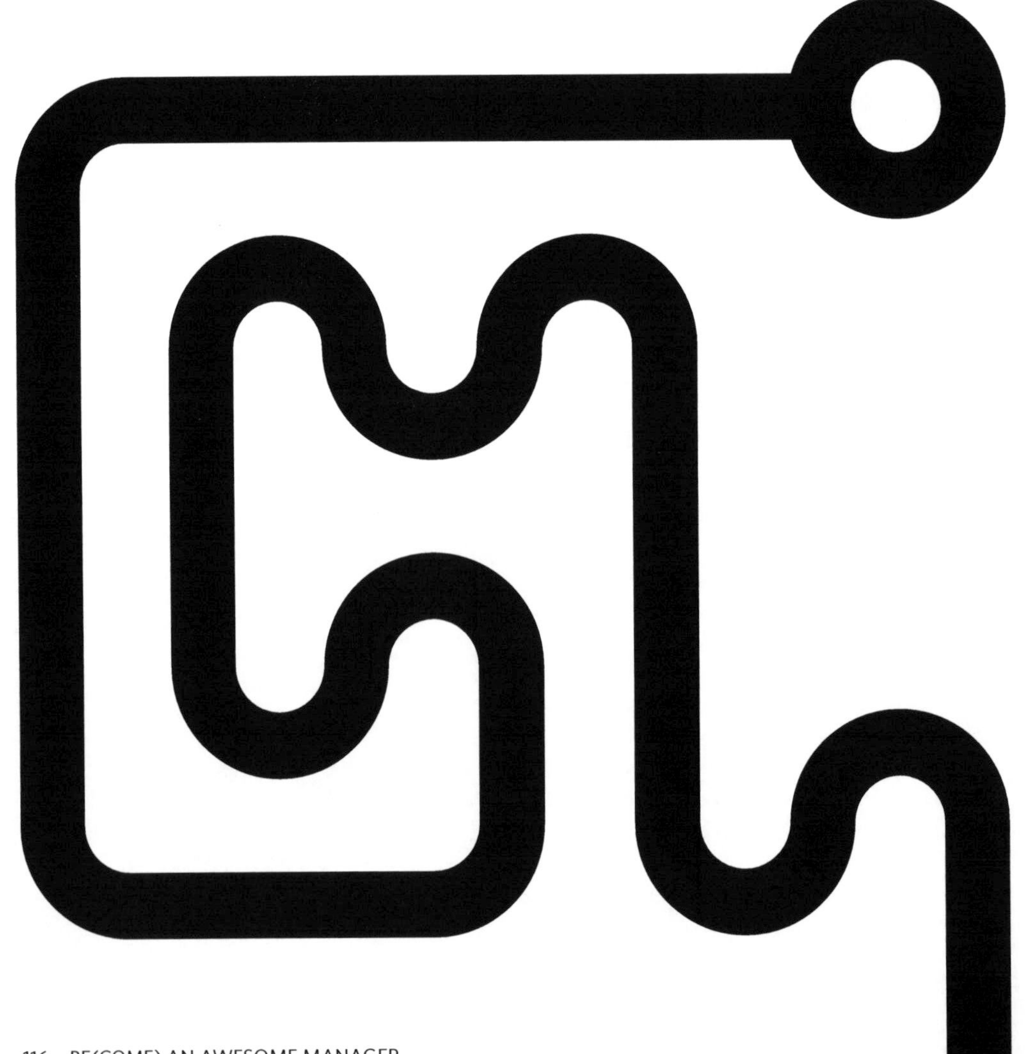

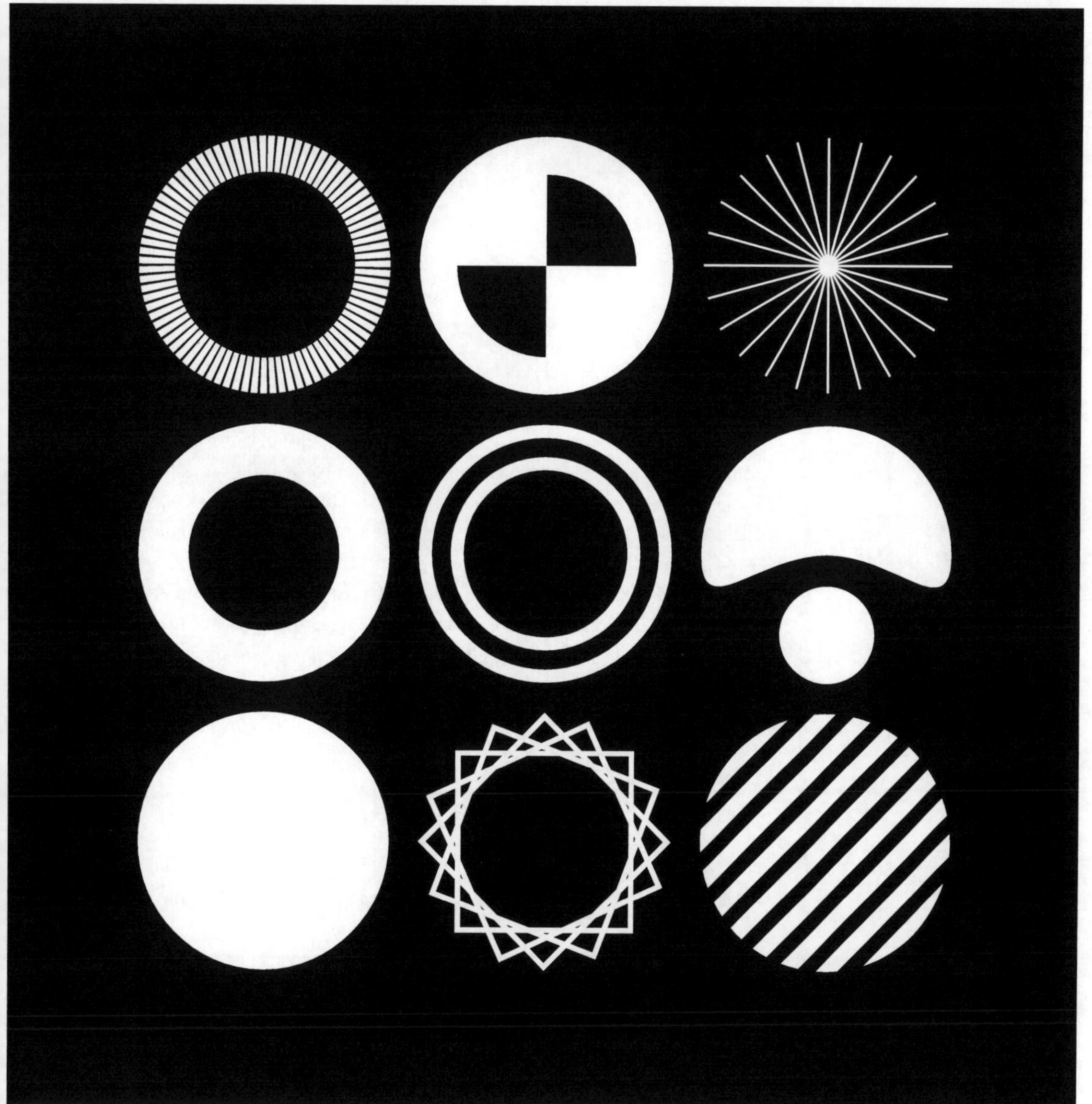

MODULE SIX

INDIVIDUALS, TEAMS, AND TEAMWORK

MODULE SIX

INDIVIDUALS, TEAMS, AND TEAMWORK

DESCRIPTION

After reviewing what constitutes a team, its purpose, different types of team configurations, team critical success factors, and components of team effectiveness and operation, this module explores the impact of cognitive style and cultural diversity on team effectiveness. Using the team role typology developed by Meredith Belbin, the nine team roles of a successful team are described each with their strengths and allowable weaknesses. Using the MBI-model (Mapping, Bridging, and Integrating), predictions can be made as to the possible team dynamics issues that are likely to occur and ways to improve team effectiveness whether the team is co-located or virtual.

LEARNING OBJECTIVES

Upon completing the learning experience, you will be able to:

- Identify different types of teams
- List the elements that make global teams more complex than domestic teams
- Differentiate between the effectiveness of a homogeneous and a heterogeneous team
- Describe how cognitive styles impact teamwork
- Describe how culture impacts teamwork
- Apply the Belbin team roles to the functioning of a team
- Apply the concepts of mapping, bridging, and integrating to a team

GUIDING QUESTION

How can I make my (and my teammates') knowledge more valuable through teamwork?

JOE's company acquired a company in a different country. Joe's manager informed him that he was going to lead a larger team comprised of his current team plus the new team at the acquired company. Joe had carefully cultivated the team culture, values and norms, and areas of expertise/knowledge for each team member. Soon he would be responsible for a team that was twice as large. Moreover, he would have employees working in another country with a different national and company culture. Already, some individuals on both teams were starting to jockey for influence and responsibility for critical tasks. Everybody knew there may be some layoffs within the newly combined organization—and the rumor mill was just getting started.

In today's work environment, more and more work is done in teams. There are many reasons for working in teams: the complexity of tasks requiring division of labor and expertise; the interdependency of tasks and processes; the need for shorter cycle times and increased productivity; the ability to create synergy and innovate; and the opportunity of team members to share knowledge and learn.

The link between individuals, teams, and organizations is profound. Individuals bring their different competencies to the team (knowledge, skills, abilities, and other person-related factors also known as KSAOs). The team shares know-how (explicit and tacit knowledge) and know-who (networks) and determines how they will work together. The organization provides resources and support to the team members through the development of processes, policies, and procedures, and its organizational culture (the ways of doing things). From an organizational perspective, teamwork is about innovation and creativity as well as knowledge sharing and preservation. Today, intellectual capital is becoming the major outcome of production and when (knowledge) workers walk out the door, they take their valuable knowledge and expertise with them.

In his 2005 book, *The Wisdom of Crowds*, James Surowiecki argues that groups of people are smarter than an elite few, better at problem solving, more innovative than a single member of the group (even an expert), and reach better decisions.[1] In that sense, in 'open source' work, the incremental voluntary efforts to contribute individual knowledge become collective through the concurrent input of different ideas.

CONFIGURING TEAMS

In a 1993 *Harvard Business Review* article entitled, "The Discipline of Teams," Jon R. Katzenbach and Douglas K. Smith try to understand what differentiates team performance, where and how teams work best, and what management can do to enhance team effectiveness. They define a team as "a small number of people with complementary skills who are committed to a common purpose, set of performance goals, and approach for which they hold themselves mutually accountable."[2] In this definition, the four key elements that define a team are:

1. A common commitment and purpose;
2. Performance goals;
3. Complementary skills;
4. Mutual accountability.

Teams are different from groups working together. While a working group is a function of what members do as individuals, team performance includes both individual results and collective work products requiring both individual and mutual accountability.

The team and team effectiveness management literature has studied different configurations of people working together resulting in different names for different types of teams. Each one of these types of—sometimes overlapping—team configurations has been studied in different contexts and shown to have different opportunities and challenges. Take a closer look at the list (see 6-1) to identify whether you have experience working on any one of those types of teams and understand their advantages and disadvantages.

These different configurations can further be grouped into three different types of teams according to the roles and authority of the people on the team:

1. Teams that recommend things;
2. Teams that make or do things;
3. Teams that run things.

Teamwork

Teamwork is a set of values that encourages listening and responding constructively to views expressed by others, giving other team members the benefit of the doubt, providing support to each other, and recognizing the interests and achievements of others. Katzenbach & Smith identify the following success factors to achieve team performance: bonding, complementary roles, trust, common

6-1. Different Team Configurations

Ad hoc team
A team brought together to consider an urgent matter and come up with a specific solution without any experience or prior agreement of how to work together.

Agile Team
Work done by multidisciplinary (Scrum) teams with flexibility and short cycles (sprints) playing different team roles (Scrum Master, Product Owner, and Developers).

Autonomous work team
A group of people granted autonomy or independence over the work they do within an organization and set their own goals and practices.

Bi-culututal team
Teams that are made up of basically two different national/cultural groups.

Co-located team
A team that is in the same location and has the ability to interact face-to-face.

Crew
A group of people who work closely together to operate a workyard, ship, boat, aircraft, spacecraft, train or repair something.

Crossfunctional team / Multi-disciplinary team
A team made up of people from different disciplinary backgrounds.

Dispersed team
A team that is spatially dispersed versus being co-located.

Extreme action team
A team made up of highly skilled members performing urgent, unpredictable, interdependent, and highly consequential tasks.

Global team
A team that is dispersed in different locations around the world and/or comprised of people from different cultural backgrounds.

Heterogeneous team / homogeneous team
Refers to the cultural diversity of the team. A homogeneous team is non-diverse while a heterogeneous teams is more diverse (token, bicultural, or multicultural team).

Hot group
A terms used by Jean Lipman-Blumen for a type of lively, high-achieving, dedicated group, usually small, whose members are turned on to an exciting and challenging task.

Intact team
A team that has the same team members over the time of the project or for a sustained period of time.

Management team
A group of individuals responsible for managing others in the pursuit of key business goals and functions.

Multicultural team
A team made up of people from different cultural background.

Natural work group
Teams working together every day and organized according to a common product, customer, or service.

Process team
A team responsible for recurring processes.

Project team
A team working on a project with a definite start and end-date.

Production team
A group of technical staff who produce something together.

Professional team
A team made of professionals who have discretionary autonomy over their work.

Self-managed team
A self-organized, semi-autonomous group of employees who set, plan, and manage their day-to-day activities and duties with limited or no supervision.

Short-term / long-term team
Teams who are on a short-term versus a long-term mission.

Small team / large team
A team that has no more than 4 to 7 members/a team that usually has more than 7 members.

SWAT team
Acronym for Special Weapons And Tactics or a group of elite team members who specialize in high-risk tasks.

Task force
A team established to work on a single defined task or activity.

Tokenn team
When only one member on the team (or a few) are diverse and become the token person.

Two-pizza team
(Just for fun) Jeff Bezos, CEO and founder of Amazon, believes that no matter how large your company gets, individual teams shouldn't be larger than what two pizzas can feed.

Virtual team
A team where members rely predominantly on Information and Comunication Technology (ICT) to accomplish their common goal—usually as a result of spatial and geographically dispersion

Source: Definitions based on multiple dictionary sources

purpose, individual accountability, a common approach and shared space, and whether the goal is considered worthy of effort.[3]

According to various sources, the critical success factors of teamwork—the things that are absolutely necessary for team success—are fairly well understood. They usually include trust, commitment, accountability, conflict management, expertise, and personal networks—but also have fun and celebrate success!

Trust—is built and earned by team members who fulfill their obligations and behave in a consistent and predictable manner. There are three types of trust: (1) deterrence-based trust—team members do what they say they will do simply because they fear they'll be punished if they don't; (2) knowledge-based trust—as members become more familiar with each other, each member knows his or her teammates well enough to predict their behavior with confidence and trust their knowledge; (3) identification-based trust—trust built on empathy and shared values where members are able to put themselves in their teammates' place.[4]

Commitment—refers to how committed each member of the team is to the project and to each other.

Accountability—is achieved when people on the team can be assured that every member will contribute and do what is expected of them. Unfortunately, many teams often have to deal with free riders or people who do not carry their share of responsibility but often get away with it, creating tension on team operations.

Conflict management—refers to the ability to manage conflict on the team, whether the team members acknowledge or not that there is a 'problem,' they will do something about it. There are vast personal and cultural differences in how to deal with confrontations among team members.

Expertise—refers to whether the team has the necessary complementary expertise among its team members to accomplish the goal. An interesting team dynamic question is whether, and under which circumstances, tasks will be assigned to team members based on their expertise or on their opportunity for learning and development.

Networks—refer to the friendships and personal networks of the team members. In the most effective teams, around half of the relationships among members are close enough to be considered friendship. If the team members have 100% friendship, the team performance drops dramatically. Friendships and networks that benefit team performance most are those formed with people outside of the group, such as business-centered relationships with people in other parts of the organization and relationships that extend into the social sphere allowing the buildup of social capital.[5]

Coordination, Cooperation, and Collaboration

Not all teamwork has or needs to be done at the same intensity. Some teamwork requires either coordination, cooperation, or collaboration.[6]

- **Coordination** is the act of managing interdependencies between activities to achieve the goal.
- **Cooperation** is working or acting together for a common purpose or benefit.
- **Collaboration** is jointly working with one another in a continuous interaction that cannot be replaced by individual work.

Collaboration

Identifying great talent is important for organizations but as long as team members don't develop the competencies to work in great teams, true collaboration will not necessarily happen. In a 2019 *Harvard Business Review* article entitled, "Cracking the Code of Sustained Collaboration," Francesca Gina argues that collaboration requires certain skills and proposes six tools for training people to work better together:[7]

1. Ensure people genuinely listen to one another

   How to teach people to listen, not talk:
   - Ask expansive (and open-ended) questions
   - Focus on the listener, not on yourself
   - Engage in 'self-checks'
   - Become comfortable with silence

2. Approach discussions with empathy not opinions

   How to train people to practice empathy:
   - Expand others' thinking
   - Look for the unspoken

3. Become comfortable with feedback

   How to make people more comfortable with feedback:
   - Discuss feedback aversion openly
   - Make feedback about others' behavior direct, specific, and applicable
   - Give feedback on feedback
   - Add a 'plus' to others' ideas
   - Provide live coaching

4. Teach people to lead AND follow (i.e., flexing)

   How to teach people to lead and follow:
   - Increase self-awareness
   - Learn to delegate

5. Speak with clarity and avoid abstraction

6. Have win-win interactions

Desirable Team Behaviors

There are a number of 'desirable' behaviors of team members that make a team member a 'good' team member:[8]

1. Treats every member of the team with respect
2. Fosters teamwork and commitment to their team project
3. Is well organized and prepared for meetings
4. Contributes to the group discussions
5. Demonstrates good listening skills
6. Is open to other viewpoints and opinions
7. Carries assigned workload
8. Demonstrates good coaching skills
9. Is considerate of time commitments of others
10. Maintains positive relationships with others
11. Takes initiative to make things better in the group
12. Has cultural and emotional intelligence
13. Is inclusive of others

Linear Stages of Group Development

In 1965, Bruce Tuckman proposed a linear model of team development where a team goes through of forming, storming, norming, performing, and adjourning.[9]

- **Forming**—a period of getting acquainted, testing, and dependence; members look for cues of acceptable interpersonal behaviors.
- **Storming**—group structuring for the tasks and roles; intra-group conflict and hostility may evolve.
- **Norming**—the members accept roles and develop cohesion; exchange of tasks begins.
- **Performing**—the group focuses on goal attainment; functional roles are accepted and interaction is more effective.
- **Adjourning**—the purpose is achieved and the group disbands.

Group Processes

Synergy and groupthink are two additional concepts that have been studied as they relate to teams and teamwork.

> **Synergy**—meaning working together—refers to whether the sum of individual performances of the members is greater (positive synergy) or smaller (negative synergy). In positive team synergy there is a 'Gestalt' effect—a combined effect where the total is greater than the sum of the parts (2+2=5) and the team performance is better than performances of individuals. But the synergy can also be negative; when the team performance is less than the sum of individual performances. The Apollo Syndrome (discussed later) is a variant of negative synergy.

Groupthink—is conformance to the way the group thinks so members no longer evaluate each other's inputs critically. Non-diverse teams and self-selected teams composed of friends are more likely to experience groupthink!

Team Size

Is there an 'optimal' team size? In general, we think of teams as smaller numbers (usually in single digits) of people working together. If the team size is small, it is easier for the members of the team to (self) manage their operations. Agile (Scrum) teams are kept small on purpose so they can remain agile. If teams gets too large, the team members must spend more time grouping themselves into smaller sub-teams and coordinating their activities. While the preference is for relatively small (e.g., two-pizza teams) to avoid many possible team dysfunctionality, today's projects often require the involvement of large numbers of people. With today's focus on project work, the complexity and global scope of these projects, agile team portfolio management (also called Agile TPM), engages teams who work on different projects simultaneously. For example, in a complex change management initiative or program that demands more preparatory work to implement, Agile TPM allows the entire project team (or multiple agile teams) to stay current on the status of each other's work, make quick decisions, as well as timely adaptations and changes.[10]

MAPPING A TEAM

While there are generic team critical success factors, each team is unique because when people join a team, they bring in their own personalities, cultures, and team roles. As a result, when working together, each team is likely to have somewhat different challenges that will need to be bridged and integrated.

Personality

When people work on a team, they bring their personality and cognitive style to the team. A cognitive style is based on habituated behavior. It refers to the way a person approaches and attempts to solve problems they encounter including work-related problems and team contributions. A person's cognitive style influences their behavior. There are a number of assessment tests to identify one's cognitive style, such as the Myers-Briggs Type Indicator (MBTI) and the Dominance, Influence, Steadiness, Conscientious (D.I.S.C.) profile, among others.

The MBTI is a personality questionnaire designed to identify certain psychological differences and classify individuals in positive terms (what they like rather than what they lack). The four contrasting MBTI styles not only line up with key features of most managerial jobs, but they also give an indication of how a person's cognitive style impacts particular aspects of teamwork in terms of establishing relations, generating information, making decisions, and choosing priorities (see 6.2).[11]

A team member also brings their personal D.I.S.C. characteristics to the team. Being high on a particular D.I.S.C. dimension can show up behaviorally on the team (especially in times of stress) but also brings with it certain fears. A team member with high 'D' Dominance tends to be impatient, result oriented, have high ego strength, and is more aggressive with a fear of being taken advantage of. A team member with high 'I' Influence tends to be emotional, friendly, people oriented, optimistic and has a fear of loss of social approval. A team member with high 'S' Steadiness tends to enjoy routine

6-2. MBTI Styles and Teamwork

Extrovert-Introvert (E-I)
Dealing with people (establishing relations)

Sensing-Intuiting (S-I)
Acquire information (generating information)

Thinking-Feeling (T-F)
Decision-making (making decisions)

Judging- Perceiving (J-P)
Establish goals (choosing priorities)

Source: Ancona, D., Kochan, T., Scully, M., Van Maanen, J., & Westney, D. E. (2005). *Managing for the Future: Organizational Behavior & Processes* (3rd Ed.). Cincinnati: South-Western College Publishing.

6-3. Fears Based on D.I.S.C Profile

High D	Being taken advantage of
High I	Loss of social approval
High S	Change
High C	Criticism

Source: History of DiSC (2003). *The DiSC® Indra® Research Report*, Inscape Publishing, 2003. https://www.discprofile.com/what-is-disc/history-of-disc/

and fears change, is loyal, possessive, and family oriented; a team member with high "C" Conscientious is more accurate, fussy, persistent, polite, and fears criticism (see 6-3).

If you know your own personality traits and those of your team members, you can identify the things about each of the other personality characteristics types; the things that others could do to work better with your style; and the things that you can do to work better with the other styles. Foremost, you begin to understand how different cognitive styles of team members may affect the functioning of the team—especially under stressful situations when people tend to go into their back-up behavior. A basic team rule coming from psychology is that "you cannot change people's personalities, but you can encourage them to adapt their behavior."[12]

Understanding the characteristics of people's cognitive style has a dual effect:

1. You have lowered your expectation, and no longer expect 100 percent tidiness from them, so you'll be happier to settle for 75 percent;
2. They feel you are accepting them for what they are, so they have no need to feel angry or resentful.[13]

Another basic management principle (one of the Basic Principles developed by Jack Zenger and Dale Miller in the 1980s) applies to teams, namely 'focus on the situation, issue or behavior, not on the person' rather than to blame or label the person and generalize. A fundamental 'frontline' management skill is to learn to differentiate the 'behavior' of the person from the 'person.'[14]

Culture

In addition to their personality, team members also bring their culture to the team. Hence, it is important—especially in diverse multicultural teams to identify how a team member's cultural profile could affect teamwork. Geert Hofstede's value dimensions can be used to map a team member's cultural profile[15] (see module on the cultural lens) and to determine how differences in power distance, individualism, uncertainty avoidance, masculinity, and short or long-term orientation may impact behaviors of team members and perceptions of them by other team members.

In her culture map, Erin Meyer identifies several dimensions that describe specific aspects of teamwork such as communicating (low vs high context), evaluating (direct vs indirect feedback), persuading (principle vs application first), leading (egalitarian vs hierarchical), deciding (consensual vs top down), trusting (task vs relationship based), disagreeing (confrontational vs avoiding confrontation), and scheduling (linear vs flexible time).[16]

Another important question related to culture is whether non-diverse (homogenous) teams are more or less effective than diverse (heterogeneous) teams. Heterogeneous teams can be token, bicultural, or multicultural ones. Team effectiveness is influenced by the diversity of their team members as diversity has both advantages and disadvantages. Advantages of team diversity are that it permits increased creativity; forces people to understand other points of view; can lead to better problem formulations, solutions and, ultimately, decisions; enables the team to be more effective and productive. Disadvantages of team diversity are that it causes a lack of cohesion, mistrust, and miscommunication; disables the contribution of valid ideas and people in terms of agreement, consensus, and concerted action; can weaken the team's efficiency, effectiveness, and productivity. The productivity of diverse teams rises due to the synergy of diversity but loses due to the increased faulty processes inherent to diverse people working together. Summarizing factors that influence the effectiveness of multicultural teams, Nancy Adler in her 2003 book, *International Dimensions of Organizational Behavior*, states that the actual productivity of a diverse team is equal to the potential productivity gain minus the losses due to faulty processes. So, if companies want the potential gains of diverse teams, they must ensure team members are equipped to resolve the faulty team processes that are more likely to occur.[17]

Team Roles

Team roles are based on cognitive styles of individual team members. Each team member has particular team roles they bring to the team. People have a psychological make-up that allows them to contribute to the team in a particular way (i.e., a team role). Team roles relate to how well one takes on 'tasks' on the team (i.e., a range of behaviors and contributions). Team role behavior is not just psychological but also environmental. Team roles are different from functional roles as they are based on individual jobs, abilities, and experience. According to Meredith Belbin, team role behavior is the result of many factors: personality, role learning, mental abilities, values, motivations, and field constraints.[18]

BELBIN TEAM ROLES

Meredith Belbin dedicated lifelong research efforts to how teams work effectively and introduced the notion of team roles. The Belbin Team roles are widely used in companies around the world but are virtually unknown in the U.S. Belbin started his team role research when he was working for NASA in the United States. He observed that teams made up of very smart people (in this case astronauts) do not necessarily outperform lesser intelligent teams. His basic research question was as follows: "How can a team of people with IQs of 120 each have a collective average IQ of 63?" He called it the 'Apollo' syndrome.[19] The easy answer to this question is that teams of similarly highly intelligent people (usually professional) do not really contribute well to the team (beyond being what Belbin called the 'Plant'). On the contrary, they usually do not listen to other team members very well and engage in a great deal of abortive debate, trying to convince the others of the validity of their points of view.

The Duality of Belbin® Team Roles[20]

According to Belbin, in a perfect team there are nine complementary team roles. All roles are necessary for team success and one role is not necessarily better than another. Each team role has strengths (the contribution people make based on their team roles) and allowable weaknesses (the price the team pays for the strength that each team member brings). The better the 'mix' of the team members, the better the team will perform. People have 'preferred' team roles. Most people can play only one to three team roles effectively. It is possible to change natural but not desirable behavior (beyond the three roles), as team members, taking on team roles they are not well suited for, will likely play the role inadequately.

The **Plant (PL)** is a 'creator' and brought into teams in order to generate new ideas. The PL is creative, imaginative, unorthodox, loves to solve difficult problems and is generally not assertive, and the ideas he brings in are not always viable. *But too much intellect and too many ideas can raise arguments!*

The **Monitor-Evaluator (ME)** is objective. The ME is brought in to evaluate all ideas for feasibility, is serious-minded, strategic and discerning, sees all options and pitfalls, judges accurately, and once the evaluation is completed, delegates the work to other team members. *But who will mobilize the team?*

The **Coordinator (CO)** is motivating. The CO is needed to control and develop the team members, is mature, confident, calm, decisive, and understands people. The CO clarifies goals, brings other people together to promote team discussions, and delegates. *But so far, no* *'real' work has been done yet on the team. Is the team getting anywhere?*

The **Implementer (IMP)** has the capacity to take practical steps and actions and is brought in to get things organized. The IM is organized, disciplined, reliable, dependable, loyal, conservative in habits, does not like change, and is good at process. *But, is anybody communicating outside the team?*

The **Resource Investigator (RI)** is outgoing. The RI finds out what's going on and needed in the outside world, is an extrovert, enthusiastic and communicative, is good at getting things out of people, gets easily bored, explores opportunities, and develops contacts and networks. *But the team can easily lose its direction!*

The **Shaper (SH)** is hard driving. The SH is brought in to give energy to the team, is challenging, dynamic, and thrives on pressure, has the drive and courage to overcome obstacles, is competitive and impatient, can be rude, and cracks the whip to keep things on track. *But a few feathers get ruffled on the team!*

The **Team worker (TW)** is diplomatic. The TW is needed to facilitate good atmosphere and dialog with the team, listens, builds team spirit and averts friction, is amiable, cooperative, mild, and perceptive, creates harmony, can be indecisive and reactive, and can't take pressure. *But are things being done to high enough up-to-date standards?*

The **Completer Finisher (CF)** is meticulous. The CF ensures that everything works to perfection and is being done according to high standards, is painstaking, conscientious, anxious, worried, searches out errors and omissions, covers all tracks, delivers on time, and can't delegate. *But, where are the experts?*

The **Specialist (SP)** is knowledgeable. The SP is dedicated to a chosen field of work; is single-minded and dedicated; is a self-starter; provides specialized knowledge and skills in rare supply; and does not like to work in groups. *But what is really making a team that has all the nine team roles played successfully?*

These nine Belbin team roles are grouped into three categories: action-oriented roles (Shaper, Implementer, and Completer Finisher); social-oriented roles (Coordinator, Team Worker, and Resource Investigator) and thinking-oriented roles (Plant, Monitor Evaluator, and Specialist).

Strengths and Weaknesses of Belbin Team Roles

The strengths and non-allowable weakness of each Belbin team role are summarized in 6-4.

In many organizations (mainly outside the U.S.), individuals complete a Belbin Self-Perception Inventory and they ask for feedback from their colleagues. Generated Belbin Individual Report helps pinpoint individual Team Role strengths and weaknesses. The results are then shared and discussed with the rest of the team.[21] When a team does this exercise, it is apparent that basing solely on team roles, each team will have specific challenges that will need to be addressed. Belbin team roles are also being used in identifying things 'to do' and things 'not to expect', when dealing with other team roles, as well as typically 'good' and 'problematic' working relationship between a boss, subordinate, and peers.

In terms of team composition, an effective team must have all team roles; people are best at playing their primary and secondary roles; and it is necessary to manage and control allowable weaknesses. In terms of construction, certain types of team roles work best together (hierarchical, peer, and subordinate relationships); there may be a gap between self-perception and observer-perception of your team role; and project cycle needs different team roles. Belbin team roles provide mapping and team confidence as team members have a common team language, understand the strengths and weaknesses of each role, and the do's and don'ts for each team role.

6-4. Belbin Team Role Strengths and Non-Allowable Weaknesses

Belbin Team Role	Strength	Weakness
Plant (PL)	Theorizes; creative intelligent thinker	Strong 'ownership' of ideas inhibiting results
Monitor-Evaluator (ME)	Judges impartially; intelligent thinker	Cynicism without logic
Coordinator (CO)	Generalizes; strong leader; promotes harmony and team spirit	Taking credit for the effort of the team
Implementer (IMP)	Applies; doer	Obstructing a change
Resource Investigator (RI)	Recognizes opportunities, creating, liaising, and motivating	Letting people and clients down by neglecting follow-up
Shaper (SH)	Drives; strong (control) leader	Inability to recover from conflict
Team Worker (TW)	Supports; promotes harmony and team spirit	Avoiding situations that may entail pressure
Complete Finisher (CF)	Perfects established systems; doer, achieving high standards	Obsessive behavior
Specialist (SP)	Expert; achieves high standards and expertise	Ignoring facts outside of area of competence

Source: Belbin® Team Role Master Trainer Certification Program, Cambridge, England (2003)

GLOBAL AND VIRTUAL TEAMS

In today's global environment, the workings of a 'global' team is of particular interest. A global team (group of people working together to accomplish a common objective) is a team that is dispersed in different locations around the world and/or comprised of people from different cultural backgrounds. Global teams have all the challenges of a team in addition to four additional complexities such as culture, distance, time, and language.[22]

The term virtual team, first coined in a 1999 paper by Guy Paré and Line Dubé, is foremost a team where team members rely predominantly on ICT to accomplish their common goal—usually as a result of spatial and geographically dispersion.[23] Some of the key challenges of virtual teams is that the team members work in different locations and do not often interact face-to-face. Virtual and remote team workers use a variety of ICT such as shareware, email, conference call, video conference, etc. Because of the need of team members to rely on ICT for completing their tasks and their lack of face-to-face communication, virtual teams are not without their challenges. Yet, with the right competencies, skills, and technology, they can succeed.

In a 2007 article in the *Academy of Management Persectives*, Arvind Malhotra, Ann Majchrzak, & Benson Rosen (2007) identified best practices for team leaders of virtual teams so they can be successful:[24]

1. Establish and maintain trust through the use of communication technology;
2. Ensure distributed diversity is understood and appreciated;
3. Manage virtual work-life cycle (meetings);
4. Monitor team progress using technology;
5. Enhance visibility of virtual members within the team and outside in the organization; and
6. Enable individual members of the virtual team to benefit from the team.

According to M. Katherine Brown, Brenda Huettner, and Char James-Tanny in their 2007 book, *Managing Virtual Teams*, effective virtual teams:[25]

- Understand their shared goals and objectives
- Know what is expected of them
- Have the technology they need to accomplish their tasks
- Know how to use the technology
- Are motivated to use the technology to perform their jobs well

Remote work is one of the fastest growing areas of work flexibility as workers are working from their home and/or a flexible office. Statistics on remote work in the U.S. indicate:[26]

- 70% of professionals work remotely at least one day a week
- 53% of professionals work remotely for at least half of the week
- In 2022, the remote workforce will be 42.5% of the total global workforce
- The flexible office market is growing at 13% rate annually

There are advantages and disadvantages of remote work for both the employer and the talent (see 6-5).[27] Organizations that use remote virtual teams employ ICT for team communication and organize regular off-site meetings for vital face-to-face interaction among the team members.

6-5. Advantages and Disadvantages of Remote Work

	Pros	Cons
Employer	• Less office overhead costs • Reduced real estate costs • Recruiting • Retention and 'stickiness' • Access to lower cost markets • Hiring globally adds cross-cultural diversity • Diversity recruiting • Easier to hire (bigger talent pool) • No need for bigger offices, no relocation cost, less immigration cases	• More administrative burden for HR, Finance, and IT • Needs different leadership skills • More complicated/nuanced performance metrics • Challenges with mixed teams • Cost of setting up legal entities • Cost of different team off sites for face-to-face connection • More communication required • More difficult to nurture and maintain company culture • New ways of supporting office safety and duty of care
Worker	• Less time/cost in commute • Less distractions for 'flow' time • Full productivity • Full flexibility • Flexibility to balance home and family needs (work-life integration) • Better nutrition (possibility of home cooked meals every day)	• More administrative burden for HR, Finance, and IT • More complicated/nuanced performance metrics • Challenges with mixed teams • Cost of setting up legal entities • Cost of different team off sites for face-to-face connection • More communication required • More difficult to nurture and maintain company culture • New ways of supporting office safety and duty of care • Protection of customer data in a virtual setting • Need for additional biometric security

Source: Lisbeth Claus, Anika Lehde and Maris Krieger (2019). The Future of Work: Rise of the Individual worker. 4th Annual Global HR Conference: Redmond, WA: Global HR Consortium/IT Roundtable

BASIC CONDITIONS FOR EFFECTIVE TEAM PERFORMANCE

According to Belbin, factors that contribute to the critical success of a team are as follows:[27]

1. There is a person in the 'chair' who leads the team;
2. There is one strong 'plant' in the team, who stimulates brainstorming and getting new ideas;
3. There is a good spread of mental abilities and skills;
4. There is a spread in personal characteristics of people that ensures wide coverage in the different team roles;
5. There is a good match between the attributes of the team members and their responsibilities; and
6. There is recognition of imbalances in the team and ability to adjust.

Deborah Ancona et al. show how team effectiveness differs from that of team operations. The key ingredients of team effectiveness are performance (did all team members contribute?), member satisfaction (how satisfied is each member of the team?), team learning (what learning occurred individually and as a whole?) and external viability (do the project and the team have viability externally?). Team operations refer to the internal processes and boundary management.[28]

Martha L. Maznevski and Celia Chui (2012) identified four basic conditions for team performance: (1) clearly defined tasks, objectives, and task definitions; (2) a team composed of the right combination of team and social skills; (3) appropriate roles; and (4) engagement in effective processes such as communication, conflict resolution, and process management.[29]

Martha L. Maznevski and Joseph, J. DiStefano (2000) identify mapping, bridging, and integrating as three skills necessary for team success. Mapping is understanding the team's compositional differences and the corresponding implications for bringing to the team different knowledge perspectives and approaches to relationship management. Bridging is communicating across those differences to ensure that each member understands the others. Integrating is bringing the different perspectives and preferences together, resolving differences among them, and building on them to generate innovative, high quality approaches to the task.[30]

Google studied hundreds of its teams to identify what made its team successful or not. They gave the research the code name Project Aristotle because of Aristotle's famous quotation that 'the whole is greater than the sum of its parts.' The study could not find patterns or any evidence that the composition of the team made any difference, but understanding and influencing group norms were key to improving team performance. Google's Aristotle project shows that the following five factors are more important for team success than who is on the team:[31]

1. **Psychological safety**—team members must be comfortable in taking risks and speaking their mind.

2. **Dependability**—every team member needs to contribute to the best of their ability and deliver high quality work.

3. **Structure and clarity**—they must be clear direction and goals and every team member must know how to get their job done.

4. **Meaning**—every team member must have the satisfaction that their contribution is a key element of success of the team.

5. **Impact**—team members must feel that what they are doing actually benefits the company and they are not wasting their time. ▮

REFERENCES

1. Surowiecki, J. (2004). *The Wisdom of Crowds: Why the Many are Smarter than the Few and how Collective Wisdom Shapes Business, Economies, Societies, and Nations* (1st ed.). New York: Doubleday.
2. Katzenbach, J., & Smith, D. (1993). "The Discipline of Teams," *Harvard Business Review*, 83(7/8): 162-171.
3. Ibid.
4. Types of Trust in Organizational Relationships (2008). *Citeman*, July 12 (Accessed: January 5 2019). https://www.citeman.com/3621-types-of-trust-in-organizational-relationships.html
5. Labianca. J. (2004). "The Ties That Bind," *Harvard Business Review* 82(10): 19.
6. Malone, T.W. & Crowston, K. (1990). "What is Coordination Theory and How Can it Help Design Cooperative Work Systems?" *Proceedings of the 1990 ACM Conference on Computer-Supported Cooperative Work*, September, 357-370.
7. Gino, F. (2019). "Cracking the Code of Sustained Collaboration," *Harvard Business Review*, 97(6): 72-81.
8. These desirable team behaviors have been developed and refined by Willamette University MBA student teams in the development of rubric for peer rating of teamwork (2002).
9. Tuckman, B. (1965). "Developmental Sequence in Small Groups," *Psychological Bulletin*, 63(6): 384-399.
10. Boskma, W., Buizer, M., van de Hoef, N, Peters, G. & Zelen, W. (2017). *Agile HR*. Amsterdam: Nubiz.
11. Ancona, D., Kochan, T., Scully, M., Van Maanen, J., & Westney, D. E. (2005). *Managing for the Future: Organizational Behavior & Processes* (3rd Ed.). Cincinnati: South-Western College Publishing.
12. Jay, R. (2000). *Build a Great Team*. London: Prentice Hall.
13. Belbin, M. (1981). *Management Teams*. Oxford: Butterworth-Heinemann.
14. Perrin, C. & Blauth, C. (2010). "The Basic Principles: Building Blocks of Trust," *Catalyst*, 39(2):9.
15. Hofstede, G. (1991). *Culture and Organizations. Software of the Mind*. New York: McGraw-Hill.
16. Meyer, E. (2014). *The Culture Map: Breaking Through the Invisible Boundaries of Global Business*. Philadelphia: Public Affairs.
17. Adler, N. (2002). *International Dimensions of Organizational Behavior* (4th ed). Cincinnati: South-Western Thomson Learning.
18. The discussion of the Belbin team roles is based on materials provided through the Belbin® Team Role Master Trainer Certification Program, Cambridge, England, 2003. https://www.belbin.com/about/belbin-team-roles/
19. Belbin, M. (1981). *Management Teams*. Oxford: Butterworth-Heinemann.
20. Belbin® Team Role Master Trainer Certification Program, Cambridge, England, 2003, https://www.belbin.com/about/belbin-team-roles/
21. Armstrong, D. (2000). "Building Teams Across Borders," *Executive Education Excellence*, 17(3): 10.
22. Paré, G. & Dubé, L. (1999). Virtual Teams: An Exploratory Study of Key Challenges and Strategies. *Proceedings of the 20th International Conference on Information Systems*, Charlotte, N.C.
23. Malhotra, A., Majchrzak, A., & Rosen, B. (2007). "Leading Virtual Teams," *Academy of Management Perspectives*, 21(1): 60-70.
24. Brown, M. K., Huettner, B. & James-Tanny, C. (2007). *Managing Virtual Teams*. Sudbury: Wordware Publishing.
25. *17 Stats About Remote Work* (2019). (Accessed: February 4, 2020). https://remote.co/10-stats-about-remote-work/
26. Claus, L., Lehde, A., & Krieger, M. (2019). The Future of Work: Rise of the Individual Worker. *Proceedings of the 4th Annual Global HR Conference*, Redmond, WA.
27. Description of the nine Belbin Team roles (2001). e-interplace, Belbin®, Cambridge, England, 2001
28. Ancona, D., Kochan, T., Scully, M., Van Maanen, J., & Westney, D. E. (2005). *Managing for the Future: Organizational Behavior & Processes* (3rd Ed.). Cincinnati: South-Western College Publishing.
29. Maznevski, M., & Chui, C. (2012). Leading Global Teams. Pp. 142-145 in Mendenhall, M. et al. *Global Leadership* (2nd ed.). London: Routledge.
30. Maznevski, M. & DiStefano, J. (2000). "Global Leaders are Team Players: Developing Global. Leaders Through Membership On Global Teams," *Human Resource Management*, 39 (2/3): 195-208.
31. Duhig, C. (2016). What Google Learned From Its Quest to Build the Perfect Team. February 25. (Accessed: November 1, 2019). https://www.nytimes.com/2016/02/28/magazine/what-google-learned-from-its-quest-to-build-the-perfect-team.html

GUIDED READING QUESTIONS

1. What is a team?

2. Identify a number of different types of teams.

3. What are the Belbin team roles and how can they be used?

4. What is mapping, bridging, and integrating in the context of team work?

FOLLOW-UP CRITICAL THINKING QUESTIONS

1. What is my major takeaway from this reading?

2. What do I already know about this subject?

3. What follow-up questions do I have about this?

4. How can I apply this in real life?

KEY TERMS

Ad hoc team
Agile team
Autonomous work team
Belbin team role
Bi-cultural team
Bridging
Colocated team
Crew
Crossfunctional team
Dispersed team
Extreme action team
Global team
Groupthink
Heterogeneous team
Homogeneous team
Hot group
Intact team
Integrating
KSAO
Large team
Long-term team
Management team
Mapping
Multicultural team
Multi-disciplinary team
Natural work group
Process team
Project team
Production team
Professional team
Self-managed team
Short-term team
Small team
Synergy
Remote team
Task force
Token team
Team
Team role
Team work
Virtual team

LEARNING ASSESSMENT

Critically reflect on the content and the different concepts in this module and rate your own competency using the assessment scale.

Competency	I never heard of it	I heard of it but have limited knowledge of it	I can reasonably explain it to others	I have used it, done it, applied it
Belbin team role	0	1	2	3
Mapping, bridging, integrating	0	1	2	3
Virtual teamwork	0	1	2	3
Remote work	0	1	2	3
Team effectiveness of multicultural teams	0	1	2	3

MODULAR-SPECIFIC ASSESSMENT

Assess how your personality impacts your team contribution:

- Take a Cognitive Style Assessment such as Myers-Briggs, big five, DISC
- Take the Belbin team role inventory: Belbin Observer AssessmentTM https://www.belbin.com/about/what-are-observer-assessments/

VIGNETTE

A PROFESSIONAL JOINS THE WORKDAY TEAM AS A REMOTE WORKER[1]

With over a decade of experience designing and implementing solutions that align people, process, technology, and financial resources in the consumer goods, non-profit higher education, federal government utilities, and national marketing sectors, Tina Alexander, PMP, SHRM-SCP, GPHR, SPHR, landed a job as Sr. Engagement Manager for Workday. This position matched her major strengths: project management, customer service, and mobilizing teams to achieve desired outcomes. However, she spent her first day at work at her home connecting through her laptop to get ready for her new job responsibilities, the company, and the team! Her letter of agreement specified she would work 50-50 remote (from home) and on the road (at Workday client sites). Workday, a company offering enterprise-level software solutions for financial management, human resources, and planning, is not unique in having a large group of its employees working remotely. What is unique, however, is how the company supports and nurtures its remote workers.

The phenomenon labeled telecommuting (in the 1970s) has grown into a reality today—called remote work. The different terms being used for this new reality—telecommuter, lone worker, isolated worker, remote worker—all have in common that these workers work at home or in a flexible office/co-shared space all or most of the time and with limited face-to-face supervision. Partly due to the expectations of a new generation of workers, the high cost of real estate in urban areas where companies are located, remote (and flexible) work is becoming the norm in the U.S. Companies are recruiting workers where they live (or want to live) and when they want to work.

One of the major management challenges of remote work is to ensure that people working in such virtual and remote environments can work effectively with others on the team and feel supported. Remote work has challenges and opportunities for both employers and workers. Nick van Der Meulen investigates the effects of flexible and remote working practices on performance in the digital workspace and describes the '*distance dilemma*' as the trade-off between opportunities for concentration (at home) and collaboration (at the office). He argues that while remote work stimulates a worker's focus through reduced distractions, it may frustrate interdependent collaborative work through reduced presence and social capital.[2] Introducing work done anytime and anywhere requires an organizational capability that is closely linked to the corporate culture and leadership style of the employer.

Here is how Tina describes her remote work experience with Workday—from day one, six months and one year later, and now more than two years as a remote worker—in her own words:

Day One—two days of orientation, four weeks of intensive training cumulating with an exam and a practicum, first assignment to lead a fortune 1000 enterprise-wide deployment, and I head home! Waking up at 6am in my own bed for the first time in more than a month. Quick shower, coffee brewing, dogs walked, load of laundry started, HR and news headlines scanned, and at my desk by 6:30am. I'm ready for the day. Armed with what I learned, partnered with a peer project manager for support, weekly check-ins with a senior leader to absorb our culture, and a daily briefing with my supervisor to ensure my questions are answered and I'm making progress. I'm on my own but, I'm not alone. At my fingertips is a wealth of information to help me do my job. I can get answers on my own through the organization-wide search engine, peer blogs, and on-demand learning modules or reach out to peers for help through instant messenger, text, email, and phone. I have everything I need to be a success. Extensive project planning, negotiating for resources, obsessing over every detail, and a deep dive into the customer's industry, organization and culture. Just over seven hours of exciting travel from door-to-door. I'm feeling prepared and looking forward to partnering with the customer to achieve their goals.

Six months into my remote lifestyle and the project is on track. I've made several professional friends. It's satisfying leading and supporting my team and contributing to the customer's success in a meaningful way. I meet with my supervisor weekly by video chat, virtually join my business unit's bi-weekly status web conference, and plan time to watch product recordings and keep up on what's new. I'm doing it! Dogs walked, coffee brewing, dinner is in the crockpot, led one and participated in another meeting, and it's 6:30am.

One year—working remotely for more than year and I am settled into my 'remote-scheduled lifestyle'. On-time and off-time are completely integrated - team meetings, customer travel, and budgets mixed with dental appointments, lawn mowing, and grocery shopping. Worktime weaves its way throughout a 14-hour day. My company keeps me informed of events and invites me to join virtually where it makes sense. Leadership encourages remote workers to participate in remote worker organized community volunteer events. I receive surprises in the mail to remind me that I am thought about. Meetings that I miss are recorded and weekly company communications broadcast news about colleagues' awards and promotions, reorganizations and new initiatives. Remote workers often tradeoff recognition for lifestyle, mentorship for self-management, and personal for professional friendships.

Two years later—although I'm still in my original role celebrating two years as a remote worker, I'm well regarded by my colleagues, teammates seek my advice, and I act as mentor to newly hired remote workers. My remote worker scheduled lifestyle includes chats with neighbors, lunch with dear friends, and personal time for exercise and long walks. Crockpot meals have been replaced with family-time dinner prep. Travel is necessary but not as glamorous as it once seemed. It's 6:30am, coffee is brewing, and I'm prepping for a status call grateful to have the chosen the remote lifestyle.

From the employer's perspective, a different management style is needed to overcome the pitfalls of remote teamwork. On the one hand, managers are no longer able to observe team members at work and give up some control through the lack of visibility. On the other hand, remote work requires a great dose of self-management of the team members. Transparency, communication and a coaching leadership style are the key success factors of this form of "new" remote work. This openness and accessibility must be supported by an "any time, any place" information and communication technology.

From the worker's perspective, working remotely can be isolating and lonely as it lacks the social interactions and connectivity that coworkers bring—though we know that navigating relationships with coworkers can be tricky as well. Remote workers who choose to work from home may also sacrifice their living space in order to make their own home office, especially for people or in places/countries where living space is more limited. This can also make it more difficult to establish a healthy work-life balance and separate the worker from their work. As the line between home and work becomes increasingly blurred with remote workers, there is a risk of burning out due to overwork. This may not be the case for individuals who lack the type of self-discipline that it typically takes in order to be successful at remote work.

REFERENCES

1. This vignette was prepared by Professor Lisbeth Claus and Tina Alexander for the sole purpose of illustrating a global HR practice for instructional objectives. Global HR in Action © 2020, Global Immersion Press, All Rights Reserved.
2. van der Meulen, N. (2016) *The Distance Dilemma: The Effect of Flexible Working Practices on Performance in the Digital Workplace.* Doctoral Dissertation, Rotterdam: Erasmus University.

GUIDED READING QUESTIONS

1. What are the challenges and opportunities of remote (team) work?
2. Who/what makes a good/poor remote worker?

MODULE SEVEN

MOTIVATION, ENGAGEMENT, AND THE EMPLOYEE EXPERIENCE

MODULE SEVEN

MOTIVATION, ENGAGEMENT, AND THE EMPLOYEE EXPERIENCE

DESCRIPTION

This module summarizes the various motivation theories and identifies how they contribute to either a motivating or demotivating work environment. We focus on the organizational context that affects engagement/disengagement as well as ways to improve the employee and worker experience.

LEARNING OBJECTIVES

Upon completing the learning experience, you will be able to:

- Describe the basic tenets of the major need, reinforcement, job characteristics, and cognition motivation theories
- Apply motivation theories to practical management situations
- Distinguish between intrinsic and extrinsic motivators
- Identify the drivers of employee engagement and organizational citizenship behavior
- Describe the components of the employee experience

GUIDING QUESTIONS

Does my motivation match my ambition?
How can employers improve the employee experience?

Roughly half of JULIE's team were long-tenured employees with over 20 years with the company. The rest were some very career-oriented professionals who she had hired over the past 5 years. The individuals on the team were motivated differently. Some, but not all, of the longer-tenured employees were focused on retaining their current positions and responsibilities until retirement while many of the employees with less than five years were anxious to learn new skills and responsibilities while bringing an 'out of the box' mindset to their jobs. Julie needed to pull the team together to motivate them to achieve the stretch goals that had been defined for the team.

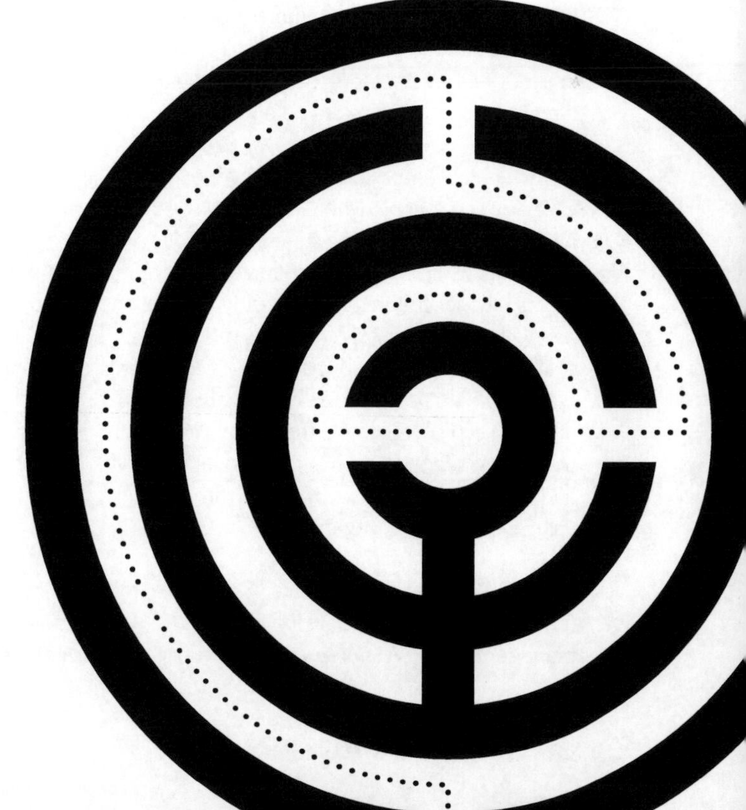

MOTIVATION

One of the overall challenges in managing any individual (including oneself), team, or organization, is designing the right structure to motivate people on these three different levels of management (the micro, meso, and macro level). It's wonderful to have workers—employees, contract workers, freelancers, volunteers, or otherwise—who are high in competencies, but what purpose does that ultimately serve if they are not motivated to excel?

Motivation is the reason an individual pursues any kind of goal. Motivation stems from a variety of wants, needs, or desires; these wants, needs, and desires themselves stem from both innate qualities and external influences (e.g., societal, cultural, or familial pressures). Motivation is personal and difficult to measure. A highly motivated person is usually identifiable by the direction, intensity, and persistence of their voluntary behavior.[1] All three characteristics of the effort must be present for true motivation: direction in terms of an individual's choices to channel one's efforts toward accomplishing a goal; intensity in how hard the person tries and expends their effort; and persistence or how long the person can sustain the effort. A highly motivated person can be described as someone who is putting in a lot of effort for a long period of time at a directed task they found to be highly desirable.

Unfortunately for organizations and individuals alike, the very people who wish to motivate others often end up doing the exact opposite. Managers, policies, and procedures, and organizational culture are frequently the reasons people become demotivated. This module examines some motivational theories to better prepare you to negate such 'organizational rain' effects (i.e. protect people from the rules and politics associated with any big-budget activity) and create environments that motivate yourself, your team, and your organization.[2]

To provide an easily applicable framework for those interested in developing their management savvy, our guiding question applies first to ourselves: Does the motivation I have match my ambition? In other words, we may all have different degrees of innate motivation—that is given behavior and not the result of learning or experience. But that does not necessarily mean we act on that motivation. That's where agency comes in, or the ability of people to act on their own behalf and impact their motivation. Viewing the motivation challenge primarily from one's own individual/micro perspective should provide insight on how best to approach motivation from both the meso (whether in a management relationship or team environment) and macro (the larger organizational context) perspectives as well.

CURRENT VIEWS ON MOTIVATION

Today's views on motivation have shifted towards engagement and experience. At the core of people's motivation is the fundamental question of whether people can really be motivated. This begs a subsequent question, namely what are we needing to motivate people to do in today's workplace?

Can People Be Motivated?

Is it even possible to motivate people, or is this a managerial wild goose chase? Theories abound on how best to motivate people; a handful of the best-tested and most widely used classic motivation theories shall be examined later in this module. People have an innate amount of motivation, but ultimately it is generally agreed upon that one cannot motivate someone if they don't want to be motivated! Efforts by managers to increase motivation—beyond the innate motivation and drive that people possess, is largely futile. However, managers can either improve the employee experience so that they are eager to show up at work and engage with others or create a 'de-motivating' environment that reduces a person's engagement.

There is no one-size-fits-all approach to motivation! The best way to move forward is to ignore the fantasy of one motivational practice to solve all your problems and instead gather a working knowledge and understanding of multiple theories. Imagine a motivational tool belt. You would not use a screwdriver to hammer a nail; you would not use a hammer to drive a screw. By outfitting your tool belt with a diverse array of tools (including traditional and progressive views) with different best-use cases and leading practices, you can better prepare yourself for many of the people management challenges you will face in your career—and at the least how to deal with a de-motivated worker.

For What Purposes Are We Motivating People?

This question is especially relevant when it comes to work performance. Every organization is unique in its mission and scope. You may find yourself working for a government agency providing public services such as roads or other basic infrastructure. A nonprofit may have a social or environmental mission with few revenue generation goals but ensuring contributions to their reserves so they can sustain their activities. Or, you may end up working for a financial services firm that is clearly profit-driven. Within each organization, disparate teams and individuals have their own purposes and functions as well. A financial analyst at a clothing brand may be focused on the costs and revenues generated by their products; a marketing person is likely thinking about how to satisfy customer needs.

Think about the different things for which people's motivation is required in the workplace to achieve top performance aligned with organizational goals: improved performance, increased productivity, being motivated to manage, change, excel, sell, learn, provide superior customer service, work together as a team, and even balance work and life. Getting people engaged in the right direction (aligned with organizational goals) is quite complex. In addition, incompetent managerial action will 'mess' it all up—i.e., create 'de-motivating' experiences.

Engagement

Since motivating people is likely somewhat of an illusion, it is important to understand the subtle distinction between engagement and motivation keeping in mind it's likely that a motivated employee will be engaged with their work. Engagement is the extent to which an employee is interacting with their work. Employee engagement (as opposed to disengagement) is a desirable condition linked to motivation of the employee and organizational outcomes. While in practice, companies are obsessed with the engagement of their employees and conduct annual satisfaction and engagement surveys, as a construct in terms of definition (conceptualization) and measurement (operationalization), engagement has not been rigorously used and tested. In spite of the focus on employee engagement during the past two decades, it is alarming to notice that studies (mainly done by consultants and not necessarily on a robust definition and measurement of engagement) show the large extent of disengagement in the global workforce—and that most people are only moderately engaged and even strongly disengaged.[3] To remedy the vagueness of the term and its measurement in management, William H. Macey and Benjamin Schneider (2008) define the underlying constructs of engagement as trait engagement, psychological state engagement, and behavioral engagement.[4]

- **Trait engagement**—positive views of life and work (proactive personality, autotelic personality, trait positive affect, and conscientiousness).
- **Psychological state engagement**—feelings of energy, absorption (satisfaction, involvement, commitment, and empowerment).
- **Behavioral engagement**—extra-role behavior (organizational citizenship behavior, proactive, personal initiative, role expansion, and adaptive).

To have an engaged workforce, organizations and their managers must get a better understanding as to what people value in their work and current job. Some interesting research findings with regard to employee engagement reveal the following:

- The things that attract employees to a job are not the same as the elements that engage them and persuade them to perform consistently well.
- Engagement is driven by an employee's immediate experience of his/her organization, within the wider context of national concerns (employment, welfare, culture).
- Employees are increasingly driven by personal motivation rather than inspired by their organization.
- Many employees feel that (senior) management is not interested in them.
- There is a clear distinction between rational and emotional factors of engagement.
- Organizations have mastered the processes that lead to effective management of the work (rational), but are less successful at the personal aspect of managing people (emotional).
- Engaged employees are more productive and have higher retention.
- Engaged employees have a sense of belonging because they can bring their authentic self to work.

Engaged employees typically perform better, are less likely to leave or burn out, and display more Organizational Citizenship Behavior (OCB). OCB is the behavior that employees exhibit above and beyond their required tasks, such as:[5]

- Does an employee volunteer extra effort to organize social events for the office?
- Does an employee take an active role in shaping new company policy?
- Does an employee contribute to the creative design of new processes that improve the way team works?

OCB can be thought of as two different types: relationship-oriented style (engagement) and task or performance-oriented style (performance). A balance of both is desirable, as stronger interpersonal relationships among employees will increase motivation and higher performance increases the organization's effectiveness at accomplishing its mission.

While viewed as a desirable state, engagement creates difficult empirical questions:

- Does engagement actually cause higher performance (causation), or are high-performing employees just more engaged (selection)?
- Do company-wide gains in engagement result in higher profits and stock valuation (and the reverse)?

Companies are paying a lot of attention to creating an engaged workforce and the manager's role is crucial in these efforts. To capitalize on the OCB of their workers, organizations must reflect on the following and get a greater understanding of:

- Why do people want to engage in OCB and go the extra mile for the organization (not something they are paid for directly)?
- Why do many people define themselves by their jobs?
- What can managers do to create an engaged workforce?
- What do employee satisfaction surveys tell us and how can they be used properly?
- What are some of the behavioral (self) and contextual (others and the organization) characteristics of an engaged employee in an organization?

In order to avoid becoming disengaged, look introspectively at your own motivation in your current job, or at the jobs of people you know and answer the following questions for yourself:

- Why am I doing what I'm doing?—this question relates to your life as well as your work;
- How will I (or other people) find meaning in life over a greatly extended period?—the so-called mid-life crisis is a relatively recent phenomenon;
- Do I know people who are in their mid-career, have achieved career goals and monetary success?—yet, they find their jobs meaningless;
- What motivates and inspires me?—this is an important question to reflect upon (with your significant life partners/friends).

Motivation and performance are partly determined by how effective people believe they can be. People's beliefs about their own capabilities lead to better performance as in a self-fulfilling prophecy (called the Galatea effect).[6] Self-efficacy—or the belief that one can do it—has also been shown to be highly correlated with organizational citizenship behavior. This is reasonable, as somebody who believes they can achieve their goals will be more likely to go the extra mile in that pursuit. Engagement also correlates with business level performance and organizational effectiveness. Engagement leads to high performance, which leads to engagement. The two feed off each other.

Fostering individual and team engagement can be a challenge for managers. We are operating in a much more uncertain world of work and there is an increase of flexible anytime-any place workers, remote workers, and freelancers. As we are now undergoing the fourth industrial revolution, many organizations now see the value in improving the employee experience on the job.

In his 2007 book, *The Three Signs of a Miserable Job*, Patrick Lencioni (2007) explores three 'red flags' to keep in mind when it comes to motivation and engagement:[7]

- **Anonymity**—feeling as though you are unrecognized, unmemorable, and easily replaceable can lead to deep dissatisfaction.
- **Irrelevance**—if your job has no sense of purpose, where is your engagement going to come from?
- **Immeasurability**—having no understanding of the effect of your efforts can leave you confused and dejected. Measuring the outcome of your inputs can provide a sense of self-worth and keep you engaged with the task at hand.

Daniel Pink in his 2009 book, *The Surprising Truth About What Motivates*, identifies three factors to increase performance and job satisfaction: autonomy, mastery, and purpose:[8]

1. **Autonomy**—our desire to be self-directed (increases engagement over compliance).
2. **Mastery**—the urge to get better skills (learning and development).
3. **Purpose**—the desire to do something that has meaning and is important (meaningful work).

A common belief is that 'give me the money' and I will be motivated. Right! Not so fast. Motivation is not just about carrots and sticks. While it is attractive to believe that higher pay and bonuses motivate, in fact money is more—in Herzberg's terminology—a hygiene factor than a motivator. When work is based on basic, mechanical skills, pay does matter. But for knowledge work (involving cognitive skills, decision-making, creativity, or higher-order thinking), higher pay does not increase performance provided it is not a job dissatisfaction (hygiene) factor. The challenge of any manager—and also for the individual worker—is to create work experiences that are engaging in the eye of the beholder.

The Employee Experience

The focus of organizational development is markedly different from the previous three industrial revolutions in which utility (1st industrial revolution), productivity (2nd), and engagement (3rd) were the core ideas shaping how organizations interact with their employees. According to Jacob Morgan, in his 2017 book, *The Employee Experience Advantage*, the 4th industrial revolution is all about 'the employee experience.' The employee experience takes a broader approach to engaging with employees, including the complete experience an employee has when interacting with an organization in their life cycle as an employee (before, during, and after). Interestingly, some companies even consider rejected applicants in their employee experience lifecycle. According to Morgan, employee experiences are influenced by three broad elements:[9]

1. The physical environment in which they work (office, manufacturing plant, campus, etc.);
2. The organizational culture;
3. The technological tools.

In the same manner that marketing focuses on the (external) customer experience, many employers are implementing programs to both monitor and improve the employee (or internal customer) experience, beginning with the first 'touchpoint' and ending with the last. Touchpoints are the emotional points of contact the employee has with the organization as an internal customer—whether through structures, systems, or people. This includes what the website interaction is like when an applicant searches for job postings, the experience of going through the application process, the selection experience, onboarding, working, and exit. Although employee satisfaction surveys are a common method of understanding the employee experience, they must not only ask the right questions at the right times, but they are often too broad and only done once or twice a year. A new way of gauging employee experience is the use of sentiment analysis. Sentiment analysis consists of using either pulse surveys or text analytics to mine various sources of data for employee opinions or sentiment rather than annual engagement surveys. Whatever tool used, the data obtained must be accurate, complete, and timely (ACT) to provide the necessary information to make evidence-based decisions. Managers and organizations must learn from the data and take actions based on it to make the employee experience richer, more positive, and better aligned with the organization's mission and culture. Where does the value lie for the organization? Well, improving the employee experience can increase motivation and productivity of your employees. Even for rejected job applicants, creating a positive experience for them can put more company ambassadors out into the world and spread your reputation as a positive employer. In a world where workers are expected to change jobs multiple times in their career, it's important to attract and retain top talent. A rock-your-world employee experience can help you do both.

CLASSIC MOTIVATION THEORIES

Everyone has probably heard of Maslow! Yet, for the past 50 years, many more theories of motivation have been proposed. While theories might sound too academic for day-to-day practitioners, theories—even if rejected—are useful to identify patterns. In organizational behavior textbooks, motivational theories are usually categorized into four buckets: need theories, reinforcement theories, job characteristics theories, and cognition theories. This section highlights the major classic theories of motivation and summarizes them in a textbox.

1. **Need theories**—focus on motivation from an individual's unique psychological needs, which can come from a variety of sources.
2. **Reinforcement theories**—concentrate more on external 'carrot and stick' methods to encourage desired behaviors and discourage undesirable ones.
3. **Job characteristics theories**—examine the relationship between a job's attributes and their effect on the worker's motivation.
4. **Cognitive theories**—explain human behavior as a careful response to new information that is largely based on the individual's past experiences and currently available information.

1. Need Theories

Needs-based theories of motivation assume that people have certain needs that must be met in order to be motivated in their performance. The motivation theories of Maslow, McClelland, McGregor, and Herzberg fall in this category.

Maslow's Hierarchy of Needs[10]

So how does Maslow's motivation theory apply to managing and being managed? You can use this theory as a framework for thinking about yourself and the people around you. Understanding where a person is in their life allows you to identify what their current needs might be. If a worker is experiencing some episode of psychological or emotional insecurity outside of the job, it may be difficult for that person to focus on achieving their full potential at work until the safety need is first taken care of. It is more pressing and therefore consumes more of that person's energy and time. On the same token, a person struggling to meet basic needs of food and shelter will find it more difficult to self-actualize. While our culture pushes people to self-actualize or reach one's full potential, self-actualization may not mean the same for different people. Working to promote satisfaction of varying levels of needs in the workplace may actually motivate people to realize their full potential on their own as they focus on the level of need that is most valuable to them in Maslow's hierarchical pyramid—even if it requires skipping some lower levels. For example, nobody would argue that Mother Theresa did not self-actualize. Yet, she often did so at the expense of the bottom two levels of Maslow's hierarchy.

McClelland's Need Theory[11]

McClelland's theory has strong implications for managers because it reflects the U.S. view of motivation (rather than a commonly held view in other parts of the world) that a person's needs structure can be changed through training programs. Understanding what motivates a person can ensure they are placed in roles that suit them. Somebody motivated by power would likely succeed in a top-level executive position, while an affiliation-driven employee may prefer to work with a consistent team in more servant leadership roles. Matching people with good roles based on their motivation profile will likely increase their effectiveness and person's work will be better matched to their needs. People with high need for achievement seek medium-risk situations where their personal effort can have a great effect on the outcome. Low-risk situations are too easy and don't allow for 'true achievement' while high-risk situations depend too much on external factors and luck to truly achieve something. Those with a strong need for affiliation desire strong relationships and enjoy feeling attachment to groups of people around them. They have a preference for work involving a high degree of personal interaction and fear rejection strongly. Finally, those with a need for power can be categorized into two types: a need for personal power and a need for institutional power. People who need personal power seek to control and direct others while people who need institutional power seek to mobilize an organization's resources to accomplish its mission. Knowing which motivating factor is the dominant one for oneself and others allows for tailoring approaches to meet their dominant need.

McGregor's Theory X and Theory Y[12]

In a typical practical context, when dealing with theoretical generalization, we should ask ourselves the triple (Amazonesque-like) question, 'What? So what? Now what?' and reflect on how we use Theory X versus Theory Y in a real-world situation. According to John J. Morse and Jay W. Lorsch in a 1970 Harvard Business Review article, academic studies performed in the 1970s indicate that neither Theory X nor Theory Y is the best approach to all situations, but both have their own best-use cases. If you are motivating employees to perform highly repetitive tasks with little requirement for creativity and high-level cognitive function, Theory X likely fits that situation. For organizations demanding lots of creativity and high-performing brain work, Theory Y would likely motivate workers to achieve their full potential.[13]

Herzberg's Two-Factor Theory[14]

The key realization to make is that motivators and hygiene factors are not a zero-sum game: the nonexistence of these factors does neither lead to satisfaction nor dissatisfaction. Hence, there is no motivation. In order to have worker motivation, it is necessary to avoid job dissatisfaction by taking care of the hygiene factors plus adding job satisfaction through motivators. Thus, if an employee is not recognized for their work (a motivator), it may lead to a lack of satisfaction but not necessarily dissatisfaction. Recognizing that employee will likely motivate them and increase their job satisfaction. Conversely (and perhaps surprisingly), a low salary (a hygiene factor) will likely contribute to job dissatisfaction, but a high salary won't necessarily make a person satisfied in their work. To truly motivate an employee, managers should clean up dissatisfaction by attending to hygiene factors and increase growth and motivation by creating positive motivator factors. One can think of a 'zero mid-point' of neutrality at which hygiene factors rest when taken care of and at which motivator factors rest when not addressed.

2. Reinforcement Theories

Reinforcement theories—also called behaviorism or operant conditioning—implies that "an individual's behavior is a function of its consequences." Skinner's behavior modification theory of motivation is the leading example of reinforcement theory. Although questionable as a theory, Skinner's approach is still well-embedded in U.S. management life and often misused!

Skinner's ABC Model[15]

B.F. Skinner was an innovator in the field of behaviorism and very popular in the post-World War II era with the popularization of the field of psychology. He used operant conditioning to both explain and influence behavior patterns. Operant conditioning explains behavior as being controlled by its consequences rather than the illusory free will. Rewarding behavior makes it likely to be repeated while punishing behavior makes it less likely to occur. To illustrate his theory, Skinner conducted a Pavlov dog-type experiment and placed a hungry rat in a box. On the side of the box was a lever and the rat would inadvertently knock this lever, releasing a piece of food into the box. The rats quickly learned to use the lever to keep dispensing more food. If you view pressing the lever as the behavior and receiving food as the positive consequence, it's clear that the positive consequence motivated the rats to perform the behavior. Removing a negative consequence further strengthens a behavior as well. Imagine the rats received an electric shock or spray of foul odor every time they pressed the lever as well. Removing that negative reinforcement would further entice them to press the lever.

Note that reinforcers (both positive and negative) 'INCREASE' the probability of the behavior to occur. People often make the error thinking that 'negative' reinforcement 'decreases'— which is false! Pay attention to the word 'reinforcement' as it always means increasing the behavior. Punishment 'DECREASES' the probability of occurring and consists of punishment and extinction. Punishment is more problematic than (positive or negative) reinforcers as it leads to suppression rather than forgetting the behavior. It can also create an environment of fear and aggression and does not tell somebody what to do; it only tells one what not to do.

Managerial applications of Skinner Motivation Theory in the workplace consist of using reinforcement schedules, feedback, and behavioral modification. Schedules for reinforcement can be fixed or variable (either interval or ratio):

- **Fixed interval schedules**—provide reinforcement at fixed time intervals (bi-weekly paychecks)
- **Variable interval schedules**—provide reinforcement at variable intervals (praise, reward, visit, unexpected)
- **Fixed ratio schedules**—provide reinforcement after a fixed number of behaviors (loyalty card)
- **Variable ratio schedules**—provide reinforcement after a variable number of behaviors (mystery shopper)

Feedback must have the following characteristics: it must be specific, immediate, and constructive. Effective feedback also needs to be timely and candid. Behavior modification is a systematic program of reinforcement to encourage desired behaviors. However, Skinner's application in management can lead to demotivating behaviors as seen in the following teamwork example where a student on a team is assigned to edit the team's paper:

- **Student performs exceptionally well**—student is asked to do it all the time and good performance is punished.
- **Student performs poorly, paper is full of errors**—student is never asked again to edit the paper and poor performance is rewarded.

- **Student performs exceptionally well**—other students do not comment on the performance, excellence does not seem to matter, and performance does not seem to matter.
- **Student cannot complete the assignment up to his/her standards because some of the sections came in too late**—student editor gets blamed for the poor grade of the paper and punished for obstacles.

3. Job Characteristics Theories

As Herzberg said, "You cannot motivate anyone to do a good job unless he (sic) has a good job to do."[16] Job characteristic theories focus on the importance of how work is actually designed in the motivation of people.

Hackman & Oldham's Job Characteristics Theory
Greg R. Oldham and J. Richard Hackman developed their job characteristics theory in the 1980s. In their job characteristics model, they explain motivational outcomes (internal motivation toward and positive feelings about a job) as the result of five core job characteristics (skill variety, task variety, task significance, autonomy, and feedback) leading to three critical psychological states: experienced meaningfulness, experienced responsibility, and knowledge of the results.[17]

The motivational outcomes of job characteristics and the motivational states are:

- High internal job motivation.
- High growth satisfaction.
- High general job satisfaction.
- High work effectiveness.

The job characteristics motivation theory takes individual differences in need for development into account by modifying motivation on an individual level using 'Growth Need Strength' (GNS) to differentiate motivation levels among people. GNS is the strength of a person's need for personal accomplishment, learning, and development.

4. Cognitive Theories

Cognitive theories of motivation (Adams' Equity Theory, Rawls Fairness Theory, Vroom's Expectancy Theory, and Locke's Goal Setting Theory) assert that people think about their choices and make decisions based on knowledge regarding equity, fairness, expectations, and goals.

Adams' Equity Theory[18]
In the early 1960s, J. Stacy Adams proposed that motivation in the workplace stems from a desire to maintain equity in social relationships with co-workers and the organization as a whole. When individuals make contributions (or inputs), they expect certain rewards (or outcomes). Equity is compared to a referent group or person one relates to or uses as a comparison group. People use four basic referent groups as comparison: self and others—both inside and outside:

- **Self-inside**—individuals seek to maximize their outcomes (rewards minus costs).
- **Self-outside**—groups develop accepted systems for equitably apportioning rewards and costs among members and will generally reward members who treat others equitably and generally punish members who treat others inequitably.
- **Others-inside**—individuals find themselves participating in inequitable relationships, they become distressed. The person who gets too much may feel guilt or shame. The person who gets too little may feel angry or humiliated.
- **Other-outside**—individuals who perceive they are in an inequitable relationship attempt to eliminate their distress by restoring equity.[19]

If a person is perceived to put in more/less effort, they feel they should be rewarded proportionally more/less than somebody who puts in more. That would be equitable. Two coworkers who put similar amounts of resources into an organization should receive similar amounts of resources in return. Breaking the perceived equitable balance results in one person feeling cheated and therefore becoming demotivated. Importantly, the person 'over-receiving' outcomes will feel guilt or shame; these negative feelings contribute to demotivation. Adams' equity theory partially explains how sometimes well-intended managerial action (giving someone an incentive such as raise, a bonus, an award, etc. can backfire if not handled in an equitable and transparent manner).

Fairness Theory[20]

The fairness theory of motivation differs from equity in that it is not measured on an input-outcome basis; rather, it is measured by a standard of fairness that assumes everybody should receive equal treatment regardless of input. People who feel they have been treated unfairly will likely not feel motivated in their work.

Vroom's Expectancy Theory[21]

If a person believes that a strong effort will allow them to meet a performance goal, meeting said performance goal will produce a reward, and that reward is highly valued by the person, then motivation should be high. Through the linkage of these factors, their effort is perceptively correlated with a valued reward. For the mathematically minded, this idea can be distilled into a simple equation: $M(force) = E \times \sum(V \times I)$. The motivation a person will have is equal to the expectancy (E) times the sum of valence (V) plus instrumentality (I). Of course, these things aren't easily quantifiable in most real-world scenarios (but has been explored extensively by academics), but the mathematical equation serves to deepen understanding of the principles underlying Vroom's theory.

Goal Setting Theory[22]

Setting SMART goals are an application of goal setting theory. SMART is an acronym for Specific (what you are trying to accomplish), Measurable (how you will measure progress and achievement of the goal), Achievable (how achievable and realistic the goal is), Relevant (how much achieving the goal matters to you and the organization), and Time-based (when will the goal be achieved). SMART goals are quite embedded in the management of performance whether for developmental or control purposes. In the performance management section of the book (Module 10), we will focus on a new way of goal setting that companies are using when they abandon the traditional performance appraisals, namely the setting of OKRs (Objectives and Key Results).

APPLYING MOTIVATION THEORIES

Each of the classical motivation theories has a golden nugget and teaches us something about how the non-innate component of motivation can be increased—provided a person has the required sufficient innate motivation. Finding a nugget in these motivation theories to apply to management is an example of contingency management. Using an eclectic management approach to motivation can serve one-self, teams, managers, and organizations and avoid creating a de-motivating environment for performance.

To tie the motivation theories back into our guiding question of, "Do my innate motivation and agency (or lack thereof) match my ambition?" we can frame each of them from an individual perspective. An interesting self-analysis to perform is to ask yourself what your ambitions are. Do you aspire to become a top-level CEO, own your own company, run a government agency, or simply become very good (or an expert) at performing a specific task for an organization? No matter your ambition, you must objectively compare your motivation level with your ambition to ensure they match each other. If they don't, you can either apply these theories to raise your motivation level or, alternatively, lower your ambitions to match your motivation (though applying motivation theory to match ambitions will likely produce more satisfying results and is recommendable). Can you find a way to ensure you are recognized for the work you do? Speak with your manager and team members to share what motivates you and how you can gain more autonomy and decision-making power in your job. All of these are viable options for increasing your motivation in the workplace to match your level of ambition. Be creative and apply these theories to help yourself. It may be uncomfortable to change the status quo initially, but you will appreciate the effort in the long run.

Now let's broaden the scope a bit. If you are managing a team, department, or entire organization, how can you apply these theories in an eclectic manner to motivate your employees? You can pull from Maslow and ensure people's lower-level needs are being met so they shift their focus to self-actualization. Or perhaps you administer a McClelland's needs assessment to your employees and ensure people are placed in roles that intrinsically motivate them. Alternatively, maybe you need to redesign your company's policies to reduce dissatisfaction and ensure fairness or redesign your rewards system at work to promote motivated behaviors. And, remember motivation is in the eye of the beholder. What motivates you as an individual does not necessarily motivate others. The tools are in your belt now. It's up to you to make good use of them.

An inclusive leader (as in DIBs) would spend time understanding the motivational drivers of each of his/her team members. Such a leader would also self-reflect as follows: what do I need to change in my leadership behavior to optimally motivate my team and my team members? Finally, here are a few questions to guide your thinking about the subject of motivation:

1. What can we learn from each theory?
2. Are these theories robust around the world, or are they geographically and culturally dependent?
3. Does contingency management (operant conditioning) work?
4. Do financial rewards work?
5. What matters most when motivating people?

Lisa Lai (2017) states that motivation is less about employees doing great work and more about employees *feeling great about their work*. She suggests the following motivation best practices for leaders:[23]

- **Share context and provide relevance**—employees are motivated when their work has relevance.
- **Anticipate roadblocks to enable progress**—employees are motivated when they can make progress without unnecessary interruption and undue burdens.
- **Recognize contributions and show appreciation**—employees are motivated when they feel appreciated and recognized for their contributions.
- **Check in to assess your own motivation**—employees feel motivated when their leaders are motivated.

A great way to understand motivation is to explore the short story of Nora Watson. Nora Watson's story comes from *Working* (1974) by Studs Terkel, in which he explored a wide scope of Americans' careers and how they feel about them through interviews. The book is very interesting and can give you some added perspective on what it means to work and different ways to go about your career. When reading this short story of a few pages ask yourself the question to answer "What can Nora, her coworkers, her manager, and the organization do to motivate her?"[24] ▮

7-1. Maslow's Hierarchy of Needs

In 1943, Abraham Maslow developed the hierarchy of needs theory to explain human motivation. A common way of representing this theory is visually with the needs pyramid, organizing psychological needs by levels of sophistication. In order from the bottom to the top of the pyramid, the needs are as follows: physiological (food, water, sleep, shelter, sex, etc.), safety (physical security, emotional security, etc.), love/belonging (friendships, family, romance), esteem (recognition, status, respect), and self-actualization (realization of full human potential). In his initial development of the theory, a person would satisfy one set of needs before moving to the next in a linear fashion. Many academics have since rethought this assumption and now consider these needs to overlap more than exist sequentially. For example, a person who is motivated to achieve self-actualization later in life may also be working toward a sense of love and belonging at the same time. That being said, it is unlikely for somebody to fully pursue higher-level needs without first satisfying the basics.

Source: Maslow, A. H. (1943). "A Theory of Human Motivation," *Psychological Review*, 50, 370-396

7-2. McClelland's Need Theory

In the 1960s, around twenty years after Maslow's hierarchy of needs theory, psychologist David McClelland created his model for understanding people's motivation in the workplace. Limiting the scope to organizational work, McClelland posited that people are motivated by three sets of needs: the need for achievement, the need for affiliation, and the need for power.

- **Achievement**—A desire to do better than other people or more effectively, to solve problems, to master difficult tasks.
- **Power**—A desire to control other people, to influence their behavior, or to be responsible for other people and their work.
- **Affiliation**—A desire to establish and maintain friendly and close relationships with other people.

A person who is predominantly motivated by achievement cherishes the opportunity to both set and accomplish goals. The person motivated by affiliation wants to work as part of a group. The person motivated by power want to control others. Most people have some mixture of the three needs with different levels of strength but one of them is the dominating motivator. His theory holds that the type of motivation that drives each individual is shaped by life experience and external culture rather than innate qualities.

Source: McClelland, D. (1961). *The Achieving Society*. New Jersey: Van Nostrand

7-3. McGregor's Theory X and Theory Y

Douglas McGregor developed Theory X and Theory Y to explain two opposing theories on how to best manage people in organizations. Each of these contrasting theories is based on different underlying assumptions about how workers feel about and behave in their jobs. Theory X (based on Frederick Taylor's scientific management theory) assumes that people resist work and must be prodded and controlled to work toward an organization's goals. This theory also assumes that people actually prefer to be treated this way because it involves less responsibility and they only care for their personal interests. Hence, Theory X calls for an authoritarian management style. On the other hand, Theory Y (based on the human relations movement) assumes that employees have intrinsic motivation, desire to work hard and solve problems, and are capable of creative problem-solving in the workplace. Theory Y—closely related with Maslow's hierarchy of needs—aims to motivate employees based on higher-level psychological needs like self-actualization; Theory Y calls for a participative management style.

Source: Morse, J. & Lorsch, J. (1970). "Beyond Theory Y," *Harvard Business Review*, 48(3):61-68.

7-4. Herzberg's Two-Factor Theory

Frederick Herzberg's Two-Factor Theory is based on a single important discovery: factors that make a person satisfied and motivated at work (motivators) are different from factors that lead to dissatisfaction (hygiene factors). Under his theory, motivators lead to job satisfaction and include achievement, recognition for achievement, the work itself, responsibility, and growth or advancement. Hygiene factors lead to job dissatisfaction and include things such as company policy and administration, supervision, interpersonal relationships, working conditions, salary, status, and security. Motivators will contribute to satisfaction and motivation at work and hygiene factors lead to a lack of satisfaction and motivation.

Source: Herzberg, F. (2003). "One More Time: How Do You Motivate Employees?" *Harvard Business Review*, 81(1): 87-96.

7-5. Skinner's Reinforcement Theory of Motivation

The ABC Model, which includes antecedents, behavior, and consequences, takes positive and negative reinforcement as well as prompting behavior (antecedent) and following behavior (consequence) into account for influencing behavior.

- **Antecedents** include company rules, policies, mission statements, goals, directives, announcements, information, and training programs.
- **Behavior** is what produces observable, measurable results and can be managed (i.e., corrected and appraised.)
- **Consequences** are reinforcers (consequences that increase the probability of behavior) and punishment (consequences that decrease the probability of behavior).

Positive reinforcement increases the probability for making behavior occur more often by contingently presenting something positive. Examples are:

- Strengthens the behavior by providing a reward or presenting a positive stimulus.
- Repeat the behavior that results in positive consequences.
- Praise, bonus, giving attention, job rotation (etc.).
- Different strokes for different folks (within and between cultures).

Negative reinforcement also increases the probability a behavior will occur by terminating, removing, or eliminating an undesirable task or situation. Examples are:

- You don't carry out the negative consequence you promised.
- Threaten someone with a consequence, but you don't carry it out.
- Strengthens the behavior by escape from an undesirable consequence (avoidance).

Punishment is the presentation of aversive stimulus decreasing the probability of the behavior to occur. Examples are:

- People get something they didn't want
- Fear deters the behavior
- Being criticized for bringing up a good idea

Extinction is withholding social reinforcement so the behavior ends. An example is ignoring productive behavior.

Source: Skinner, B. F. (1972). *Beyond Freedom and Dignity*. New York: Vintage Books.

7-6. Hackman & Oldham's Job Characteristics Theory

Five core job characteristics:

1. **Skills variety**—the degree to which a job requires various activities, requiring the worker to develop a variety of skills and talents.
2. **Task variety**—the degree to which the job requires the jobholders to identify and complete work with a visible outcome.
3. **Task significance**—the degree to which the job affects other people's lives.
4. **Autonomy**—the degree to which the job provides the employee with significant freedom, independence, and discretion to plan out the work and determine the procedures in the job.
5. **Feedback**—the degree to which the worker has knowledge of the results.

Three critical psychological states:

1. **Experienced meaningfulness**—if a person feels that their work is meaningful (this is largely subjective to the individual), they will be more motivated to show up and give it their all. Sometimes framing the work in a meaningful way can change a person's attitude and motivation towards their job.
2. **Experienced responsibility**—giving employees a high degree of responsibility and autonomy is essential to creating motivation. Somebody who feels micromanaged will not have the space to take ownership over their work and feel as though they are truly in control. Empowering people by entrusting them with responsibilities motivates them to take control and work hard to succeed.
3. **Knowledge of the results**—finally, results (knowledge of outcomes) must be communicated to employees. Often times, employees play a small role in a larger project and don't see the end result of their labor. This can be very demotivating. Seeing how work makes an impact on the world can help people understand the 'why' of their career.

Source: Hackman, J. R. & Oldham, G. R. (1975). "Development of the Job Diagnostic Survey," *Journal of Applied Psychology*, 60(2):159-170.

7-7. Adams' Equity Theory of Motivation

People's motivation levels depend on the extent they perceive that they are treated fairly, in terms of inputs and outputs in comparison to others. Inputs (resources a worker gives to an organization) include things like time, effort, loyalty, and personal sacrifice—though this is not by any means an exhaustive list. Outcomes returned to people based on their inputs can be both positive and negative; they include salary, benefits, recognition, and job security—but again, this is not exhaustive. These short lists are merely provided to give you an idea of the types of factors included in both inputs and outcomes under this model. People validate the exchange by comparing their input and outcomes with those of others (referent groups) to assess whether there is equity—or comparable outcome to input ratios—for each worker. In work relations, there is positive and negative equity.

- **Positive equity**—comparison in which another person receives greater outcomes for similar inputs.
- **Negative equity**—comparison in which a person receives lesser outputs for similar inputs.

Source: Adams, J. S. (1963) "Toward an Understanding of Inequity," *Journal of Abnormal and Social Psychology*, 67, 422-436.

7-8. Rawls' Fairness Theory of Motivation

Based on John Rawls' theory of "justice as fairness," the equity theory of motivation was expanded. Rather than focusing on individuals' perceived equity in relation to their peers, fairness theory considers a person's perception of fairness based on their internal standard of fairness. There are two main types of fairness (or justice)—procedural and distributive.

- **Procedural fairness**—refers to the consistency involved in following the company's policies and procedures. For example, for one employee, the procedures are followed to the letter while for the other employee the procedure is intentionality overlooked which creates tension between the employee, the manager, and other employees.
- **Distributive justice**—refers not to the fairness of the procedure but to the material outcome of an organization's procedures. Getting passed over for a promotion or not receiving the same job benefits as other employees are examples of distributive injustice.

Source: Rawls, J. (1985). "Justice as Fairness: Political not Metaphysical," *Philosophy and Public Affairs*, 14:223-251.

7-9. Vroom's Expectancy Theory of Motivation

In the 1960s, Victor Vroom defines motivation as the cognitive process that goes into selecting an action among the possible range of actions and explains why and how an individual selects one behavioral option over another. People are motivated to behave in ways that produce valued outcomes, which depends on the individual's personal values and desires. Three factors are considered as an individual makes behavioral decisions: expectancy, instrumentality, and valence.

- **Expectancy**—the expectation that an effort will result in a desired performance.
- **Instrumentality**—how influential the expected performance is on producing a desired outcome.
- **Valence**—the relevance of the reward/outcome to a person, or its value.

Source: Vroom, V. H. (1964). *Work and Motivation*. New York: Wiley.

7-10. Locke's Goal Setting Theory of Motivation

In the late 1990s, Edwin Locke proposed the goal setting theory of motivation and the importance of creating goals in motivating a person. By setting goals and committing oneself to them (in terms of choice, effort, persistence, and cognition), goals become more specific and its attainment quantifiable.

Source: Locke, E. (1996). "Motivation through Conscious Goal Setting," *Applied and Preventive Psychology*, 5(2):117-124.

REFERENCES

1. Pinder C. (1998). *Work Motivation in Organizational Behavior*. New Jersey: Prentice Hall.
2. Goffee, R. & Jones, G. (2007). "Leading Clever People," *Harvard Business Review*, 85(3): 72-79.
3. Harter, J. & Mann, A. (2016). *The Worldwide Employee Engagement Crisis*, January 7 (Accessed: July 15, 2017). https://www.gallup.com/workplace/236495/worldwide-employee-engagement-crisis.aspx.
4. Macey, W., & Schneider, B. (2008). "The Meaning of Employee Engagement," *Industrial and Organizational Psychology*, 1, 3-30.
5. Organ, D. W. (1988). A Restatement of the Satisfaction-Performance Hypothesis. *Journal of Management*, 14(4): 547-57.
6. Babad, E. Y., Rosenthal, R., & Inbar, J. (1982). Pygmalion, Galatea, and the Golem: Investigations of Biased and Unbiased Teachers. *Journal of Educational Psychology*, 74, 459-474.
7. Lencione, P. (2007). *The Three Signs of a Miserable Job*. San Francisco: Jossey-Bassey.
8. Pink, D. (2009). *Drive: The Surprising Truth About What Motivates Us*. New York: Riverhead Books.
9. Morgan, J. (2017) *The Employee Experience Advantage: How to Win the War for Talent by Giving Employees the Workspaces they Want, the Tools they Need, and a Culture they Can Celebrate*. New York: John Wiley & Sons.
10. Maslow, A. H. (1943). "A Theory of Human Motivation," *Psychological Review*, 50, 370-396.
11. McClelland, D. (1961). *The Achieving Society*. New Jersey: Van Nostrand.
12. McGregor
13. Morse, J. & Lorsch, J. (1970). "Beyond Theory Y," *Harvard Business Review*, 48(3): 61-68.
14. Herzberg, F. (2003). "One More Time: How Do You Motivate Employees?" *Harvard Business Review*, 81(1): 87-96.
15. Skinner, B. F. (1972). *Beyond Freedom and Dignity*. New York: Vintage Books.
16. Herzberg, F. (2003). "One More Time: How Do You Motivate Employees?" *Harvard Business Review*, 81(1): 87-96.
17. Hackman, J. R. & Oldham, G. R. (1975). "Development of the Job Diagnostic Survey," *Journal of Applied Psychology*, 60(2): 159-170.
18. Adams, J. S. (1963) "Toward an Understanding of Inequity," *Journal of Abnormal and Social Psychology*, 67, 422-436.
19. Walster E, Traupmann J, Walster GW. (1978) "Equity and extramarital sexuality," *Archives of Sexual Behavior*, 7(2): 127-141.
20. Rawls, J. (1985). "Justice as Fairness: Political not Metaphysical," *Philosophy and Public Affairs*, 14, 223-251.
21. Vroom, V. H. (1964). *Work and Motivation*. New York: Wiley.
22. Locke, E. (1996). "Motivation through Conscious Goal Setting," *Applied and Preventive Psychology*, 5(2): 117-124.
23. Lai, L., (2017). Motivating Employees is Not About Carrots or Sticks, *Harvard Business Review*, June 27 (Accessed: December 20, 2019). https://hbr.org/2017/06/motivating-employees-is-not-about-carrots-or-sticks.
24. Terkel, S. (1974). *Working: People Talk About What They Do All Day and How They Feel About What They Do*. New York: The New Press.

GUIDED READING QUESTIONS

1. How are each of the motivation theory categories different?

2. What can I do now to motivate myself at school and/or in my career?

3. Is there anybody I need to engage with to increase my motivation? Maybe a supervisor, professor, or peer?

4. Does a higher salary increase motivation?

5. What is the difference between engagement and motivation? Can you have one without the other?

6. Why is the employee experience important from the perspective of the individual and the organization?

FOLLOW-UP CRITICAL THINKING QUESTIONS

1. What is my major takeaway from this reading?

2. What do I already know about this subject?

3. What follow-up questions do I have about this?

4. How can I apply this in real life?

KEY TERMS

Cognition theories
Employee experience
Engagement
Equity
Expectancy
Fairness
Hygiene factors
Job characteristics theories
Motivation
Motivators
Need theories
Negative reinforcement
Operant conditioning
Positive reinforcement
Reinforcement theories
Self-actualization
Theory X
Theory Y
Valence

LEARNING ASSESSMENT

Critically reflect on the content and the different concepts in this module and rate your own competency using the assessment scale.

Competency	I never heard of it	I heard of it but have limited knowledge of it	I can reasonably explain it to others	I have used it, done it, applied it
Theories of motivation	0	1	2	3
Organizational citizenship behavior	0	1	2	3
Self-efficacy	0	1	2	3
Engagement	0	1	2	3
Employee experience	0	1	2	3

MODULAR-SPECIFIC ASSESSMENT

David McClelland Motives
McClelland developed a need questionnaire to determine a person's motivation profile by measuring the predominant need.
http://media.johan.snobohm.nu/McClelland.pdf

The Self-Motivation Quiz
Measures how self-motivated you are.
https://www.mindtools.com/pages/article/newLDR_57.htm

General Self-Efficacy Scale (GSE)
A self-reported measurement of your self-efficacy
https://www.drugsandalcohol.ie/26768/1/General_Self-Efficacy_Scale%20(GSE).pdf

VIGNETTE | ARE YOU OR DO YOU KNOW A NORA WATSON?[1]

Your motivation, engagement and experience at work are vital not only for positive business outcomes but also—for most people—associated with leading a more meaningful life. Gallup conducts regularly employee engagement polls. These polls have consistently shown disengagement of a substantial number of employees. In 2018, Gallup reports that 34% of U.S. workers are 'engaged' and 13% are 'actively disengaged.' Although the latest poll reveals that engagement percentages are the highest in Gallup's history and active disengagement are at a new low, there is still plenty of room for improvement when it comes to an engaged and motivated U.S. workforce.[2] Hence, creating a motivating work environment and paying attention to improving the employee experience is one of management's priorities.

In his 1974 book, Working, Pulitzer Prize winner Studs Terkel interviewed different workers for his oral history of mostly disenchanted workers. The stories were published in a book entitled, *Working: People Talk About What They Do All Day and How They Feel About What They Do*. One of the stories, *In Search of a Calling*, is about Nora Watson—a demotivated and disengaged white-collar worker.[3] Nora's story of a disenchanted editor and medical writer still resonates today and is often used to refer to the roots of employee disengagement.

One of the things making Nora's story still relevant today, in light of the 2020 context of working, is that we either all know a Nora or have, at one time or another in our working life, been a Nora ourselves. Not surprisingly, many management development programs use Nora Watson as a case study. In reading Nora's story, it feels as if we are talking about today and we can put a face on a Nora![4] In addition, the story has plenty of information allowing us to analyze the (dys)functionalities at each levels of analysis: Nora (micro level), her colleagues and boss (meso level), and the organization and publishing industry (macro level).

As a team member or manager, or even for yourself, watch out for a Nora (or Jason) and take action to create an engaging work environment and fulfilling employee experience.

REFERENCES

1. This vignette was prepared by Professor Lisbeth Claus for the sole purpose of illustrating a global HR practice for instructional objectives. Global HR in Action © 2020, Global Immersion Press, All Rights Reserved.
2. Harter, J. (2018). Employee Engagement on the Rise in the U.S., August 26 (Accessed: February 7, 2020). https://news.gallup.com/poll/241649/employee-engagement-rise.aspx
3. Terkel, Studs (1997). *Working: People Talk About What They Do All Day and How They Feel About What They Do*. New York: The New Press.
4. A reprint of the Studs Terkel's chapter is at *Article Reprints* (Accessed: January 5, 2020). http://faculty.wwu.edu/dunnc3/rprnts.terkel-nw.html

GUIDED READING QUESTIONS

1. What management issues do you see at the different levels of analysis: Nora (micro level), her colleagues and boss (meso level), and the organization and industry (macro level)?
2. What action steps can be taken by the different personas to re-engage Nora and/or create a more engaging environment?

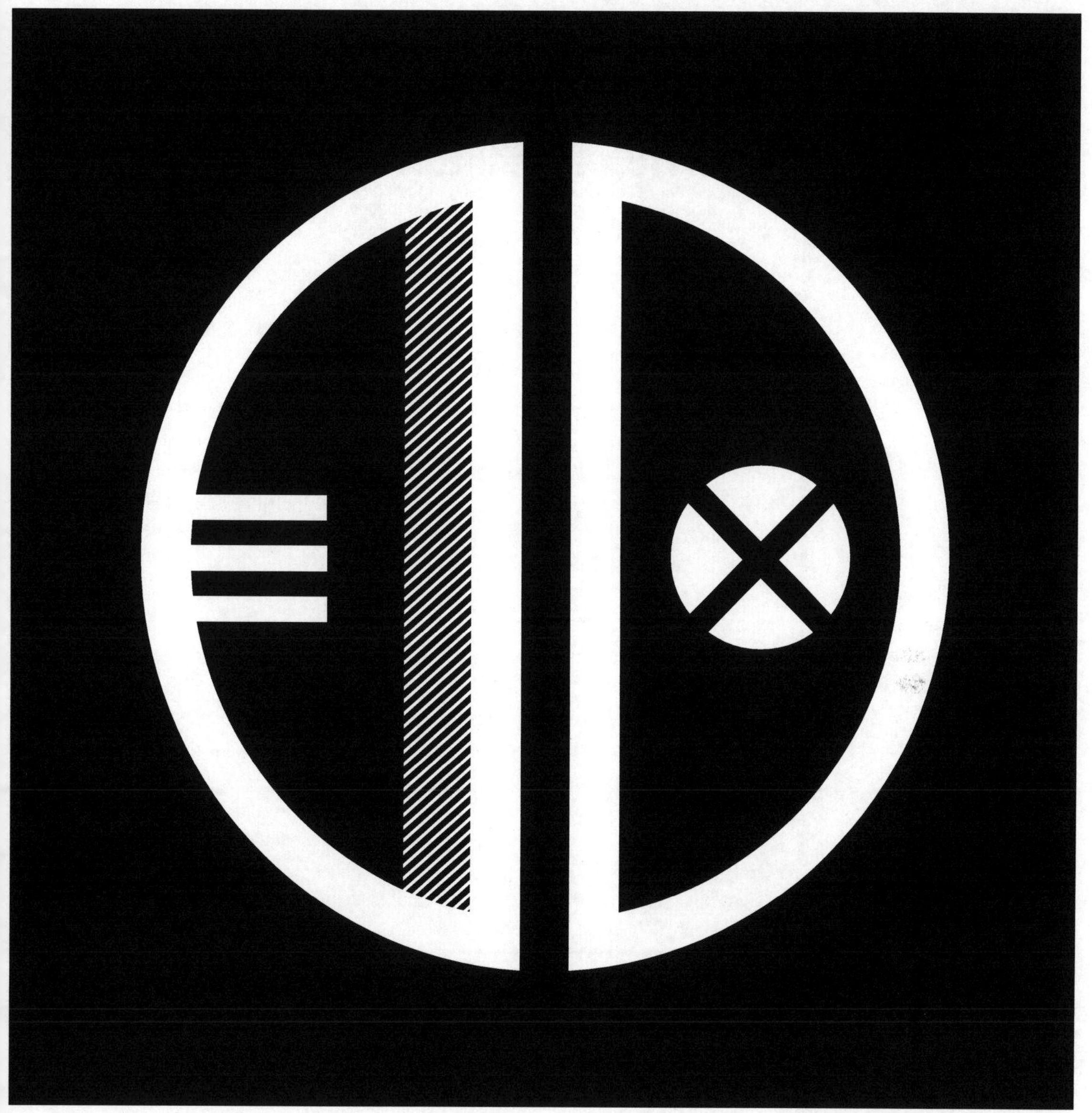

MODULE EIGHT

DECISION-MAKING AND BEHAVIORAL ECONOMICS

MODULE EIGHT

DECISION-MAKING AND BEHAVIORAL ECONOMICS

DESCRIPTION

This module explores the way people make decisions based on bounded rationality, willpower and self-interest (*homo sapiens*) rather than economic rationality (*homo economicus*). It further shows how unconscious biases, choice architecture, and behavioral nudging impact individuals and teams in organizations.

LEARNING OBJECTIVES

Upon completing the learning experience, you will be able to:

- Distinguish between conventional and behavior economics models
- Distinguish between System I and System II thinking
- Identify heuristics and biases in decision-making
- Define choice architecture and behavioral nudging

GUIDING QUESTION

How can I become aware of and reduce my unconscious biases?

It wasn't going to be easy. ELIZABETH knew her Sales Team had to start using the new Customer Relationship Management (CRM) system to track the status of potential contracts, provide contact information, probability of closing the deal, estimated Annual Contract Value (ACV), and the specific reasons why a customer decided not to purchase the product. Individuals on her Sales Team complained that entering the data into the CRM was time-consuming and administrative, taking away valuable time when they could be selling. They had a point. Elizabeth knew some salespeople were purposely refusing to enter any data because they were trying to protect their sales pipeline from other salespeople or did not want Elizabeth to know what, how, and when they did all week. As the VP of Sales, Elizabeth was responsible for proving an accurate sales forecast to the CFO and CEO so that decisions could be made in terms of current and future investment to support the growth of the company. How could she get the team to update the CRM regularly with accurate info?

Compensation & Benefits automatically enrolls its eligible employees in a plan allowing them to save for retirement through employer and employee contributions and gives workers a possibility to opt out in case they don't wish to be in the retirement plan. Setting participation in the plan as the default and having employees opt-out (rather than opt-in) increases the probability that employees participate in the benefits plan.

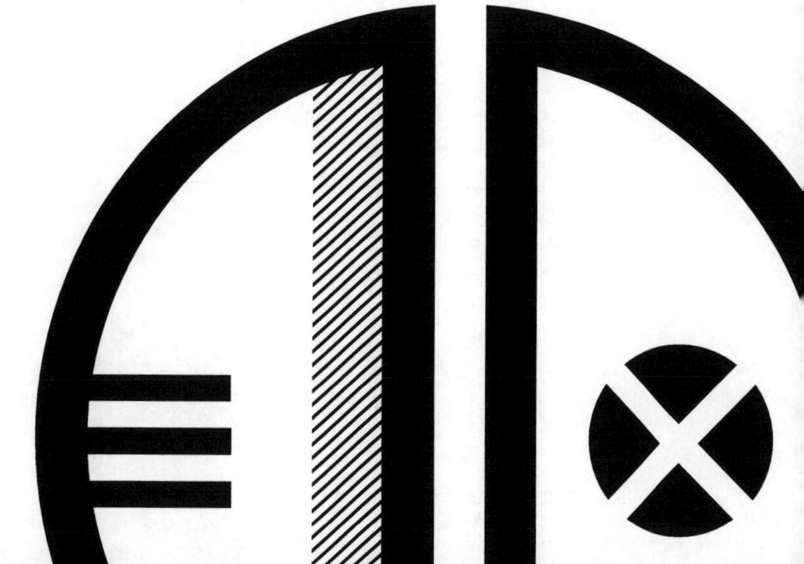

BEHAVIORAL ECONOMICS

Neoclassical economic theories are being supplanted by behavioral economics (the combination of psychology and economics), an off-shoot of heterodox economics.[1] Whereas the conventional economic model posits that people act as rational, self-interested agents concerned with maximizing utility, behavioral economics challenges this economic rationality with the idea that people act as humans (thinking automatically) rather than economic actors (thinking reflectively).[2]

System I and System II Thinking

Managers can find many insights in the lifelong work of Daniel Kahneman and Amos Tzervsky on decision-making.[3] System I and System II thinking refers to two cognitive systems or modes of thinking. System II thinking is aligned with conventional economic models in which decision-making is rule-bound, rational, deliberate, and self-aware. It is the controlled way of thinking best summarized by the words slow and deliberate. System I thinking is aligned with the behavioral economic model in which decision-making is intuitive, instinctive, and uncontrolled. In contrast to the reflective and conscious mode of System II thinking, System I thinking is rapid and automatic. In a nutshell, System I thinking is automatic, fast, intuitive, instinctive, effortless, based on gut reaction, uncontrolled, unconscious, skilled, and uses associative thinking while System II thinking is reflective, slow, rational, self-conscious, controlled, self-aware, rule following, an effortful mental activity, and a combination of deductive/inductive thinking.

Although most people toggle back and forth between System I and System II thinking depending on circumstances, human nature is not purely rational. It is bound by three distinct traits:

- **Bounded rationality**—constraints in our available information, time, and capacity to think leading to the adoption of heuristics/ rules of thumb.
- **Bounded willpower**—people take actions conflicting with their long-term goals and interests.
- **Bounded self-interest**—people are affected by factors beyond their economic self-interest and are often willing to sacrifice their own self-interest to help others.[4]

These psychological traits at the roots of our judgments should inform HR practices, policies, and programs and the way we manage and are being managed. Recognizing bounded rationality, willpower, and self-interest, behavioral economics can inform management practices to reduce the unconscious bias in decision-making. By being aware of common heuristics and unconscious biases, we can develop an architecture and use behavioral nudging—a small push in the right direction—to allow people to make better, healthier, and safer decisions.[5] In other words, the way managers present choices to their employees has an enormous impact on the decisions workers will make. In the public government sector, marketing and creative professionals have used such choice architecture to guide consumers in their decisions.

Heuristics

We are all very, very busy. We simply do not have the time to think everything through and analyze each decision in depth. Instead, we use a mental short cut and rely on common sense rules (a rule of thumb) that allow us to solve a problem quickly. In other words, people do not make decisions based on complete and reliable information. Instead of attempting the impossible—deliberately analyzing and thinking of everything (using reflective System II thinking), we use simple rules of thumb or heuristics to make quick decisions (using automatic System I thinking).

Below is a short description of a few heuristics that have been identified:[6]

- **Anchoring**—people tend to 'anchor' the value of something based on their first exposure to a number, taking it as a basis and further adjusting in the direction they think is appropriate. For example, the number of hours it usually takes to complete a task for a particular project that is acceptable (and feasible), gives employees an anchor for orientation. People can be influenced in a subtle way by being given a starting point (or anchor) for their thought process.

- **Availability**—people assess the likelihood of risk by how readily examples come to mind. If they can easily think of relevant examples, they are far more likely to be frightened and concerned than if they cannot. For example, someone who has experienced a layoff in the past, will perceive their chances of being laid off again much higher than someone who has never been fired. People tend to judge risk higher than the actual occurrence of events if they recall such an event, but the probability of risk is distorted for those who can't recall such a concrete event.
- **Representativeness**—the likelihood that A belongs to B is judged by how similar A is to their image or stereotype of B (misperception of randomness). While stereotypes often have a kernel of truth, prejudices can creep in when comparability and frequency deviate. This often happens when certain characteristics of diverse co-workers are judged in a stereotypical manner. For example, assuming that an older worker will not have the stamina of a younger one.
- **Framing**—the way things are framed leads people to different conclusions. Framing works because people tend to be lazy and passive decision makers. This means that management can be a powerful push in the right direction. Framing can be represented in terms of gains versus losses in a positive or negative way or as a threat versus an opportunity. Yet, sometimes management fool employees by presenting the company's information through inappropriate framing. Framing is not only used extensively in marketing advertising but also in management. For example, management tends to frame the situation of a company's financial (or other) results (or lack thereof) in their communications and defines (i.e. frames) the situation as a mere cause for concern or a real crisis.
- **Loss aversion**—people avoid decisions that will lead to loss. People hate losing. We prefer avoiding losses over acquiring equivalent gains. Our automatic system reacts very emotionally to losses. We feel miserable when we lose and happy when we win. As a result, we tend to make decisions that avoid losses. Loss aversion can also be a nudge that pushes us to resist change, even if the change is in our benefit. For example, the possibility of loss aversion can stand in the way of change and innovation because the possibility of a possible failed new project (even if it is a great learning experience) is viewed as being worse than the praise for success.

The fact that people make decisions in the ways described above has consequences for the behavior of managers and employees alike. However, HR also uses these heuristics in recruitment, selection, performance management, benefits, and other practices. HR must become aware they— just like anyone else—are subject to their own unconscious biases.

Cognitive Biases

Cognitive biases are hidden beliefs and prejudices shaped by our past experiences and the environments in which we were socialized. They are learned stereotypes (often based on racial and gender stereotypes) that are automatic, unintentional, deeply engrained. These biases have the ability to significantly affect our behavior and decisions. We are often unaware of these biases—hence the name 'unconscious' bias. Yet, there is a great deal of controversy about the extent to which such biases are truly unconscious. A number of other biases compound the unconscious bias, such as the affinity bias (liking people who are like us better), the halo effect (valuing things about a person more because you like them), perception bias (assuming something based on your stereotypes), confirmation bias (confirm your pre-existing assumptions), and groupthink (being influenced by how the dominant group thinks).

There are many examples where (un) conscious biases can creep in. For example, HR can reduce the selection bias by eliminating the applicant's name (and other personal information) on resumés, CVs and application forms when they present the candidates to managers or can opt for replacing the human selection process with artificial intelligence (representativeness). HR also should avoid providing benefits that may be too generous and may need to be rescinded (loss aversion). It is better to let employees choose from a series of fixed benefits that are sustainable. HR can also frame information by presenting it in a more positive manner where the focus lies on the opportunity (framing). Regarding performance management, HR can anchor a performance goal by setting it high yet realistic and attainable. The same can be applied to salary negotiations in recruiting or response options in an employee survey (anchoring).

Choice Architecture

As mentioned before, people make countless choices every day. If we had to think consciously about all these choices, we would barely get things done. Most choices we make are automatic, intuitive, and impulsive. Nudging takes advantage of this through a choice architecture. A choice architecture manipulates the way people make decisions by organizing the context in which they do so. While keeping the freedom of choice, people are nudged toward the desired choice. Usually only a limited set of choices is created allowing for better decision-making.[7] For example, a job announcement may say something like, "most people who like this job also like..." the options for a benefit plan are limited to two or three choices at the most.

Much like the parent who offers a child several healthy choices in snacks, a choice architect utilizes a form of libertarian paternalism that allows for freedom of choice in a paternalistic way that better assures good behavioral decisions. In progressive companies, HR focuses on developing choice architecture that aligns with their organizational culture to influence employees to live longer, healthier, and better lives. For example, in the cafeteria of your workplace, healthy snacks can be placed at eye level and less healthy candy at the bottom or at the top so they are less obvious. You still give people a choice, but facilitate the designated choice rather than the desired choice. The role HR plays in designing the context of employee decision-making in progressive companies is captured by Richard R. Thaler and Carl S. Sunstein in their 2008 book, *Behavioral Nudging*, which proposes that "choice architects can make major improvements to the lives of others by designing user-friendly environments."[8]

Nudging

One aspect of choice architecture is nudging. A nudge is a gentle push in order to draw someone's attention. Nudging utilizes cheap and easy interventions to change behavior in predictable ways without forbidding any options, or significantly changing economic incentives.[9] Typically, people's behavior is regulated through laws, regulations, policies, information, and even financial incentives. However, these methods are not always successful and can be rather expensive. People do not always make rational choices to follow the rules or act in their best interest. Thaler and Sunstein propose that by appropriately implementing incentives and nudges, we may be able to improve people's lives and solve some of society's major problems.[10]

Many biases in decision-making present opportunities for HR to nudge themselves, co-workers, and employees toward making more appropriate decisions for themselves and the organization. Nudging can also be used in large HR transformation and change management projects. Imagine that your organization wants to introduce a new way to cooperate between the silos, share knowledge, or stimulate people from different departments to better support each other. The chosen physical environment is open and transparent with different types of workspaces and opportunities for informal consultation. Your employees find this new office layout nice but have problems working in this environment. They prefer to work as they have always done. This is not necessarily because their decisions and behaviors have become automated. We are creatures of habit and have difficulties changing our behavior. It requires time and intensive support. Appealing to common sense and reason may be insufficient. To really change, people may need to be nudged a bit. When changing processes, it is possible to seduce employees to work in a different way by concrete interventions in the workplace and through finding an appropriate nudge. HR can nudge employees to take the stairs rather than the elevator by simply placing strips on the ground. It is amazing how small changes in the physical environment can lead to behavioral change.

DECISION-MAKING

Managing is about making decisions. While some of our daily decisions are easy, others are tough. Managers make many decisions on a broad spectrum ranging from relative certainty to broad uncertainty.

Decisions under Certainty

When making decisions under certainty, there is a known probability of occurring. But even certainty is never 100%. There is always a risk. Risk is defined as the probability of occurring times the magnitude of the risk. With risk also comes opportunity. That's why we talk about risk mitigation or managing risk to be able to continue to pursue opportunities. We have a lot of 'risk' probabilities in the management of organizations such as business risks, continuity risk, and financial risk. We manage enterprise risks by assessing them, taking preventive steps, having policies and procedures, training people, and buying insurance! Yet we often overlook that we also have human capital risks in organizations (or enterprise 'people' risk)—such as the probability of being sued, people leaving us because of poor managers, sexual harassment, wrongful termination, discrimination, safety incidents, accidents, duty of care incidents, etc.

Decisions under Uncertainty

When making decisions under uncertainty, we do not know the probability of occurring. We may also experience black swan incidents or things that have a low probability of occurring but high impact and magnitude of loss. Managing is becoming more uncertain due to rapid changes in the world of work and the worker. The most important job of any executive is to make decisions—even under uncertainty and chaos. As managers, we also have the discretionary ability to make such decisions. But today, there is an expectation for evidence-based decision-making. This is largely the result of the many hidden traps often turning the decision-making process into a flaw.

Drivers of Managerial Decision-Making

Several elements underpin managerial decisions such rational, psychological, legal and regulatory, and ethical drivers:

- **Rational drivers**—left brained-decisions are based on reasoning, evidence, and decision-making criteria (System II);
- **Psychological drivers**—decisions, judgments, and choices are often driven by emotional responses and influenced by our unconscious biases (hidden decision-making traps);
- **Legal and regulatory drivers**—decisions are also driven by the broader macro legal and regulatory environment, organizational policies and procedures, code of ethics, and the cost of compliance and non-compliance;
- **Ethical drivers**—moral considerations also come into play as we thrive to make ethical and sustainable decisions.

Hidden Traps

John S. Hammond, Ralph L. Keeney and Howard Raiffi, in a 2006 Harvard Business Review article, discuss a number of hidden traps in managerial decision-making based on the work of behavioral economists that we described above.[11]

- **Anchoring trap**—when considering a decision, the mind gives disproportionate weight for the first information it receives and anchors it;
- **Status-quo trap**—a strong bias toward alternatives that perpetuate the status quo;

- **Sunk-cost trap**—making choices in a way that justifies past choices;
- **Confirming-evidence trap**—seeking out information that supports our existing instinct or point of view while avoiding information that contradicts it;
- **Framing trap**—the way a problem is framed influences the choices that are made—gains vs losses; different reference points;
- **Estimating and forecasting trap**—when making estimates under uncertainty, our minds never become calibrated as we do not get clear feedback about the accuracy of our estimates. We either fall into the overconfidence, prudence trap, or recallability traps;
  - *Overconfidence trap*— we tend to be overconfident of the accuracy of our estimates;
  - *Prudence trap*—when faced with high-stakes decisions, we tend to adjust our estimates or forecasts to be on the safe side;
  - *Recallability trap*—because we base our predictions about future events on our memory of the past, we can be overly influenced by dramatic events.

While these traps are common in our decision-making, it is important to become aware of these traps and how they operate in the day-to-day managerial environment.

Decision-Making Tools

There are a number of different tools available in a manager's decision-making toolkit: stakeholders, decision-making roles, rational matrix-type choices, return on investment, and evidence. It is up to managers to use the appropriate tool based on the situation at hand.

- **Stakeholder maps**—identifies who the different (internal and external) stakeholders are; the respective requirements of each party (responsibilities and rights) in the relationship; and fair treatment considerations. Knowing the stakeholders and their interests applies the political lens to decision-making.
- **Decision-making roles**—Use of an analysis of the roles of everyone involved in the decision-making process. Using the RAPID acronym, the context of the decision is clarified based on the following possible role each person plays in the decision; do they have the authority to Recommend, Agree, Perform, Input, or Decide.[12] By clarifying the roles in the decision-making process, one sets clear expectations regarding the scope of one's influence.
- **Rational choice decision-making**—uses a decision matrix type tool (such as a two-by-two grid or preference matrix) in making the most optimal decision.
  - A *two-by-two grid* juxtaposes two different variables each with two options. The 2x2 grid is a typical MBA kind of perspective. Yet, different sets of grids, by selecting different variables, are good diagnostic tools that can clarify the merit of alternative choices. An example of a two-by-two grid is looking at the advantages and disadvantages of remote work from the perspective of the employee/worker versus the employer.
  - A *preference or decision-making matrix* uses multiple criteria and prioritizes and weighs the criteria in a grid format. It requires the collection of data that are salient to the decision.
- **Return on investment**—the ROI of a given decision should always be part of the decision-making toolkit. The ROI estimator is a simplified tool contrasting the ease and cost of implementation with the expected productivity return you'll experience.[13]
- **Evidence-based decision-making**—grounded primarily in data and the use of appropriate data analysis to make the decision. This is where predictive analytics comes in or using past data to find patterns that predict the future.

Whatever the decision requires, as managers, double check your decisions by asking yourself the following questions:

- Is the decision ETHICAL—right or wrong?
- Is the decision FAIR to workers—according to procedural and distributive justice?
- Is the decision GREEN—in terms of the carbon footprint?
- Is the decision-making process TRANSPARENT—open for scrutiny?
- Is the decision SUSTAINABLE—in the long run?
- Is it GLOBALLY deployable—what localization is required?
- Is it SCALABLE—can we do it throughout the organization? ■

REFERENCES

1. Silim, A. (2017). *What is New Economic Thinking? Three Strands of Heterodox Economics That are Leading the Way*. April 25 (Accessed: January 5, 2019). http://evonomics.com/new-economic-thinking/
2. Kahneman, D. (2011). *Thinking, Fast and Slow*. London: Penguin Group.
3. Kahneman, D. & Tversky, A. (1983). "Choices, Values and Frames," *The American Psychologist*, 39(4): 341-350.
4. Tversky, A. & Kahneman, D. (1974). "Judgment Under Uncertainty: Heuristics and Biases," *Science*, New Series, 185(4147): 1124-1131.
5. Thaler, R. &. Sunstein, C. (2008). *Nudge: Improving Decisions about Health, Wealth and Happiness*. New York: Penguin Books.
6. Ibid, p. 6.
7. Ibid, p. 8.
8. Ibid, p. 11.
9. Ibid, p. 22.
10. Ibid, p. 24.
11. Hammond, J., Keeney, R., & Raiffa, H. (2006). "The Hidden Traps in Decision-Making," *Harvard Business Review*, 84(1): 118-126.
12. Rogers, P., & Blenko, M. (2006). "Who has the D? How Clear Decision Roles Enhance Organizational Performance?" *Harvard Business Review*, 84(1): 52-61.
13. Everett, B. (2019). How to Assess ROI of Project Implementation. January 2 (Accessed: January 16, 2020). https://www.tmsatoday.org/index.php?option=com_dailyplanetblog&view=entry&category=strategy&id=230:how-to-assess-roi-of-project-implementation.

GUIDED READING QUESTIONS

1. What is the difference between System I and System II thinking?

2. What is heuristics?

3. What is a choice architecture?

4. What is behavioral nudging and how can it be used in management?

5. What are different unconscious biases (and their examples) that affect our decisions?

6. What are common hidden traps in decision-making?

FOLLOW-UP CRITICAL THINKING QUESTIONS

1. What is my major takeaway from this reading?

2. What do I already know about this subject?

3. What follow-up questions do I have about this?

4. How can I apply this in real life?

KEY TERMS

Anchoring
Anchoring trap
Availability
Behavioral economics
Bias
Bounded self-interest
Bounded rationality
Bounded willpower
Certainty
Choice architecture
Confirming-evidence trap
Data mining
Decision-making
Decision-making roles
Decision-making traps
Estimating and forecasting trap
Framing
Framing trap
Heuristics
Loss aversion
Nudging
Overconfidence trap
People analytics
Preference matrix
Prudence trap
Recallability trap
Representativeness
Risk
Sentiment analysis
Stakeholder map
Status-quo trap
Sunk-cost trap
System I thinking
System II thinking
Two-by-two grid
Uncertainty
Unconscious bias

LEARNING ASSESSMENT

Critically reflect on the content and the different concepts in this module and rate your own competency using the assessment scale.

Competency	I never heard of it	I heard of it but have limited knowledge of it	I can reasonably explain it to others	I have used it, done it, applied it
System I and Sys-tem II thinking	0	1	2	3
Heuristics	0	1	2	3
Decision-making traps	0	1	2	3
Behavioral nudging	0	1	2	3
Choice architecture	0	1	2	3

MODULAR-SPECIFIC ASSESSMENT

Implicit Association Test.
A test that measures one's unconscious bias whether related to race or gender.
Source: http://www.understandingprejudice.org/iat/index2.htm

VIGNETTE

NUDGING EMPLOYEES INTO HEALTHIER BEHAVIORS[1]

People sometimes make irrational and/or informed decisions when it comes to their own behavior. As a result, they often don't do what's good for them or act in their best interest. Nudging—or a small push in the right direction—allows people to make better, healthier, and safer decisions. Behavioral nudging (and the work of Richard Thaler & Carl Sunstein, in their 2008 book, *Nudge*)[2] was originally intended for policy makers, but now has widespread application in the workplace.

The most common workplace cited example of behavioral nudging is the automatic enrollment of employees in a company's elective retirement plan. Rather than opting into enrolling in the plan, the company automatically enrolls the employee—even with an optimal contribution amount deducted from their paycheck—and gives them the opportunity to opt-out if they wish. This form of 'choice architecture' gets around the so-called 'inaction' of people to enroll (or opt-in) and anchors them into a savings contribution that is more advantageous for them in the long run retirement planning. Behavioral nudging can be used in different ways in the workplace to initiate behavior (engage people to do something they otherwise would not have done); spur people into action (make them do it voluntarily) and shape existing behavior (ensure they keep doing it). Behavioral nudging in the workplace tries to counter many of the decision-making traps people tend to fall in and provides employees with choices that are good for them.

Different soft and hard tools are being used to implement behavioral nudging from marketing communication tools (such as text messages, reminders, alerts, pop up messages, lumpy mailers, scratch-off, games, creative signs, infographics, personalized messages, etc.) to using data, data mining, dashboards, apps, and a variety of interactive tools allowing for individual and social comparisons and benchmarks. Nudging can be done through all types of visual, verbal, and virtual feedback including workplace design and Artificial Intelligence (AI). Simplification, through default options, a rather limited set of choices, and easy to follow directions, is fundamental to nudging people to adopting the desired behavior. Yet, the key to nudging is empowering people with choices rather than imposing rules or forcing and controlling them.

There are many examples of the use of nudging in the workplace around benefits, health and wellness, waste reduction, learning, engagement, and overall better management:

- Enroll employees automatically in a retirement or benefit plan;
- Increase participation in wellness programs (weight loss, fitness, and smoking cessation);
- Alert people to get preventive health check-ups and screenings;
- Increase compliance with medical treatment plans for chronic conditions;
- Promote better nutrition by increasing healthy food options and decreasing unhealthy options in cafeteria;
- Encourage the use of stairs rather than elevators through signage;
- Reduce paper usage by setting the default on front & back printing;
- Increase participation in training programs;
- Suggest micro learning opportunities
- Send customized messages about learning opportunities to employees;
- Remind managers to provide feedback;
- Increase manager effectiveness;
- Built in electronic pop-up messages (not attaching a file, sending after work e-mails, etc.) ;
- Give employees a voice through sentiment analysis;
- Reduce waste.

Humu, a behavioral change technology company, co-founded by CEO Laszlo Bock (formerly the Senior Vice President of People Operations at Google, Inc. and author of the bestselling book, *Work Rules*[3]) has a mission to make work better by driving behavioral changes with the power of people science, machine learning, and love. The goal is to empower every employee and manager to do better and be better today and every day by nudging people to focus on metrics that matter—whether organizational performance, retention, individual happiness, inclusion, or innovation.

Through a primary diagnostic based on various sources of data customized for each organization, companies decide which behaviors each person needs to change to maximize what matters for themselves, the team, and the organization. Then, employees and managers get AI-driven nudges including small reminders and notes via email, text message, Slack, Yammer, or however people communicate in the company. Nudges show up at just the right time to help people be a little bit better, try something new, or make their environment a little more inclusive. These 'nudges' or reminders are timed at just the right time to impact behaviors in a positive fashion. Laszlo Bock and his company wants to drive performance and happiness at scale through a behavioral science and technology solution. A Nudge Engine® or set of algorithms that powers the nudges, starts tying off nudges inside the company—all while being transparent, giving different people voice, and empowering employees.[4]

REFERENCES

1. This vignette was prepared by Professor Lisbeth Claus for the sole purpose of illustrating a global HR practice for instructional objectives. Global HR in Action © 2020, Global Immersion Press, All Rights Reserved.
2. Thaler, R. &. Sunstein, C. (2008). *Nudge: Improving Decisions about Health, Wealth and Happiness.* New York: Penguin Books.
3. Bock, L. (2014). *Work Rules Insights from Inside Google That Will Transform How You Live.* New York: Grand Central Publishing.
4. High, P. (2019). *Former Google HR Chief Laszlo Bock Aims to Revolutionize People Management with Humu.* September 9 (Accessed: January 29, 2020). CIO Network, https://www.forbes.com/sites/peterhigh/2019/09/09/former-google-hr-chief-laszlo-bock-aims-to-revolutionize-people-management-with-humu/#2ea31fda6000

GUIDED READING QUESTIONS

1. What is behavioral nudging?
2. How can behavioral nudging be used as a positive force in the workplace?
3. Is behavioral nudging considered manipulation?

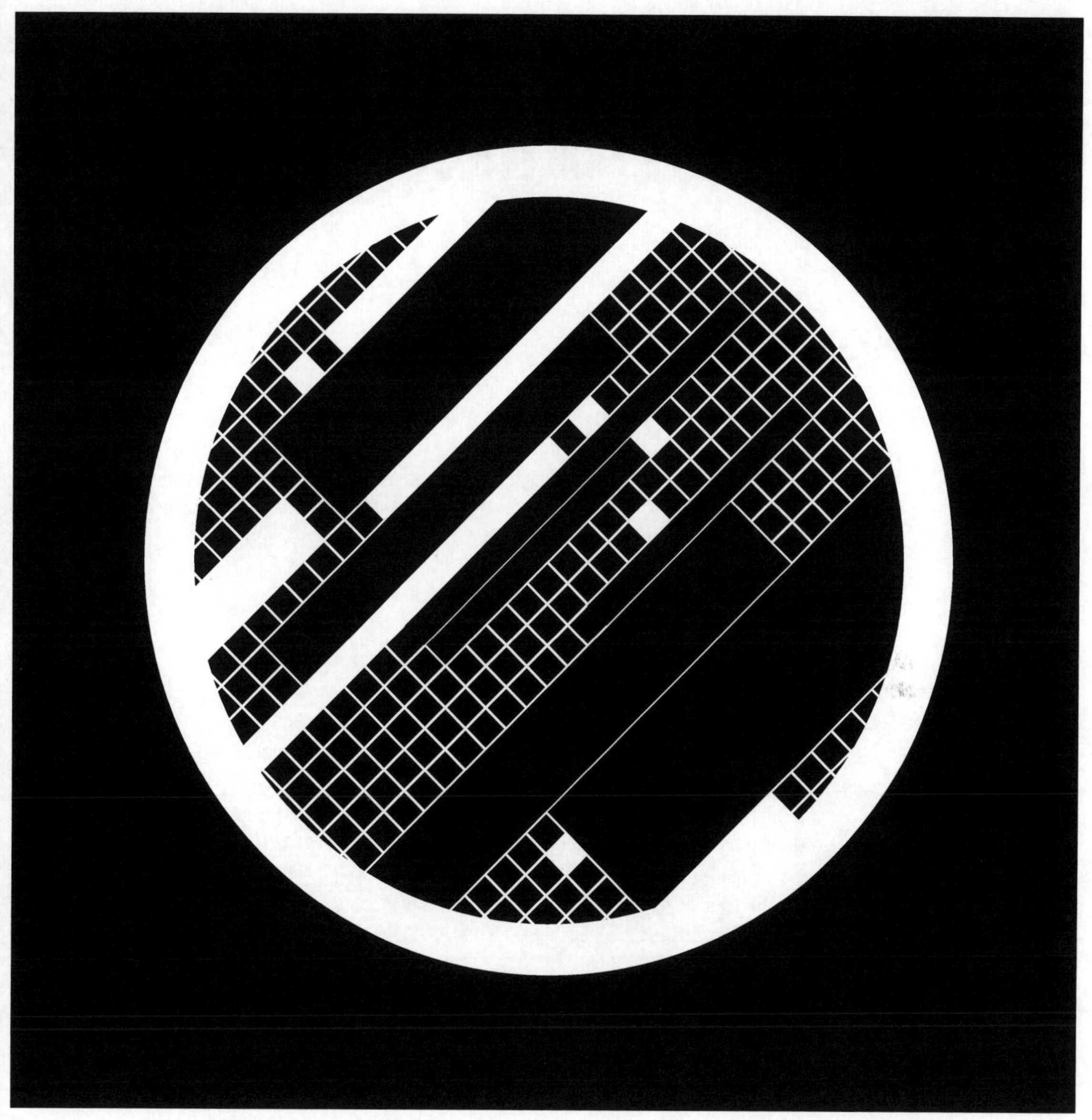

MODULE NINE

HR DIGITIZATION AND PEOPLE ANALYTICS

MODULE NINE

HR DIGITIZATION AND PEOPLE ANALYTICS

DESCRIPTION

This module focuses on the digitization of people management and evidence-based knowledge for decision-making. We review the use of people analytics, data mining, sentiment analysis, and A/B testing in managerial decision making and apply design thinking to management solutions.

LEARNING OBJECTIVES

Upon completing the learning experience, you will be able to:

- Provide examples of digitization of HR processes
- Define people analytics
- Differentiate between different types and sources of data
- Distinguish between descriptive, predictive, and prescriptive analytics
- Distinguish between impact, effectiveness, and efficiency of people processes
- Identify steps in using HR analytics
- Describe data mining applications
- Conduct A/B testing
- Identify uses for sentiment analysis
- Apply design thinking applies to management
- Use design thinking tools such as employee experience mapping, touch point management, and rapid prototyping

GUIDING QUESTION

How do I make evidence-based decisions?

ROGER leads global training operations at Facebook. He has developed a comprehensive training dashboard that shows insightful analytics that go well beyond the traditional metric of completion of training. He took a comprehensive look at training data to see which employees improved post-training, what amount of the improvement can be traced back to the specific training opportunities, if the training improvements can be replicated in other employees, and what the Net Promoter Score (NPS) for each training course was.

INIYAN is a successful team lead supporting customer service at Amazon based in Pune, India. He recently deployed a tool called Nostradamus at his site. This Artificial Intelligence tool converts 20+ employee attributes that produce leading indicators about the likelihood of an employee leaving the company. Those insights provided actionable information and context for his managers to hold "Stay Interviews" with the employees at risk. As a result of this rollout, Iniyan and his team were able to reduce attrition by 30% in the last three months and increase employee engagement by 14%.

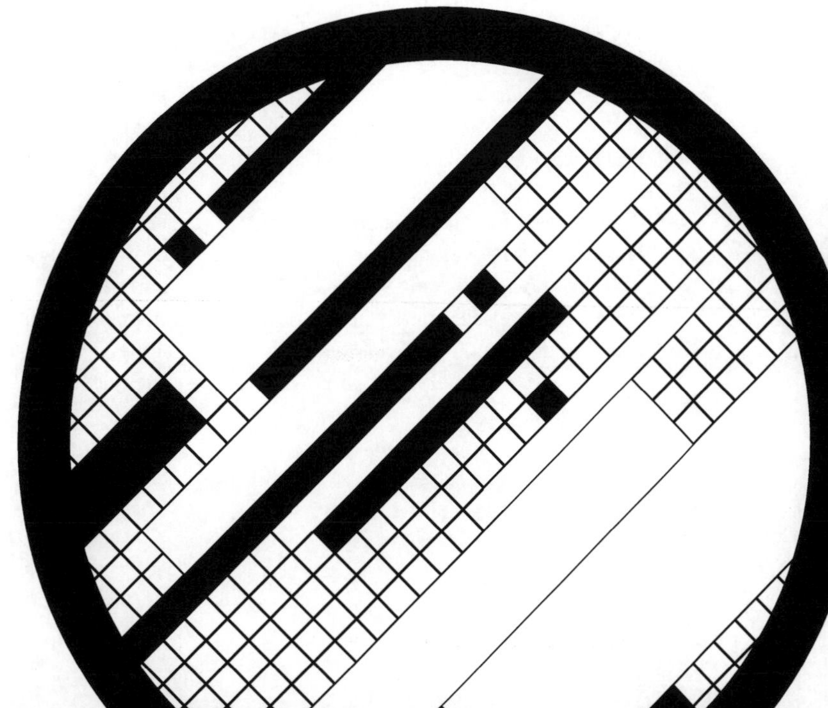

DIGITIZATION OF PEOPLE PROCESSES

Digitization is using a variety of technologies (social, mobile, data analytics, and the cloud) to make management and HR activities more efficient, effective, connected, and evidence-based. Digitization focuses both on information and communication technology (ICT) and the use of data, fundamentally changing the structure of work and the experience of the worker.

- **Information technology**—including apps, social networking tools, and platforms often driven and supported by Artificial Intelligence (AI) and the Cloud. Organizations are investing—in terms of people, systems, and vendors—in a variety of digital technologies to run their operations more efficiently.
- **Communication technology**—various communication and applications (apps) are being used (including chat tools, voice and video conference calls, project management, document and file sharing, etc.) to allow workers to communicate, connect, and collaborate better.
- **Data**—a variety of ways to explore and analyze people data to identify patterns and use evidence as a basis for decision making.

HR processes are now being digitized and many of the activities previously done by people can now be done by computers and shared and accessed by more people. There are many examples of the digitization of HR processes and activities:

- Use AI to digitize the end-to-end recruitment to hire process
- Provide tools to communicate and collaborate face-to-face and virtually
- Match people, skills, and strengths to learning and employment opportunities
- Use Cloud Technology, Artificial Intelligence, and Chatbots to answer (tier 1) HR questions
- Provide collaborative communication and social networking tools
- Identify traits of great managers
- Give people a voice and respond in real time to their sentiments regarding the employee experience
- Nudge people to behave in ways leading to greater wellbeing
- Identify high risk employees who are likely to leave the organization

Digitization of HR processes gives organizations unprecedented scaling opportunities. While in many instances, the digitization of people processes takes HR out of the picture in terms of transactions, it also augments the value of HR. Digitization creates space and time for HR to do more meaningful and strategic work focused on the performance and development of talent, allowing for better and more empowered experiences. Companies like Amazon, Unilever, Siemens, Microsoft, and Google are leading the way when it comes to digitizing HR. Digital tools not only facilitate the connection between companies and talent, they also provide enormous amounts of people data to analyze.

PEOPLE ANALYTICS[1]

HR is often accused of not being strategic! To have a legitimate 'seat at the table' with senior management, strategic global HR decision-making must be grounded in data and evidence. While other management disciplines exceedingly rely on data for decision- making, HR is generally lagging behind in this area. The adage, "*what gets measured gets done*!" is frequently mentioned. The saying (and its slight variations) is often attributed to various people from the 19th century scientist Lord Kelvin to 20th century management gurus Peter Drucker, W. Edwards Deming, and Tom Peters. Whatever the origin of the old cliché, it is generally accepted that measuring something focuses one's attention, provides data and helps us to improve the process. Today, some have gone even further and posed the question, "*What if we understood our talent better than we understand our customers*?" They know, unequivocally, that "*the key to sustainable competitive advantage is in creating a data-driven, talent-centric company culture*."[2]

"If HR wants to play a strategic role in organizations, it needs to develop its ability to measure how HR decisions affect the business and how business decisions affect HR."[3] Organizations that use data correctly can see positive results in terms of improved financial performance, increased productivity, reduced risks and costs, and faster decision-making capabilities. Companies that use data as a sixth sense, combined with experience, make more informed decisions, execute faster, operate with less bureaucracy, drive higher engagement, eliminate surprises, and have many talent benefits.[4] In summary, the benefits of HR analytics for organizations are numerous. HR analytics allows for decision-making based on evidence rather than judgment, measures the value contribution of HR practices, links HR to business outcomes, shows the value of HR investments, provides indicators of talent management, and is a new tool for strategy.

What are People Data Analytics?

People, or HR analytics, goes by many names that are all essentially the same basic concept: using data strategically. A number of related names (with varying nuances) are used for referring to the use of data in HR organizational decision-making, including terms such as: HR analytics,[5] talent analytics,[6] human capital analytics,[7] evidenced-based HR, business analytics,[8] big-data analytics,[9] metadata analytics, integrated analytics,[10] and process analytics.[11] Managing with HR analytics has been referred to as being the next level of management focusing on the "technology of human accomplishments."[12] Such data-driven organizations have also been called "decoded companies."[13] As a result, a working definition of HR analytics must be comprised of much more than previously used HR metrics and tools. The focus on data as a basis for decision-making has gained prominence due to a number of factors. Not all organizations use analytics to the full extent and there are degrees to which data are used in talent management.

People analytics can be defined as using a variety of HR and organizational data for the benefit of both meeting employee needs (soft HRM) as well as strategic decision-making (hard HRM) by organizing, analyzing, and presenting that data in a meaningful way and giving it predictive power through the application of statistical techniques. In data-driven organizations, the focus on people analytics has gone beyond any of the tools IT provides for the HR team. With a focus on benefits adoption, sentiment analysis, key population retention, and social engagement, people analytics projects include mining data from dozens of tools, but none that would classically be considered HR tools. While HR tools provide the standard data (turnover trends, performance data, diversity numbers) very well, the numbers are more reactive than proactive and the metrics provide no indication of what is really happening in the ranks. The focus of HR analytics, currently, is to also catch non-structured data—the social and information consumption metrics that indicate interest, business engagement, broad feedback sentiment, and thought leaders within the business management. It also focuses on news and social tools provided by other parts of the business. These tend to be very dynamic environments and occur within real-time data feeds. HR is looking for ways to make sense out of the noise, which has been a tremendous challenge to their internal business intelligence (BI) teams. After years of trying to groom internal talent, we are now seeing HR utilize IT skills and external knowledge workers more as a result of the predictive power of HR analytics in decision-making.

People analytics refers to the utilization of organizational data, external data, and HR data to meet employee needs (or soft HRM) as well as (hard) HRM needs such as strategic decision making. There are many technical terms involved, such as data warehousing (smart saving of available data) and business intelligence (making company and other data actionable). Data used in hard HR is organized, analyzed, and presented in a meaningful way through statistical techniques that allow for prediction. In order to be effectively implemented, HR analytics requires organizations to support their talent management decisions with data and then measure the effectiveness, efficiency, and impact of those decisions.[14]

Global organizations—as a result of their size and global reach—are sitting on an unprecedented treasure trove of employee-related data they can use strategically for decision-making. One of three leading trends in the future of HR has been identified as the use of talent analytics for competitive advantage.[15] The ability of HR to play a strategic role now requires grounding decision-making in data analysis. HR practitioners must understand the purpose, processes, and uses of HR analytics for the benefit of their global organization. Of particular interest is the ability of global organizations to evaluate how HR policies and practices are leading to different outcomes in various employee segments and parts of the world.

The Data Analysis Chain

A logical data analysis chain shows how data organized in a meaningful way becomes information and then, once analyzed, leads to evidence-based knowledge that allows for grounded decision-making (see 9-1).

Data—It all starts with raw data. Data in itself is not very valuable unless it is organized in a meaningful way. Data is "*any information that can be measured, captured, or visualized about any activity or decision that is happening within an organization.*"[16] There are different types of data: meta (big) data and other not-so-big data; quantitative and qualitative data; self-reported and ambient data.

- **Meta data**—are big data available on servers in massive data bases. These types of data are used particularly well with data mining in search of patterns in large databases.
- **Not-so-big data**—are more readily available in organizations and can be structured or unstructured.
- **Structured data**—have a higher degree of organization and can be more easily retrieved from a relational database into a spreadsheet.
- **Unstructured data**—such as emails and pictures lacks organization and, hence, is more costly to organize.

Data can be *quantitative* (such as numbers, surveys, log files, sensors) or *qualitative* (such as text, videos, pictures).

9-1. Data Analysis Chain

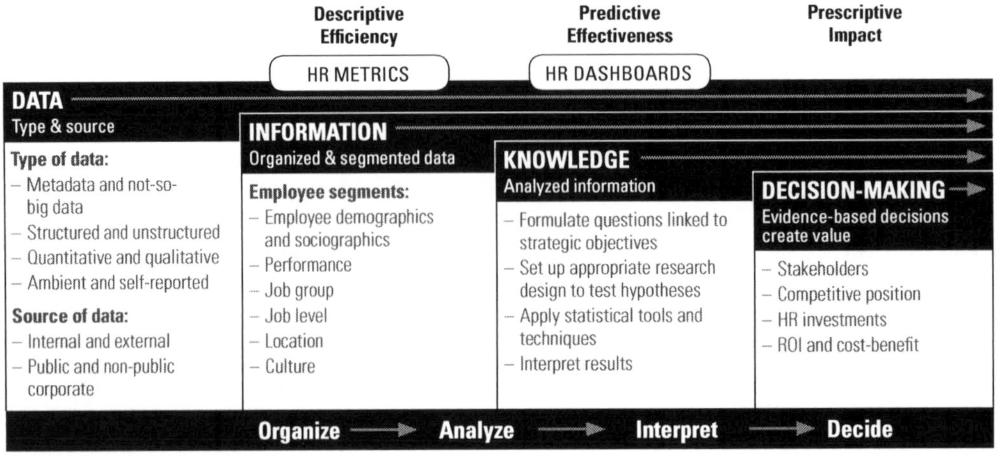

Descriptive Efficiency — HR METRICS
Predictive Effectiveness — HR DASHBOARDS
Prescriptive Impact

DATA Type & source

Type of data:
- Metadata and not-so-big data
- Structured and unstructured
- Quantitative and qualitative
- Ambient and self-reported

Source of data:
- Internal and external
- Public and non-public corporate

INFORMATION Organized & segmented data

Employee segments:
- Employee demographics and sociographics
- Performance
- Job group
- Job level
- Location
- Culture

KNOWLEDGE Analyzed information

- Formulate questions linked to strategic objectives
- Set up appropriate research design to test hypotheses
- Apply statistical tools and techniques
- Interpret results

DECISION-MAKING Evidence-based decisions create value

- Stakeholders
- Competitive position
- HR investments
- ROI and cost-benefit

Organize → Analyze → Interpret → Decide

Source: Claus, L., Baker, S., & Ely, J. (2015). Global HR analytics. Pp. 5-33 in Claus. L. (ed.), *Global HR Practitioner Handbook*, volume 3. Silverton, OR: Global Immersion Press

Self-reported data requires manual input from the user (such as surveys) while *ambient data* is automatically collected about a behavior of a user without the user having to actively enter each data point.[17] Ambient data have several advantages over self-reported data: they are usually already collected and available, organizations can track employee behaviors without requiring a behavior shift, and the influence of personal biases is reduced.[18]

Data come from different sources and can be internal or external to the organizations, and public or non-public corporate data. *Internal data* refer to the ambient and self-reported data the organization owns as part of their enterprise while *external data* are data available in the market place (purchased or available free of charge). Public corporate data are disclosed and open, while non-public corporate data are more strictly governed by privacy issues.

Information—Only when data are organized meaningfully does it become information. Information can then be used by an employer as 'internal' customer data. In the same way that organizations segment their 'external' customer data, they can organize their internal employee data based on personal characteristics (such as demographics and sociographics) and/or structural characteristics (such as job groups, job levels, department, and location).

Knowledge—Through analysis, information becomes knowledge. Inquiries linked to the strategic objectives of the organization, through appropriate research design, hypotheses testing, and the application of statistical techniques information turns existing information into explicit knowledge that is grounded in evidence. This supplements the existing tacit knowledge of HR practitioners that is mostly grounded in experience.

Decision-making—Evidence-based knowledge can then be interpreted to allow decision-makers and stakeholders to act upon and make grounded decisions. Such decisions create value for the organization as they guide stakeholders based on analytics rather than perceptions and allow for better quantification of the cost-benefit and return on investment (ROI) of HR investments.

Data sources are increasing dramatically and the tools necessary to combine them and make sense of it at the rate of change they become available is intimidating. The problem is that the more sources for data and the faster they become available, the more valuable they will likely be—but combining data from internal and external sources at the same time is challenging and takes high skill.

Implementing People Analytics

Several how-to-steps have been identified for introducing and using people analytics. They include focusing HR on assessing measures related to critical business outcomes, creating evidence-based teams and leadership, identifying and collecting ambient and self-reported data, analyzing that data with appropriate statistical methods so that the organization can learn from the past and predict future trends, and building and executing an HR analytics program that sticks. Figure 9-4 represents a linear roadmap for the implementation of HR analytics projects from start to finish. The roadmap consists of four distinct phases: (1) scope the project; (2) assemble the team; (3) manage the data; and (4) make strategic decisions.

1. **Scope the Project**—identify a feasible project and understand the capabilities and limitations of the organizational data, link it to organizational objectives, identify the research question and design, and then identify the type and source of data required.

In order to get started, HR must identify a feasible HR analytics project for the organization. Often, a good place to start is with your existing HR metrics, HR scorecard, or dashboards that will encourage curiosity about the data and their correlations. In a global organization, the choice of such a project is likely one with global implications for testing the robustness of any HR decision, activity, process, or policy across borders. Ideally, the project should be linked to organizational objectives and focus on expected key performance indicators. This allows HR to formulate the research question in terms of the relationships they will investigate and the appropriate research design and the HR outcomes they are trying to impact. In order to realistically do so, they must understand the capability of their organizational data and the type and source of data required. This engenders several questions that must be considered in scoping an HR analytics project:

- Which HR process or activity do you wish to analyze?
- Do you have a good picture of the issues?
- Do you know which gaps need to be investigated?
- What relationship(s) will you investigate?
- What are the variables related to the issue that you are investigating?
- How is this linked to your organizational objectives?
- What are common HR metrics related to this topic?
- What HR outcomes are you trying to impact?
- What does good look like and what does great look like?

2. **Assemble the Team**—identify members of the core team who have analytical interests and capabilities, identify the stakeholders and decision-makers, then galvanize them with the knowledge of the importance and limitations of the data.

The idea for an HR analytics project—and to some extent the scoping of that project—is likely to be initiated and driven in an organization by an HR team member who has an affinity for data and a curiosity for inquiry. Yet, it is vitally important for the development of a data-driven mentality to assemble a team to jointly execute the project and contribute to an organizational culture of analytics.

Data skills are at a premium and it is rare for many organizations to find people with the capabilities for advanced analytics (modeling, prescriptive, and predictive) within their ranks. The teams always consist of people with a penchant for data, but more and more, HR will have to leverage key technical skills outside of HR to just help with data management and modeling. Now more than ever, data experts are critical, and HR may have to utilize those without any HR knowledge as numbers are numbers. Organizations have done so similarly in the past with microchips and LEAN/ Six Sigma projects--they bring in technical expertise to augment the skills within an organization, and then find the line and staff people who have interest in data and can provide context to the data expert, but can rarely produce the data models and do not have the technical skill to do so.

The core analytics team should consist of individuals with the required analytic competencies—both from the creative design of the research question to the skills of data retrieval, statistical analysis, and interpretation. For maximum impact, the core team should be supported by the stakeholders and decision-makers that are affected by the analytics project under consideration. Ideally, the analytics project initiator and driver should have the leadership capability to energize followers (core team and stakeholders/decision-makers) rather than pursue solo thinking on the project. This will greatly enhance the integration of analytics in the daily workings of HR going forward. Several questions that must be considered in assembling the team:

- Who are the members of your core team who have the required competencies to execute the data retrieval, data collection, statistical analysis, and visualization of the results?
- Who are the organizational stakeholders for this HR analytics project?
- Who are the decision-makers involved?

3. **Manage the Data**—acquire, protect, analyze, interpret, and present the results of the data visually. This is where the analytical and statistical skills come into play. Each HR analytics project will have to

rely on someone—internal or external to the organization— with data retrieval and statistical analysis expertise but, equally important, the skill of visualizing the data for easy understanding. The following questions must be considered in managing the data:

- What specific (employee) data do you need?
- What type of data do you already have and what will need to be collected?
- Where (internally/externally) does HR get the data?
- Who owns that data in the organization?
- How does HR obtain that data?
- What resistance do you expect?
- Who has the skills to retrieve the data?
- What data privacy concerns are involved?
- How will you protect the data?
- How will you store and archive the data?
- What analytical tools and statistical techniques will you need to use?
- Who has the skills to conduct the analysis?
- How will you visually represent the data and what will your sample dashboards look like?

Data privacy and management have become huge concerns and get bigger every day. Part of the challenge is that many organizations are shifting to outsourced hosting and supplies, and these Software as a Service (SaaS) solutions pass data back and forth to the corporation as well as to other off-site providers. Half of the challenge of analytics is making these connections and then combing the data back together when returned to the enterprise. The desire for timeliness and the capabilities available with big data solutions provide a potential constant stream of unstructured data. The old model of normalizing and loading data in a structured fashion is becoming too slow for the pace of business and information (especially when considering predictive and prescriptive analytics).

4. **Take Strategic Action**—present and discuss the evidence-based results to stakeholders, suggest managerial action, and participate in evidence-based decision-making based on results.

The final steps of the people analytics roadmap is to use the knowledge derived from the data and use the evidence to make decisions with greater predictive value. The core HR analytics team is now in a position to present and discuss the evidence-based results to the broader stakeholders and decision-makers and suggest managerial actions based on their results.

The following questions must be considered while making strategic decisions:

- How do you interpret the data?
- What types of evidence-based actions can the organization take with these HR analytics results?
- How will you turn data into actionable insights?
- What analytics will you integrate in the daily working of HR going forward?

Finally, evaluate the impact of these decisions on both the organization and HR itself. The value of HR analytics to talent management practices throughout the HR life cycle has been well documented. Tracking things enables one to find patterns and themes in the data and identify hotspots that require action. Measuring and tracking human behavior requires the use of qualitative as well as quantitative tools.

Common Analytical Techniques

A number of analytical techniques such as data mining, sentiment analysis, and A/B testing are being increasingly applied to guide talent management decisions by managers. This allows HR to fully participate in decision-making supported by data that show HR and organizational impact. Thus, HR becomes an integral and legitimate partner on par with other management disciplines.

1. Data Mining

Data mining extracts and examines data from a large database to identify patterns. Using large quantities of past enterprise data allow HR to make not only better data-driven decisions, but also build more predictable models. In a 2017 *Harvard Business Review* article, Paul Leonardi and Noshir Contractor argue for better people analytics. They propose that rather than simply mining the attributes of employees, the people's interactions are equally if not more important. They argue for the use of relational analytics to examine—what they call the digital exhaust of a company—and find structural signatures in social networks (as mined in e-mail exchanges, chats, file transfers, etc.).[19] In the last few years, there has been a shift toward mining and using employee data generated from a variety of sources. Internal social media tools, article comments, management presentation feedback forums, and other venues for comment are producing tremendous volumes of unstructured data. Organizations are using text analytics and other modeling tools to determine such metrics as turnover risk, the 'true' knowledge workers in the company, highly networked and skilled individuals, and key communication channels for audiences in which the organization wants to increase retention. The systems are still owned by other groups—mainly in IT through collaboration or workplace capability teams—but this is the space where employees are engaging and confirming their adherence to initiatives, commenting on strategies, and discussing business direction. HR metrics that are predictive and prescriptive need to look for the earliest signs possible indicating population movement, and these unstructured networks provide insights into the narrative. As the next generation enters the workforce, the use of social tools and feedback capabilities at work will only increase, and a sustained effort at mining this data and doing trend analysis or forecasting is what will likely lead to the best predictive measures.

Examples of data mining:

- Examine patterns as it applies to various HR functions over the life cycle of an employee
- Mine data of a vendor they use (such as benefits, expense report management, travel data, etc.) to identify specific trends and utilization patterns
- Understand which employees are at risk for turnover
- Identify factors associated with above average performance and great managers

2. Sentiment Analysis

Sentiment analysis consists of using either pulse surveys or text analytics to mine various sources of data for employee opinions or sentiment. The data is usually collected from emails, various social media platforms and the Internet in an ambient way, or by asking a sentiment question on a sample of the workforce on a regular basis. This method is not new and has been in use in marketing (customer sentiment) and academic circles to predict trends and election results. Sentiment analysis allows HR to use social networks across the company, identify and measure employee emotions, motivations and engagement, and better understand work-related attitudinal and behavioral aspects of the employees. It helps measure cultural change and gather data if what your organization is doing works for different employee groups. The use of sentiment data provided by employees—whether in an ambient or self-reported manner—carries with it many issues when it comes to the privacy of employee data, even if the data is company owned.

Examples of sentiment analysis:

- Many companies start the workday by asking employees a sentiment question (how do you feel about...) regarding their real time employee experiences and take immediate action based on the results customized to the sentiment in different parts of the company and the work. Think about an electronic score board at HR headquarters that displays the comparative employee sentiment worldwide, by area, department, or even by specific manager.
- At particular times or for specific purposes, employers can identify specific concerns through text analysis of the social networks across the company.

3. A/B Testing

A/B testing compares two variants (A and B) of a modality to see which one performs better. Such testing is commonly used in market research where potential customers are divided in two groups and each group is presented with a different option to see which one is more attractive. HR can also test the attractiveness of different modalities of various rewards or compare employee satisfaction with various HR touchpoints. In A/B testing two different modalities are compared. A is the 'control,' usually the current system that is considered the champion. B is the treatment or challenger—a modification of something we are trying to test or improve. In a small-scale experiment, users are randomly assigned to either group A or B. Metrics that determine the success of the intervention are calculated and compared until sufficient (statistically significant) evidence is gathered to determine whether the decision to introduce a new modality is a good or bad decision. With this kind of experiment, HR can come to a conclusion in a more sustainable and evidence-based way to implement a change initiative.[20]

Examples of A/B testing:

- Develop two different versions of a learning tool (online and classroom) and see which one has better learning outcomes
- Test two different incentive systems and see which one produces the greatest discretionary effort
- Offer two versions of a benefit and compare utilization patterns

Creating value with HR analytics requires organizations to be able to support talent management decisions with data. In order to know one's employees as well as they are known as consumers[21] and be able to measure the efficiency, effectiveness, and impact of HR,[22] organizations must be able to answer a number of questions with data in various areas of talent management (such as HR workforce and succession planning, talent analytics, recruitment and applicant tracking, selection, compensation and benefits, payroll delivery, performance management, employee retention and turnover, leaves of absence, global mobility, human capital risk/safety and security, office capacity, leadership identification, assessment and development, training and development, diversity and inclusion, work-life balance, HR policies and procedures, HR processes, and organizational change).

Challenges in People Analytics

In spite of the many benefits that people analytics provide and the growing interest in data, global organizations face a number of challenges when it comes to implementing an evidenced-based approach to HR management.

Cost of HR data investment—it is not uncommon for HR to lack data to justify its worth, use the wrong data, or produce unquantifiable returns.[23] Yet, the development of meaningful global HR analytics for the organization requires strategic planning as collecting and retrieving data can have considerable costs associated with them. Unless the collection of ambient and self-reported data is planned carefully, it usually requires a considerable investment of HR time and cost.[24] One should keep in mind that cost considerations are important in getting to HR analytics. The basic HR metrics of the past (and present) such as turnover, diversity, etc. are relatively low cost to acquire and are getting easier with improved HRIS tools. But the true business intelligence projects in HR are more costly as they require time and headcount to push predictive and prescriptive metrics. Such analytics may require over 10X the investment compared to standard metrics, and once developed these models developed cannot just be 'created and then walked away from.' They need constant feeding and management to produce results. As a result, HR needs to change its mindset regarding investments in this area. Creating the next level of statistics—beyond what a single system can show—can be quite expensive and time consuming.

Global data integrity—HRIS and other enterprise-wide systems are major internal sources of data providing the global organization with valuable employee data. Yet, there are many data integrity problems associated with the use of these systems for global operations. Besides the integrity of the data-in terms of accuracy, timeliness, and completeness—data collection for a global organization may lack validity and reliability. Apparently similar data collected from one place to another may not mean the same thing due to the incompatibility of different systems, measures, and cultural interpretations.

Big brother perception—the exploitation of employee data for the benefit of the strategic objectives of an organization tends to engender a big brother perception by employees, even when legal and ethical standards are met by the employer. Self-reported data does not trigger the same big brother reflex as the use of ambient data. If an employee does not want to share his/her information, they simply don't fill it in. Ambient data has the advantage of being collected without their intervention.[25] But, it also tends to be viewed as more invasive of one's privacy. Which employee data belong to the public vs. private domain is likely to be interpreted differently around the world.

Employee data protection—a major challenge for global organizations is properly managing the way in which data are acquired, analyzed, stored, and used, and how to safeguard and protect that employee information.[26] Organizations must keep in mind the ethical and privacy dimensions in the storing, usage, and dissemination of any employee data, whatever the type. In countries where data privacy is subject to strict legislation (for example, the European Union's general data protection regulation or GDPR), compliance issues must be understood and strictly enforced.[27]

Cultural organizational change—for many organizations, instilling a data mindset in HR will require a personal and organizational culture change. It involves getting everyone on board including HR, IT, line managers, colleagues, and employees. In addition, the desire to use data may have different levels of acceptability within the same organization in different parts of the world as different regions, industries, and functional disciplines likely have different perceptions as to the utility and role of data.[28]

HR numeracy skills gap—analytics use a wide array of statistical and analytic techniques at different levels of complexity. HR practitioners often have a skills gap when it comes to utilizing and analyzing data. It is not uncommon for HR to leave the HRIS to IT and rely on business analysts. HR is often unable to retrieve & analyze the data and/or develop meaningful metrics and dashboards for decision-making.[29] As a result, HR often lacks the right metrics and analytic models and the data-based decision-making capabilities that are necessary to influence business strategy. Many HR organizations do not have skills in analysis, research design, and data interpretation within the function.[30]

The limits of artificial intelligence

Both humans and AI have limitations when it comes to biases. While AI is often touted as a way to reduce the unconscious biases of humans, algorithms are developed by people and incorporate their biases. Vivian Ming in her research on machine learning in hiring points out that algorithms mine large sets of data based on correlations rather than causal relationships. A widely cited example is the gender bias inherent in Amazon's failure of their AI recruiting to hire women as they based the algorithm on their existing male-oriented data. Ming suggests that unless we understand the causal factors, algorithms run the risk of replicating our implicit biases.[31] The question remains, which biases are easier to change? People or machines?

Applicability to management—it has been noted that not all management decisions and personnel matters may lend themselves to analytics and that some may be well and appropriately informed by instinct. Hence, HR has a challenge in "*knowing when to run with the numbers and when to run with their guts.*"[32] In addition, there is often resistance in HR organizations to rely on analytics. This is largely based on the notion that talent analytics is de-humanizing HR by putting people into data and making human capital decisions that produce the required return on investment (ROI) rather than finding a sustainable sweet spot. The question of which activities lend themselves best to HR analytics is still being debated.

In addition to using data analytics and IT, organizations are exploring design thinking to find innovative ways of working together and develop capability for rapid design of prototypes, experimentation, and the scaling of innovative practices throughout the organization.

DESIGN THINKING

The origin of design thinking dates back to the 1950s with the development of creativity techniques and new design methods in the 1960s. L. Bruce Archer was the first author to use the term 'design thinking' in his book Systematic Methods for Designers (1965).[33] Design thinking is an alternative to classical linear processes and is based on creativity, logic, intuition, and data as evidence. Simply stated, it is a way of thinking and working to solve complex problems in a practical and creative manner and to develop (read: design) new products and services. As a result, it is often used in innovation.

Design thinking is an iterative process where multi-disciplinary teams work together. Design thinking always starts from the (needs of the) client who is then also involved in the co-creation. A design thinking process usually—according to the source consulted—consists of (four to six) different phases:[34]

1. **Empathize**—understand
2. **Observe**—listen
3. **Define**—define the problem
4. **Ideate**—generate ideas
5. **Prototype**—develop a prototype
6. **Test**—test the proposed solution

Concretely, design thinking can be used for most HR-related challenges that matter to companies such as: increasing retention; decreasing stress, burn out, and absenteeism; fostering a new organizational culture; and redesigning HR processes. It can also help design innovative solutions that improve the employee experience as consumers of HR products, services, and processes along the employee life cycle. By applying design thinking, HR gets a more realistic picture of the specific challenges from the perspective of employees by mapping the employee experience including all interactions (touchpoint management) with HR and the organization.[35] This allows HR to redefine the challenges employees encounter—not from the perspective of HR but from the point of view of employees—and design creative and workable solutions based on feedback and data (rapid prototyping). The power of rapid prototyping is that, very quickly, many possible solutions are generated that are simple to implement. The simplicity and speed of this model can help HR improve the employee experience and the various touchpoints rather than focusing on the HR process itself. In other words, in design-centric culture, HR gets to understand and improve the employee's emotional experience with the organization. In design thinking, three core principles apply:[36]

- **Empathy**—HR understands the problems employees face;
- **Imagination**—HR proposes creative solutions to improve the employee experience;
- **Experimentation**—HR tests, improves, and optimizes the solution with feedback and data.

There are different tools for each phase in the design thinking process. We zoom in on a few: namely employee experience mapping, touchpoint management, and rapid prototyping.

Employee Experience Mapping

How to win the war for talent by giving employees the workspaces they want, the tools they need and a culture to celebrate? This is the theme of *The Employee Experience Advantage* by Jacob Morgan. He looks at three factors (the physical environment, technology, and organizational culture) that have a positive or negative impact on how employees interact with HR and experience the organization.[37] Developing employee experience maps allows HR to gain insight into what their employees are doing, thinking, and feeling rather than looking at HR practices from the perspective of the provision of HR services. It allows HR to acquire a more empathetic understanding of how employees experience the touchpoints with the HR organization and how to improve them, if needed, by focusing their HR budgets, time, and resources on improving or redesigning these interactions. This helps HR to better conceptualize what it means to belong to the organization, measure various aspects of belonging, and implement a culture where everyone belongs, albeit in different ways.

Touchpoint Management

Employees have different interactions (touchpoints) with HR during their life cycle with their employer. Touchpoints are the emotional points of contact the employee has with the organization as an internal customer—whether through structures, systems, or people. Once an employee experience map has been designed, it is critical for the HR team to develop an inventory of all the touchpoints the employee has with the processes, products, and services that HR provides and through which channel (virtual or face-to-face) these touchpoints are experienced.[38]

A few examples illustrate the importance of managing HR touchpoints:[39]

- How do new applicants perceive their contacts with you as an employer—when they are invited for an interview, whether they get hired or rejected as an applicant, during their first day at work, or after a long period of absence?
- How do remote workers get support and coaching from their managers when they have limited face-to-face interactions?
- How easy is it for employees to navigate the self-service HR portal?
- What opportunities for development and growth do employees have in your organization?
- How well are they supported and coached by their managers?

Each touchpoint can be experienced either positively by employees (a great experience) or are viewed negatively (pain points). HR must provide a seamless set of services that enable work productivity and improve the overall employee experience and must handle all the touchpoints with people (managers, HR, and co-workers), tools, systems, policies, and procedures—from the employee's point of view rather than the HR process and delivery perspective. Note that the employee experience is not necessarily uniform for each employee as one segment or group of employees is likely to experience the various touchpoints with HR somewhat differently. Therefore, it is good to identify different customer personas. A persona is an ideal type of a typical employee who is representative of a group of people with similar behavioral characteristics, needs, and experiences. In the same way that marketing segments its customers with personas to better understand potential customer, so too can personas be used to better understand employees and approach them more effectively in a customized manner. For example, an older worker has different wants and needs and, therefore, may experience the benefit policies in a totally different manner than a millennial worker. The global standard that you have for certain HR practices (i.e., non-smoking or alcohol consumption rules) is likely experienced differently in various geographies where you operate. The labeling of the employment status according to different people working on the same team (employee vs. freelance) is likely going to affect their sense of belonging and work experience. The greater flexibility afforded to some employees (usually based on their rank or status) is likely experienced differently from the worker who has limited or no opportunity for flexibility.Hence, employee experience mapping is not a one-size-fits-all proposition. It has to be customized for each persona (demographics, job function, work location, etc.). Thus, it is necessary to use the lens or overriding filter through which a particular persona views the employee journey. Multiple maps must eventually be developed based on the wants and needs of the segmented employee persona groups.[40]

Rapid Prototyping

Design thinking uses prototypes to explore possible solutions.[41] Rapid prototyping is a collective noun for different techniques that make it possible to quickly develop prototypes. Call it a form of experimentation, where a preliminary rough original model—representing the embodiment of an idea—is built quickly to allow questions to be asked and choices to be made. It is a minimum viable product that represents the least amount of effort to run an experiment and get feedback.[42] Designing these prototypes in various iterations is a social, rather than a personal activity. Once the front-end analysis has been done, designing and developing a rapid prototype for an HR-centered design idea usually takes about two hours, wherein a team using an established development protocol can deploy rapidly in terms of piloting, testing and later refining the prototype. Rapid prototyping is a design technique that can be used by global HR teams to develop innovative customer-centric services for their employees and pilot and refine them for wider deployment. It is all about being open-minded, experimenting with new solutions, and going forward with working solutions.

Experimentation and Scaling

As a result of access to information technology and data in real time, people initiatives are becoming more agile and experimentation and scaling is becoming more prominent:

- **Experimentation**—rather than deploying a new initiative using waterfall project management approach, each innovative people initiative goes through experimentation, or a tentative test or trial to see whether the intent reaches its intended objective and whether the experiment can be successfully scaled throughout the company. The new motto is, 'experiment, experiment, experiment!' Experimentation also changes the nature of failure—making even a 'no-go' initiative successful because of its opportunity for learning from mistakes.
- **Scaling**—only after successful experimentation is scaling considered or expanding the initiative throughout the organization at minimal additional cost and greater efficiency.

Without a doubt, information, technology, and data are playing a key role in people management today. While there are many ethical and governance challenges associated with the increased use of information technology, artificial intelligence, and the management of personal data, digitization and analytics can augment people management activities and give greater transparency and evidence-based grounding to management decisions. ▮

REFERENCES

1. This module is an update of previous publications: Claus, L., Baker, S., & Ely, J. (2015). Global HR Analytics. Pp. 5-33 in Claus. L. (ed.), *Global HR Practitioner Handbook*, volume 3. Silverton: Global Immersion Press; Claus, L. & Baker, S. (2018). The Global HR Stack: External and Internal Tools and Methodologies Impacting HR. Pp. 35-63 in Claus. L. (ed.), *Global HR Practitioner Handbook*, volume 4. Silverton: Global Immersion Press; Claus, L. & Arens, L. (2019). *#ZigZagHR: Why the Best HR is no Longer HR*. Silverton: Global Immersion Press.
2. Segal, L., Goldstein, A., Goldman, J., & Harfoush, R. (2014). *The Decoded Company*. New York: Portfolio.
3. Lawler, E.E., Levenson, A., & Boudreau, J.W. (2004). HR Metric and Analytics: Uses and Impacts. *CEO Publication*, G04-8(460), May.
4. Harvard Business Review Analytics Services (2012). *The Evolution of Decision-Making: How Leading Organizations are Adopting Data-Driven Cultures*. Boston: Harvard Business School Publishing.
5. Boudreau, J.W. & Ramstad, P. M. (2004). "Talentship and Human Resource Measurement and Analysis: From ROI to Strategic Organizational Change," *CEO Publication*, G 04-17(469), September; Levenson, A. (2004). "Harnessing the Power of HR Analytics," *Strategic HR Review* 10: 28-31; Fink, A. & Mark Vickers, M. (2011). "Fresh Approaches to HR Analytics," *People & Strategy*, 34: 3; Nolan, S. (2011). "HR Analytics," *Strategic HR Review*, 10 (2004); Carey W. Worth, "The Future Talent Shortage will Force Global Companies to Use HR Analytics to Help Manage and Predict Future Human Capital Needs," *International Journal of Business Intelligence Research*, 2, 11; Fitz-Enz, J. (2010). *The New HR Analytics: Predicting the Economic Value of your Company's Human Resources*. New York: American Management Association; Lawler, E.E., Levenson, A., & Boudreau, J. W. (2004). "HR Metric and Analytics: Uses and Impacts," *CEO Publication* G 04-8(460), May; Mondore, S., Douthitt. S., & Carson, M. (2011). "Maximizing the Impact and Effectiveness of HR Analytics to Drive Business Outcomes," *People & Strategy*, 34(201): 20-27.
6. Goodwin, B. (2013) "The Emerging Technologies Transforming How HR Works," *Computerweekly.com*, July 16, 16-17; Big Data in HR: Building a Competitive Talent Analytics Function—the Four Stages of Maturity. Bersin & Associates, 2012.
7. Levenson, A. (2011). "Using Targeted Analytics to Improve Talent Decisions," CEO Publication, G 11-03(591), January; Harris, J.G., Craig,E., Light, D. (2010). "The New Generation of Human Capital Analytics," *Accenture*; Fitz-Enz, J. (2009). "Predicting People: From Metrics to Analytics," *Employment Relations Today*, 36: 1-11.
8. Davenport, T. H. (2006). "Competing on Analytics," *Harvard Business Review*, 84 (1): 2-10.
9. Brown, B., Court, D., & Willmott, P. (2013). "Mobilizing Your C-Suite for Big-Data Analytics," Insights, November (Accessed: October 1, 2015). http://www.mckinsey.com/ insights/business_technology/mobilizing_your_c_suite_for_big_data_analytics; Roberts, B. (2013). "The Benefits of Big Data," *HR Magazine*, October, 21-29.
10. Mondore, S., Douthitt, S., & Carson, M. (2011) "Maximizing the Impact and Effectiveness of HR Analytics to Drive Business Outcomes, *People & Strategy*, 34(201): 20-27.
11. Ibid.
12. Hamel, G. (2011). *Gary Hamel: Reinventing the Technology of Human Accomplishment*. May 21 (Accessed: January 10, 2015). http://www.managementexchange.com/video/gary-hamel-reinventing-technology-human-accomplishment.
13. Segal, L., Goldstein, A., Goldman, J., & Harfoush, R. (2014). *The Decoded Company*. New York: Portfolio.
14. Boudreau, J.W. & Ramstad, P. (2007). *Beyond HR: The New Science of Human Capital*. Boston: Harvard Business School Press.
15. Critical themes that will shape the future of HR management. Thought Leadership Retreat, San Diego, CA, September 29-30, 2013, SHRM Foundation and Economist Intelligence Unit.
16. Segal, L., Goldstein, A., Goldman, J., & Harfoush, R. (2014). *The Decoded Company*. New York: Portfolio. 163.
17. Ibid.
18. Ibid.
19. Leonardi, P. & Contractor, N. (2018). "Better People Analytics," *Harvard Business Review*, 96 (6): 74-81.
20. Kohavi, R. & Thomke, S. (2017). "The Suprising Power of Online Experiments,"*Harvard Business Review*, 95 (5): 4-82.
21. Segal, L., Goldstein, A., Goldman, J., & Harfoush, R. (2014). *The Decoded Company*. New York: Portfolio.

22. Boudreau, J.W., and Ramstad, P. (2007). *Beyond HR: The New Science of Human Capital*. Boston: Harvard Business School Press.
23. Levenson, A. (2011). "Using Targeted Analytics to Improve Talent Decisions," *CEO Publication* G 11-03(591), January.
24. Segal, L., Goldstein, A., Goldman, J., & Harfoush, R. (2014). *The Decoded Company*. New York: Portfolio.
25. Ibid.
26. Bersin, J., Houston, J., & Kester, B. (2015). "Talent Analytics in Practice: Go from Talking to Delivering on Big Data," in *Global Human Capital Trends: Engaging the 21st Century Workforce* (Deloitte University Press, 2014)111-135 (Accessed: October 4, 2015). http://dupress.com/wp-content/uploads/2014/04/GlobalHumanCapitalTrends_2014.pdf
27. Lubbe, J. (2018) "The New EU's General Data Protection Regulation," Pp. 64-86 in Claus, L. (Ed.), *Global HR Practitioner Handbook*, volume 4, Silverton: Global Immersion Press.
28. Levenson, A. (2011). "Using Targeted Analytics to Improve Talent Decisions," *CEO Publication* G 11-03(591). January, 4.
29. Lawler, E.E., Levenson, A., & Boudreau, J.W. (2004). "HR Metric and Analytics: Uses and Impacts," *CEO publication* G04-8(460), May; Bennett, C. & Collins, L. (2015). "HR and people analytics; Stuck in Neutral," Pp 71-77 in *Global Human Capital Trends* 2015 (Deloitte) 71-77, (Accessed: October 1, 2015). http://www2.deloitte.com/content/dam/Deloitte/at/Documents/humancapital/hc-trends-2015.pdf;
30. Ming, V. (2019). *Human insight remains essential to beat the bias of algorithms: Better data can improve AI's ability to spot correlations but will not ensure fairness.* December 3 (Accessed: January 17, 2020). https://www.ft.com/content/59520726-d0c5-11e9-b018-ca4456540ea6
31. Davenport, T.H. (2006). "Competing on Analytics," *Harvard Business Review*, 84(1): 2-10.
32. Archer, B. *Systematic Method for Designers* (1965). London: Council of Industrial Design.
33. Martin, R. (2009). *The Design of Business: Why Design Thinking is the Next Competitive Advantage*. Boston: Harvard Business Review Press.
34. Mazur, A.H., Zucker, J., Sivak, M., Coombes, R. & Van Durme, Y. (2017) *Reimagine and Craft the Employee Experience: Design Thinking in Action*. Deloitte Development LLC. (Accessed: December 20, 2018). https://www2.deloitte.com/content/dam/Deloitte/be/Documents/consulting/Deloitte%20%20Reimagine%20&%20Craft%20Employee%20Experience%20-%20Design%20Thinking%20in%20Action%20POV.pdf
35. Bersin, J., Solow, M. & Wakefield, N. (2016). *Design Thinking: Crafting the Employee Experience*. https://dupress.deloitte.com/dup-us-en/focus/human-capital-trends/2016/ employee-experience-management-design-thinking.html.
36. Morgan, J. (2014). *The Future of Work: Attract New Talent, Build Better Leaders, and Create a Competitive Organization*. New York: John Wiley & Sons.
37. O'Connor, N. (2016) *How to Build an Experience Map*. (Accessed: January 15, 2017). https://medium.com@wnialloconnor/how-to-build-an-expereince-map-5e55b7ee43f32.January 25; Risdon, C. (2011) The anatomy of an experience map. (Accessed: January 15, 2017). http://adaptivepath.org/ideas/the-anatomy-of-an-experience-map/November 30.
38. Clapon, P. (2016) *Your Guide to Employee Experience Mapping*. (Accessed: January 15, 2017). http://www.gethppy.com/employee-engagement/guide-employee-experience-mapping; *Employee Journey Mapping* (2012). http://touchpointdashboard.com/2012/11/employee-journey mapping
39. Yohn, D.L. (2016). "Design your employee experience as thoughtfully as you design your customer experience," *Harvard Business Review Human Resource Management blog*, December 8. (Accessed: January 15, 2017).
40. Kolko, J. (2015). 'Design thinking comes of age', *Harvard Business Review*, 93 (9): 66-7.
41. Kelley, T. & Kelley, D. (2013). *Creative Confidence: Unleashing the Creative Potential within Us All*. New York: Crown Business.

GUIDED READING QUESTIONS

1. How can HR digitization augment HR?

2. What is the field of people analytics?

3. What is the process for using data in (people) management?

4. How can different data analytic tools that can be used in the manager's decision making toolkit?

FOLLOW-UP CRITICAL THINKING QUESTIONS

1. What is my major takeaway from this reading?

2. What do I already know about this subject?

3. What follow-up questions do I have about this?

4. How can I apply this in real life?

KEY TERMS
A/B testing
Data
Data mining
Digitization
Evidence-based decision
Information
Leading and lagging indicators
Sentiment analysis

LEARNING ASSESSMENT
Critically reflect on the content and the different concepts in this module and rate your own competency using the assessment scale.

Competency	I never heard of it	I heard of it but have limited knowledge of it	I can reasonably explain it to others	I have used it, done it, applied it
Data analytics	0	1	2	3
Digitization	0	1	2	3
A/B testing	0	1	2	3
Data mining	0	1	2	3
Sentiment analysis	0	1	2	3
Design thinking	0	1	2	3
Rapid prototyping	0	1	2	3
Experience mapping	0	1	2	3
Touchpoint management	0	1	2	3

MODULAR-SPECIFIC ASSESSMENT
Excellence in People Analytics Survey
A short survey measuring level (foundational, intermediate, advanced, or excelling) of the people analytics discipline in your organization.

Source: Jonathan Ferrar and David Green, Insight222, https://www.myhrfuture.com/survey

VIGNETTE

INNOVATION AT AMAZON THROUGH CULTURE AND HR TECHNOLOGY[1]

By Peter Vermeulen

The world's most successful companies acknowledge their most valuable resource is their people. And Human Resources (HR), when properly invested in, is a lynchpin to their success. Innovative HR systems are being introduced at a dazzling pace, and HR departments and practitioners must keep up. Attracting the best and brightest talent is a highly competitive game. Employees today are used to fast, intuitive, effective technology as consumers and they expect this from their employer as well. For those contemporary employees choosing where to work, the line separating traditional companies and companies with innovative, high-technology systems is increasingly obvious. The talent gravitates to progressive companies with creative cultures and leading-edge HR technology. Where traditional companies make do with pen-and-paper and semi-automated solutions, progressive companies gain a competitive advantage not just in acquiring top talent, but in all aspects of supporting them with an engaging organizational culture relying on data and technology. Employees expect instantaneous, exhaustive technological systems: HR must be no different.

Amazon is a prime example of a company taking advantage of every opportunity technology presents. In October of 2019, I left Amazon after two incredible years as HR Head. While there, I saw first-hand just how seriously the company takes applying technological advantages to every problem set including its workforce. In order to do so, Amazon gathers far more data than traditional companies do, and treats it with scientific complexity. That data and analysis provides Amazon with actionable insights that have provided enormous gains in managing its workforce, HR and across the entire company. I explore two interrelated themes: how Amazon has leveraged different forms of information technology to accomplish its HR objectives and how decisions are supported by a principled organizational culture. Amazon is uniquely positioned to discover innovative technological solutions by virtue of its status as one of the largest e-commerce and technology-integrated companies on the planet. Yet, that isn't why they've been so successful at integrating them. Amazon demands a culture of creativity, efficiency and innovation—and companies of any size should take note. Discrete, arbitrary, or random technological solutions are insufficient to meaningful change: a risk-tolerant, innovative culture must be embraced to achieve profitable success.

Amazon's (HR) Successes through Big Date, Artificial Intelligence, and More

Despite HR being considered overhead rather than a profit center, HR is responsible for maintaining a well-trained, highly engaged, well-supported workforce crucial to exceeding customer expectations and creating value for the internal customer. And Amazon, recognizing this, has piloted and championed products and processes that leverage high-technology solutions, including AI, cloud computing, data mining, and crypto analytics, in furtherance of the company's HR and talent objectives. The following examples of Amazon's successes can help other HR professionals around the world rock the boat of their own businesses.

***'Lights out'*—Recruitment, Selection, and Onboarding through Algorithms**

In October 2019, Amazon had approximately 660,000 employees and 63,000 vacancies.

For most HR professionals, those numbers may boggle the imagination. It is estimated that an average company in the U.S. has approximately 100 employees. In contrast, Amazon needs to find, hire, and place employees on a scale several orders of magnitude greater and needs to bring in 60,000 wage associates annually. To keep the enormous machine moving, a scalable recruitment and election solution was absolutely necessary, but one that did not sacrifice quality of hire or applicant experiences. Amazon implemented a process termed 'lights-out.' Initially, the salesforce was used to find wage associates, but by using AI all applicants were brought through the recruitment and placement process—all with no human recruiter involved. The process occurred 'in the dark,' or 'lights-out.' Applicants were found, solicited, given personality, capability and language tests online. Those who met the threshold were extended offers and invited to a training class. As a result, 60,000 new hires were placed without HR teams needing to be involved directly. Through the implementation of this 'lights-out' approach, Amazon was able to recruit and onboard a massive amount of talent to locations all around the globe. On analysis, the gaining teams in the field never experienced significant downtime, and quality of hire and employee experience remained at the same, if not better levels than previous, human-based hiring processes.

'Nostradamus'—Retention through Data Mining and Stay Interviews

Retaining valuable employees is a classic conundrum in HR. The cost of attrition to a company can be devastating, especially in terms of the high cost of replacing an employee. Amazon sought ways to understand, anticipate, and act on employees' reasons for departing a job. The Amazon solution came to be named Nostradamus, after the 16th-Century, purported French seer who published predictions and prophecies. The system mined employee data—far more data than a human team could ever handle—and analyzed metrics, attributes, and changes about them. Nostradamus converted all the data about employees into actionable insights for managers. Those insights provided information and context for decision makers and managers to positively influence employee outcomes in terms of retention. In total, 28 attributes were identified that could produce leading indicators about the likelihood of an employee leaving the company. These ranged from the ordinary (gender, performance rating, and years of service), to the complicated (level to which the employee was represented in diversity in the work center as well as engagement and participation data), to the slightly more obvious (recency and frequency of LinkedIn profile updates). Amazon compared a group being analyzed by Nostradamus against a control group and found Nostradamus to have a 70% accuracy rating in predicting which employees would leave the company. Most importantly, however, Nostradamus' findings were used to hold "Stay Interviews"—interviews held with contented team members to find out what about the workplace was satisfying to them. Stay Interviews have a distinct advantage over the more common "Exit Interviews" as they provide opportunities to 'get ahead of the bang,' and make changes that could improve conditions for all employees and reduce attrition. The roll-out of Nostradamus saw a sharp reduction in regrettable losses—to more than 30% in certain business units. There was also a marked uptick in employee engagement—attributed to employees feeling a stronger connection with their manager and the business overall.

'Chatbots'—Answering Tier 1 HR Questions

With more than 600,000 employees to serve, answering Tier 1 questions represents an impossible level of effort for HR associates at Amazon. Questions like 'how many days off an employee has' waste an HR teams' time and pull them away from questions and interactions that require critical thought and a trained perspective. To that end, Amazon added AI-driven employee conversations for Tier 1 support by using chatbots. Highly trained chatbots provide instant, accurate responses to common queries. Meanwhile, with chatbots handling rote, simplistic requests, HR teams were able to engage with employees in more complex, one-on-one issues. In typical Amazon fashion, the results of the experiment were evaluated and the initial roll-out of the pilot was not scaled because it didn't show marked impact on HR efficiency as so much time and effort needed to be invested in quality control of the chatbot support. However, the pilot programs, despite their learning curves, were considered a success and chatbot support was very well received in some areas (such as India) and will be receiving further global deployment.

'Connections'—Daily Employee Sentiment Analysis

Due to its size, Amazon's employees represent a city (if not a country) and understanding the morale, direction, and desires of all its members is as important to management as elections are to a political entity. Taking advantage of the fact that nearly every single employee is logged on to a digital device at the start of their workday, Amazon instituted Connection or a daily sentiment question for every employee. Every day, a new question gets posed and each employee in a large division (Corporate, Global Operations, etc.) receives the same question. Questions like "Is your manager good at handling stress?" "Do you feel valued in what you're doing?" "Do you have the necessary resources to complete your tasks?" are designed to elicit straightforward feedback about efficiency, management, and corporate lifestyle. Drivers on the road, customer service reps, forklift drivers, software developers, and VPs— all 660,000 employees answer this daily question! This wealth of data and insights are immediately turned into recommendations for managers and are available any time. Normally, this much data would be staggering. But not only does Connections parse and process the results, it also aggregates them and delivers them to relevant stakeholders in real time. Connections enables every manager to be aware of what's going well with their teams and what opportunities for improvement exist, in real-time.

'Voices of Associates'—Giving the Frontline Employee a Voice

For management teams throughout Amazon, resolving quality-of-life issues or emergent problems with production can often be a game of catch-up. A long lag time can form between a problem emerging and management knowing about it. This can mean that despite workers knowing about an issue for weeks, it's not until production slumps, profits dip, or morale nose dives that solutions get considered. Voice of Associates (VoA) is a virtual board to which associates can post a question or comment (anonymously if they'd prefer) and receive management's attention immediately. Other associates can interact with posted questions or comments, voting them up or down making VoA a real-time barometer to indicate which needs are most pressing. Often things that can seem trivial, such as for example the food quality in the canteen for instance or cleanliness of the bathrooms, but these issues are actually top-of-mind for associates. For managers to be able to see, first-hand and immediately, the concerns that are most pressing means understanding problems from the perspective of the employees, and having the data to resolve them quickly. Amazon's implementation of VoA gives associates on the frontline a voice to ask questions of management and provide comments about their (good and bad) work experiences. Creating the forum and making management accountable in a time-frame of days, rather than weeks or quarters, resulted in employees feeling valued as the data supported. Deployment of VoA in work centers resulted in higher engagement and correlated with lower attrition. Combining VoA with Connections gives managers enough data to provide a leading instead of a lagging analysis. Rather than having to wait until emergent problems were causing widespread issues, managers could create word cloud analysis of Connections and VoA responses to get ahead of high-interest topics in the mind of employees.

'Forte'—Finding Your Super Performance Strength

Performance reviews are a necessary instrument for any company and Amazon is no different. Providing helpful feedback to employees while highlighting a roadmap for success can get mired in paperwork, be stymied by human emotion and reaction, and overlooked or given short shrift. In looking for a way to highlight strengths while also providing useable feedback, Amazon developed Forte. In fencing, the forte of the blade is the part closest to the hilt. This section of the blade is the strongest, and least likely to bend out of the way of an attacker's thrust, which is why a parry should be taken on the *forte*. At Amazon, they adopted this figure of speech not just as a way to approach performance reviews, but as a cultural approach: "*What's your super power*?" is asked in many different contexts throughout the business. When an employee's annual review comes due, employees can opt into a "360-degree performance feedback." This supplements the yearly appraisal with an opportunity for the employee, managers, peers, and other stakeholders to consider the employee's *forte*. The system generates simple questions for the review stakeholders: What does this person do particularly well (What is their *forte*)? What growth opportunities do you see for this person? In addition to self-assessment from the employee and assessments from managers, the Forte system generates a detailed report about their strengths and what aspects of their work they're best at and can remain committed. This commitment to a growth mindset and utilization of the integrated feedback system means employees get acknowledged for their best work and utilized to their best advantage.

'Hallmark'—Celebrating Milestones

Good management and good HR is often simply based on thoughtfulness. At a fast-paced company like Amazon, it's very easy for normally thoughtful and considerate people to overlook important milestones and dates of employees. The Hallmark application is an easy way to be reminded of work anniversaries, birthdays, and other important dates. The system pushes notifications to managers and leaders to make sure they have the opportunity to reach out to employees and associates to commemorate and celebrate important milestones in their life and career. Legendary is the symbolism of the changed color of the batch for employee who reach a milestone anniversary with the company. The system also makes sure that wherever the employee may be, the manager can reach out to them, whether they're on-site, remote, or on a leave of absence. Making sure everyone gets thought of and acknowledged leads to a positive and rewarding employee experience.

These are just a few of the innovative, progressive technological and data solutions Amazon has deployed. But these are the successes as the failed or aborted projects that didn't bear fruit are not listed. Amazon is successful at finding progressive and innovative HR solutions not just because of the technology, but also because of its culture. Even the best technology can't be implemented if the company doesn't embrace the idea that 'things can be done better.' And that is truly the key to Amazon's success—its culture of innovation.

Amazon's Culture of Innovation

Amazon has written and published lengthy internal documentation that explains their company ethos. Unsurprisingly for a company that was start-up sized just 20 years ago, a central tenet is innovation and invention. But it's not Amazon's embrace of innovation that sets it apart: it's their acknowledgment of the risk involved. Trying new approaches is risky to both profits and careers. Introducing a new technology, changing existing processes, developing a new system could all be expensive boondoggles. But in Amazon's own words, "*To invent you have to experiment, and if you know in advance that it's going to work, it's not an experiment.*" Key to Amazon's success is their dedication to innovation and to protecting risk takers. This attitude, fostered in their 14 Leadership Principles, is a rich soil for ideas to take seed in.

The 14 Leadership Principles—You Better Live Them!

Amazon disseminates 14 Leadership Principles to its associates. They are the explicit concepts to guide team members and leaders at all levels. The list starts with "Customer Obsession" and includes "Frugality" and "Have Backbone," but the one we'll focus on is #3: "Invent and Simplify."

> *"Leaders expect and require innovation and invention from their teams and always find ways to simplify. They are externally aware, look for new ideas from everywhere, and are not limited by 'not invented here.' As we do new things, we accept that we may be misunderstood for long periods of time."*

Amazon leads the way in technological solutions to HR problems not because of their unique position as an e-commerce and technology-forward company. They lead the way because there is one, unified message: all members of Amazon's teams are expected to continually look for new and creative ways to solve problems. A company can purchase all the technology, all the widgets, and all the systems they want. If its employees truly don't feel empowered to innovate and take risks, growth will halt. For Amazon, if it serves the customer and helps the process, you and your team should be empowered to try it out, and 'critically' allowed to fail. But, there's more to innovation than just good ideas. Where many companies get held up is in how to propose, initiate, and get approval for their ideas. Enter Amazon's three-part document known as the DOC, press release, and frequently asked questions. This three-part document can be written by any Amazon employee (an "Amazonian") with a big idea to explain the idea, justify its *raison d'être*, and answer all external and internal questions. Anyone at any level in the company can write one. The documents are simple yet very detailed and highly uniform.

Amazon's DOC Writing—Ban the PowerPoint™!

The DOC is a six-page single-spaced document written out in a long narrative essay-style single-spaced format with complete sentences and paragraphs (no PPT-style bullet points!). It contains all nuances, principles, and features of the intervention. The concept is clearly described (conceptualization), the data are provided and measures of success identified (operationalization), and the processes and support needed to make the intervention successful are clearly explained (execution).

Press Release (PR)—Dream Big

The press release (PR) portion is written from the perspective of the hypothetical future, after the proposed product has been released. From small tweaks to Alexa's functionality one-day delivery for PRIME customers, the PR portion is always short. Invariably, it is at most one-and-a-half pages long and follows a templated format.

Frequently Asked Questions (FAQ)—But Focus on the Details

The frequently asked questions (FAQ) portion is two parts: the first addresses all questions a customer may have about the product, the second all the questions any internal stakeholder may have. Combined with the PR, the document doesn't merely explain the product, it also helps guide teams once the product gets approved. Engineers, sales, marketing, and executive should all be able to use the PRFAQ after its approval as a starting point for their own research and work. One appeal of the PRFAQ is that its simplicity helps restrain scope creep. If all stakeholders don't get a clear idea of the proposed new product in a page and a half, it's likely unrestrained, and a bad product. If there are questions a stakeholder might ask in the future that aren't covered in the FAQ portion, it's likely not well-considered enough to begin work.

If a DOC and PRFAQ get approved and funded, a team is created to champion the project. At Amazon, such a team has an ideal size and is dubbed "a two-pizza team." These follow the Agile project management methodology and don't actually have anything to do with pizza, except that their size should roughly be no bigger than what could be fed by two pizzas. Any smaller and they may not have the time and bandwidth to bring the product to market. Too large, and the team will get dragged down by its own weight. The entire PRFAQ process helps to restrain random, arbitrary changes while encouraging customer-focused, profitable proposals that get finished rapidly.

Progressive Companies Find Clever Solutions

As should be obvious by now, Amazon has taken very seriously the challenge of finding innovative solutions to common HR problems. Some of these changes are simply by necessity: finding and hiring 60,000 employees every year would require an unsustainably large HR pool. But most of the changes are by design and aimed at creating a culture that ensures every employee is heard, guarantees each work center is optimized, and getting people with the right talents doing what they are best at. All these improvements are made possible thanks to a culture of innovative improvement in HR.

In their book, *#ZigZagHR: Why the Best HR is No Longer HR* (2019), Lisbeth Claus and Lesley Arens wrote that "*HR needs a dose of chutzpa: the arrogance, guts and impudence to rock the boat*." Keeping up with ever-changing technologies and finding ways to integrate them into HR practices takes hard work and ambition! Not every company is going to have the problems that face Amazon, and very few are going to have the resources. Yet the lessons Amazon can provide about good governance and forward-thinking solutions are crucial to any and all HR professionals. The world will soon be split between companies who embrace traditional HR practices and those companies who embrace progressive, high-technology solutions and systems. Big data,

AI, machine-learning, automation; these are all tools companies will need to take advantage of if they seek to win the talent war.

REFERENCES

1. This vignette was prepared by Peter Vermeulen for the sole purpose of illustrating a global HR practice for instructional objectives. Global HR in Action © 2019, Global Immersion Press, All Rights Reserved.
2. Claus, L. & Arens, L. (2019). *#ZigZagHR: Why the Best HR is No Longer HR*. Silverton, OR: Global Immersion Press

GUIDED READING QUESTIONS

1. What are the objectives of Amazon's various initiatives (such as Lights Out, Nostradamus, Chatbots, Connections, Voices of Associates, Forte, and Hallmark) and how are they supported by data and technology?
2. How does the Amazon culture support innovation?

MODULE TEN

MANAGING PEOPLE, PROCESSES, AND PROJECTS

MODULE TEN

MANAGING PEOPLE, PROCESSES, AND PROJECTS

DESCRIPTION

This module looks at value-added activities and professional skills in managing people, projects, and processes in traditional and progressive organizations with a special focus on agile management tools and techniques.

LEARNING OBJECTIVES

Upon completing the learning experience, you will be able to:

- Define project, process, and agile management
- Describe the tools of process management
- Describe the tools of waterfall project management
- Describe the tools of agile project management

GUIDING QUESTION

What would make my organization more agile?

RALPH woke up at 2am and could not fall back to sleep. His mind was racing as he reflected on all the day-to-day tasks and responsibilities for his team. It was frustrating that his team was asked to do more and more by his boss without any additional headcount. His boss frequently asked for the status of the team's projects and initiatives that were critical to the successful launch of a new product that was projected to result in significant revenue. Ralph considered how he might best leverage his people and current and new processes to maximize his team's effectiveness.

WHAT ARE WE MANAGING?

In the workplace, managers are responsible to manage work (output) and people (performers doing the work). Managers have higher accountability as they are ultimately responsible for ensuring that the work is done by the team. Work consists of routine (process) and non-routine (project) work. Managing work entails managing not only the design and organization of the work but also the processes, projects, and people responsible for work outcomes. Organizations rely on professional tools to manage the work done by people. In managing routine work, individual and teams rely on process management while project management is used for managing non-routine work.

- A **process** is an ongoing endeavor consisting of a series of tasks and activities that help deliver a product or service outcome. In that sense, we talk about a manufacturing process, a billing process, a risk management process, etc. Delivering a monthly payroll is an example of a process. Process management focuses on delivering and optimizing business processes so they meet organizational goals in a timely and cost-effective manner at the required quality.
- A **project** is a one-shot undertaking resulting in defined deliverable products, limited by time and resources. Project management is a set of tools and techniques that guide the initiation, planning, execution, monitoring/controlling, and closing of a project.

Traditional process and project management are considered a part of operations management—each coming with a set of methodologies and professional skills. In addition to traditional process and project approaches, progressive process management also focuses on reengineering and agile project management. In this module, we juxtapose these traditional (continuous quality improvement) process management and (waterfall) project management practices with more progressive practices such as process reengineering and agile project management. But, ultimately, the people management component is central to successfully using these professional methodologies and tools within the organization and require specific people competencies and situational leadership to be successful.

PROCESS MANAGEMENT

Traditional process management focuses on continuous improvement of existing processes. The Japanese concept of 'Kaizen' (meaning improvement) is at the core of process management. When dealing with routine and recurring work, the focus is improving existing processes and optimizing them by reducing and eliminating defects.

Total Quality Management

The focus of Total Quality Management (TQM) is on improving the quality of products and services through continuous improvement of internal processes. TQM with its roots in the 1930s, was further formulated in the 1950s in Japan, and only flourished in the United States in the early 1980s. The main TQM thought leaders and contributors are:

- **Walter Shewhart**—considered the father of statistical process control;
- **Edward Deming**—initiated statistical analysis and quality control in Japanese engineering and established TQM as a management field;
- **A.V. Feigenbaum**—focused on the quality cost management (costs of prevention, appraisal, and failure);
- **Philip B. Crosby**—focused on zero defects in quality management;
- **Joseph M. Juran**—focused on total quality control and managerial involvement;
- **Kaoru Ishikawa**—famous for his cause-and-effect diagram; developed a specific Japanese brand of total quality management.

TQM is based on eight foundational principles:[1]

1. **Customer-focused**—the level of quality is ultimately decided by the customer;
2. **Total employee involvement**—all employees participate empowered as individuals and teams to focus on continuous improvement;

3. **Process-centered**—process thinking and TQM tools are fundamental;
4. **Integrated system**—horizontal processes interconnect (siloed) functions;
5. **Strategic and systematic approach**—quality management is fundamental to achieving the organization's vision, mission, and goals;
6. **Continual improvement**—stakeholder's expectations are met through continuous improvement;
7. **Fact-based decision-making**—data on performance measures are key;
8. **Communications**—employees at all levels are aware of strategies, method, and timeliness.

One of the cornerstones of process management is known as the PCDA cycle or circle (also called Shewhart and Deming cycle/circle):

- **Plan**—plan and direct;
- **Do**—perform and deploy;
- **Check**—monitor and review;
- **Act**—revise and improve.

A 'Responsibility Assignment Matrix' (called RACI charts) describes the responsibility (i.e., Responsible, Accountable, Consulted, Implement) of various roles for completing tasks and deliverables in a project or business process. TQM empowers teams involved in the work output of a product or service—through training and measurement—to strive for quality and continuously improve the processes involved in producing that quality. Today, these TQM concepts are present in their daily operations through modern quality management systems—whether in manufacturing or service industries.

- **Six-Sigma**—initially applied to manufacturing but now extensively used for service—is an example of the integration of process management techniques to reduce the probability of errors, reduce or eliminate waste, and have greater quality. The key measure is that errors should not exceed six sigma from the mean or 3.4 defects per million.
- **Customer obsession**—refers to constantly listening to the customer and testing, enhancing and improving the customer experience. Customer obsession is the first of 14 Leadership Principles at Amazon: "*Leaders start with the customer and work backwards. They work vigorously to earn and keep customer trust. Although leaders pay attention to competitors, they obsess over customers.*"[2]

Reengineering

Reengineering consists of radically rethinking (even disrupting one's) processes to obtain radical improvement rather than single digit continuous improvement. Reengineering—also known as business process reengineering—was introduced by Michael Hammer in the 1990s. While continuous improvement allowed for incremental improvement, the context of the 1990s required more dramatic improvements to compete in a global market place. In their 1993 book, *Reengineering the Corporation*, Michael Hammer and James Champy defined reengineering as the "*fundamental rethinking and radical redesign of business process to achieve dramatic improvements in critical measures of performance such as cost, service, and speed.*"[3] Instead of focusing on statistical process control tools for incremental improvement, they advocate the use of information technology to produce these dramatic results.

Process Management Tools

The seven TQM tools (see images below)[4] are rather elementary but very useful in Statistical Process Control (SPC):

1. **Fishbone diagram**—also called cause and effect fishbone or 'Ishikawa' diagram—identifies the root causes of a problem in a visual manner. Factors that may contribute to the cause of the problem are looked at by category: people, management, process, environment, equipment, and materials.

> *Example: The '5 Whys' is an application of the fishbone diagram used in brainstorming to find the root causes of a problem by asking the question at least five times before finding the issue(s) related to a problem.*

2. **Control chart**—shows how a process (historically) changes over time indicating a central line for the average, an upper limit for the upper control limit (UCL), and a lower line for the lower control limit (LCL). These limits predict the expected range of outcomes of a process and show whether a process is in control. It also allows us to explore the special causes of the variation.

   Example: Student evaluations of professors can be plotted over time using a control chart to identify whether their teaching evaluations are within the control lines.

3. **Pareto chart**—is a distribution diagram represented as a vertical bar graph where values are plotted in decreasing order of relative frequency (left to right) and the right side of the vertical axis shows the cumulative percentage in a line graph. It is based on the Pareto principle, or the 80/20 rule, that states 80% of problems are caused by 20% of the causes.

   Example: In an employee satisfaction survey, the major reasons for employee dissatisfaction can be identified and show which top reasons make up the majority of the complaint so dealing with these few issues bring the greatest value.

4. **Check sheet**—is a sheet that captures both quantitative (tally sheet) and qualitative data and shows how many times (check) the value occurs.

   Examples:
   Check sheet: making a 'to do' list for daily tasks and checking them off.
   Tally sheet: recording class attendance.

5. **Histogram**—plots quantitative continuous data with the ranges of the data grouped into intervals with no gaps between adjacent bars.

   Example: Assigning workloads on a team to different people and looking at it on a bar chart.

6. **Scatter diagram**—posts the values of two variables—one along the X-axis and the other along the Y-axis--to determine whether there is a relationship (positive or negative) or no relationship.

   Example: Whether there is a relationship between work absenteeism and weather conditions.

7. **Flow or run chart**—shows data in a time sequence and identifies whether a process is stable over time.

   Example: The time sequence of hiring, turnover, terminations, relocations, etc.

While these seven process management tools are elementary, their use is powerful when everyone in the organization uses these tools to manage their day-to-day processes by collecting, sharing, and analyzing the data (see figure 10-1). Can you think of processes in your organizations that would benefit from using these tools to provide data on how well your processes are working and where they can be improved?

PROJECT MANAGEMENT

In today's work environment, more and more work is done as a project where several individuals contribute to the desired outcome.

What is a Project?

A project is "*a series of tasks and activities that has a stated goal and objectives, a schedule with defined start and end dates, and a budget that sets limitations on the project's dedicated use of both monetary and human resources.*"[5] Project management is an applied professional skill. Project resources are any quantifiable factors (except time) that are needed or consumed for completing the planned work. Basic types or resources are people, money, equipment, materials, and supplies. Note that time is not a resource but a function of the amount of resources used in a project. Traditional project management is 'waterfall' project management while 'agile' is a more recent form of project management.

10-1. The seven TQM Tools

Cause-and-effect ('fishbone' or Ishikawa) diagram

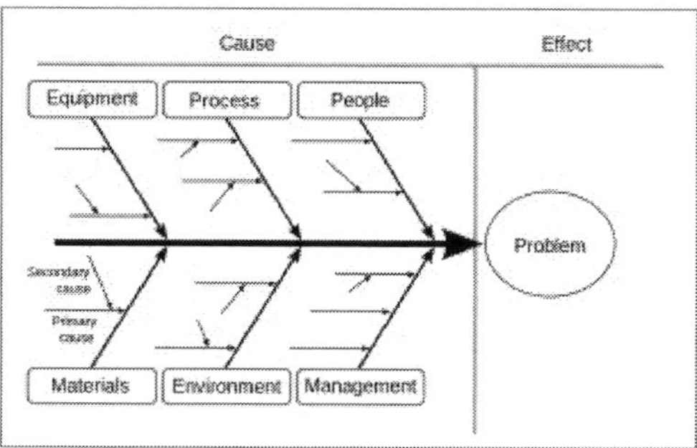

Control Chart

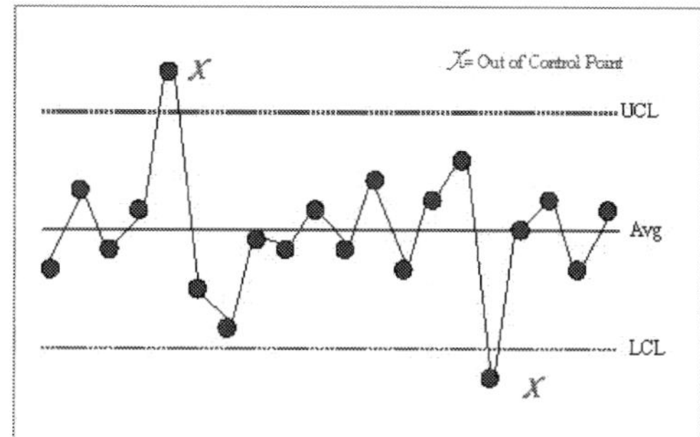

Pareto Chart

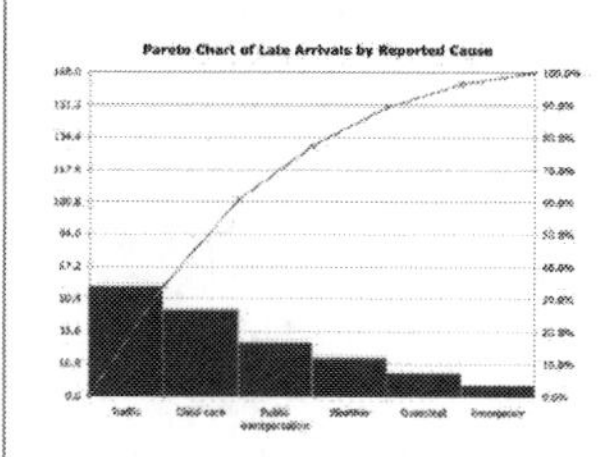

Check Sheet

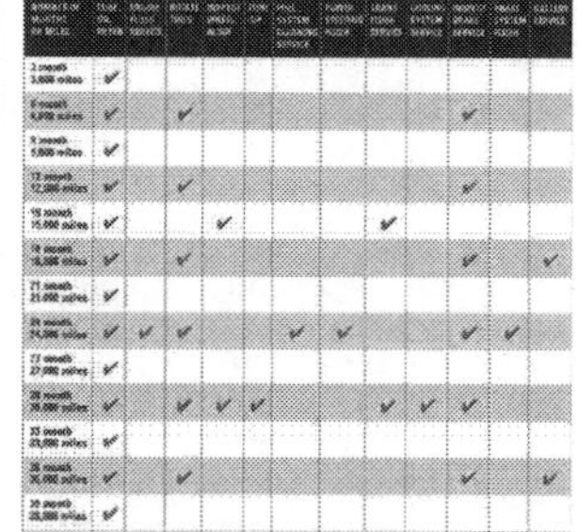

Historgram

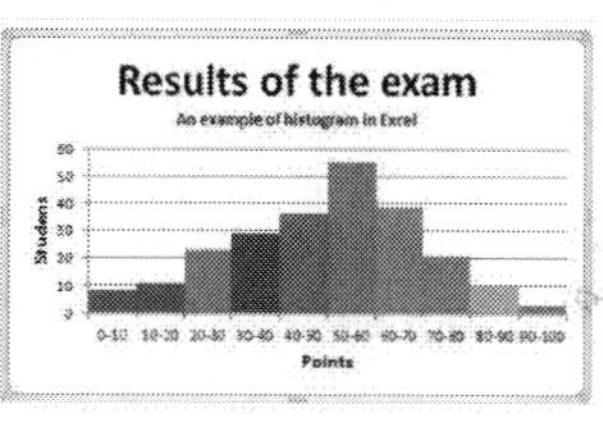

Scatter Diagram

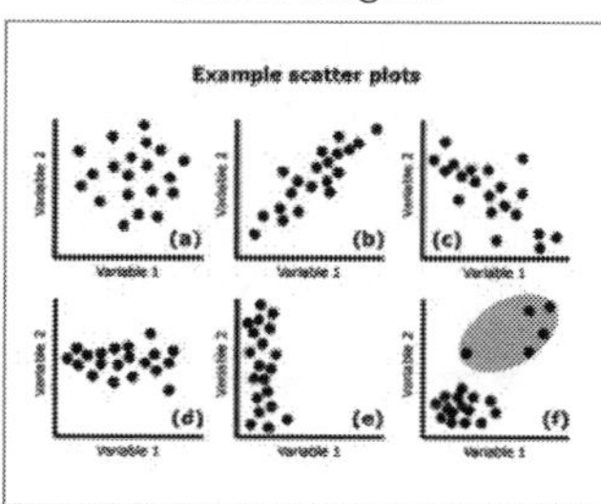

Run Chart

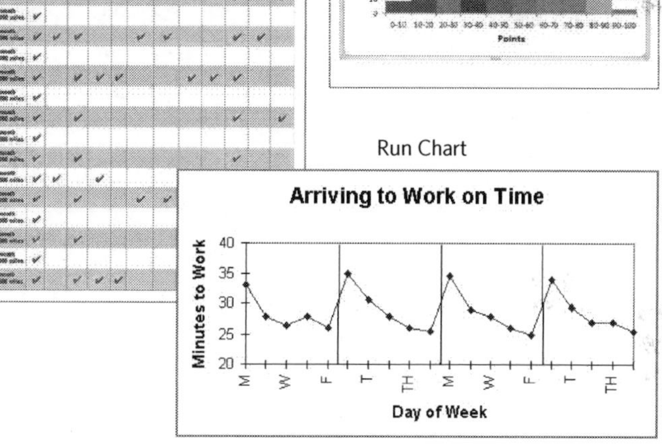

Source: Various Google Images

Waterfall Project Management

The project management life cycle is based on a systematic staged approach that includes the following project stages: initiating, planning, executing, monitoring/controlling, and closing the project. Waterfall project management is process oriented—we make a plan and follow it. The 'Iron Triangle' is a classic waterfall PM concept. It states that change in one of the key elements or constraints of the project—scope, budget, or schedule (also called the triple constraints)—will affect the quality of a project. The focus is on making trade-offs regarding the scope, quality, cost, and time elements of the project.

The Project Management Body Of Knowledge (called PMBOK) was codified by the Project Management Institute (PMI) responsible for professional certification.[6]

Waterfall project management is organized around:

- 5 project management processes (project life cycle);
- 10 knowledge areas (critical functions);
- 47 processes;
- 614 outputs, tools and techniques.

Waterfall Project Management Tools

According to PMI, the PMBOK consists of 10 critical waterfall project management functions. There are specific processes (47) and tools[7] within each of these functions (See 10-2).

1. **Scope management**—includes the processes (6) required to ensure the project includes all the work required, and only the work required, to complete the project successfully;
2. **Time management**—includes the processes (7) required to manage the timely completion of the project;
3. **Cost management**—includes the processes (4) involved in planning, estimating, budgeting, financing, funding, managing, and controlling costs so the project can be completed within the approved budget;
4. **Quality management**—includes the processes (3) and activities of the performing organization that determine quality policies, objectives, and responsibilities so the project will satisfy the needs for which it was undertaken;
5. **HR management**—includes the processes (4) that organize, manage, and lead the team;
6. **Communications management**—includes the processes (3) that are required to ensure timely and appropriate planning, collection, creation, distribution, storage, retrieval, management, control, monitoring, and the ultimate disposition of project information;
7. **Risk management**—includes the processes (6) of conducting risk management planning, identification, analysis, response planning, and controlling risk on a project;
8. **Procurement management**—includes the processes (4) necessary to purchase or acquire products, services, or results needed from outside the project team;
9. **Stakeholder management**—includes the processes (4) required to identify the people, groups, or organizations that could impact or be impacted by the project, to analyze stakeholder expectations and their impact on the project, and to develop appropriate management strategies for effectively engaging stakeholders;
10. **Integration management**—includes the processes (6) and activities to identify, define, combine, unify, and coordinate the various processes and project management activities within the Project Management Process Groups (initiating, planning, executing, monitoring/controlling, and closing).

Agile Project Management[8]

Agile project management originated in software development. The approach to design and deliver software is now applied to other types of work and management. In contrast with waterfall project management, agile requires very little upfront planning. Agile focuses on user requirements and delivering customer value. The agile interactions among the team members and customers are more important than the standard operating procedures and plans. Agile management is an iterative incremental method of managing a project in a highly transparent, flexible, and interactive manner. Agile is iterative, collaborative, incremental, quick, and value focused. It allows the project team to respond quickly to changing requirements of the client and the environment. Projects are implemented quickly, refined and improved, morphing into ongoing new projects. One hundred percent perfection is not expected but speed and agility are key. Agile is a way of organizing work done by multidisciplinary teams with flexibility and short cycles. Agile project management requires engaged self-organized teams that provide predictable outcomes with very little upfront planning. Agile has become synonymous with flexibility and the ability to change.

Agile Project Management Tools

Agile working methods are Kanban, Scrum, and Agile Portfolio Management (APM).[9]

1. Kanban

Kanban is a Japanese visual board method with three columns: to do, busy, and done. Team members use post-it notes or an electronic board. Everyone sees what the team is busy working on and what the status of the task is. Each day, new tasks can be added and not everyone is dependent on the tasks of the others. Kanban is mainly used for operational tasks and execution of process work on teams of 10 to 12 people (maximum). The main advantage is that it provides an overview of all tasks and activities, makes them visible to the team and reduces the work pressure of the team. Kanban is very easy, takes little time to introduce (daily 15-30 minutes combined for the whole team), and is inexpensive to implement (all it requires is wall space and a board). It eliminates periodic team review, daily status, activities, and individual to do lists.

2. Scrum

Scrum is a self-organized agile team of 5-9 highly engaged people from different disciplines playing different team roles (Scrum Master, Product Owner, and Developers). Scrum requires following a set of required components: project charter development, assembling a Scrum team with defined roles, user stories and personas, product backlog, backlog grooming, release plan, chunking, sprint, daily scrum, burndown chart, and sprint retrospective.

An agile **project charter** is a one-page narrative that includes the vision (what, how, why), the mission, and the success factors.

- **Project vision**:
  - A single sentence that describes the expectations for the product
  - Created by the product owner and agreed upon by the Scrum team
  - Should answer the what, how, and why questions related to the purpose of the project
- **Project mission:**
  - What everyone will do to accomplish the vision

10-2. Waterfall Project Management Functions and Processes

Function	Processes
Scope Management	1. Plan scope management 2. Collect requirements 3. Define scope 4. Create work breakdown structure (WBS) 5. Validate scope 6. Control scope
Time Management	1. Plan schedule 2. Define activities 3. Sequence activities 4. Estimate activity resources 5. Estimate activity duration 6. Develop schedule 7. Control schedule
Cost Management	1. Plan cost manage-ment 2. Estimate costs 3. Determine budget 4. Control costs
Quality Management	1. Plan quality management 2. Perform quality assurance 3. Control quality
HR Management	1. Plan HR management 2. Acquire project team 3. Develop project team 4. Manage project team
Communications Management	1. Plan communications management 2. Manage communications 3. Control communications
Risk Management	1. Plan risk management 2. Identify risks 3. Perform qualitative risk analysis 4. Perform quantitative risk analysis 5. Plan risk responses 6. Control risks
Procurement Management	1. Plan procurement 2. Conduct procurement 3. Control procurement 4. Close procurement
Stakeholder Management	1. Identify stakeholders 2. Plan stakeholder management 3. Manage stakeholder engagement 4. Control stakeholder engagement
Integration Management	1. Develop project charter/ statement of work (SOW) 2. Develop project management plan 3. Direct and manage project work 4. Monitor and control project work 5. Perform integrated change control 6. Close project or phase

Source: *A Guide to the Project Management Body of Knowledge*, PMBOK Guide, 6th edition (2017). Project Management Institute.

- **Success criteria:**
  - Simple one-sentence tests to make sure the project accomplished its mission

A **scrum team** is an agile work team where individual team roles are based on the strengths of the team members. There are three roles in scrum teams: Product owner, Scrum master, and Developers or members of the delivery team. In the various iterations (sprints), the team may want to change those roles so everyone on the team gets to experience them.

- **Scrum Master**—ensures work gets done by tracking progress and removes the obstacles to optimize the team's productivity.
- **Product Owner**—empowers the connection between the team and the project's client by ensuring deliverables meet client's expectations.
- **Delivery Team**—delivers the product following the product owner's expectations through the completion of daily tasks.

User stories are the stories collected from different users (personas) to better understand the deliverable. User stories are crafted based on the user role or persona. User stories are written down as a script in the format:

- As a <user role>,
- I want/need/can, etc. <goal>
- so that <reason>

User stories are collected by talking with the various users (client) and identifying what they want out of the project/product. Customer demographics often provide cluster personas.

The **product backlog** is the collection of user stories that make up the wish list of the users. It is a list of high-level product requirements (based on user stories) that are implemented as product features and functionality. Once the product backlog is established, it will need to be groomed (backlog grooming), released (a release plan), and planned for sprints (chunking).

Backlog grooming prioritizes the work (based on user stories) for next sprint using a task board, sets a timeframe for completion, and keeps the backlog up to date.

A **release plan** is a collection of sprints (from 2 to 12) based on the prioritized user stories in the product backlog. The release plan establishes the duration of the sprints and the planning of multiple sprints within a release. Larger user stories are broken down into manageable chunks and the amount of work involved is estimated by the team. Estimates are usually done in buckets of 1, 2, 4, or 8 hours or 2, 3, 5, or 0 days with in-between estimates falling into the larger bucket.

Chunking means splitting the final release into smaller chunks or sprints, prioritizing the larger tasks and making the project more manageable and easier to deliver.

A **sprint** is a time-constrained (time-boxed) iteration milestone to build a manageable chunk of a deliverable ship-ready 100% complete product increment. The ultimate project deliverable is broken down into blocks and weekly assignments (called chunking) for release. During the sprint, the team intensively focuses to complete a deliverable chunk of the project and releases it for client review. During the sprint, team members keep track of their work through a Scrumban—a Kanban task board with three columns: to do, work in progress, done. Team members agree in advance and describe what 'done' means so everyone has the same image of the standard when done.

The **daily scrum** is a stand-up meeting that doesn't exceed a time limit of 30 minutes. The meeting is scheduled at a regular time—often first thing at the start of the workday—to accommodate all team members. Daily stand-up meetings allow the team to have a short, productive, and honest meeting where individual members hold each other publicly accountable for delivering the work expected from them. The scrum master leads this short stand-up meeting. The entire team stands up and each person gets maximum three minutes to answer the following questions:

- What did I do yesterday? OR, what have I completed since the last meeting?
- What am I doing today? OR, what will I do before the next meeting?
- Are there any obstacles in my way? AND, what are they?

Note that stand-up meetings are not dragged-on meetings where only one hour of productive work gets done; one-sided meetings with one or two members dominating the discussion or making all the decisions; sit-down meeting and time for everyone to settle in and get comfortable; a time for 1:1 problem solving; a freeform time to talk about other work and non-work-related things (unless it was an obstacle to completing your task).

The **burn down chart** monitors the completion of a sprint, the work that remains to be done, and the estimated completion time. It is a day-by-day measure of the amount of work that remains in a sprint (trends towards zero). The slope (work remaining/time) is the burndown velocity based on the average rate of work done each day.

Sprint retrospectives ensure regular sprint review done at regular intervals by the team and the client. Two types of retrospectives are popular with agile teams: the starfish and racecar retrospectives. Starfish retrospectives asks the following questions about the sprint activities: what should we do more, less, start, stop, and keep. The racecar retrospective asks a number of questions by using the metaphor of a racecar (what makes us go faster or what drives us?), a parachute (what slows us down?), an abyss (a bump in the road and what obstacles are we expecting?), and a bridge (how can we overcome or bridge those obstacles?)

3. *Agile TPM (Team Portfolio Management)*
Professionals often work on different teams and several projects that are dependent upon one another. TPM allows us to stay in touch with each other's work and adapt quickly to stay on course. TPM provides insight in everything the team does and wants to do, connections between ambitions, activities and people, as well as focus toward what is jointly important. Agile TPM uses the circles or ring image. The middle point represents the ambitions of team members and where they are going in the next period; the inner circle entails the projects and activities the team is currently working on; and the outer ring is what the team needs and shares.

WATERFALL VS AGILE PROJECT MANAGEMENT

Contrasting waterfall with agile does not mean one is better than the other. Each project management approach has advantages and disadvantages, and is applicable for particular situations and types of projects.

Waterfall project management is best suited for large (engineering) projects based on past experience and use large teams. The well-defined plan, control, and structure of work lend themselves better for stable environment with a greater degree of certainty. There is usually a single source of accountability (executives). There is big project design planning done up front and the project is broken down into phases. While the senior project manager relies on the accountability of each project team member, the ultimate accountability lies at the top management level.

Agile is best suited for smaller, complex, and innovative projects that require flexibility and adaptability to changing needs. The large deliverables are broken down into smaller chunks. Teams usually cannot rely much on past experience because the product is not defined at the project start. Team accountability lies at the co-worker and middle management level.

Although agile is increasingly being applied to management and especially HR,[10] Darrell K. Rigby, Jeff Sutherland, and Hirotaka Takeuchi in their 2016 *Harvard Business Review*, "Embracing agile," argue that agile management is too slow to be applied in management. They identify that leaders do not really understand agile and, therefore, continue to use conventional management practices that undermine agile projects.[11]

BENEFITS OF MANAGING WORK WITH PROCESS AND PROJECT TOOLS

There are many benefits of organizing project work provided team members are proficient in the skills required for project management. Managing projects in a systematic way using these professional waterfall and/or agile management skills provides a common language, tools and techniques, more empowered work, increased accountability, limited free riding, reduced meeting times, distributed work over a span of time, ability to meet changing client requirements, and increased client satisfaction. ▮

REFERENCES

1. *What is Total Quality Management* (TQM) (Accessed: January 5, 2020). https://asq.org/quality-resources/total-quality-management.
2. *Leadership Principles*. (Accessed: January 15, 2020). https://www.amazon.jobs/en/principles
3. Hammer, M., & Champy, J. (1993) *Reengineering the Corporation: A Manifesto for Business Revolution*. New York: Harper Collins.
4. *Seven Basic Tools of Quality*. (Accessed: January 5, 2020). https://www.whatissixsigma.net/7-qc-tools/
5. *SHRM Learning System*. Alexandria, VA, 2017.
6. *A Guide to the Project Management Body of Knowledge*, PMBOK Guide, 6th edition (2017). Project Management Institute.
7. Ibid.
8. The description of agile management is based on: Claus, L., & Baker, S. (2018). The Global HR Stack: External and Internal Tools and Methodologies Impacting HR. Pp. 35-63 in Claus. L. (ed.), *Global HR Practitioner Handbook*, volume 4. Silverton: Global Immersion Press; Claus, L. & Arens, L. (2019). *#ZigZagHR: Why the Best HR is no Longer HR*. Silverton, OR: Global Immer-sion Press.
9. Boskma, W., Buizer, M., van de Hoef, N, Peters, G. & Zelen, W. (2017). *Agile HR*. Nubiz.
10. Cappelli, P. & Tavis, A. (2018) "HR goes Agile," *Harvard Business Review*, 96(2): 46-52.
11. Rigby, D.K., Sutherland, J. & Takeuchi. H. (2016). "Embracing agile," *Harvard Business Review*, 94(5): 41-50.

GUIDED READING QUESTIONS

1. What is the difference between a process and a project?

2. How does continuous improvement differ from reengineering?

3. What are the seven TQM tools? Provide a workplace application for each.

4. How does waterfall project management differ from agile project management?

5. What is Kanban?

6. What is Scrum?

7. For which type of projects are waterfall vs agile project management better suited?

FOLLOW-UP CRITICAL THINKING QUESTIONS

1. What is my major takeaway from this reading?

2. What do I already know about this subject?

3. What follow-up questions do I have about this?

4. How can I apply this in real life?

KEY TERMS

Agile project management
Backlog grooming
Burn down chart
Chunking
Communication management
Continuous improvement
Cost management
Daily scrum
HR management
Kanban
Personas
Process
Procurement management
Product backlog
Product owner
Project
Project charter
Quality management
Responsibility assignment matrix (RACI)
Reengineering
Release plan
Risk management
Scope management
Scrum
Scrum Master
Scrum Team
Six Sigma
Sprint
Spring retrospective
Stakeholder management
Standup meeting
Team portfolio management (TPM)
Time management
Total quality management (TQM)
User story
Waterfall project management
Work breakdown structure

LEARNING ASSESSMENT

Critically reflect on the content and the different concepts in this module and rate your own competency using the assessment scale.

Competency	I never heard of it	I heard of it but have limited knowledge of it	I can reasonably explain it to others	I have used it, done it, applied it
Process management	0	1	2	3
Project management	0	1	2	3
TQM	0	1	2	3
Six Sigma	0	1	2	3
Customer obsession	0	1	2	3
Reengineering	0	1	2	3
Agile management	0	1	2	3

MODULAR-SPECIFIC ASSESSMENT

12 Questions to Ask Your Organization About Agile Adoption

Is your organization ready for agile management? Twelve quick questions allow to determine if an organization can adapt to Agile and be successful.

Source: Nanjundappa, N. (2012). 12 Questions to Ask Your Organization About Agile Adoption, August 9. https://www.solutionsiq.com/resource/blog-post/12-questions-to-ask-your-organization-about-agile-adoption/

VIGNETTE

AGILE AND AGILE HR LITE[1]

In response to the demands imposed by the 4th industrial revolution, HR competencies—in terms of traditional HR knowledge and functions—have to be augmented with new skills, tools, and capabilities. HR must do what IT has coined as 'stack'—manage people and processes across an organization using a collection of technologies and solutions. Along with the traditional HR capabilities, these tools are derived and layered—literally stacked—from related management disciplines long ignored by HR. Agile management is one of the four pillars of the 'HR stack' (later renamed '#ZigZagHR-Stack') and an integral part of a new, progressive, and flexible HR architecture.[2]

Three basic principles are at the core of agile, namely the primacy of the customer, descaling work for small teams, and the organization as a network.[3] The application of these agile principles requires a cultural and structural transformation in the way people work in organizations There are two ways in which agile and HR come together. First, HR supports the agile organization by developing the culture and structure necessary for agile and ensuring people have the needed competencies to use prevalent agile methods. Second, HR manages its own function, processes, and staff in an agile manner. Agile concepts and tools have already shown promise in their HR applications responding to the disruption challenges and are defining a new future for HR.

There is a lot of buzz in HR about agile today. For over a decade, Agile HR pioneers and influencers—such as Riina Hellström (Finland) and Pia-Maria Thorén (Sweden)—are promoting the learning and development of agile competencies among HR practitioners and have helped HR people and their organizations move towards a culture of increasing agility. As of today, 300-plus HR professionals worldwide are the signatories of the Agile HR Manifesto aiming to work according to its principles. Yet, agile HR—or even 'agile lite,' the application of general principles without adopting all the tools and protocols from the tech world[4]—is still in its infancy in most companies beyond recognizable IT/data-driven adopters such as Amazon, Apple, Facebook, Google, and Microsoft. One notable exception is ING, a global bank with 50,000 employees headquartered in the Netherlands.

To meet the evolving expectations and needs of its external clients (i.e., users of bank services), ING needed to become lean and flexible as an organization. Internally, this required a change in its long-held, traditional, siloed organizational culture and the introduction of collaborative processes throughout the bank. This digital transformation of ING—from a traditional bank to an agile bank—led to both cultural and structural changes. New and existing employees needed onboarding in the new ways of thinking and working and work required a re-organization. The agile structure of the bank looks as follows:

- '**Squads**'—small interdisciplinary teams collaborating together and responsible for end-to-end processes. Task product owner is responsible for what the squad does, the product backlog, and determining priorities;
- '**Chapters**'—members of different squads from the same discipline. Chapter leads are responsible for how jobs are tackled;
- '**Tribes**'—a collection of squads connecting with one another and assuming coordination among squads (less than 150 people). Tribe leads are responsible for knowledge sharing, establishing priorities, budget allocation, and interfacing with other tribes;
- **Agile coach**—coaches individuals and squads and allows them to grow.

This agile structure allows people to collaborate and connect with others in a broader ecosystem within the bank as well as with the services of other companies customers rely on.

In the same vain, HR at ING Bank added an agile overlay to its HR structures. It connects the HR Business Partners (who are supporting the management team and business leaders in their unit), People Services (the administrative transactional HR activities) and Communities of Excellence (HR thought leaders in their field of expertise who share best practice). Squads focusing on four different areas (ways of working; craftsmanship & leadership; talent acquisition & management; and performance management) now overlay the HR organization. This partial restructuring of the HR organization allows HR decisions to be made at the level of expertise, empowers people to experiment with HR solutions that are co-developed with customers, customized to employee needs, and tested out through iterations and experimentation. The HR organization is not only becoming more flexible but throughout their career, HR people can move more easily from project to project, gain new experiences, and learn. As agile means flexibility, the structure is evolving as the needs are changing. As Maarten Van Beek, HR Director Benelux for ING, reflects "*Agile HR is more than a methodology and a skillset. It is a philosophy that not only fits the digital tempo of the bank itself, but rewards and encourages learning and collaboration in HR and throughout the bank.*"

One of most valuable aspects of Agile for HR is the frequent touchpoints to get customer feedback. Traditional HR says to employees, "*we know what you need and is best for you as an employee, HR will create a program that adds value, and you will use it since the HR initiative will be great for you.*" Agile HR says, "*based on your feedback we see a need, we want your input from brainstorming to implementation, and we want the HR program to be a value to you so you can support and use it.*"

REFERENCES

1. This vignette was prepared by Professor Lisbeth Claus for the sole purpose of illustrating a global HR practice for instructional objectives. Global HR in Action © 2020, Global Immersion Press, All Rights Reserved.
2. Claus, L., & Baker, S. (2018). The Global HR Stack: External and Internal Tools and Methodologies Impacting HR. Pp. 35-63 in Claus. L. (ed.), *Global HR Practitioner Handbook*, volume 4. Silverton: Global Immersion Press; Claus, L. & Arens, L. (2019). *#ZigZagHR: Why the Best HR is no Longer HR*. Silverton, OR: Global Immersion Press.
3. Dunning, S. (2018). *Can HR Become Agile*? March 11 (Accessed: February 6, 2020). https://www.forbes.com/sites/stevedenning/2018/03/11/can-hr-become-agile/#462fb5284ae3
4. Cappelli, P. & Tavis, A. (2018) 'HR Goes Agile', *Harvard Business Review*, March-April, 96(2):46-52.
5. For a detailed overview of Agile at ING Bank, see: Van Beek, M. & Abelen, E. (2016). *Creating Sustainable Impact with Agile HR*. October 26 (Accessed: February 6, 2020). https://www.youtube.com/watch?v=phLjOUxkhFk

GUIDED READING QUESTIONS

1. What is agile?
2. How is agile applicable to HR?

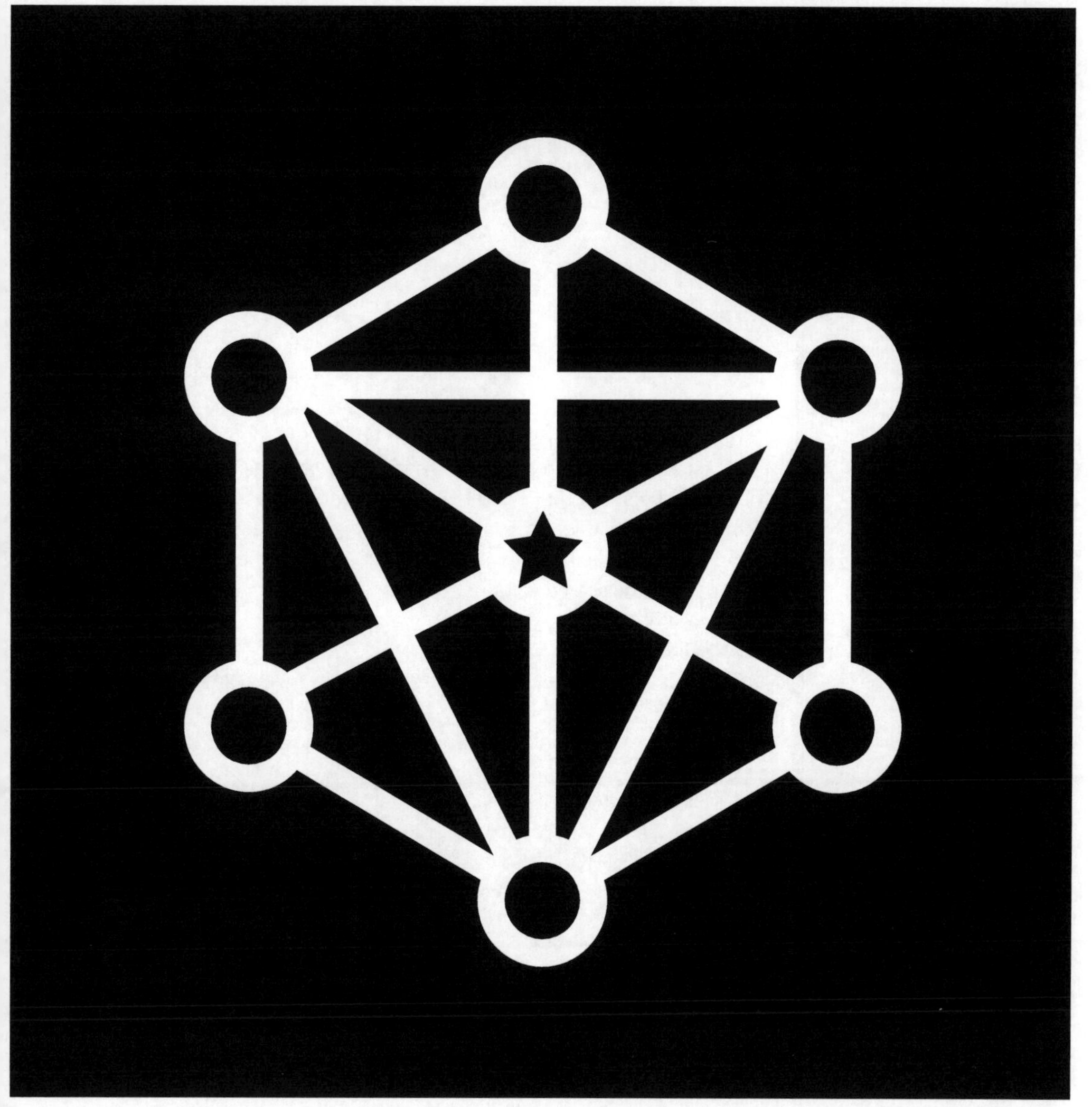

MODULE ELEVEN

TALENT MANAGEMENT REINVENTED

MODULE ELEVEN

TALENT MANAGEMENT REINVENTED

DESCRIPTION

Companies have been using a combination of different strategic and tactical talent management approaches and processes to ensure they have the talent they need to meet their objectives. This module introduces a new talent management paradigm (dynamic open talent) to build capacity and meet workers' expectations in the context of the current 4th industrial revolution.

LEARNING OBJECTIVES

Upon completing the learning experience, you will be able to:

- Describe the 'dynamic open talent' paradigm
- Identify the value of different talent management strategies
- List and define talent management tactics

GUIDING QUESTION

How does a company build capacity and acquire and retain high performing talent?

STEVEN manages the Global Mobility team at a large pharmaceutical company. His team was asked to partner with Global Marketing teams from around the world to build digital marketing capabilities in China. Steven and his team helped the business craft a plan to inpatriate three high potentials in digital marketing roles from China to the headquarters in Switzerland for a short-term assignment and orchestrate a long-term expatriation assignment of an Australian digital expert to Beijing for a period of three years.

JADEN and ANDRE are both talented millennials with superb credentials and newly minted university degrees. While Andre is pursuing a job and career with an established employer, Jaden prefers to string together a number of gigs as a freelancer. Andre believes that being hired as an employee will provide him with a steady income, more benefits, and greater security while Jaden prefers the flexibility to work hard for intense periods of time and then take time off to travel the world.

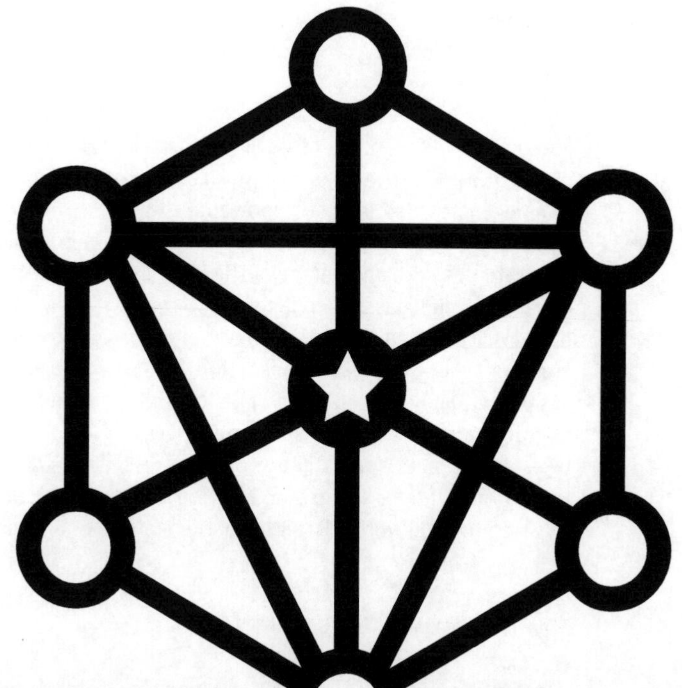

IS TALENT MANAGEMENT PASSE?

Simply defined, talent management is the ability to attract, develop, and retain talent—beyond talent acquisition—and encompasses the entire experience of the employee journey. Rapid changes in demographics, technology, and globalization are globally impacting the context of work and the worker. This new context is disrupting the current talent management practices of HR as they have known for the last two decades. Progressive companies have realized talent management practices of most companies are no longer meeting the needs of workforce. Instead, they now focus on developing a meaningful employee experience to attract and nurture the skill set they need rather than relying on their established HR practices.

Talent management is the key differentiator and a major—if not "the" major—source of competitive advantage. Today, it is appropriate to ask ourselves the question, "*Is talent management passé*?" Nowadays, managers need to think about developing talent for 2-4 years, not 20-40 years. Prospective talent might be more interested in a 'career' brand versus an 'employer' brand. Some have concluded that the 21st century context of work and the worker requires us to rethink traditional talent management policies, practices, and structures as the talent management practices developed and refined during the past two decades were good and have served us well, but they are no longer sufficient today and definitely won't be in the future.[1]

Paradigm shifts do not necessarily abolish some of the true and proven best practices of the old thinking—provided they still add value—but instead radically change the discourse. Let's illustrate this with an analogy of the half-empty/half-full glass when it comes to the evolving HR and talent management practices. Traditional HR focuses on transactional activities mainly related to compliance and operational issues (glass half-empty). This type of HR practice can still be observed in many organizations worldwide—typically in small companies with HR departments staffed primarily with administrative personnel. Strategic talent management designs and optimizes processes to serve the competitive human capital needs of the organization as the primary HR customer (glass half-full). As the context is changing dramatically today, there is a need to rethink HR's value proposition once again and redesign talent management— to fill the half-full glass yet again, this time to capacity (or all the way to fullness) by focusing on the employee/worker customer experience and looking for the sweet spot where talent management practices are good for both the worker AND the employer. That's what new talent management architecture in progressive companies is all about.[2]

THE NEW TALENT MANAGEMENT ARCHITECTURE

The new personalized and customized talent management architecture is simple, authentic, responsive, and transparent. The new talent management value proposition is evolving from talent acquisition—grounded in policies and procedures—to designer or architect of worker experiences. Building a new organizational talent management architecture involves a great deal of thinking to design a productive and meaningful experience in the physical, technological, and cultural environment of our companies through solutions that are compelling, enjoyable, simple, and customized for different employee personas. HR and talent management must get away from a 'one program fits all' mentality and think about building an organizational talent architecture that allows customizing programs to specific employee segments. The architecture is all about creating an employee experience through HR solutions that are at the intersection of the need and expectations of the employees and the talent requirements of the organization. Yet, HR and talent management must still meet existing requirements in terms of building capacity and being legally compliant, culturally appropriate, equitable, and fair. The true talent management challenge is about a commitment to truly make a difference in the life of organizations and their talent—whether they are employees or part of the larger contingent workforce.

Capacity Building

Organizations need to build capacity and develop the resources necessary to pursue their mission, achieve their vision, and execute on their strategic objectives. Capacity building is the process by which organizations acquire, develop, and retain the competencies and the capabilities to perform at a greater capacity. Building capacity by developing and strengthening the human and organizational resources is one of the most critical activities of management. It requires competencies, capabilities, and capacities supported by an organizational infrastructure and management culture.

- **Competencies**—or the knowledge, skills, abilities and other person-related factors (KSAOs) of its talent and their level of engagement;
- **Capabilities**—or the collective ability of teams (and/or systems) to do something either inside or outside the system including the quantity and quality of the workforce need;
- **Capacity**—or the processes of education, development, and change enabling people, organizations, and systems to innovate and respond to organizational needs.

Capacity building starts with workforce planning or "a disciplined business process that ensures that current decisions and actions impacting the workforce are aligned with the strategic needs of the enterprise"3 and entails an organizational skill gap analysis aligning short-term workforce planning with the current shorter average job tenure of an employee. Capability building must be supported by an organizational infrastructure, workplace locations, equipment, and workplace operations embedded in an overall organizational culture nurturing the employee experience (EX).

Workforce Expectations

Talent is a competitive advantage. After all, people—and their capacity to learn and innovate—are a main differentiator in creating competitive advantage. As a result, to attract and retain that talent, employers are required to consider new workforce expectations of different segments of the workforce with regard to diversity and inclusion, pay equity, development, flexibility, and global opportunities.

- **D&I**—the talent expects diversity, inclusion, and belonging and the ability to pursue their passion in an authentic manner;
- **Equity**—there is a growing desire of the talent for greater equity in terms of pay and opportunities;
- **Development**—the talent expects learning and development opportunities, fluidity, and opportunities for upskilling (learning or teaching workers new skills) and reskilling (learning or teaching workers new skills to be able to do a different job in or outside the company);
- **Flexibility**—the talent expects greater flexibility in working from anywhere at any time;
- **Global opportunities**—the talent wants to explore work opportunities around the world and take advantage of cross-border deployment and companies want to attract the talent, wherever the talent resides in the world.

STRATEGIC TALENT MANAGEMENT CHOICES

When it comes to talent management, (global) organizations must answer some fundamental questions and make a number of strategic choices based on their answers to these questions.

Talent Management Approach

Revolves around the question: Which talent management approach should global organizations use?

The leading talent management approaches that have evolved during the past decades are being challenged by a more dynamic and open talent paradigm. As the standard for talent management is rising, today's successful global organizations may favor one strategic approach. They tend to incorporate many elements of the different approaches in the management of their human capital and experiment with new ways of thinking augmented by information technology and artificial intelligence.

Geographic Location

Revolves around the question: Where will organizations deploy their people around the world? Global organizations must decide where in the world their talent pool is needed both today and the future, and where they will physically, as well as virtually, locate their human capital geographically taking into account geopolitical issues and concerns. Such intricate HR planning takes both a short- and long-term view in terms of where the needs of the organization are (and likely will be) with regard to international expansion, customer growth, and company resources (raw materials as well as human competencies). The location of human capital— and the corresponding nexus of work—has tremendous cost, productivity, and tax ramifications for global organizations. Increasingly, the use of a remote workforce is being considered—letting the work migrate to where the talent lives rather than bringing the talent to the office.

Global Sourcing

Revolves around the question: What employment status will organizations grant their human capital? Global organizations tend to use a combination of hired employees (i.e., developed inside the organization, sourced outside of the organization and brought in, or insourced in shared services), co-sourcing, outsourcing, and open sourcing of human capital. Each sourcing choice has advantages and disadvantages, but the total configuration and balance of different sources of human capital also have tremendous organizational implications. These choices are not just a question of internal and external sources of recruitment, but strategic decisions as to where to integrate the human capital in the supply chain of goods and services. Not only does the type of sourcing have cost implications for organizations, but it also blurs the lines of traditional employment contracts and extends the notion of human capital as both customer (employee) and supplier (contactor). While it may provide the organization with added flexibility in finding the talent when needed and HR planning, it engenders a number of other considerations regarding the rights and obligations of the employer and the worker—whether it's an employee or a part of the contingent workforce such as contractor, freelancer, or gig worker.

Global Deployment

Revolves around the question: How will organizations deploy their human capital across borders?
Global organizations must decide whether they will deploy employees locally or across borders and determine which staffing approach is most appropriate for their employees (e.g., ethnocentric, polycentric, regiocentric, or geocentric staffing).[4]

Global-Local Staffing Plans

Revolves around the question: How do global organizations develop worldwide staffing plans?
The implementation of talent management strategies must be reflected in the tactical staffing plans. Global HR staffing plans are not just the sum of the local country staffing plans, but an integration of the organization's local and global needs. To truly reflect the competitive advantage that an organization can achieve through global talent management, the functional talent management processes must be globally integrated through the design of company-wide processes that are adaptable to local requirements in their implementation. Although talent management processes are standardized in their design, local staffing challenges must be understood and localized to meet local legal and cultural requirements.

Global Recruiting and Retention

Revolves around the question: How do global organizations effectively recruit and retain their human capital in each location?
The use of social media in the recruitment process for globally mobile employees is now well entrenched in global organizations. Yet, recruitment practices differ widely based on the legal and cultural environments in the local country. Retention strategies also vary widely by the local context. As a result,

recruitment and employment practices will require 'glocalization'— or a balanced approach between standardized and localized practices.

THE NEW TALENT MANAGEMENT SCENE

With the aging workforce, globalization, and the capabilities of information technology, the increasing need to find a competent workforce and attract the best is ever present. While few employers focus on developing and managing employees with the same effort they dedicate to acquiring them, many companies have implemented employee pulse surveys (daily, monthly, quarterly, annually) to help ensure that a workplace has high morale and retention. With the growing appeal of the gig economy, the allure of self-employment and entrepreneurship, the weakening social contract between employers and employees, the expectations for flexibility, and concerns for work-life integration of a generation of people who may have to work much longer, getting talent on board is only part of the equation.

Digitization has fundamentally changed the structure of work and the worker. To 'uberize' something (the business model of Uber's core service consists of an on-demand transportation technology based on an app connecting drivers and riders and a dynamic pricing algorithm to balance supply with demand) is a term that is now applied to the workforce, meaning to optimize supply and demand of talent via similar methods in order to create an 'on-demand' market.[5] Uberization of talent and the workforce is driven by three converging factors of the digital age: companies need more agility and flexibility; the younger generation thinks entrepreneurially; and digital tools facilitate the connection between companies and talents. The fundamental forces driving change in the future of work requires different organizations and approaches to strategy, talent, and work.

Two individual worker characteristics impact talent management namely the skill level of the worker and new expectations of the workforce.

- **Skill level of the worker**—high-skilled labor usually enjoys a skill premium with either deep T-shaped knowledge (having a skillset in a specialty combined with broader general knowledge) or broad M-shaped knowledge (having more than one specialty skillset in addition to the broader integration of those specialty fields) and is poised for great employability augmenting artificial intelligence. However, the rest of the labor continuum faces big challenges. Low-skilled labor is bound by minimum wage requirements and is likely to be eliminated and disrupted by new technologies. Medium-skilled talent is vulnerable to becoming irrelevant unless they continue upgrading their skills through lifelong learning.
- **New workforce expectations**—the changing expectations of the workforce are largely attributed to millennials are defined by culture, passion, meaning, and collaboration. Millennials also have a different value system, mainly seeking autonomy, technology, and flexibility.

The talent also expects a new social contract in response to the changing socio-political and legal environments. The old social contract of the 3rd industrial revolution focused on commitment and stability. However, this contract has slowly become irrelevant. Employees expect employers to act as a social enterprise, which leads to a dynamic open talent market that needs to be managed and reconciled by various stakeholders.

DYNAMIC OPEN TALENT[6]

'Dynamic Open Talent' (DOT) is a strategy to reduce the uncertainty of the supply and demand of labor in a firm at the global level by engaging diverse workers in various employment/work arrangements. This is done in a flexible and agile manner across the internal and external boundaries of the organization to meet the human capital needs of the firm, the expectations of the talent on their career journey, and the broader needs of society.

DOT is an ecosystem with five interrelated dimensions (portfolio of talent, flexibility, work agility, talent fluidity, and technology/data enabled) and has argumentation for it grounded in professional and academic literature (see 11-1).

Portfolio of Talent

Talent portfolios today are similar to an operational supply chain decision. Non-employees as talent have generated a stream of new employment categories and classifications, causing an ill-defined area of work to form on the talent continuum. The dual status reference (employee vs. contractor) is likely due to legal reasons since for an employer, having the correct classification is important. It goes beyond legal compliance and involves many HR-related policies and practices. It is important to develop a standard employment classification for the non-employee workforce around the world due to its growth on the talent continuum.

Flexibility

Talent increasingly desires flexibility—the ability to work anytime and anywhere—ever since technology untethered the worker from the workplace. This presents new challenges and opportunities for the employer, although now organizations must use different criteria to determine how flexible they can be with their talent.

Work Agility

Agile, now applied to management, has become a necessity in today's workplace. Work agility places talent in an assignment rather than a role, which can be quickly set up and easily changed. This means that for talent acquisition, top talent is catered to for its strengths rather than attempting to fill an existing position with someone weaker. In this dynamic open talent market, people move freely from project to project and organization to organization due to the application of agile HR.

11-1. The Dynamic Open Talent Model

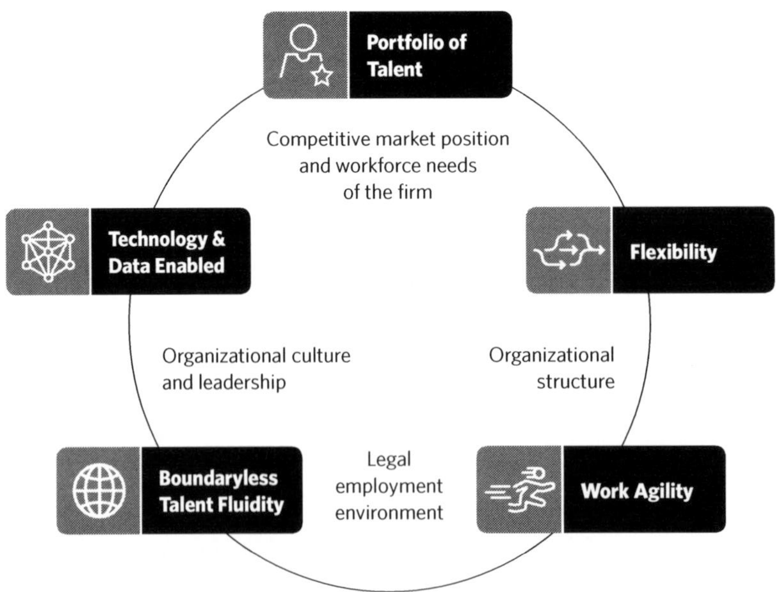

Source: Claus, L. & Monaghan, D (2019). *Dynamic Open Talent: A Template for Developing, Implementing, Supporting and Measuring a Dynamic Open Talent (DOT) Strategy for a Global Company*. Woodinville, WA: HR Roundtable and Global HR Consortium.

Boundaryless Talent Fluidity—Talent moves fluidly across the boundaries in a dynamic open talent market. 'Hoarding talent' or purposely not identifying high performers so they are not removed from specific department to develop and grow in another part of the organization is the opposite of internal talent fluidity. Internal talent mobility refers to the movement of employees within an organization, tending to be focused on lateral moves, new assignments, and shorter project-based initiatives. The focus of internal talent mobility is to let people try new roles, experiment, and stretch themselves. Boundaryless and protean careers focus on individual career development. A boundaryless career focuses on equalizing the power relationship between the manager and talent by letting people move more freely within the organization, while a protean career focuses on a personally meaningful and purposeful career. External mobility is a career path that allows workers to move beyond the organization and allows the talent to focus on employability and build more resilient careers.

Technology and Data-Enabled—New technology is the backbone of the dynamic open talent market enabled through the utilizations of integrated platforms, tools, and data, offering many opportunities as well as many issues. Some companies do not have the technology and analytical skills to operate in this new environment, while others are unable to protect private data despite their push to use it. Even the companies making informed decisions with technology still have a lot to learn from the data. The new technology creates new challenges around employee and customer data privacy and authenticity (i.e., is also the person we think he/she is).
A sustainable talent management system of a successful organization focuses on balancing the three constituencies: the internal customer or talent (employee & contingent workforce); the external customer the organization serves; and ultimately the stock and other stakeholders. A dynamic open talent approach to talent management directly contrasts a static and closed talent approach. The closed approach was better fit for a world of work

11.2. Open vs Closed Talent Management Systems

Closed	Open
Hierarchy	Networks
Jobs	Roles
Employees	Workforce
9-5 office	Work anytime anywhere
Siloed	Open & transparent
Decision-making without data	Evidence-based decision-making
Different systems	Integrated platforms
Metrics & benchmarks	Predictive analytics

and the worker that had greater certainty and stability (3rd industrial revolution). A dynamic open talent approach is more suited for the uncertainty and talent shortages in the 4th industrial revolution and the needs and expectations of its key stakeholders, namely the talent, the organization, and the society at large (see 11-2).

As the external context of work is pushing employers to be more open in their talent management approaches, some companies (such as Amazon, Uber, Google, Siemens, and Unilever, to name a few) have led the way adopting the five dimensions of dynamic open talent way beyond hiring people on the talent continuum. However, this means talent management, as it has evolved over the past quarter century, is totally obsolete. On the contrary, there are valuable lessons to be learned from existing talent management approaches. Therefore, in the next section, we review the evolution of talent management and the respective value of each approach. Companies can no longer 'copy and paste' HR best practices from others. Employers must learn to experiment, customize while they 'continue' to do what adds value, 'stop' doing what does not add value, and 'start' innovating with new practices. We call that '#ZigZagging' in HR.[7]

EVOLUTION OF TALENT MANAGEMENT

Since the 2001 publication of The War for Talent by Michaels, Handfield-Jones et al., the term talent management has popped up.[8] Talent management has become the essence of global success for organizations. In spite of high unemployment rates in many parts of the world, organizations are vying for the often-scarce high level competencies of available talent and perfect fit between people within the organization itself.

The human capital challenges faced by global organizations have become known as 'global talent management' (GTM) challenges. They include the need to: (a) reduce and remove talent in order to lower the cost of operations; (b) locate and relocate operations around the world; and (c) obtain equally competent talent anywhere in the world at lower wages.[9] Talent management is the set of sustainable organizational strategies that uses human capital to the competitive advantage of the organization, as well as a portfolio of integrated HR activities that result in getting the right number of people in the right location at the right price with the right competencies and motivation.[10] Hence, the definition of talent management includes both strategic and tactical components

Various strategic approaches to talent management have come to the forefront of HR management literature during the past two decades. These views on talent management have been proposed by various thought leaders in their bestselling management books. Each one has discussed talent management approaches using contributory knowledge from a particular business discipline.

Traditional HR Approach

The traditional HR approach to talent management is based on competency management, performance management, succession planning, and internal development of the talent pipeline, with a focus on high potential identification and the acceleration of talent at various levels of the organization. Labor is sourced both internally and externally. In this approach, HR is often forced to switch between recruitment and retrenchment as a result of fluctuating economic cycles. It is now widely recognized that transactional HR activities are table stakes (or hygiene factors) which are a necessary condition, but by and of themselves do not add value to the organization.[11]

Traditional talent management processes in use today were developed 50 years ago and are no longer appropriate for today's uncertain world. Internal development is too slow and risky, and outside hiring is too expensive and disruptive to the organization.[12] While all of the traditional tactical HR talent management components need to be in place, relying solely on tactical HR processes and failing to use a more strategic approach to talent management may not add value to the organization or achieve its intended strategic objectives in terms of human capital contribution.

Talent 'churn' is not a sustainable approach to talent management. HR must develop a talent management strategy that focuses both on recruitment and retention of talent. In the age of jobs having a high probability of being disrupted and/or taken over by artificial intelligence, HR must focus more on roles (open approach) rather than jobs (closed approach) and include the upskilling and reskilling in its workforce planning.

Signaling and Stratification Approach

Based on Ed Michaels, Helen Handfield-Jones, and Beth Axelrod's 2001 book, *The War for Talent*,[13] this talent management approach applies marketing concepts of signaling and stratification to talent management. In order to effectively attract, develop, and retain the best talent, organizations focus heavily on creative HR practices. This is done through signaling an attractive employee value proposition (EVP) to the potential market of employees and the use of employment branding before, during, and after employment. By focusing on an EVP ("Why should I come and work for you?"), companies attract the best talent because they are 'the best place to work.' Four basic brand propositions that attract employees are:

1. **Go with the winner**—employees are most interested in growth and advancement;
2. **Big risk, big rewards**—employees value advancement and compensation;
3. **Save the world**—employees need an inspiring mission;
4. **Lifestyle**—employees seek flexibility and a good fit with the boss.

Once on board, employees are stratified into A-B-C employees through the performance management system. Each of these stratification levels has to be managed appropriately to achieve employee and organizational goals. Organizations manage their talent by investing heavily in the A-players,[14] growing B-contributors solidly,[15] and acting decisively with C-players.[16]

(2.) What we learned from this approach that still applies today is that talent is not uniform whether in its performance, persona (who they are) or expectations (what they want). Finding the sweet spot between what's both good for the worker and the employer, contributes to making the worker an internal customer and stakeholder of the organization.

Decision-Science Approach

In their 2007 book, *Beyond HR*, John Boudreau and Peter Ramstad[17] develop the notion of pivotal talentship. Talentship is building organizational effectiveness by improving decisions that affect or depend on human capital where they make the biggest strategic difference. Only a small number of all jobs are pivotal (i.e., the performance of talent and organization in these roles makes the biggest difference). Thus, an investment in pivotal talent yields marginal (a small change produces a large increment) rather than average value.

According to Boudreau and Ramstad decision science for talent includes five elements:

1. **A decision framework**—defines the logical connection between the decisions about a resource and the organization's ultimate goals. Investments in programs and practices produce performance of organization elements and talent pools and lead to the organization's sustainable strategic success.
2. **Management system's integration**—includes integrating management systems outside of the HR function as well as talent management systems within the HR function.
3. **Shared mental models**—a common understanding of the talent decisions outside of the HR function with executives, managers, supervisors and employees.
4. **Data, measurement, and analysis** aligned with the decision framework and measures to support strategic decisions. HR programs must consider three anchor points: efficiency (how investments affect programs and practices), effectiveness (how programs and practices affect talent and organizational pools), and impact (how talent and organization pools affect sustainable strategic success).
5. **Focus on optimization**, namely how decisions can optimize the return from a resource by balancing trade-offs and optimize a portfolio of HR practices against the organization's unique resource opportunity costs and constraints.

What we learned from this approach that still applies today is that the workforce is made up of pivotal talent key to organizational success and other talent that can more easily be replaced. While not all talent is created equal—and is rewarded differently—all workers need a certain amount of investment to align their work with the goals of the organization.

Supply Chain Management Approach

In his 2008 book, *Talent on Demand*, Peter Cappelli[18] develops a supply chain perspective by applying operations principles to talent management. This talent management framework is based on four core principles for matching talent supply and demand while reducing uncertainties:

1. Make and buy to manage demand-side risk;
2. Reduce the uncertainty in talent demand;
3. Earn a return on investment in developing employees;
4. Balance employee interests by using an internal market.

The first two talent management principles aim at reducing the uncertainty on the demand side. Organizations should both 'make and buy' to manage risk by underestimating the need for talent and hiring from outside to make up for shortfalls. To adapt to the uncertainty in talent demand, they must make better talent predictions. This is done by having smaller cohorts come in more frequently, breaking up development programs into shorter units, and creating an organization-wide pool that can be allocated among different units. The other two principles aim at reducing the uncertainty on the supply side. This is achieved by improving the return on investment in developing employees, getting employees to share in the cost of development, and maintaining relationships with former employees. Finally, employers need to preserve the investment in employees by balancing employee-employer interests.

What we learned from this approach that still applies today is that talent is the key resource of the organization that must be managed like all other operational resources including the decision to make (as employees) and/or buy the talent (as independent contractors).

The Strategic Management Approach
In their 2009 book, *The Differentiated Workforce*, Brian Becker, Mark Huselid, and Richard Beatty[19] argue for a strategic human capital approach that consists of a four-step process built upon the previous talent management approaches:

1. Identify the strategic capabilities of the organization.
2. Identify 'A' positions in those core capabilities.
3. Place 'A' players in these positions.
4. Get buy-in for the human capital plan throughout the organization.

Such a strategic differentiation of the workforce is believed to have a positive impact on the overall performance of the organization. People capability are a strategic comparative advantage and companies must match the talent with these core capabilities.

Globally Integrated Approach
When using a globally integrated talent management approach, people management strategies are looked at from a global rather than a purely domestic perspective. The opportunity to tap into talent is much broader in a global market than a domestic market. Global organizations must make a number of specific staffing decisions with regard to their human capital. A global organization that uses a globally integrated talent management approach has been called a 'talent factory.'[20] Talent factories are organizations that marry *functionality* (rigorous talent processes that support strategic and cultural objectives) and *vitality* (emotional commitment by management that is reflected in their daily actions). The 'functionality wheel' of talent management includes HR processes such as sourcing, assimilation, development, deployment, performance management, rewards, engagement, and retention. The 'vitality wheel' focuses on the commitment, engagement, and accountability of four distinct groups in the organization: the top executive team, line management, human resources, and the talent pool itself.

A talent management approach that works in one part of the world may not work in another one and will need to be localized to scale effectively in a different legal, structural, and cultural environment.

Today, companies have incorporated elements of these six different approaches in their talent acquisition practices and the building of their employee talent capacity (see 11.2).

TALENT MANAGEMENT TACTICS
In spite of the digitization of HR, the fundamental talent management building blocks have not really changed and must be in

11-2. Traditional Talent Management Approaches (1990-2015)

Discipline	Approach	Concept
HR	Traditional HR	Switch between recruitment and retrenchment of talent. Focuses on recruitment rather than retention of talent.
Marketing	Signaling and stratification	Consider workforce as internal customers. Have an attractive employee value proposition. Segment the talent based on performance.
Management	Decision science	Pivotal talent makes the biggest difference and must get a disproportionate share of investment.
Operations	Supply chain management	Reduce the uncertainty of the supply and demand for talent.
Strategy	Strategic management	Put 'A' players in 'A' positions.
Global	Global integration	Integrate 'functionality' and 'vitality' of the talent. Localize standardized HR processes.

place. The talent management buildings blocks are: plan for talent; acquire talent; deploy talent; and develop and retain talent. Managing each of these tactical functions with optimized processes allow for a portfolio HR effect of results (see 11-3).

Today, many aspects of these HR tactics can be augmented with information technology and artificial intelligence. The benefits include scaling, reducing the unconscious bias, and giving more access and control to the talent by eliminating the middle (HR) person.

TALENT MANAGEMENT ANALYTICS

No talent management strategy is complete without data analytics. There are three kinds of metrics that organizations can use to better understand and evaluate the impact of HR activities and to influence business strategy and performance.[21]

- **Efficiency**—relates to how well the HR function does its basic administrative tasks (e.g., productivity and cost measures).
- **Effectiveness**—is whether HR programs and practices have the intended effect on the people or talent pools toward which they are directed (e.g., training and development, satisfaction surveys, talent management metrics).
- **Impact**—relates to the impact of HR programs and practices on developing and optimizing the capabilities and core competencies of the organization (e.g., changes in performance of business processes when talent is improved and HR practices are introduced).

SHOULD TALENT MANAGEMENT BE A PROFIT CENTER?

An interesting idea coming out of the dynamic open talent approach is whether HR should become a profit center for the organization rather than simply an overhead staff function. This question goes much farther than a focus on return on investment (ROI) of an HR intervention. Instead, it calls for whether companies with successful talent management approaches should sell their processes, systems, learning, and data capabilities to other companies as a product and become a profit center. This is a conversation progressive HR companies are starting to have. For example, Amazon has developed several people management tools (e.g., a tool to predict retention) but is not keen on sharing this as they like to retain their comparative advantage the tool provides and keep the intellectual property in house. Other companies such as IBM and Microsoft are actively selling their talent management applications and processes to other HR departments. Several ex-CHROs of leading companies have also started their own companies selling HR solutions—products and services—to other companies. ▌

11-3. HR Talent Management Tactics

Plan for talent	HR planning and forecasting	What is quantity and quality of the future workforce?
	Competency management	What are competency models for successful positions?
	Job analysis	What does the job (work packages) entail?
	Job specification	What are the required competencies?
	Job alignment	How are the various positions aligned and rewarded?
	Job evaluation	What is the job valued at?
	Replacement planning	Who will replace any existing positions that open?
	Succession planning	How will I replace my pivotal and leadership positions?
Acquire talent	Employer branding	How and where will I brand myself as an employer?
	Recruitment	What recruitment channels will I use?
	Selection	What selection mechanisms will I use?
	Hiring	What are my hiring practices (including background checks)?
	Background checks	Can the hiring of this potential worker lead to negligent hiring?
	Onboarding	How will I onboard people (total orientation) into their jobs and new positions?
	Ramping up	How long does it take employees to ramp up?
Deploy talent	Staffing choices	What staffing choice and tactics will I use?
	Redeployment	How can I redeploy people (rather than firing them) and proactively reskills?
	Global mobility	Which people will need to cross borders?
Develop and retain talent	Employee experience	What are the experiences of the employee during the employee life cycle?
	Employee engagement	How are employees inspired, empowered, and enabled to reach performance?
	Performance management	What set of activities allows employees to reach performance goals?
	Total rewards	What are the tangible and non-tangible rewards employees received for work done?
	Learning and development	What activities are focused on learning, improving performance, and developing new skills?
	High potential and leadership	How is talent identified and developed in the organization?
	Retention management	How do we create a job and work environment that encourages employees to stay with their current employer?
	Work-life integration	How do we integrate work and life activities?

REFERENCES

1. Claus, L. and Arens, L. (2019). *#ZigZagHR: Why the Best HR is No Longer HR*. Silverton: Global Immersion Press.
2. Claus, L. (2019). "HR disruption: Why We Must Reengineer Talent Management," *Business Quarterly Review*, 22(3): 207-215.
3. Dan L. Ward and Rob Tripp, (2013). Positioned Strategic Workforce. Planning That Gets the Right Person in the Right Job." New York: AMACOM, American Management Association, January 9.
4. Perlmutter, H., & Heenan, D. (1974). "How Multinational Should Your Top Managers Be?" *Harvard Business Review*, 52(6): 121-132.
5. Chamorro-Premuzic, T. (2014). *The Uberisation of Talent: Can the Job Market Really Be Optimised?* March 21 (Accessed: July 25, 2019). https://www.forbes.com/sites/tomaspremuzic/2014/03/21/theuberisation- of-talent-can-the-job-market-really-beoptimised/# 4aaf1d81dded.
6. Claus, L. & Monaghan, D (2019). *Dynamic Open Talent: A Template for Developing, Implementing, Supporting and Measuring a Dynamic Open Talent (DOT) Strategy for a Global Company*. Woodinville: HR Roundtable and Global HR Consortium.
7. Claus, L. and Arens, L. (2019). *#ZigZagHR: Why the Best HR is No Longer HR*. Silverton: Global Immersion Press.
8. Michaels, E., Handfield-Jones, H., & Axelrod, B. (2001). *The War for Talent*. Boston: Harvard Business Press.
9. Claus, L. (2013). "Global Talent Management: An Overview." Pp.117-137 in Lisbeth Claus (ed.), *Global HR Practitioner Handbook*, volume 1. Silverton: Global Immersion Press.
10. Ulrich, D., & Brockbank, W. (2005). *The HR Value Proposition*. Boston: Harvard Business Press.
11. Cappelli, P. (2007). "Talent Management for the Twenty-First Century," *Harvard Business Review*, 86(3): 74-38.
12. Michaels, E., Handfield-Jones, H., & Axelrod, B. (2001). *The War for Talent*. Boston: Harvard Business Press.
13. Ibid.
14. Goffee, R., & Jones, G. (2007). "Leading Clever People," *Harvard Business Review*, 85(3):72-79.
15. DeLong, T., & Vijayaraghavan, V. (2003). "Let's Hear It for B Players," *Harvard Business Review*, 81(6): 96-102.
16. Axelrod, B., Handfield-Jones, H., & Michaels, E. (2001). "A New Game Plan For C Players," *Harvard Business Review* 80(1): 80-88.
17. Boudreau, J., and Ramstad, P. (2007). *Beyond HR: The New Science of Human Capital*. Boston: Harvard Business School Press.
18. Cappelli, P. (2008). *Talent on Demand: Managing Talent in an Age of Uncertainty*. Boston: Harvard Business Press.
19. Becker, B., Huselid, M., & Beatty, R. (2009). *The Differentiated Workforce: Transforming Talent Into Strategic Impact*. Boston: Harvard Business Press.
20. Ready, D., & Conger, J. (2007). "Make Your Company a Talent Factory," *Harvard Business Review*, 85(6): 68-77.
21. Boudreau, J., and Ramstad, P. (2007). *Beyond HR: The New Science of Human Capital*. Boston: Harvard Business School Press.

GUIDED READING QUESTIONS

1. How is 4th industrial revolution impacting talent management?
2. Which strategic talent management choices must (global) organizations make?
3. What is dynamic open talent?
4. How does the 'traditional HR' approach view talent management?
5. How does the 'marketing' approach view talent management?
6. How does the 'supply chain management' approach view talent management?
7. How does the 'decision science' approach view talent management?
8. How does the 'strategic' approach view talent management?
9. How does the 'globally integrated' approach view talent management?
10. What are common tactical HR practices in 'plan, acquire, deploy, and develop'?

FOLLOW-UP CRITICAL THINKING QUESTIONS

1. What is my major takeaway from this reading?

2. What do I already know about this subject?

3. What follow-up questions do I have about this?

4. How can I apply this in real life?

KEY TERMS

Competency management
Contingence workforce
Descriptive analytics
Design thinking
Effectiveness
Efficiency
Employee experience
Experience mapping
Employee engagement
Employee value proposition
Employer branding
Future of work
Global mobility
High potential
Hiring
HR planning and forecasting
Impact
Job alignment
Job analysis
Job evaluation
Job specification
Learning and development
Onboarding
Performance management
Persona
Predictive analytics
Prescriptive analytics
Ramping up
Rapid prototype
Recruitment
Redeployment
Remote worker
Replacement planning
Retention management
Selection
Staffing
Succession planning
Talent management
Total rewards
Touchpoint
Touchpoint management
Workforce planning
Work flexibility
Work-life integration

LEARNING ASSESSMENT

Critically reflect on the content and the different concepts in this module and rate your own competency using the assessment scale.

Competency	I never heard of it	I heard of it but have limited knowledge of it	I can reasonably explain it to others	I have used it, done it, applied it
Dynamic open talent	0	1	2	3
Traditional HR approach to talent management	0	1	2	3
Marketing approach to talent management	0	1	2	3
Supply chain management approach to talent management	0	1	2	3
Decision science approach to talent management	0	1	2	3
Strategic management approach to talent management	0	1	2	3
Globally integrated approach to talent management	0	1	2	3
HR tactics	0	1	2	3

MODULAR-SPECIFIC ASSESSMENT

How would you rate your organization/company on each of the following dimensions of an open talent management system?

Very hierarchy-based	1	2	3	4	5	**Very network-based**
Focus on jobs	1	2	3	4	5	**Focus on roles**
Mostly employees	1	2	3	4	5	**Mostly contract workers**
Work in office 9-5	1	2	3	4	5	**Work anytime anywhere**
Siloed	1	2	3	4	5	**Open & transparent**
Decision-making without data	1	2	3	4	5	**Evidence-based decision-making**
Different stand-alone systems	1	2	3	4	5	**Integrated platforms**
Metrics & benchmarks	1	2	3	4	5	**Predictive analytics**

Source: Adapted from Claus, L. & Monaghan, D (2019). *Dynamic Open Talent: A Template for Developing, Implementing, Supporting and Measuring a Dynamic Open Talent (DOT) Strategy for a Global Company.* Woodinville: HR Roundtable and Global HR Consortium.

VIGNETTE

ENGAGING AND RECRUITING THE BEST CANDIDATES VIA SOCIAL MEDIA AND HR ANALYTICS AT CLEVELAND CLINIC ABU DHABI IN THE UNITED ARAB EMIRATES[1]

In a fiercely competitive talent acquisition climate aimed at acquiring and keeping the best talent, how does one convince talented professionals from all over the world to quit their current job for a new employment opportunity in Abu Dhabi? That is exactly the situation faced by the Talent Acquisition Department of the Cleveland Clinic in Abu Dhabi, UAE. From 2012 through 2014, they used data analytics through social media to build and acquire their pipeline and meet their recruitment goals for a hospital that was not yet in operation but still under construction.

Cleveland Clinic Abu Dhabi, a Mubadala Company, is an extension of the Cleveland Clinic Health System in the USA. This new world-class multispecialty hospital on Al Maryah Island in Abu Dhabi was scheduled to see patients in 2015. Using the U.S.-based Cleveland Clinic model of care, the 364 (expandable to 491) bed hospital was to be staffed with North American board certified (or equivalent) and Health Authority Abu Dhabi licensed physicians. While the physical construction of the building was taking shape, the talent acquisition team had the challenge of building a deep pipeline and keeping these candidates engaged until the official opening of the hospital in 2015. With 85% of the workforce coming from overseas, the talent acquisition team faced a number of additional recruiting challenges: recruiting for a future opportunity rather than a current opening; a lengthy offer-to-start time frame; recruiting candidates (and their families) to move to Abi Dhabi; fierce competition to hire local talent due to Emiratization (nationalization) targets; global competition for professional talent with healthcare and related subject matter expertise; minimal digital interaction with the global community; and limited global awareness of Abu Dhabi as a work destination choice (compared to Dubai).

The global recruiting initiative covered as many as 60 countries with a primary focus on the UAE and other English-speaking countries. Out of a global population of 10 million LinkedIn potentials, there were 700,000 LinkedIn potential candidates in their target markets in MENA (Middle East and North Africa), India, and the Philippines alone. The talent acquisition team used data on the supply and demand of health care professional globally and plotted them to find hidden gems in large supply/low demand locations. This enabled them to differentiate their potential recruitment pool and prioritize specific regions to be targeted on LinkedIn. The team used different webpage versions (or skins) depending on whether the target was IT, Medical, Junior, or Senior staff. For talent that was not as active on LinkedIn, for example nurses, they relied on Facebook and other traditional recruitment methods. Keeping in mind they had to recruit 15% locally, they also developed employer brand awareness through a digital 'come into our office' open house with videos about open positions from three perspectives—the hiring manager, career development, and other employment opportunities. This campaign alone resulted in 8,400 views, 18,000 minutes of video watched, 140 shares, 71 likes, and 0 dislikes. At local events, they digitized the recruitment rooms with touch screen and iPad check-in features. Over 800 UAE nationals participated in these events allowing HR to build a robust local talent pipeline.

Once they reached potential recruits, they had to sell them on the CCAD employee value proposition to entice professionals to move to the UAE. They focused primarily on professional attractiveness such as working for a brand new world-class medical facility, building something from the ground up, being part of a top-notch medical team, and various professional development opportunities. But they also emphasized attractive pay and benefits, the adventure of living as an expatriate in a vibrant city, and opportunities to explore other parts of the world due to their central location.

In April 2015, on the eve of festivities for the grand opening of the hospital, Kevin Ferra, Director of Talent Acquisition, and his team not only had exceeded their recruiting targets, they were able to hand over the logistics of international assignment management to a well-trained and prepared global HR team. As Kevin reflected, "*Today's global recruiter relies on more than HR knowledge and traditional recruitment methods. Modern recruitment relies on savvy professionals who must be able to integrate marketing, social media and HR analytics tools and techniques to attract and acquire the right talent.*"

REFERENCES

1. This vignette was prepared by Professor Lisbeth Claus for the sole purpose of illustrating a global HR practice for instructional objectives. This vignette is based on interviews with the HR team at the Cleveland Clinic Abu Dhabi and information taken from https://www.youtube.com/watch?v=oCfLazebXY4

GUIDED READING QUESTIONS

1. What would attract a successful healthcare professional to leave their current position and accept a job offer at CCAD?
2. What are nationalization targets (e.g., in Qatar, Saudi Arabia, UAE) and how do they impact recruiting?
3. What is the role of social media (especially LinkedIn and Facebook) in global recruiting?

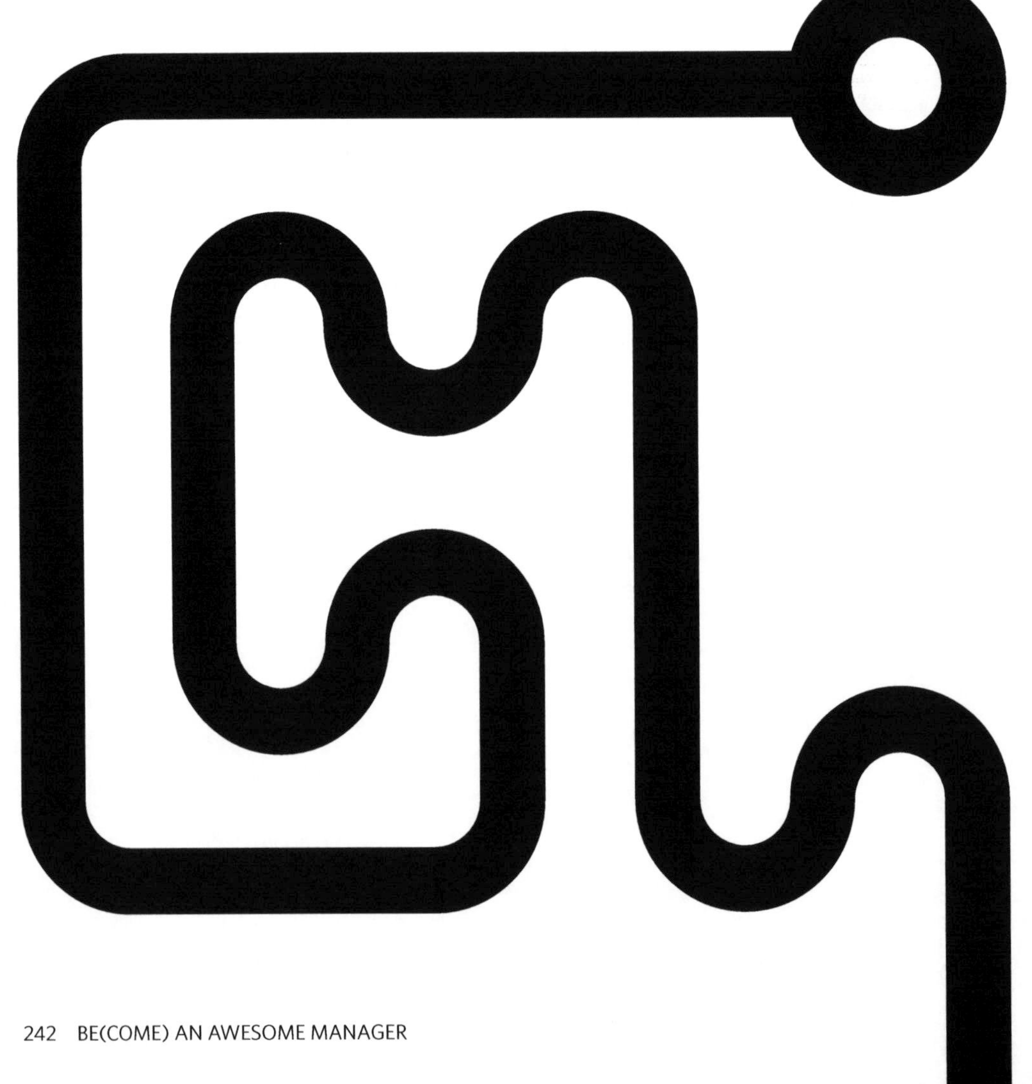

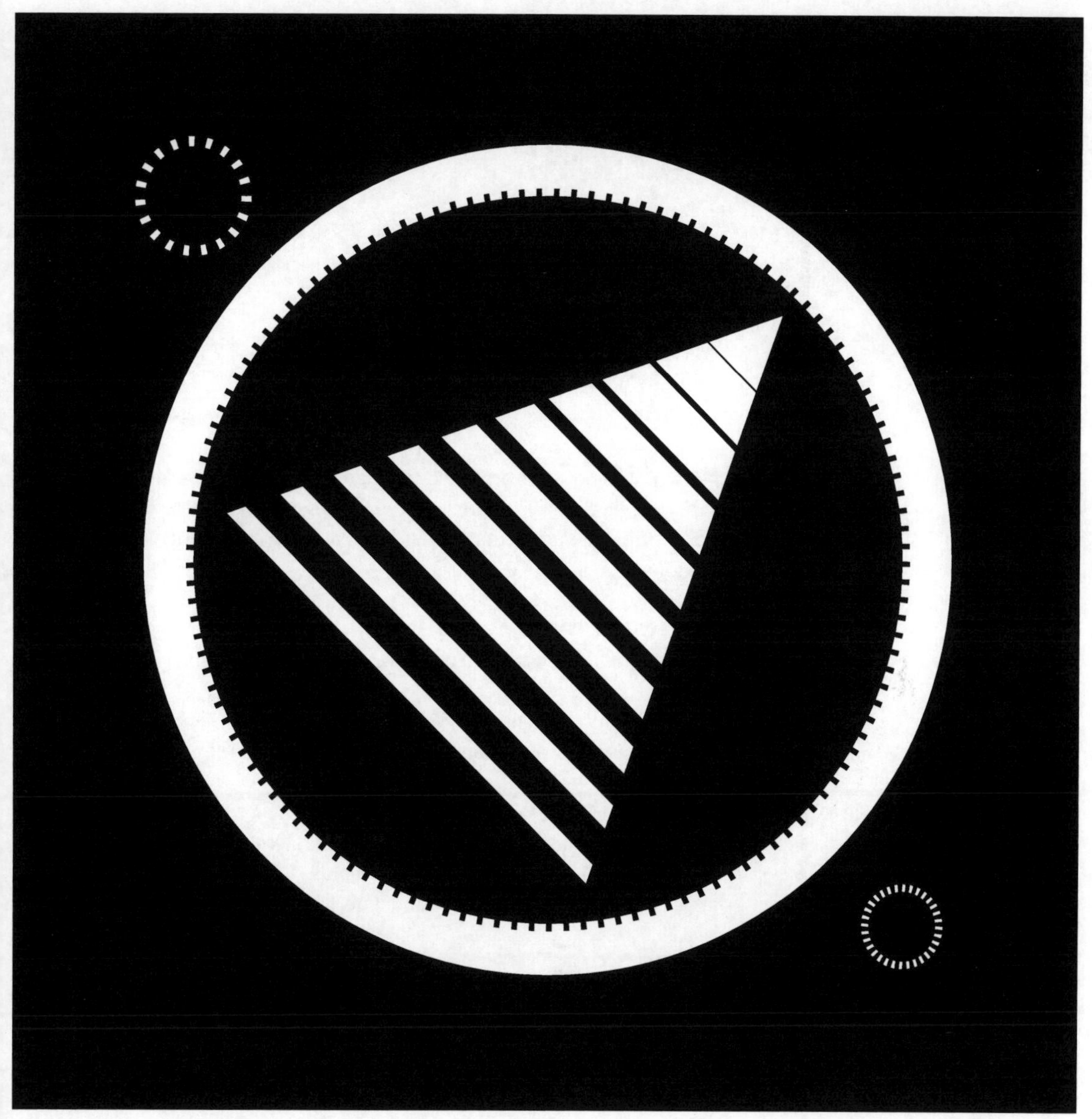

MODULE TWELVE

PERFORMANCE MANAGEMENT

MODULE TWELVE

PERFORMANCE MANAGEMENT

DESCRIPTION

This module evaluates evidence-based knowledge about performance management, the new performance management paradigm adopted by high performing organizations and the managerial skills required to manage employee performance based on an employer's prevailing organizational performance culture.

LEARNING OBJECTIVES

Upon completing the learning experience, you will be able to:

- Describe the components of the performance management wheel
- List the dimensions of a sound performance management system
- Explain the split egg concept
- Explain the set-up to fail syndrome
- Determine the reliability of different types of raters and rating systems
- Identify different performance appraisal biases
- Analyze reasons for abolishing annual performance reviews

GUIDING QUESTION

Who is responsible for performance?

JORGE managed a team based in France, California, and China. Two months ago, his company eliminated performance review ratings and allowed managers the option of moving away from the traditional annual performance review form. Jorge's preference was to have a consistent process with the same form for all his employees. He also knew that he wanted to share valuable and actionable feedback versus 'checking a box' to complete a process. He asked some of the employees on his team for their thoughts. The employees in France reminded him that he was required to complete a formal written 'performance appraisal' every year for them as required by law; they saw no reason for change. The employees in California were innovative and had coworkers at other companies that raved about having a more informal monthly 'check-ins' with their manager focused on achievements, challenges, and goals for the next month. The employees in China were hesitant about receiving individual specific feedback that may compare them positively or negatively to their peers. They preferred more group or team-based feedback. Jorge thought about it for a few minutes as he made some fresh tea and wondered how he might have to utilize multiple feedback tools and methods based on the employee's cultural and individual preferences for the cadence and depth of performance feedback.

TRADITIONAL PERFORMANCE MANAGEMENT

The vast field of people performance management can practically be broken down into a number of questions: What is performance management? What is the purpose of performance management? Who is responsible for people performance? Does performance really matter? How reliable are performance reviews? How is performance managed effectively?

Defining Performance Management

Performance management (PM) is the organizational system that manages all aspects of employee performance.[1] PM is defined as a designed, implemented, and evaluated intervention for the purpose of managing the performance of employees so performance at the individual, team, and organizational levels results in achieving strategic objectives and overall desired performance. Note that this definition of employee PM is much broader than the traditional individual annual performance appraisal (PA) practice that is being questioned today by some leading global organizations.[2]

Performance review or appraisal is only one tactical component of a larger PM system. PM is often represented as a 'performance wheel' where managers establish performance standards, evaluate people performance on a regular basis, and develop a follow up plan based on that evaluation. Each of the components of the wheel comes with specific action steps for the manager (see 12.1):

12-1. The Performance Management Wheel

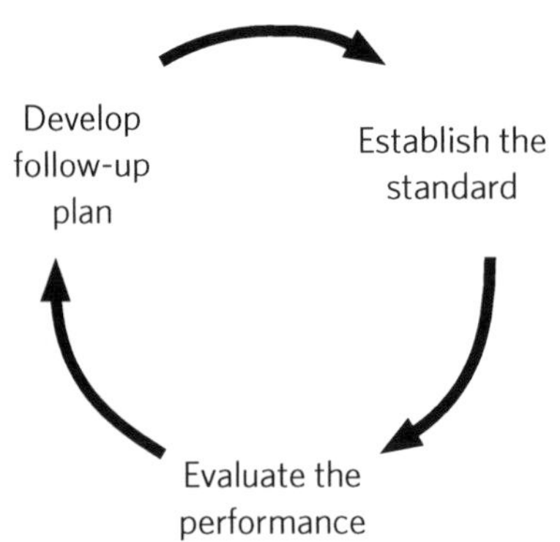

Establish the standard—Define the expected performance from employees in their position.

- Set goals and objectives for area of responsibility
- Identify job requirements
- Determine and communicate clear job expectations to employees
- Acquaint employees with the PM process

Evaluate the performance—conduct periodic performance reviews of individuals who are part of a team.

- Complete PA form
- Conduct performance review meeting
- Distinguish between satisfactory performance and performance needing improvement
- Link performance to reward structure

Develop follow-up plan—for performance that meets or does not meet standards.

- Draft a developmental action plan for those meeting performance standards so they can grow
  - Set goals and objectives for next performance period
  - Identify resources and opportunities for growth
- Draft a performance improvement plan for those not meeting performance standards
  - Monitor 90-day performance through a performance improvement plan (PIP)
  - Conduct a new performance appraisal meeting

During the past 50 years, academic researchers in the fields of psychology and sociology have made major evidence-based contributions to understanding this important management practice.

Purpose of Performance Management

With the focus on talent management in global organizations and the desire to attract, engage, and retain high-performing employees, a workable PM system that is 'relevant, sensitive, reliable, acceptable, and practical'[3] has been and remains one of the keys to the competitive human capital advantage of the global organization.

According to Wayne Cascio in a classic 1982 article, a workable PM system must have the following characteristics:

- **Relevant**—there must be a clear linkage between performance standards and organizational goals. The performance dimensions rated in the performance appraisal instrument must correspond to the critical job elements;
- **Sensitive**—must differentiate between individual performance compared to others and individual performance compared to self (personal development);
- **Reliable**—must result in a consistency of judgment;
- **Acceptable**—to those who will use it;
- **Practical**—must not interfere with ongoing operations.

Based on the belief that 'what gets measured, gets done,' the periodic performance review is used to measure worker performance, develop employees, measure their contribution, document their performance, and give employees some form of self-expression.

- **Development**—a performance review allows managers to identify areas of performance with competency gaps: between what is expected from the employee and what they realize; between currently needed competencies and future organizational needs.
- **Measure contribution**—a performance review ascertains the contribution of the individual worker to the organization and links it to the reward system and development opportunities.
- **Documentation and administrative control**—managers also use a performance review to document performance and support employment decisions in compliance with anti-discrimination legislation and labor contracts.
- **Subordinate expression**—the periodic performance review is a way (and often the only one) for employees to express themselves with regard to their needs, career path, and performance justification.

The challenge with managing performance is that it is a multi-dimensional concept which ensures employees have work duties, skills, and enthusiasm for their work, accomplishes the required quality and quality of work, and are ready to innovate

- **Work duties**—the worker must understand the work duties (see below the split egg concept) and how they align with organizational objectives.
- **Work skills**—the worker must have the work skills (competencies or knowledge, skills, abilities, and other person-related factors or KSAOs) to perform those work duties.
- **Work enthusiasm**—the worker must be motivated, engaged, and enthusiastic about work duties and get along well with others.
- **Quantity and quality of work**—the worker must have a standard output in terms of quantity and quality required by the job.
- **Innovation**—the worker must have the capacity to continuously improve, innovate, and change.

Responsibility for Performance

Whose fault is it when an employee or worker does not perform? At an individual level, using the age-old heuristic that 'performance is motivation times ability,' it is possible to blame performance that does not meet standards on the individual and classify their performance to different degrees of ability or motivation. When put into a two-by-two table, workers are classified by having either: low motivation and low ability; high motivation and low ability; low motivation and high ability; or high motivation and high ability—each best handled

12-2. Performance is Ability Times Motivation

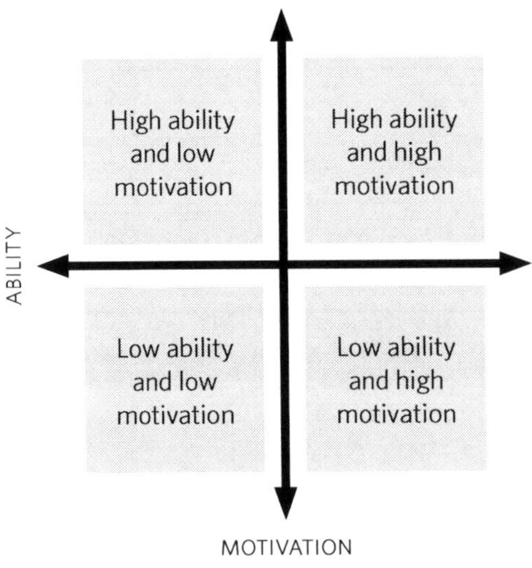

with a different managerial approach. Yet, often managers fail to deal with performance whether good or bad (see 12-2)! At a team level, managers can pick players that may excel in certain aspects and then combine them (in a MoneyBall manner) on a team where they support each other's strengths/weaknesses.

- **High motivation and low ability**—provide training to fill the performance gap due to skill deficiency, focus on the person's strengths, and try to match the person's skills with business needs;
- **Low motivation and low ability**—should we retain this person after having a crucial conversation that the situation is not sustainable?
- **High motivation and high ability**—provide stretch assignments, high exposure, sponsoring and mentoring, do not hoard this talent but provide internal opportunities for career growth;
- **Low motivation and high ability**—why is this person not engaged? Is the low motivation due to external and personal factors or internal organizational issues? Is this person burned out?

It is commonly believed people performance is a function of the quality of leadership to which they are exposed. Performance is the outcome of a system created by the leadership behavior. In other words, performance (whether good or bad) always reflects on the manager, as poor performance of employees is usually a direct result of management action or inaction. In reality, when an employee's performance that meets or exceeds expectations, the success should be attributed to the employee's abilities and motivation. However, when the employee does not meet performance expectation, the failure should foremost reflect on the manager. Do you agree or not?

Jean-François Manzoni and Jean-Louis Barzoux in a 2002 *Harvard Business Review* article (and book) developed what they called the 'set-up-to-fail' syndrome.[4] They claim the boss can largely be blamed for an employee's poor performance. There is a causal relationship between leadership of the boss and the performance of the subordinate. Employees perceived to be mediocre or weak live up to the low expectations their managers have for them. The 'set-up-to-fail' syndrome is both self-fulfilling and self-reinforcing. The 'compatibility' between boss and subordinate can have a significant impact on a manager's impressions. It is 'self-fulfilling' as the actions of the manager contribute to the very behavior that is expected from weak performers. It is 'self-reinforcing' as the low expectations of the manager are being fulfilled by the weak subordinate. The weak subordinate triggers more of the same behavior, which in turn triggers more of the same behavior by the boss. This then becomes a vicious circle. The manager compares weaker performers with stronger performers and makes assumptions of in-group relationships (based on mutual trust and reciprocal influence) and out-group relationships (based on rules, policies, and authority). Hence, managers are controlling toward weak performers! Managers attribute the good things that happen to weak performers to external factors (luck) rather than their own efforts and ability. Success of high performers is theirs and the occasional failures are attributed to external factors. This has consequences for both weak and strong performers. Weak performers are deprived of autonomy on the job, feel undervalued, and shut down emotionally and intellectually on the job, while strong performers can experience overload and burnout. According to Manzoni and Barzoux, managers can interrupt the 'set-up-to-fail' syndrome by taking the following steps:

- Create the right context for the discussion;
- Use the intervention process to come to an agreement on the symptoms of the problem;
- Arrive at a common understanding of what might be causing the weak performance in certain areas;
- Arrive at an agreement about performance objectives and on the employee's desire to foster the relationship for the future.

Does Performance Really Matter?

The relationship between the performance of a person and the importance of the work they do is not clear cut, as individual performance must be aligned to organizational goals. Paul Evans developed the 'split egg' concept regarding a person's performance by focusing on the importance of working below and above the split egg.[5] The bottom of the egg represents the operational role (70%) of a person fulfilling the essential functions of their job responsibilities. It gets the person hired because of the competencies and the agency (read: motivation and discipline) they possess to do the job as expected. It also can get someone fired if they don't perform. Working below the split egg is being an effective manager and doing the right things in the operational role. The top of the egg represents a person's project role (30%) above and beyond their specific job duties and corresponds more to lateral work in the organization. It is being an effective leader by participating in various project roles. The project roles are what gets the performer noticed, promoted, and showcases their leadership capabilities and high potential status.

Ideally, people who know their job perform on the 70-30 percentage split below and above the split egg. When starting a new job or position, the performer usually experiences an opportunity cost due to the learning curve of performing a new job in a different context and devotes most of their time (perhaps 100% or even 120%) working below the egg to meet job expectations. In principle, effective performance below the split egg is required to make a person keep their job and not get them fired! But, after an initial ramping up period (three to six months), the performer will be able to achieve the same productivity in less time and will slowly start working above the egg. They can now devote up to 25-30% of their time to lateral projects. This will get them noticed, identified as a high potential candidate, and likely considered for promotion. When a person is comfortable in their job, the distribution of the work performed changes as they tend to perform more work above the split egg—sometimes even to the extreme—70% above and 30% below the egg. This can have a number of consequences. Above the split-egg work usually produces a greater amount of individual job satisfaction as that work tends to be based on the person's strengths. The employee likes that work better than their 'real' job responsibilities and must be careful not to neglect their core job functions. It may also lead them to work on projects that may not be in the best interest of the company unless it leads to innovation. However, working above the egg is only good if the employee continues to deliver what is required below the split egg or has an opportunity to automate or delegate some of these tasks! But, if the worker can do their job in 30% of their time, the job should be enriched or enlarged so that it is challenging. This is where the rule of thumb of reinventing one's job responsibilities every 12 to 24 months comes in so no one gets too comfortable in their job but continues to grow and be challenged.

Types of Traditional Performance Appraisals

Traditional (annual appraisal) performance reviews have become very sophisticated in terms of types of rating methods such as; categorical, comparative, narrative, the 9-box grid, 360-degree multi-rater feedback, or other methods (see 12-3).

12-3. Traditional Performance Rating Methods

Categorical rating methods	
Graphic scale method	Lists a number of traits and a range of performance for each (either a 1 to 5 scale or meets, exceeds, or fails expectations).
Checklist	List of statements and checks the items on the list that describe the performance of the employee.
Forced choice	Requires checking a list of statements (or pairs of choices) that are most or least like the behavior of an employee.
Comparative methods	
Ranking	A person's performance is ranked with that of others from best to worst.
Paired comparison	A person is paired and compared with another employee.
Forced distribution	A predetermined number or percentage of people fall in each performance category (i.e., curve).
Narrative methods	
Essay	A short narrative is written about a person's performance.
Critical incident	The manager records incidents of good and undesirable performance.
Field review	The manager and someone other than the manager (HR, manager's manager) cooperate in the review.
Other methods	
MBO Management by Objectives	Where specific objectives are set and evaluated. Based on Peter Drucker's work (1954),[6] advocating that bosses should set the company's overall goals and then, in discussion with each worker, agree on a subset of goals to align with the goals of the company and develop SMART (specific, measurable, actionable, realistic, and time-sensitive) objectives.
BARS Behaviorally Anchored Rating Scales	Quantitative ratings are anchored to narrative critical incidents (spe-cific behavior examples).
9-box grid	A visual tool that maps the employee's performance with their potential. By rating each dimension (performance and potential) on low, moderate, to high scale, a 9-cell grid is created. Then the employee's strengths and weaknesses can be discussed with a view to evaluate organization's talent pool for either succession planning (top right quad-rant) or termination (lower left quadrant). The tool was popularized by Jack Welch at General Electric and received its share of criticism in terms of reliability of rating and the labeling of people.
360-degree multi-rater feedback	In 360 evaluation, multiple raters inside and outside the company assess employee performance. The idea is that multiple raters will in-crease the accuracy of the judgment. It is important to understand that different raters evaluate different performance components.

Reliability of Performance Reviews

Academic researchers have accumulated a wealth of evidence regarding performance management, mainly related to its validity (is the construct measuring the intended performance valid?) and reliability (are different raters obtaining the same rating?). Performance ratings are inherently biased due to the rating method, the rater-ratee dyad, or the issues related to 360 degree evaluation (see 12-4).

Traditional PM Skills

Managerial skills for action required for managing performance in a traditional setting when PAs are still being conducted are:

- Manage A-B-C employees
- Prepare and conduct a performance appraisal meeting
- Develop a performance improvement/ development plan
- Handle a crucial conversation
- Mentor and be mentored

We will focus in detail on these traditional day-to-day people management issues in module 13.

ABOLISHING PERFORMANCE APPRAISALS[8]

The traditional PA has become passé! It usually began with top-down, cascading organizational and personal objectives, once-a-year appraisals, mainly backward-looking reviews using some type of multi-rater 360-degree feedback tool that resulted in a one-dimensional single end-rating that was in turn linked to compensation and promotion decisions. It also included a short-term, forward-looking performance improvement plan (PIP) for employees who failed to meet expectations and, in some cases, a more long-term personal development plan (PDP) for those who met or exceeded expectations.

What's wrong with this traditional PA and review system that has evolved over the last decades and was touted as a best practice by many leading global organizations, including General Electric? The traditional performance review—developed in the era of personnel management and perfected in the latter part of the 20th century—was a product of an emerging modern multinational corporation (MNC). Yet, in today's context, it is disruptive and counterproductive. It no longer fits the new global organization and the world of work in the 21st century that requires agility, reliance on data, and responsiveness to the needs, expectations, and requirements of the millennial generation.

12-4. Rating Methods Biases

Halo/Horn effect	Employee is extremely competent in one area and therefore rated high in all categories (halo); Employee receives low ratings in every category be-cause of very poor performance in one (horn).
Recency	Appraiser gives more weight to recent occurrences than long-term ones.
Strictness/leniency	One person may view the same behavior and rate it a 9, while another may give it a score of 5 (strict); others may be reluctant to give low scores (lenient).
General, non-specific evaluation	Indicates a poor effort or lack of 'frame-of-reference' (FOR) training; General statements that are not operationalized.
Mixing description and judgment	Judging the person rather than the behavior.
Lateness	Putting the appraisal off until there is no adequate time to do a good job and provide feedback.
Poor documentation	Both findings (ratings) and action steps must be documented, especially if the appraisal is used for positive or negative employment decisions.
Central tendency	All employees are rated within a narrow range.
Rater-ratee biases	There are many known unconscious biases issues with rater-ratee dyads based on gender, age, nationality, affective regard, and type of rater. Many empirical studies have shown that the same performance is rated differ-ently (hence unreliable) when the above characteristics of the rater and rate are changed.
Issues with 360 evaluations	While 360-degree ratings increase the reliability of the rating by increasing the number of raters, they may also lead to issues with the use of poorly-designed, non-validated systems; failure to understand which performance dimension is being rated by which type of rater; failure to take into ac-count the biases inherent in the different types of raters and the rater-ratee context; usage of the same (standardized) or different (localized) systems around the world; and failure to look at the impact of culture.[7]

While there may have been a long-standing gap between what is known and practiced when it comes to PM, recent discourse about abandoning the 'traditional' PM system and replacing it with a more effective approach to managing employee performance (in the framework of the 21st century world of work and the worker) is a good example of convergence between HR concepts, theories, and practices.

There is a plethora of reasons why 'rank and yank' performance review systems may not work anymore today.[9]

1. Disliked by Managers and Employees
The widely practiced annual PA is an exercise that is generally disliked by both managers (raters) and employees (ratees). "*Managers don't like doing appraisals. Employees don't like getting them. Perhaps that is because they all suspect what the evidence shows: such performance reviews don't work.*"[10] Managers and HR tend to support performance reviews 'because we have always done it.' There are also cultural and structural reasons why performance appraisals are done. The French need written reviews by law; the Dutch tend to be more direct (give me the straightforward feedback right away); other cultures like Japan may not want to have negative or critical feedback whether in writing or in person. Also, some managers verbally give critical feedback but then water down the performance review in writing or vice versa. The dreaded reviews, often done by ill-prepared managers and forced-curve impositions by management, put both managers and employees in the awkward position of focusing on employee weaknesses rather than on strengths, and on past performance rather than on future capabilities. Managers are not motivated to invest time in annual PAs and often themselves have negative experiences of the process as receivers (or ratees) throughout their careers. Hence, they do the minimum required to meet the expectations of HR with regard to PA meetings and documentation. It is simply an additional burden that has low priority on a long to-do list.

2. Time Consuming
Annual PAs are extremely time consuming in terms of preparation and meeting time for both managers and employees and, hence, have a high financial cost for the organization. Adobe reported that the complex infrastructure required to support performance reviews required 80,000 hours from 2,000 managers, or the annual full time equivalent (FTE) of 40 employees.[11] Deloitte reported that their old PM system (an annual 360-degree feedback) cost them 2 million hours a year.[12] That time is usually spent on the mechanics of doing reviews rather than on coaching and developing employees toward improved performance.[13]

Estimating the time it takes of all involved for administering a traditional annual performance appraisal, a conservative estimate is four 'people' hours per employee. This translates to 40 'people' hours for 10 employees or one full-time equivalent (FTE) per year for 500 employees being reviewed. Multiply these time estimates with the hourly rate of employees, managers, and managers' managers and the cost of conducting reviews is considerable. In addition, managing poor performers (i.e. the so-called 'C' employees) toward an 'up or out' standard (i.e. preparing the written review, discussing the review, monitoring progress, providing constructive feedback, developing a performance improvement plan (PIP), and documenting the process) is also very intense and time consuming for managers and takes time away from working with A and B performers.[14]

3. Not Adapted to the Current Needs of Today's Worker
The traditional performance management system fails to meet the needs of millennial workers. Not only are the expectations of the millennial generation different from those of their predecessors, but also by 2025 the millennials are expected to represent 75% of the global workforce.[15] Millennials tend to place a greater value on fairness, regular feedback, coaching, development, professional career advice, and transparency. Managing performance is the most frequent engagement

driver for the millennial generation and is one of its top drivers. PM is also the number one overall driver during millennial interviews.[16] In addition, millennials typically do not stay in a job for long, so the traditional annual or semi-annual PA may not be timely. The millennial's need for feedback that is timely (without delay), frequent (often), and delivered in a certain way (clear and specific) is of utmost importance for their engagement.

4. Not Adapted to Agile Work

Global organizations recognize the rate of change impacting their business is happening at an increasing speed. Competitive and geopolitical challenges have an impact on their business almost daily and are tracked and reported in their reporting cycles, requiring quick adjustments to company goals, objectives, and tactics. The performance drivers of knowledge work have also changed as the performance dimensions are now more focused on skills, attitude, customer empathy, innovation, and teamwork.[17] An annual or semi-annual PA of employees impacting the achievement of the goals of the organization does not support the rapidly changing realities of operating globally today. Fast-paced and agile management requires an ability to redirect performance in a timely and just-in-time manner. Yet, the traditional PM system does not align with the current nature of work in (especially IT-driven) agile environments.

5. Negative Impact on Employees

The effect of the performance review also comes at a high psychic cost for employees. It alienates high performers, demoralizes employees, creates animosity, and damages employee engagement.[18] One of the fundamental principles governing human behavior (i.e., so-called 'hardwired behaviors') is that we tend to use emotions as the first screen for all information received. This is especially true in receiving a PA. While several performance dimensions may have been rated as excellent for an employee, it is the lower rated one that receives the most focus, and the employee will tend to remember that one rather than the others.[19]

The process of defensiveness—automatic in the face of criticism—can also lead to a belief of weakness, lack of effort for improvement and damaged manager-employee relationships. Employees are also negatively impacted when there isn't a high degree of differentiation and recognition of the top performing employees in their organization. Imagine an employee receiving an average rating when he/she is aware that a peer received the same rating—and perhaps even a higher 'merit' increase or award—yet did not work as hard or make as much of an impact on the business. Like a sports team, strong performers want to play on a winning team with other star performers. The only employees who are a comfortable with low differentiation are those who tend to be average employees who crave stability.

6. Low Reliability and Validity

Academic research on performance ratings has shown PA ratings have low reliability and validity as a result of a number of factors: the rater-ratee configuration, conscious and unconscious biases of the raters, the idiosyncratic rater effect, and specific circumstances that may bias the ratings. The structural characteristics of the rater and the ratee—such as gender, age, nationality, race, affective regard, etc.—and the social context of performance appraisals are shown to reduce rating outcomes.[20]

A lot of attention is currently being paid to the impact of the unconscious bias in HR processes such as selection of new hires, promotion decisions, leadership identification, and performance ratings. These hidden biases operate at the implicit unconscious level and influence how managers perceive others and make decisions, even though managers think they are objective and fair. These unconscious biases are especially strong when it comes to attributes of traditionally disadvantaged groups—such as gender, age, race, and national origin—being evaluated. The idiosyncratic rater effect is also frequently discussed. It indicates that what is being measured in PAs is the rating perception of the manager (as rater) rather than the actual behavior of the employee (as ratee). Deloitte found that assessing someone's skills is subjective and says more about the rater than the ratee because people rate other people's skills inconsistently.[21]

The reliability and validity of the performance ratings may also be biased due to other motives:

- Raters and managers may inflate or deflate appraisals for various reasons such as their affective regard towards the ratee, power struggles amongst managers, their own role as manager, and excessive competition among team members. In some cases, managers (raters) may hesitate to give a poor or average performer a lower rating due to the unique skillset or knowledge the employee has that may be difficult to replace. All organizations have employees who have a highly desired skillset or knowledge of legacy systems that are imperative to retain. Some managers may allow themselves to be held hostage by these employees, provide higher performance ratings than justified, and may ignore the true value of the PA process. As a result, they focus on the desirability of the skillset rather than the performance of the individual employee.
- There may be a discrepancy between the content of the conversation with the employee during the PA meeting and the documentation recorded in the employee's record. Managers may be willing to communicate more direct constructive feedback during the review meeting with the employee but soften anything in the written appraisal as a means of documentation. Records related to the PA have been shown to become a liability in terms of lawsuits related to terminations.[22] Managers inherently want to 'balance' any constructive feedback with positive feedback, and this provides valuable documentation for the plaintiff.
- It is not uncommon in many global organizations, particularly in the high-tech industry, for an employee to have more than one manager during a transitional 12-month period. Due to frequent reorganizations and the fast-paced nature of work, an employee may have been assigned to different managers during the year-long review period. This means managers may not want to address a performance issue and just wait for the 'next manager' to deal with it in six months in a fast-growing high-tech company. The employee may complain their 'new' manager does not know of their accomplishments earlier in the review period. If the 'previous' manager is required to write the review, then the employee may complain the manager ignored more recent accomplishments. Rarely would two managers provide a consistent and objective performance review of the same employee.
- Given that many employees operate in a matrixed organizational structure, the ability of the different managers to provide an accurate view of an employee's performance is limited. As a result, the manager who has limited sight of the employee's performance is more likely to provide an 'average' rating for both the low and the high performer.
- Some companies have a forced curve and a calibrating process by which managers provide feedback on employees and the performance ratings of managers from other functions or departments. In these cases, some of the managers pre-negotiate the ratings before the official discussion with other managers who are involved in the process. In these situations, the process is tainted by the alliances developed among managers to support one's recommended performance rating. Many employees also know how to manipulate the traditional performance review system by improving their performance in the last couple of months leading up to the rating process by completing key deliverable products, working longer hours to show commitment, etc. and thereby creating a 'recency' effect which is a well-known bias in performance ratings. Such an unreliable PA system is then linked to employment decisions such as promotions, demotions,

and terminations, merit increases and compensation. The compensation system is often not shared with employees thus creating more distrust. So now, employees do not trust how their ratings were determined and do not trust the compensation system that determined their compensation award.

7. Negative Influence of Forced Ranking

Although many companies continue to grade employee performance on the curve, it does not accurately reflect the way people perform. Forced rankings label employees as star, average, and low performers (i.e., A-B-C employees) and rations the number of high-performance ratings by typically allowing no more than 10-to-20% of the employees to get a star rating. It forces the bottom 10% to get a low rating, creating 'losers' in the group. Even if the team is made up of high performers, someone is still at the bottom. The majority of the employees are rated in the middle and considered more or less average. As a result, forced bell curve rankings diminish the value of top performers and push many mid-level performers toward the bottom.[23] The forced ranking also does not differentiate between a skills gap versus a performance gap. Yet, many decisions (i.e., promotions, demotions, and terminations) are then linked to these forced ratings.[24] On the other hand, occasionally using a forced curve may be a very effective method to clean out some dead weeds, especially when it has not been done for several years.

The imposition of a forced curve also can lead to manipulation:

- Some managers may refrain from acting against poor performers so they can use them to meet the bottom 5-to-10% target for their employees based on the bell curve. This unintended consequence of the forced curve philosophy results in the cost of continuing to employ poor performers, negative impact on departmental performance, as well as a negative impact on team morale.
- In some cases, a calculated manager may even temporarily hire a person to do the job of the poor per-former essentially doubling the cost for the organization.
- New employees may also be at a disadvantage, since there may be a culture in the organization in which a new hire can rarely be rated as a high performer during their first or second year of employment due to the perceived time to 'learn about the company and make an impact'. Imagine new hires at a company who are motivated to make a major impact on their new employer only to learn from their peer group they can expect only average ratings for the first year or two!
- Managers frequently deflect blame for an employee's poor performance on the forced curve of a PA, stating, "I would not have given you this low rating but HR required me to do it because I must meet a forced curve." This response results in a negative outcome for both the employee and the manager. It is demotivating and may, in some cases, encourage the employee to take legal action against the company and claim they are being treated unfairly and/or discriminated against.

8. Poor Link to Employee Engagement and Performance

In theory, a traditional PM system is supposed to cascade top-down goals and objectives and create alignment across the organization and with other HR objectives (such as engagement, compensation, and performance). In reality, for many organizations, the PA process has merely become a 'check box' exercise. This is perpetuated by the fact that employees do not necessarily know the objectives of other employees in their department or cross-functionally and whether their coworkers' objectives are aligned with their own. The practice of annual PAs does not necessarily drive employee engagement and high performance. The feedback provided during the PA does not always lead to improved performance (i.e. drive employee engagement and higher performance).[25]

Many surveys have supported the fact that employees tend to resign their position based on negative experiences with their manager. Employee engagement surveys often focus on the way employees are treated by their managers (rather than the company) as a main indicator of employee engagement, the likelihood of making significant contributions to the company, and the predictors of employee retention. Yet, one should also question whether the PM system ultimately results in a more engaged employee. If not, it should be eliminated and replaced with a more engaging manager-employee practice.

9. Focus on Weakness Rather Than on Strengths of the Employee

By their very nature, traditional PAs highlight the weaknesses of employees—so they can be improved and developed—rather than their strengths. An important goal of the PA has been to identify performance gaps so they can be improved and/or document the weaknesses of the employee in case of dismissal. Although no one argues weaknesses must be improved and brought up to par, it is through freeing one's strengths that the greatest performance is achieved. Therefore, high performing individuals and teams should focus on utilizing and building on their strengths rather than simply improving their weaknesses.[26]

10. Failing to Provide True Coaching and Feedback

Annual (or biannual) PAs tend to provide one-way feedback rather than actual coaching.[27] The time that managers spend with each employee during the review process is mostly devoted to reviewing the final ratings on each dimension of the PA form, illustrating these ratings with (positive and/or negative) critical incidents that have been observed during the review period, and identifying areas needing improvement. At the end of the review meeting, goals may be set for the next year. This process provides limited opportunities for true feedback and coaching.

11. Limited Support From HR

Over time, PAs have devolved from HR managing the process to the managers doing the actual reviews. HR teams are usually so lean that they do not have the time to support the performance review process with frame-of-reference training in order to improve the performance and accuracy of the rating, process the written performance reviews, and coach managers on how to improve their reviews. Many HR departments also do not have the resources to read, review, and coach managers on the performance reviews they submit. Furthermore, HR has minimal influence and authority in encouraging managers to improve their performance reviews. Managers would argue they have just as much incentive to ignore HR in writing and communicating performance feedback as part of a traditional PA process. These activities are generally time consuming and not very rewarding for either the manager or the employee.

12. Limited Global Applicability

When the Western concept of PM is viewed from an international perspective, an added layer of complexity emerges largely due to the varying cultural and structural contexts in which global HR is implemented. There is a concern with the implementation of a management process developed and tested in the West and applied to a different context (i.e. different national cultures, laws, and markets). Can a well-established Western practice, such as employee PM, be transferred to another external context and retain its intended value? In this way, the global applicability of a PM system and an annual PA—designed at headquarters and rolled out internationally to the local employees of a global organization—has been questioned in terms of its design, implementation, and evaluation.[28]

There are also many cultural aspects related to the traditional PA system that provide an employee with direct feedback and a specific rating/rank. In some Asian cultures, a more soft and circuitous process for giving feedback is expected, and 360 multi-rater feedback does not work as intended in high power distance and high context cultures.[29] When considering the various issues affecting global PM and the complexities involved in evaluating the performance of international assignees,[30] it is fair to state that the PM system—designed and perfected in an Anglo-Saxon context—may have limited global applicability. While in general, the purpose and principles of the PM system may be standardized by a global organization, the implementation will always require a certain amount of localization.[31]

Polarized Reactions to Abolishing Performance Appraisals

The practice of abolishing performance appraisals spread in American progressive organizations like wildfire and created a lot of discourse with arguments on both sides indicating that whether one abolished the practice or not. Things had to change in how performance is reviewed.

Peter Cappelli and Anna Tavis in a 2016 *Harvard Business Review* article elaborated on business reasons to drop performance appraisals.[32]

1. The return of people development—companies are under competitive pressure to upgrade their talent management efforts.
2. The need for agility—rapid innovation is a source of competitive advantage and future needs are continually changing.
3. The centrality of teamwork—moving away from forced ranking and from appraisals' focus on individual accountability makes it easier to foster teamwork.

Another view is expressed by Lori Goler, Janelle Gale, and Adam Grant in a *Harvard Business Review* article that same year entitled, "Let's not kill performance evaluations yet."[33] The authors argued that "*Performance is always rated in some manner. If you don't have formal evaluations, the ratings will be hidden in a black box*," and then list benefits of performance evaluations: making things fair (fairness); being transparent (transparency); and developing people (self-development).

In spite of these different views on the value of performance appraisals, a new performance management paradigm has developed in recent years and been adopted by many companies.

THE NEW PERFORMANCE MANAGEMENT PARADIGM

While most traditional PA systems and forms in global organizations have the same main process characteristics (i.e., objectives/goals, actual performance to objectives, written manager summary of performance, performance ratings, etc.), the new paradigm is producing very different components and features based on the needs and characteristics of the global organization (such as industry, sector, size, performance philosophy, organizational culture, etc.).

Fifteen years ago, the performance review forms and systems of global organizations were very similar. Today there is much more variety in performance tools and methods available to consider and ranging from low- to high-tech. Many global organizations have in the past tried to 'modernize' their performance review systems and regularly updated them. One could argue the changes in PA were mostly superficial—such as transitioning their traditional hard copy form to an electronic version or adding multi-source raters and linking employee ratings to their balanced scorecards. While many organizations have converted their hard copy appraisal forms to a more high-tech online version, the transition from hard to electronic copy is more akin to automation and does not address any of the fundamental issues of a traditional PM system. The paradigm shift that is going on today in PM is more profound and constitutes a new way of looking at employees and their performance. The core features of the performance management shift from old to new focus on: ongoing informal reviews; future-oriented, short-term objectives and key results goal setting; feedback and coaching conversations with employees; developing employees; simple and transparent systems for both managers and employees, decoupled from compensation; and piloting diverse approaches based on the organizational culture.

While the transformation of PM has been very diverse among the global companies that have replaced their traditional PM systems, a number of core features seem to be prevalent:

- Focus on OKRs (Objectives and Key Results) rather than KPI (Key Performance Indicators);
- Provide RTF (real-time feedback);
- Encourage frequent coaching conversations and data points by engaging in continuous performance management (CPM);
- Take steps to reduce the unconscious bias;
- Focus on strength management;
- Take advantage of teachable moments.

Organizations have made many major transitions in the past decades as a result of globalization, information technology, and other trends impacting HR. These transitions have included evolving traditional hierarchical organizational structures to flatter and matrixed organizations, replacing command and control management styles with more autonomous and empowered workforces, annual employee satisfaction surveys with regular engagement and employee sentiment pulse taking, and waterfall with agile software development. The latest major organizational change now requires a repositioning of the PM system and a replacement of the 'rank and yank' system with a new performance review model.

There are many driving and restraining forces for changing the PM system in a global organization. We would be remiss not to state that a 'rank and yank' PA system may have its advantages and that not everyone in the organization is necessarily ready to adopt the modern PM system. Some voices in HR circles have even cautioned against it.[34] Therefore, it is important to explore the factors that facilitate the change as well as the obstacles that resist it.

With regard to facilitating the change, the following leading practices are recommended:

- Involve stakeholders in the design;
- Create greater transparency of the process and results;
- Hold the manager accountable for ongoing coaching and feedback;
- Decouple compensation from review;
- Link performance management to the organizational culture;
- Conduct frame-of-reference training.

In the best of worlds, performance management is not just between the manager and the talent. It is a feedback and support system between individuals, the team, and the manager—much like a wheel with spokes. The manager is in the middle and the employees are collaborating with each other to achieve their development and performance goals in alignment with organizational objectives. The key is regular feedback to the talent. ▮

REFERENCES

1. Claus, L., & Briscoe, D. (2008). "Introduction to the Special Issue on Global Performance Management," *European Journal of International Management*, 2(2): 128-131.
2. Claus, L., & Hand, M. "Customization Decisions Regarding Performance Management Systems of Multinational Companies: An Empirical View of Eastern European Firms," *International Journal of Cross-Cultural Management* 9(2): 237-258.
3. Cascio, W. (1982). "Scientific, Operational, and Legal Imperative of Workable Performance Appraisal System," *Public Personnel Management*, 11:367-375.
4. Manzoni, J., & Barsoux, J. (2002). *The Set-up-to-Fail Syndrome: How Good Managers Cause Great People to Fail*. Boston: Harvard Business School Publishing
5. Evans, P. (2012). *Combining People and Organizational Development—What Really Works*. Greece: AHRMIO Annual Conference. (WFPMA, 2004, Thessalonica, Greece)
6. Drucker, P. (1954). *The Practice of Management*. New York: Harper.
7. Claus, L., & Hand, M. "Customization Decisions Regarding Performance Management Systems of Multinational Companies: An Empirical View of Eastern European Firms," *International Journal of Cross-Cultural Management* 9(2): 237-258.
8. This section is based on: Claus, L., & Baker, S. (2013). The New Global Management Performance Management Paradigm. Pp.165-200 in Lisbeth Claus (ed.), *Global HR Practitioner Handbook*, volume 3. Silverton: Global Immersion Press.
9. Ibid.
10. Pfeffer, J. (2009). The Trouble with Performance Reviews. June 30 (Accessed October 1, 2015). https://www.bloomberg.com/news/articles/2009-06-30/the-trouble-with-performance-reviewsbusinessweek-business-news-stock-market-and-financial-advice
11. Sutton, B. (2014). How Adobe got Rid of Traditional Performance Reviews. February 6 (Accessed October 1, 2015). https://www.linkedin.com/pulse/20140206114808-15893932-how-adobe-got-rid-of-traditional-performance-reviews/
12. Buckingham, M., & Goodall, A. (2019). "Why Feedback Fails," *Harvard Business Review*, 97(2): 92-101.
13. Stanleigh, M. (2012). New Directions for Performance Management. April 15 (Accessed October 1, 2015). https://bia.ca/new-directions-for-performance-management/
14. Axelrod, B., Handfield-Jones, H., & Michaels, E. (2001). "A New Game Plan For C Players," *Harvard Business Review*, 80(1): 80-88.
15. Big Demands and High Expectations: The Deloitte Millennial Survey Executive Summary, 2014, (Accessed October 1, 2015). http://www2.deloitte.com/content/dam/Deloitte/global/Documents/About-Deloitte/gx-dttl-2014-millennial-surveyreport.pdf.
16. Gilbert, J. (2011). "The Millennials: A New Generation of Employees, A New Set of Engagement Policies," *Ivey Business Journal*, September-October 2011.
17. Barry, L., Garr, S., & Liakopoulos, A. (2014). Performance Management is Broken. Pp. 45-52 in Jeff Schwartz et al. (eds.), *Global Human Capital Trends 2014: Engaging the 21st Century Workforce*. Hartford: Deloitte University Press.
18. Ibid.
19. Nicholson, N. (1998). "How Hardwired is Human Behavior?" *Harvard Business Review*, 76(4): 134-147.
20. Levy, P., & Williams, J. (2004). "The Social Context of Performance Appraisals: A Review and Framework for the Future," *Journal of Management*, 30(6): 881-905.
21. Jõgi, O. (2015). Reinventing Performance Management: A Deloitte Case Study. April 13 (Accessed October 1, 2015). https://www.business.com/articles/reinventing-performance-management-a-deloitte-case-study/
22. Keynes, J. (2011). *The Legal Case for Eliminating Performance Reviews*. March 30 (Accessed October 1, 2015). http://www.shrm.org/legalissues/legalreport/pages/eliminatingperformancereviews.aspx
23. Barry, L., Garr, S., & Liakopoulos, A. (2014). Performance Management is Broken. Pp. 45-52 in Jeff Schwartz et al. (eds.), *Global Human Capital Trends 2014: Engaging the 21st Century Workforce*. Hartford: Deloitte University Press.
24. Bersin, J. (2014). *The Myth of the Bell Curve: Look for the Hyperperformer*. February 19 (Accessed October 1, 2015). http://www.forbes.com/sites/joshbersin/2014/02/19/the-myth-of-the-bell-curve-look-for-the-hyper-performers/

25. Barry, L., Garr, S., & Liakopoulos, A. (2014). Performance Management is Broken. Pp. 45-52 in Jeff Schwartz et al. (eds.), *Global Human Capital Trends 2014: Engaging the 21st Century Workforce*. Hartford: Deloitte University Press.
26. Buckingham, M., & Goodall, A. (2015). "Reinventing Performance Management," *Harvard Business Review*, 93(4): 40-50.
27. Stanleigh, M. (2012). New Directions for Performance Management. April 15 (Accessed October 1, 2015). https://bia.ca/new-directions-for-performance-management/
28. Claus, L. (2008). "Employee Performance Management in MNCs: Reconciling the Need for Global Integration and Local Responsiveness," *European Journal of International Management*, 2(2): 132-152.
29. Rowson, A. (2002). "Using 360 Degree Feedback Instruments Up, Down and Around the World: Implications for Global Implementation and Use of Multi-rater Feedback," *International Journal of Selection and Assessment*, 6(1): 45-48.
30. Claus, L., Lungu, A., & Bhattacharjee, S. (2011). "The Effects of Individual, Organizational and Societal Variables on the Job Performance of Expatriate Managers," *International Journal of Management*, 28(1): 249-271.
31. Vance, C. (2006). "Strategic Upstream and Downstream Considerations for Effective Global Performance Management," *International Journal of Cross Cultural Management*, 9(1): 123-141.
32. Cappelli, P., & Tavis, A. (2016). "The Performance Management Revolution," *Harvard Business Review*, 10(94): 58-67.
33. Goler, L., Gale, J., & Grant, A. (2016). "Let's Not Kill Performance Evaluations Yet," *Harvard Business Review*, 94(11): 90-94.
34. Lawler, E. (2015). Performance Management: The Three Important Features You're Forgetting. April 15 (Accessed October 1, 2015). https://www.forbes.com/sites/edwardlawler/2015/04/15/performance-management-yet-another/#1eeb6d262d9c

GUIDED READING QUESTIONS

1. What is the difference between performance management and performance appraisal?

2. What is the performance management wheel?

3. What are the essential requirements of a workable PM system?

4. What is the 'split-egg' concept?

5. What is the 'set-up-to-fail' syndrome?

6. Describe different types of rating methods.

7. What are common reliability and validity issues in PA?

8. What are traditional PM managerial skills?

9. What are the reasons why 'rank and yank' systems of PA may no longer work?

10. What are progressive PM managerial skills?

FOLLOW-UP CRITICAL THINKING QUESTIONS

1. What is my major takeaway from this reading?

2. What do I already know about this subject?

3. What follow-up questions do I have about this?

4. How can I apply this in real life?

KEY TERMS

A-B-C employees
Assessment center
BARS (Behaviorally Anchored Rating Scales)
Biases
Checklist
Comparative methods
Competency gap
Critical incident
Essay
Field review
Forced choice
Forced distribution
Frame-of-reference training
Graphic scale method
Heuristic
Idiosyncratic rater effect
KSAOs (Competencies or knowledge, skills, abilities, and other person-related factors)
MBO (Management by Objectives)
Managerial skills
Narrative methods
Paired comparison
Performance appraisal/Performance review
Performance dimensions
Performance Improvement Plan (PIP)
Personal Development Plan (PDP)
Performance management
Performance management instrument
Performance management paradigm
Performance management wheel
'Rank and yank' performance review system
Ranking
Ratee
Rater
Rating system
Reward structure/system
Self-expression
'Set-up-to-fail' syndrome
SMART objectives
'Split egg' concept
Strategic objective
Teachable moment
9-box grid
360-degree evaluation/assessment/ performance management

LEARNING ASSESSMENT

Critically reflect on the content and the different concepts in this module and rate your own competency using the assessment scale.

Competency	I never heard of it	I heard of it but have limited knowledge of it	I can reasonably explain it to others	I have used it, done it, applied it
PM wheel	0	1	2	3
Split egg concept	0	1	2	3
Set up to fail syndrome	0	1	2	3
Idiosyncratic rater effect	0	1	2	3
P=M x A	0	1	2	3
Performance rating biases	0	1	2	3
Performance rating methods	0	1	2	3
Abolishing PA	0	1	2	3

MODULAR-SPECIFIC ASSESSMENT

The Via Character Strengths Survey, VIA, Institute on Character. Assessment that lets you identify your top strengths. https://www.viacharacter.org/Account/Register

VIGNETTE

"OPEN EXCHANGE" AT DMG WORLD MEDIA[1]

DMG World Media, an international exhibitions company leader in home and consumer shows, is a relatively small (fewer than 1,000 employees), yet international company. Developed mainly through acquisitions of other small businesses, dmg world media is not an asset-based company, but an intermediary that rents exhibit space and creates exhibits marketed and sold by their teams of employees. Employees are based in the UK, the US, Canada, Dubai, Australia, New Zealand, and Beijing. dmg world media's success is heavily dependent upon high levels of employee performance. According to Warren Girling, Executive Vice President of HR, "*We have a culture of how we manage our people to get that high performance. We select groups of highly motivated and developed people who understand their customers and the business. And, we have an ongoing discussion on how we perform.*"

The company's previous HR-driven PM system was similar to that of many others in that it utilized a rating scale from 1 to 5 that was linked to a % merit increase. This traditional system, particularly its once-a-year reference point performance appraisal, no longer fit the needs of the business or its organizational culture. The merit increase was highly distorted because market forces in this business have a greater impact on salary increases than merit. Additionally, managers considered the system too time consuming and wanted more of a report card type of approach. Moreover, some of the newly acquired companies were often so small that they had no formal experience with performance management.

The new PM system, *Open Exchange*, was developed by a small group within the company, including the three most senior Executive VPs, HR, and selected employees from around the world. The group started with only a blank sheet and a vision that had previously been defined by the company. This vision, or business statement, was developed in the form of a constitution *because constitutions* are the broad foundation documents of modern societies. Yet, much like a standard constitution, not every single word of *dmg world media's* business statement applies to every day-to-day activity. The core elements of *dmg world media's* constitution are that they are the leader in their field, getting things done in a very un-bureaucratic and decentralized way by understanding the customer's business. Performance is the common purpose behind which the company unites as it reviews every set of results regularly, exhibit by exhibit.

Essential performance dimensions were identified by looking at their own high performers and asking, "*If we think about our best/most successful people and customers we love to work with, what are their essential characteristics?*" These essential qualities are sought in the people who join the company, and major features of the new PM system were based on checking performance against these "essentials." Rather than an annual affair, performance review is now done by managers, event by event. As employees work in small teams, they know when someone on the team is not performing and inform the manager. Not only do underperforming people feel peer pressure, but they are required to sit down with the manager, who is held accountable for solving the problem. It is dmg world media's strong belief that when someone has a performance problem, the appraisal is not the right place to discuss it. Performance problems cannot wait for a period review.

In the new performance reviews, employee performance is regularly reviewed by the manager and categorized into one of three groups: Employees are either (1) exceptional performers; (2) great but not exceptional performers; or (3) great people but not trainable or right for the job. Exceptional performers are the role models. Great employees may have the essential skills but also some blind spots that can be improved upon. That's where training is an option. The manager completes a grid of training analysis needs and coaches the employee to work on areas needing improvement. Employees who struggle with job know-how and perform poorly on more than one of the essentials must complete a face-to-face action plan. For those below expected level, training is rarely an option. Most of the time, there are multiple reasons for unacceptable performance: lack of skills, competency, motivation, or simply the wrong person in the wrong job. Sometimes there are bad hires, bad promotions, and bad placements. At *dmg world media*, heavy focus is on bringing in the right people and putting them in the right jobs.

Managers document performance because the company recognizes that some of the best performers need management confirmation of their accomplishments and stroking. Documentation is the recording of a positive. Negatives are handled outside of the performance appraisal process. Although *dmg world media* does not have a common single workplace and is dispersed throughout different countries, they successfully use a standardized PM system. This is possible because the employees from different national cultures are held together by a single common product (the exhibitor business), common personalities (the type of people who work in the exhibitor business), and a similar organizational culture (their constitution). In addition, they are flexible, adaptable, and willing to be elastic based on these common principles.

REFERENCES

1. This vignette was prepared by Professor Lisbeth for the sole purpose of illustrating a global HR practice for instructional objectives. Global HR in Action

GUIDED READING QUESTIONS

1. How is performance management at *DMG World Media* different from traditional performance management systems at other companies?
2. What was the impetus for developing a different performance management system at *dmg world media*?
3. Can a standardized performance management system be used effectively with managers and employees from different cultures in an international company?

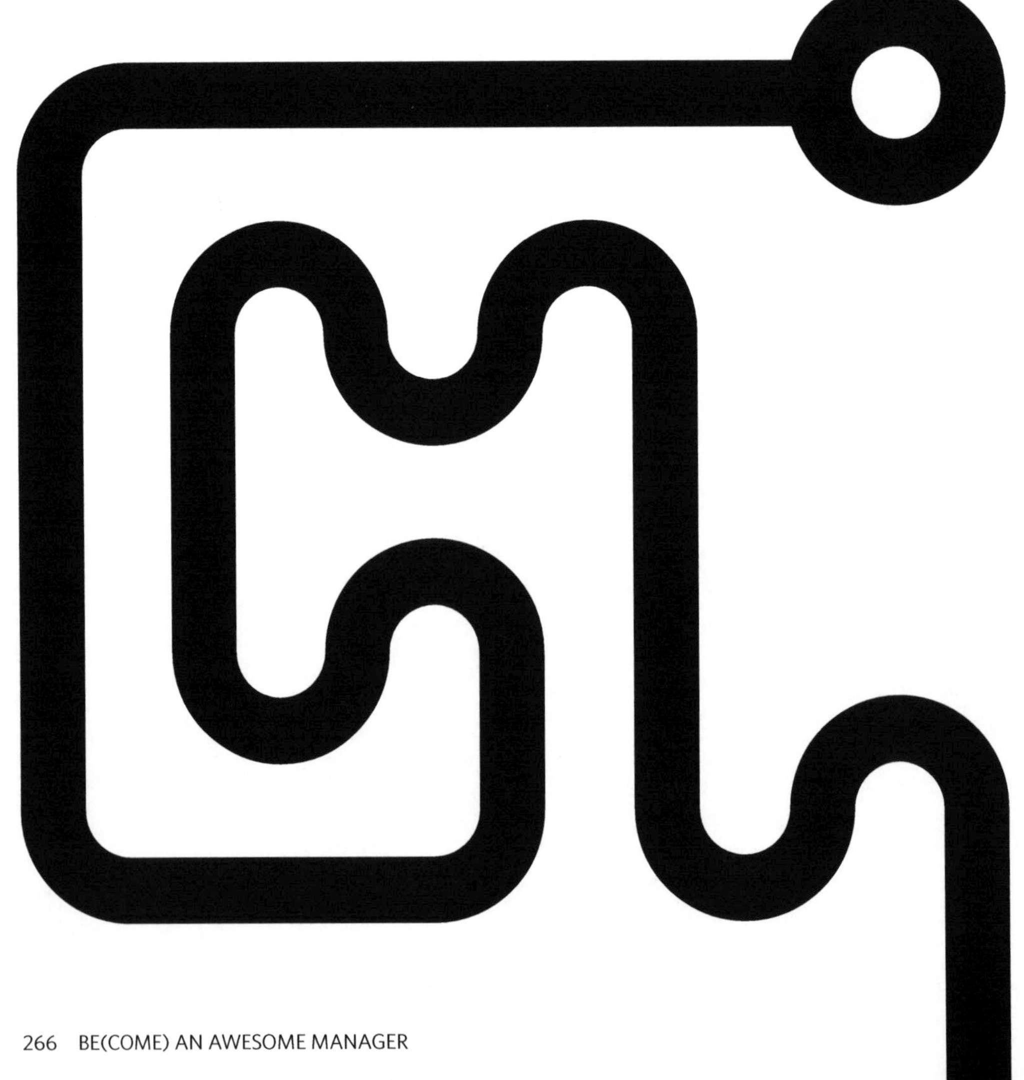

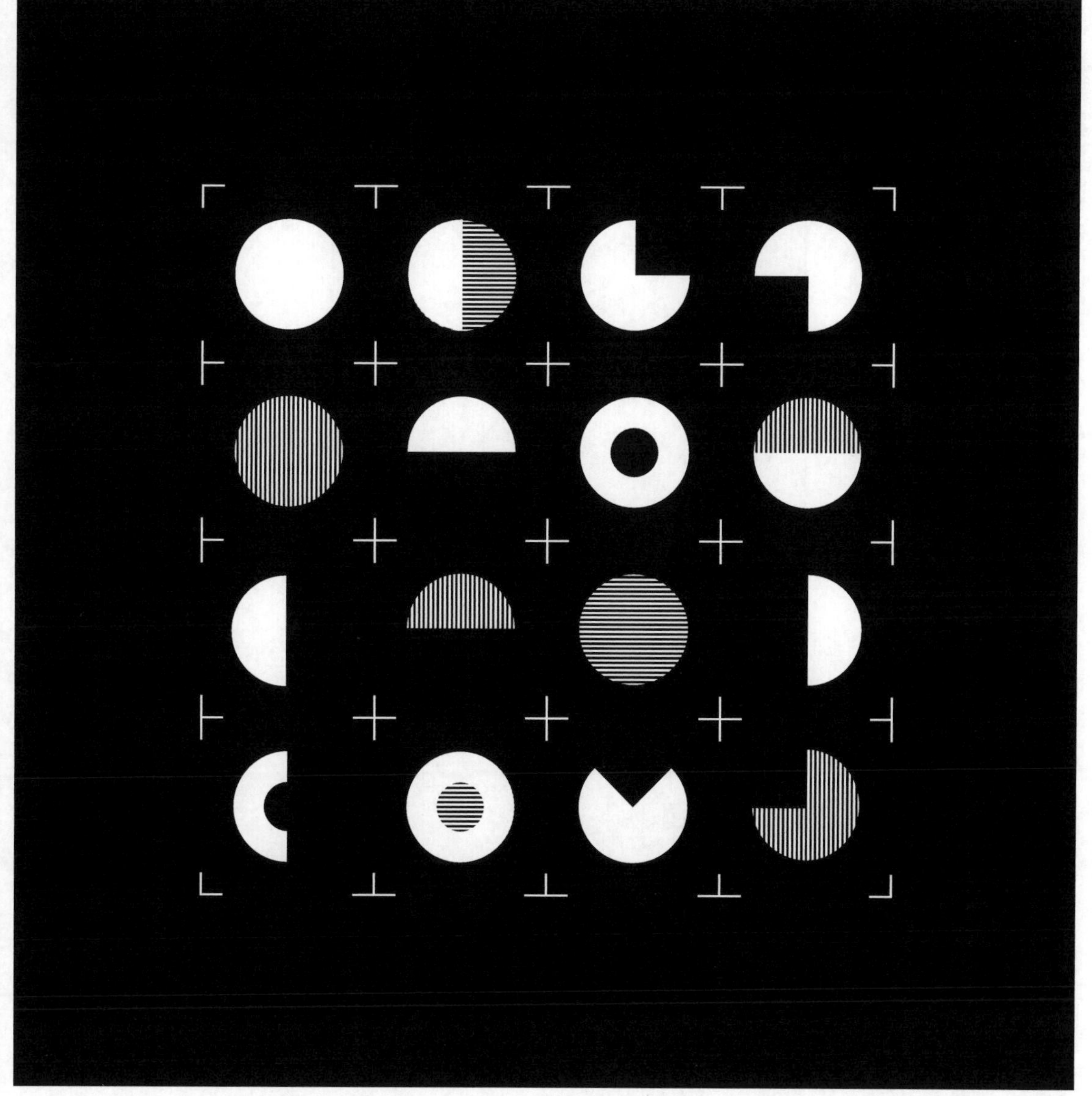

MODULE THIRTEEN

DAY-TO-DAY PEOPLE MANAGEMENT

MODULE THIRTEEN

DAY-TO-DAY PEOPLE MANAGEMENT

DESCRIPTION

This module spotlights developing managerial skills for traditional and progressive work environments including contingency management (based on A-B-C worker classification), crucial conversations, coaching, teachable moments, and developing Objectives and Key Results (OKRs).

LEARNING OBJECTIVES

Upon completing the learning experience, you will be able to:

- Distinguish between day-to-day managerial skills in traditional and progressive organizations
- Develop specific skills in managing A-B-C employees
- Develop an action plan
- Have crucial and coaching conversations
- Write OKRs

GUIDING QUESTION

How do I improve my day-to-day managerial skills?

RAFAELA had worked for managers with different leadership styles. Some were directive while others had more of a coaching style; she knew that they were supportive and wanted her to succeed. Some managers were personable while others were highly introverted and minimized any interactions with the employees on the team. Some leaders were able to effectively motivate their employees to achieve stretch goals through teamwork and celebrating successes. Rafaela even remembered a boss who threatened everybody on the team that he would fire them if they did not achieve a specific objective–it must have worked because the team achieved the objective! Rafaela reflected on what was the best leadership style as the company announcement was being written about her promotion to Director of Engineering.

This module focuses on developing day-to-day managerial skills used in traditional and progressive work environment contexts.

THE BASIC PRINCIPLES

Over 30 years ago, every new manager for a large retailer was required to attend a "Front-Line Manager' training program developed by a company called Zenger-Miller. As the title of the program suggests, the training was meant to develop managerial skills for inexperienced professionals who worked in the trenches and now managed people on the front-line! After going through the program, high-potential employees were urged to volunteer for a train-the-trainer series and become certified to teach the new leadership development skills in-house to others. The training did not look anything like an organizational behavior/ management course in an MBA program, but dealt with concrete steps to manage day-to-day situations: how to delegate, how to provide constructive feedback, how to solve problems, how to manage change, etc. The core of the managerial skill set was based on 'The Basic Principles' as timeless building blocks of trust. Over time, the set of basic principles grew to six fundamental behavioral guidelines:

1. **Focus on the situation, issue, or behavior, not on the person**—rather than blame, label, and generalize.
2. **Maintain the self-confidence and self-esteem of others**—rather than demean and threaten.
3. **Maintain constructive relationships with your employees, peers, and managers**—rather than withhold help, information, or resources.
4. **Take initiative to make things better**—rather than complain and wait for others to act.
5. **Lead by example**—rather than tell others, show them the way.
6. **Think beyond the moment**—rather than promote a personal agenda.

These basic principles are a framework for managerial action and apply whether one operates in a traditional or progressive framework.

ZIGZAGGING BETWEEN TRADITIONAL AND PROGRESSIVE MANAGEMENT STYLES

In their 2019 book, *#ZigZagHR: Why the Best HR is no Longer HR*, Lisbeth Claus and Lesley Arens explore new ways of managing to respond to the changing context of work and the worker.[2] While traditional management—based on the 3rd industrial revolution—has served us well in the past, it is no longer sufficient today now that we are in the midst of a 4th industrial revolution. As the values and the norms of the workforce are evolving, we must explore new ways of thinking and doing in managing organizations for today and the future. This does not mean *tabula rasa*! Besides, that is also impossible for most companies that have legacy systems. Instead, we must #ZigZag between traditional managerial practices that still work today and new practices introduced and used in progressive companies.

In traditional organizations, *structure* is central focusing on the functions of management such as planning, organizing, leading, and controlling:

- **Planning**—create a detailed action plan aimed at one or more organizational goals.
- **Organizing**—how to distribute resources and organize employees according to the plan.
- **Leading**—connecting with employees on an interpersonal level.
- **Controlling**—evaluate the results against the goals.

But in fact, it is really not about 'management' (the position that is held) but 'managing' while integrating these four functions of management seamlessly.

Traditional day-to-day managerial skills are largely based on contingency management—managing depending on the situation. Managing focuses on different approaches to A, B, and C employees, preparing and conducting performance reviews, having crucial or difficult conversations, and coaching & mentoring. In progressive organizations, it's all about the *culture* and the employee experience. Managing focuses on reducing the unconscious bias, developing and using Objectives and Key Results (OKRs), giving and receiving feedback in real time (RTF), having regular coaching conversations, and responding to teachable moments.

Obviously, the ability to #ZigZag between traditional and professional day-to-day managerial skills is very important for achieving personal, team, and organizational performance. In this module, we discuss these day-to-day managerial skills.

DAY-TO-DAY MANAGERIAL SKILLS IN TRADITIONAL ORGANIZATIONS

Traditional day-to-day managerial skills focus on managing A, B, and C employees, preparing and conducting performance reviews, coaching and mentoring, and having crucial or difficult conversations with employees.

Managing A-B-C-Players

In their now classic 2001 book, *The War for Talent*, Ed Michaels, Helen Handfield-Jones, and Beth Axelrod differentiated between A, B, and C-players in assessing people's performance.[3] They suggested investing in those people who consistently deliver results and inspire others (A-players); affirming and developing solid performers who meet expectations but have limited upward mobility (B-players); and acting decisively to raise the performance of employees who deliver barely acceptable results or remove them from the workplace (C-players). Jack Welsh, Chairman and CEO at General Electric from 1981 to 2001 who often talked about the critical importance of human resources, popularized managing the performance of A-players (20% of the workforce), B-players (70%) and C-players (10%) differently. Ideally, an organization would have 70-80% of A-players, 20-30% of B-players, and no C-players at all. Let's dig deeper into the profile of these different players. What do they want and what is the best way to manage them day-to-day?

1. C-Players

The profile of the C-player is one of an employee who underperforms either due to lack of motivation, lack of abilities, or both. In the "performance is motivation times ability" (P=M x A) heuristic, C-players are in the bottom left cell of the two-by-two (low motivation and low ability) matrix. The C-player is often not 'managed' properly, put in the wrong job, or their skills have not kept up with the new work demands.

In a 2002 *Harvard Business Review* article entitled, "A new game plan for C-players," Beth Axelrod, Helen Hanfield-Jones, and Ed Michaels elaborate on why people (managers and co-workers) tolerate low performers or fail to deal with them.[4] They argue that confronting low performers is fraught with emotional, ideological, and practical barriers:

- **Emotional**—we work with them, have a friendship relationship, and empathize with them.
- **Ideological**—we believe they can become B-players, have a degree of loyalty to them, and want to be fair.
- **Practical**—we fear litigation and find the process too onerous to manage.

The authors propose a number of alternatives for managers with C-players. Doing nothing is NOT a viable choice but managers have the following alternatives in dealing with C-players:

1. Improve their performance from C to B or even A.
2. Move the C-player to a job that better matches his/her skills (may be a demotion).
3. Have them leave the company (through voluntary separation or termination).

The best practice managerial action is to manage C performers in the following way:

- Identify C-players by evaluating their talent and distributing employee performance along an assessment curve.
- Agree on explicit action plans that articulate the improvements or changes C performers must achieve within three to twelve months—known as the traditional Performance Improvement Plan or PIP.

- Provide the necessary coaching, support, and resources to assist the C performer to make the necessary improvements.

Managing a C-player is a lot of work for a manager! While it may be compelling to do nothing, managerial action is essential for the individual, the team, and the organizations. C-players are not necessarily happy in their failure to perform up to the standard as their lack of performance impacts the entire team. Let's not immediately dismiss them but try to support their turnaround efforts. As a general rule, when C-players are no longer ignored, but supported, they are likely to improve. In the U.S., managers often make the mistake of aggressively documenting the C-player's PIP and setting such high expectations for the C-player to turn around that the employee cannot realistically achieve them in the 90-day period, causing them to leave the company—only for them to come back and sue the employer for constructive discharge, where the employee resigns as a result of the manager setting unrealistic performance expectations and creating a hostile work environment.

The manager needs to be able to 'diagnose' a C-player before proceeding with a 90-day view and ascertain whether it is a 'can't do' or 'won't do', a skill issue or an attitude issue. Most managers will try to help an employee with a skill issue if the C-player is willing and able to learn. An attitude issue may not justify 90 days but having a coaching conversation. A performance issue may need a more crucial conversation with some tight deadlines. In that case, micro-manage the performance of the C-player by restricting their job responsibilities so the employee can focus on improving their performance, get necessary training, resources, and coaching support for a relatively short period of time (90 days or so). Hopefully, the manager gains the trust of the C-player, sends the message that they really want to help them improve, and acknowledge small improvements when they occur. Managers also can protect the C-player from the set-up-to-fail syndrome other co-workers have attached to them and fail to take the small improvement steps seriously. The organization must hold its managers accountable for carrying out the action plan and support the employee.

2. B-Players

B-players are steady performers due to their commitment and solid contributions to the organization. They play an important role in the success of the organization. They are not necessarily less intelligent than A-players but have different personalities and temperaments. B-players bring enormous value to the organization: their stability makes them particularly important contributors to the organizational memory; they are less frightened about restructuring; they are internal resources to mentor less experienced employees through transition, stress, and change; they are less affected by management shake-ups; and they usually ignore political infighting and go about their work; they are, in many ways, the steady backbone of the organization.

According to Thomas DeLong and Vineeta Vijayaraghavan, in a 2003 Harvard Business Review article "Let's hear it for B-players," there are plenty of misconceptions about B employees such as: everybody is the same; everybody wants the same things out of work; everybody wants to be promoted; and everybody wants to be a manager. Yet B-players have certain communalities: they have an aversion to calling attention to themselves; they place a high premium on work-life balance and highly value the time they spend with family and friends; and assume one of a limited number of distinct organizational types as recovered A-players, truth tellers, go-to people, and middlings:[5]

- **Recovered A-players**—they have been A-players, scaled back their ambitions for more time with family. But if successfully managed, they can pinch hit in time of crisis.
- **Truth tellers**—individuals with a zeal for honesty and reality in their interactions with superiors. They are often functional experts, may be politically naïve, and prefer work rather than career.

- **Go-to-people**—have an extraordinary feel for the organizational processes and norms. They can be extremely helpful during organizational change and uncertainty as they are unaffected by the turmoil and can be a stability anchor for co-workers.
- **Middling**—are less competent than other B-players but somehow hang in there without becoming a C-player.

3. A-Players

The typical profile of the A-player is that they know their worth, are organizationally savvy, often ignore corporate hierarchy, expect instant success (such as rapid promotion, high-end compensation, etc.), are well connected, have a low boredom threshold, and won't thank you for their success.[6] While in fact A-players often get the least attention at all from managers—as they don't really have performance issues—A-players require special managerial attention if organizations want them to thrive and retain them. A common mistake is to put A-players in charge of C-players as A-players like to play with other A-players!

A-players have a bias for thinking and action and thrive on innovation. In their 2014 book, *How Google Works*, Eric Schmidt and Jonathan Rosenberg propose the following best practices in managing 'smart creatives': place culture at the top of their list; give them the ability to dissent; and make arguments based on data.[7] DeLong and Vijayaraghavan recommend that managers protect A-players from 'organizational rain' or the rules and policies associated with any big-budget activity in an organization.[8]

Performance Management Skills

Traditional organizations tend to rely on periodic performance reviews. While there are many pitfalls to such annual or bi-annual performance appraisals (as discussed in module 12), if the organization still uses performance reviews, it is important for managers to conduct them as skillfully as possible to reduce their pitfalls. Many of the enterprise systems (such as Workday) also have performance management modules that automate, document, and streamline some of the performance review process.

To increase the reliability and validity of the performance appraisals, HR can conduct frame-of-reference (FOR) training with managers and employees and focus on the process itself, critical incidents, and the development of action plans for improvement or further development.

1. The PA Process

Performance appraisal is just one component of the performance management wheel. The manager (and employee) completes the performance appraisal form used by the company and conducts a performance review meeting with the ratee. The manager then must assess whether the employee's performance is 'satisfactory' (meets and or exceeds expectations) or the performance 'needs improvement' (fails to meet expectations) and drafts a Performance Improvement Plan (PIP) for employees who do not meet performance or a Performance Development Plan for employees meeting and exceeding performance (PDP). For a PDP, the manager monitors the employee's performance (usually for 90 days in the U.S. and countries where this approach is legally supported) and conducts a follow-up performance appraisal meeting. In many cases, a company may provide a (lucrative) severance package and avoid the 90 days. In a PDP, the manager, jointly with the employee, sets goals and objectives for the next performance period; identifies resources and opportunities for growth; and links the performance to reward structure (i.e., merit increases).

2. Critical Incidents

One of the managerial skills in completing the performance appraisal is for the manager to write a narrative that justifies the rating rather than simply providing a numerical rating. More and more companies (and automated PA systems) are dropping numeric ratings in favor of such narratives. This is where critical incidents come into play. A critical incident is a technique where the manager keeps a log of positive and negative critical incidents based on the quantitative (work output) and qualitative (interactions with customers and co-workers) behaviors of the employee. These incidents provide examples of positive (good) or negative (bad or unacceptable) behaviors. These critical incidents are then used to write a narrative that focuses on behavior and can be discussed with the employee during their review. Employees may be asked when completing their performance appraisal form to do the same for themselves. While writing critical incidents over a six- to twelve-month period of time reduces the 'recency' bias in performance appraisals; it is not a substitute for a manager to deal with positive and negative critical incident long after they have happened!

3. Developing an Action Plan

Action plans are great tools for managers to support their employees in reaching performance goals. As mentioned above, action plans can be used for improving employee performance (a PIP) or further developing employees (PDP). Both action plans follow the same steps and are jointly crafted and agreed upon by both the manager and the employee:

- **Step 1: Goal**—identify an improvement or development goal. When setting a goal, you must clearly identify where the employee should be when the goal is successfully achieved.
- **Step 2: Specific objectives**—write at least three objectives that will help accomplish that goal. Use the SMART format. SMART is an acronym for Specific, Measurable, Achievable, Result-oriented, and Time bound.
- **Step 3: Action plan**—develop a multi-step action plan for achieving the objective. Each goal (and the related SMART objectives) should include a multi-step action plan. When outlining a plan, indicate the various action steps that need to be taken to accomplish the goal (steps), how long it will take to achieve the various action steps (time) and the overall results (measurement).

The ability of managers to work with employees to develop an action plan lies at the basis of coaching and mentoring.

Coaching and Mentoring

Coaching and mentoring are not tools for disciplinary measures or corrective actions but are ways for managers to develop their employees to reach higher performance.

Coaching is an integrated set of actions aimed at boosting the performance of an individual or team. It requires a context of trust and understanding, the use of 'ask' not only 'tell,' agreement on the goals, optimizing opportunities to have ongoing and ad hoc feedback, periodically planning a coaching session of greater depth, a recognition by the line manager of the obligation to coach, and the organizational incentives to do so.[9] Coaching "*focuses on helping another person learn in ways that let him or her keep growing afterward (...) and on holding a person accountable for his or her goals.*"[10] Optimal coaching requires a context of trust and understanding between the coach and the mentee and an agreement on the goals so opportunities to perform are optimized. It requires ongoing and ad hoc feedback.

Developing coaching as an organization capability requires tools and support for managers to be coaches. A common model for coaching is the GROW model developed by John Whitmore is the standard for the International Coach Federation (ICF) dedicated to professional coaching. The acronym stands for Goal, Reality, Option, and Will.[11]

- Goal—what do you want?
- Reality—where are you now?
- Options—what could you do?
- Will—what will you do?

In a 2019 *Harvard Business Review* article entitled, "The Leader as Coach," Herminia Ibarra and Anne Scoular recommend that in order to cope with disruptive change, companies need to reinvent themselves as learning organizations and adopt a new approach where leader serve as coaches. Managers ask questions instead of providing answers, support employees instead of judging them, and facilitate their development instead of dictating what has to be done. Yet, most managers don't feel they have the time and they are not good at it! They suggest basic steps for developing coaching capability in managers:[12]

1. Articulate the 'why'
2. Model the behavior
3. Build capability throughout the organization
4. Remove the barriers

Mentoring is "*(...) a relationship between two individuals based on a mutual desire for development toward career goals and objectives. The relationship is a non- reporting one and replaces none of the organizational structures in place.*"[13] While coaching is more task and short-term oriented—concrete issues that need to be addressed and skills to be developed—mentoring is more relationship and long-term oriented—to share guidance for professional and personal success. In some cases, we speak of reverse mentoring, when much younger and less experienced employees mentor older and often higher-level bosses in a specific area of experience—for example social media skills, IT skills, etc.

Crucial and Fierce Conversations

There are times when we have to have a real conversation with our subordinates or co-workers. Some may have excellent performance but exhibit behavior that is unacceptable. Others may be free-riding on a team or not carrying their share of responsibilities. Or, as is often the case with managing C-players, managers often fail to have a real conversation with the person until it is too late.

There are many books out there that suggest ways to have such conversations that are crucial, difficult, and fierce. While these books are more experience than evidence-based, they contain practical nuggets that managers can adopt to see whether the suggested best practices for providing true feedback work for them. Having crucial conversations with others apply not only at work but also in one's private life. In their book, *Crucial Conversations*, Kerry Patterson, Joseph Grenny, Ron McMillan, and Al Switzler focus on how to deliver a tough message.[14] A crucial conversation is a discussion between two or more people where (1) the stakes are high; (2) opinions may vary; and (3) emotions run strong. People have different response modes including silence, violence, or dialogue. The authors suggest the following best practices in crucial conversations:

- **Work on yourself before working on others**—more often than not, we do something to contribute to the problems we're experiencing.
- **Aim for a dialog**—ask yourself, what do I want for myself, the other(s), and the relationship?
- **Create a shared pool of knowledge**—ask clarifying questions to encourage others to add their knowledge to the 'shared pool.'
- **Embrace 'and'/'or' when making decisions**—rather than making a choice between either/or thinking, consider a third option that is a compromise.
- **Create a safe environment for voicing productive conflict**—establish mutual purpose in conversations with others.
- **Use contrasting**—what you DO mean and what you DON'T mean—to rebuild safety when others misinterpret your intent in the discussion.
- **Don't confuse stories with facts**—we tend to add meaning to the action we observed. See/Hear → Tell a Story → Feel → Act.
- **State the path that led to your story**—Facts → Mental story → Other Story → Truth.
- **Don't jump to conclusions frequently**—these conclusions are often fraught with unfair assumptions and inadequate facts. Perception might not be reality: a manager saying to an employee, "you are not paying attention to what I say," is different from a manager who says, "every time you look at your PC or mobile phone during the meetings, I think you are not paying attention."

In her book, *Fierce Conversations*, Susan Scott argues that unreal conversations are incredibly expensive for organizations and individuals.[15] Instead, a fierce conversation is "one in which we come out from behind ourselves into the conversation and make it real." The most valuable thing during a fierce conversation is finding a way to "say the things that can't be said." Fierce conversations "interrogate reality," provoke learning, tackle tough challenges, and enrich relationships. It is the difference between "ground truth"—available for general circulation and often seen as propaganda—and "official truth"—seldom offered for public consumption.

The author suggests the following best practices in confrontations and giving feedback:

- Each of us owns a piece of the truth;
- Healthy relationships require appreciation and confrontation;
- Avoid using praise as a lead-in to a confrontation;
- Fierce conversations cannot be dependent on how others respond;
- For a leader, there is no trivial comment—something you might not even remember saying may have had a devastating impact on someone looking to you for guidance and approval and something you said years ago may have encouraged and inspired someone who is grateful to you to this day;
- As a leader, you get what you tolerate.

These crucial and fierce conversations are difficult, and this type of constructive feedback is often not given at work. Not having a crucial or fierce conversation when needed is a missed opportunity for both the manager and the employee. When a manager does not hold people accountable to a continual higher standard of expectations at work when they are not performing—at least not at the level they are capable of—it impacts the entire team. It's really important that someone gives critical feedback, provided it is honest, the person cares, has the other's best interest in mind, and wants the receiver of the feedback to succeed.

DAY-TO-DAY MANAGERIAL SKILLS IN PROGRESSIVE ORGANIZATIONS

When progressive organizations started to abolish their performance appraisal systems, they focused on a different set of managerial activities aimed at reducing the unconscious bias, developing objectives and key results, introducing real-time feedback, having coaching conversations, and focusing on strength management and teachable moments.

1. Unconscious Biases

An unconscious bias is a bias that happens automatically when making decisions. An unconscious bias affects our perceptions, decisions, and interactions and is the result from making quick judgments and assessments of people and situations automatically (unaware) influenced by our background, cultural environment and personal experiences. When making decisions fast and without data, we fill in the gaps with the 'unconscious' bias. It can be positive—helping us to process information quickly and efficiently--or negative—making decisions that are not objective. Remember, previous modules on behavioral economics and performance management both elaborated on the unconscious bias in management decisions and ratings.

2. Objectives and Key Results (OKRs)

OKRs are a management practice to set and share short-term employee, team, and organizational objectives and measure and report progress toward achieving the intended *key results* so everyone can develop personal competencies while focusing their performance on organizational results. First formally introduced by John Doerr at Intel in the 1990s, OKRs are not new in management per se, but some aspects such as connectivity, sharing, transparency, and agility are made possible through IT applications, the changing nature of work, and the needs of current workers.[16]

Precursors to OKRs are Management by Objectives (MBO),[17] SMART objectives,[18] balanced scorecards,[19] and Key Performance Indicators (KPIs).[20] They are all fundamentally aimed at aligning individual performance with organizational performance. Recently, many global organizations (such as Intel, Google, General Assembly, LinkedIn, Oracle, Twitter, Sears, Uber, and Zynga to name a few) have embraced OKRs.

The 'O' of OKR, stands for "*What do I want to accomplish?*" (Objectives) that are personally meaningful, significant to the company, and aspirational.[21] Each employee has agreed upon goals developed top-down and bottom-up. The 'KR' (Key Results) stands for "*How will I accomplish the objective?*" in terms of means, time frames, and measurable results. From both—the manager's and the employee's points of view—key results must be concrete in terms of metrics such as, "*Achievement of these specific metrics will confirm my success,*" or "*Success in achieving this objective is defined by these metrics...*"

Employees are asked to set individual OKRs (usually about three) on a quarterly basis. They meet one-on-one with their manager or the team. The various individual OKRs are then discussed and negotiated in a larger group, resulting in departmental OKRs. These are then presented and discussed with the entire organization (e.g., through a town hall meeting or posting). OKRs are developed and agreed upon through both a bottom up and a cascading down process in terms of sharing and aligning objectives and results at all levels of the organization (i.e., individual, group, and organizational level OKRs). Progress on the OKRs are tracked and shared on a weekly basis and the status is regularly updated. At the end of the quarter, results are reviewed and new objectives are set.

It should be noted that OKRs must be separate from performance appraisals, must not impact compensation, and are not an alternative to performance reviews. While writing, OKRs may look deceptively simple and easy, they should not be equated to setting SMART objectives or developing action plans. In order for OKRs to be aligned throughout the company, it will require training of managers and employees to develop and orchestrate them.

In addition to being flexible and agile to respond to changing conditions, there are many benefits to the use of OKRs:[22]

- Aligns individual and organizational goals;
- Imposes disciplined thinking in the planning of work priorities;
- Helps focus the efforts and results of employees on agreed upon issues;
- Informs everyone regarding what's important to work on;
- Enables more accurate communication;
- Provides a means to see progress and accomplishment;
- Fosters transparency and accountability for everyone in the organization (top-down, bottom up, and cross-functional);
- Separates OKRs from performance reviews;
- Promotes risk taking by setting aspirational and stretch objectives;
- Develops the entire enterprise.

The main advantage of OKRs is that they allow employees and managers to be realistic about what they want to achieve based on the organization's strategic business goals. Employees are encouraged to consider stretch objectives and key results with the goal of attainting 60 to 70 percent of them. Since the OKRs are public, employees can view the OKRs of others to ensure a consistent level of stretch across the organization. The key results for each objective provide a specific and easily understandable metric that indicates success. In this way, there is an implied individual and organizational accountability that facilitates teamwork across the global organization.

Since the OKRs are purposely not tied to compensation, there is a lack of incentive for the employee to 'sandbag' their goals and objectives to maximize compensation. Some organizations keep their traditional performance review process intact for purposes of compensation rewards even after implementing OKRs. Although there may be some overlap between employee objective setting as part of the performance management process and their OKRs, they really should be kept as two separate systems when employed together with the performance objectives linked to employee accountability and OKRs for work alignment purposes in the organization. If OKRs replace performance reviews as a method for determining compensation awards, the advantages of OKRs will disappear and the system will become a cosmetic name change for performance appraisals.

3. Real-Time Feedback (RTF)

An important managerial skill is to be able to provide to others. The feedback can be positive or negative; instant or delayed; social (your performance is better or worse than others) or self-comparative (against yourself); done in person or through an app.

Feedback—often given as constructive criticism or negative feedback—may lead to discomfort, especially in a classroom or work environment. The focus on developmental feedback leads to growth and continuous performance improvement. This demands a great deal of intellectual engagement with ideas and people you may find uncongenial or even wrong. Feedback raises awareness of strengths & weaknesses (or areas for improvement) and identifies actions to be taken to improve/optimize performance. Progressive companies that no longer use performance appraisals create a transparent culture where people (managers and co-workers) can provide honest and supportive feedback in real time, allowing people to quickly correct their behavior. Feedback is a term often used in the performance management process with the goal of improving the performance of an individual or a team. The feedback giver does not have to be a person of authority or in a management role and can be a peer or colleague. However, effective feedback does require that the giver has a trusting relationship with the receiver. Feedback is typically a short, concise, and empathetic conversation.[23] RTF gives information to employees on their performance frequently and shortly after it happens. This allows employees to make small incremental corrections toward improved performance.

Continuous Performance Management (CPM) in the form of Continuous Performance Feedback (CPF) replaces the annual performance review in progressive companies. According to John Doerr—the initiator of OKRs at Intel—CPF stands for conversation, feedback, and recognition.[24]

- **C = Conversation**—*"an authentic, richly textured exchange between manager and contributor aimed at driving performance."*
- **F = Feedback**—*"bi-directional or networked communication among peers to evaluate progress and guide future improvement."*
- **R = Recognition**—*"expressions of appreciation to deserving individuals for contributions of all sizes."*

In a 2019 *Harvard Business Review* article, "Why feedback fails," Marcus Buckingham and Ashley Goodall explore how various feedback theories—based on the premises of let me tell you, let me teach you, or let me show you—may not be as successful as we thought in improving a person's performance.[25]

- **Theory of the source of truth**—other people are more aware of your weaknesses than you are of your own. Others help you by showing what you cannot see yourself. But humans are unreliable raters and idiosyncratic rater effect produces systematic errors. Hence, **let me tell** you may not be an effective way to provide feedback!
- **Theory of learning**—you lack certain abilities you need to acquire, so others should teach you. But criticism inhibits the brain's ability to learn. People grow more learning from their strengths than their weaknesses. Hence, let me teach you may not be an effective way to provide feedback!
- **Theory of excellence**—performance is universal, analyzable, desirable, once defined it can be transferred from one person to another. But excellence is idiosyncratic, can't be defined in advance, and is not the opposite of failure. Things cannot be learned by studying failure. Hence, let me show you may not be an effective way to provide feedback!

Millennials and Gen Z workers are very keen at getting instant feedback in real time as they value (and expect) to grow and develop at work. While Millennials want feedback, they prefer positive feedback and may be particularly sensitive to feedback that is negative or constructive. As mentioned earlier, someone giving such critical feedback must provide it in an honest manner, show they really care, and have the millennials best interest in mind if they want the millennial worker not to perceive the feedback as an attack. In providing feedback and help people excel, Buckingham and Goodall suggest the feedback giver considers the following:

- **Look for outcomes**—recognize what excellence looks like and acknowledge people when they do something the right way ("That! Yes that!"); not just for praise but for learning.
- **Replay your instinctive reactions**—describe what you experience when excellence in someone catches your attention; explore the nature of excellence.
- **Never lose sight of your highest priorities and interrupt**—interrupt and direct when you see something that really works; allowing to rest and digest it what makes it work.
- **Explore present, past, and future**—start with the present when dealing with a problem and look at the three things that work right now; when you or someone had a problem in the past, what did they do that worked; when looking at the future, what do you actually want to happen, what do you already know you need to know.

Feedback by people who know us and care about us is very powerful, especially when they tell us how the behavior (positive and negative) they observe impacts them and others. In our zeal to help people improve performance, we often only focus on what people do wrong. Instead, *"if you see somebody doing something that really works, stop her and dissect it."*[26] In giving feedback, ask people questions such: What does great look like? Describe a moment when you are happy and fully effective and successful in your role? What are you doing? How do others behave around you?

4. Coaching Conversations

At the core of the new performance management paradigm is the role of managers as coaches. The annual performance appraisal is replaced with ongoing coaching conversations between the manager and the employee. A coaching conversation is a two-way conversation that stimulates thinking, growth, and change that leads to action. It develops people and unleashes their potential. A coaching conversation is simply a short conversation where the manager inquires with the employee regarding a project and gets an answer to the following questions:

- How has it been going?
- What have you done that has gone well?
- What might you have done differently that might have made your results even better?
- What did you learn from the project that you are going to apply to the next project?

Managers are held accountable for engaging in these coaching conversations with their employees on a regular basis. Many organizations align at least some of the feedback and coaching conversations to their company values. This allows the employee to self-assess their performance, aim at improvement and development, and produce performance results in alignment with the core values of the organization. Some employers require some quick online documentation that a conversation took place. Others may use regular pulse surveys with their employees to ensure that such conversations are actually taking place regularly.

Google has gone to great lengths to identify the traits and associated behaviors of high performing managers grounded in analytics.[27] Through the analytics obtained in Google's Project Oxygen, they identified the eight traits of high performing managers—noteworthy is that many of these traits relate to day-to-day managerial soft skills:

1. Be a good coach
2. Empower; don't micromanage
3. Be interested in direct reports, success and well-being
4. Don't be a sissy: be productive and results-oriented
5. Be a good communicator and listen to your team
6. Help your employees with career development
7. Have a clear vision and strategy for the team
8. Have key technical skills so you can advise the team

> *NOTE FROM THE AUTHORS: We do not like the wording of, "don't be a sissy" (emphasis own), as the terms denotes a person regarded as effeminate or cowardly. Yet, it is the official wording in Google's Project Oxygen!*

In replacing its annual performance cycles with a simple snapshot of job-impact evaluation, Google believes these two questions only need to be asked to peers every six months:

1. What's one thing person x does really well and should continue doing?
2. What's one thing person x could improve on in order to have more impact?

In his 2013 book, *The End of Performance Review*, Tim Baker provides a 'Five Conversations Framework' for managers wanting to start coaching conversations with employees.[28] Over a period of five months, the manager starts a conversation about different and expanding spheres of topics (climate review; strengths and talents; opportunities for growth; learning and development; innovation and continuous improvement) each with specific content and key 'how' and 'what' questions. Note that 'why' questions are avoided in coaching conversations.

The approach used in positive coaching—a trend in sports coaching—is to prepare and train 'double goal' coaches or coaches who balance the goal of winning with the second, and more important, goal of teaching life lessons. The most helpful feedback for young athletes developing their potential does not consist of praise for good performance or criticism for bad performance. Positive coaching focuses on having people understand they control three key variables, namely their level of *effort*, whether they *learn* from experiences, and how they respond to *mistakes*.[29]

5. Strength Management

In a classic 2005 *Harvard Business Review* article entitled, "Managing oneself," Peter Drucker introduces the notion a person can only perform really well based on their strengths and that strengths are a matter of personality (i.e., their cognitive and learning style). Hence, a person must try to work hard to improve the way they perform from the base of their given strengths. People discover their own strengths as a result of feedback.[30]

The focus on strength management in many global organizations is based on the following:[31]

- Spending time on employee weaknesses takes time and energy away from the development of their strengths.
- Employees must bring their weaknesses up to the bar, especially those that stand in the way of their strengths.
- It is really difficult to turn a weakness into a strength, but it is possible to stop or minimize the impact of the weakness.

6. Teachable Moments

Employee development is critical in the new performance management system. But rather than relying on extensive HR development (HRD) interventions, managers are being urged to take advantage of teachable moments—identified on the spot or through analytics—and provide customized just-in-time training interventions based on the needs of the employee and the job. A teachable moment is an unplanned event during the day that managers can use as a learning opportunity for employees. A teachable moment allows for quick knowledge transfer. Teaching moments can be uploaded and stored in a training portal—by either managers or employees—especially if the same "teaching moment" repeats itself and the learning is useful for others in the organization.

A teachable moment allows for just-in time customized advice and teaching when the employee needs it the most and can apply it immediately. A teachable moment intervention incorporates three important components of training effectiveness:[32]

- **Context**—meaningful and relevant for the learner at the time they need it;
- **Practice**—apply what they learn in their day-to-day job;
- **Feedback**—get immediate feedback for improved performance.

When a teachable moment is recognized—either through data or direct observation by the manager—the training intervention should be provided to the employee in a customized way. Many global organizations are letting managers and employees develop their own very short training interventions (e.g., a three- to five-minute how-to video) and putting them on the company's training portal for others to share. A rule of thumb for managers is that when the same thing needs to be explained frequently (more than three times) and it is of vital importance to performance, they (or their employee) should consider finding or putting together an online resource to quickly make the coaching available to all.

DAY-TO-DAY MANAGERIAL SKILLS SET

Your day-to-day managerial skill set should include both traditional and progressive management skills. As a successful manager and team member, you will need to be able to—depending on the type of organization you work in—

- Use contingency management depending on the situation.
- Use different approaches to manage A, B, and C employees.
- Prepare and conduct periodic performance reviews of your organizations.
- Write positive and negative narrative critical incidents you observe.
- Have crucial or difficult conversations with employees when needed.
- Coach others (and be coached).
- Mentor others (and be mentored—including reverse mentoring).
- Develop OKRs.
- Provide real-time feedback.
- Engage in coaching conversations with others.
- Manage others (and self) based on strengths.
- Identify and use teachable moments.

These skills require practice, resilience, and emotional intelligence to work with others in an agile manner and at a sustainable pace. ▮

REFERENCES

1. Perrin, C., & Blauth, C. (2010). *The Basic Principles: Building Blocks of Trust*. Tampa: AchieveGlobal.
2. Claus, L. & Arens, L. (2019). *#ZigZagHR: Why the Best HR is no Longer HR*. Silverton: Global Immersion Press.
3. Michaels, E., Handfield-Jones, H., & Axelrod, B. (2001). *The War for Talent*. Boston: Harvard Business Press.
4. Axelrod, B., Handfield-Jones, H., & Michaels, E. (2001). "A New Game Plan For C-players," *Harvard Business Review* 80(1): 80-88.
5. DeLong, T., & Vijayaraghavan, V. (2003). "Let's Hear It for B-players," *Harvard Business Review*, 81(6): 96-102.
6. Goffee, R., & Jones, G. (2007). "Leading Clever People," *Harvard Business Review*, 85(3): 72-79.
7. Schmidt, E., & Rosenberg, J. (2014). *How Google Works*. New York: Grand Central Publishing.
8. DeLong, T., & Vijayaraghavan, V. (2003). "Let's Hear It for B-players," *Harvard Business Review*, 81(6): 96-102.
9. Landsberg, M. (1997). *The Tao of Coaching*. Santa Monica: Knowledge Exchange.
10. Frankovelgia, C. (2010). *The Key to Effective Coaching*. April 28 (Accessed: January 11, 2020). https://www.forbes.com/2010/04/28/coaching-talent-development-leadership-managing-ccl.html#14cba13338e0
11. Whitmore, J. (2009). *Coaching for Performance: People Skills for Professionals* (4th ed.). Boston: Nicholas Brealey.
12. Ibarra, H. & Scoular, A. (2019). "The Leader as Coach," *Harvard Business Review*, 97(6): 110-119.
13. American Association of Pharmaceutical Scientists (AAPS). (2017). *What is Mentoring?* (Accessed: June, 2018). https://www.aaps.org/uploadedFiles/Content/Career_Center/Professional_Development/ What_is_Mentoring.pdf.
14. Patterson, K., Grenny, J., McMillan, R., & Switzler, A. (2012). *Crucial Conversations: Tools for Talking When Stakes are High*. New York: Mc Graw-Hill.
15. Scott, S. (2001). *Fierce Conversations: Achieving Success at Work & in Life, One Conversation at a Time*. New York: Berkley Books.
16. Doerr, J. (2018). *Measure What Matters: How Google, Bono, and the Gates Foundation Rock the World with OKRs*. New York: Penguin.
17. Drucker, P. (1976). "What Results Should You Expect: A Users' Guide to MBO," *Public Administration Review*, 36(1):1 2-19.
18. Doran, G. (1981). There's a SMART Way to Write Management's Goals and Objectives," *Management Review*, 70(11): 35-36.
19. Kaplan, R. & Norton, D. "The Balanced Scorecard: Measures That Drive Performance," *Harvard Business Review*, 70(1): 71-79.
20. Parmenter, D. (2010). *Key Performance Indicators: Developing, Implementing, and Using Winning KPIs* (2nd ed.). New Jersey: John Wiley & Sons.
21. Nickols, F. (1997). "Don't Redesign Your Company's Performance Appraisal System, Scrap It! A Look at Costs and Benefits," *Corporate University Review*, May-June, 54-59.
22. Ibid.
23. Harley, S. (2013). *How to Say Anything to Anyone: A Guide to Building Business Relationships That Really Work*. Denver: Greenleaf Book Group Press.
24. Doerr, J. (2018). *Measure What Matters: How Google, Bono, and the Gates Foundation Rock the World with OKRs*. New York: Penguin.
25. Buckingham, M., & Goodall, A. (2019). "Why Feedback Fails," *Harvard Business Review*, 97(2): 92-101.
26. Ibid.
27. Devos, K. (2015). "Learnings from Silicon Valley: Ground Zero of the Entrepreneurial Competence," *HR Builders*, 15(1).
28. Baker, T. (2013). *The End of the Performance Review: A New Approach to Appraising Employee Performance*. London: Palgrave Mamillan.
29. Bornstein, D. (2011). The Power of Positive coaching. New York Times, October 20. (Accessed: January 19, 2020). https://opinionator.blogs.nytimes.com/2011/10/20/the-power-of-positive-coaching.
30. Peter F. Drucker, "Managing oneself," *Harvard Business Review* 83, 1 (2005): 100-109.
31. Buckingham, M. (2007). *Go Put your Strengths to Work: 6 Powerful Steps To Achieve Outstanding Performance*. New York: Free Press; Roberts, L., Spreitzer, G., Dutton, J., Heaphy, R., & Barker, B. (2005). "How to Play to Your Strengths," Harvard Business Review, 83(1): 45-80.
32. Segal, L., Goldstein, A., Goldman, J., & Harfoush, R. (2014). *The Decoded Company*. New York: Portfolio.

GUIDED READING QUESTIONS

1. What day-to-day managerial skills are included in traditional organizations?

2. What day-to-day managerial skills are included in progressive organizations?

3. What is the profile of an A employee?

4. What is the profile of a B employee?

5. What is the profile of a C employee?

6. What is the difference between a performance improvement plan and a performance development plan?

7. What is constructive discharge?

8. What is (are) ...?
   - Contingency management
   - Critical incident
   - Crucial conversation
   - Coaching
   - Mentoring
   - OKRs
   - Real-time feedback
   - Strength
   - Teachable moment

FOLLOW-UP CRITICAL THINKING QUESTIONS

1. What is my major takeaway from this reading?

2. What do I already know about this subject?

3. What follow-up questions do I have about this?

4. How can I apply this in real life?

KEY TERMS

A employee
Action plan
B employee
Balance scorecard
C employee
Coaching
Controlling
Constructive discharge
Critical incident
Crucial conversation
Feedback
Fierce conversations
Go-to-people
Key performance indicators
Leading
Management by objectives
Managing
Mentoring
Middlings
OKRs
Organizing
Performance appraisal
Performance appraisal process
Performance development plan
Performance improvement plan
Performance management
Performance review
Planning
Recovered A-player
Real-time feedback
Reverse mentoring
SMART objectives
Strength management
Teachable moment
The Basic Principles
Truth tellers
Unconscious bias

LEARNING ASSESSMENT

Critically reflect on the content and the different concepts in this module and rate your own competency using the assessment scale.

Competency	I never heard of it	I heard of it but have limited knowledge of it	I can reasonably explain it to others	I have used it, done it, applied it
Contingency management (A, B, C)	0	1	2	3
Critical incident	0	1	2	3
Crucial conversation	0	1	2	3
Coaching	0	1	2	3
Mentoring	0	1	2	3
OKRs	0	1	2	3
Real-time feedback	0	1	2	3
Strength	0	1	2	3
Teachable moment	0	1	2	3

MODULAR-SPECIFIC ASSESSMENT

The Leadership Motivation Assessment
MindTools
The quiz helps you find out how much you want to lead.
https://www.mindtools.com/pages/article/newLDR_01.htm

VIGNETTE

GLOBAL LEADERSHIP—THE VALUE OF LOCAL ORIGINS FOR GLOBAL SUCCESS[1]

By Thomas Belker[2]

It was snowing hard in November 2010 on a back country road somewhere in Germany. Traffic came to a standstill and with it a group of OBI Human Resource (HR) managers. They were on their way to a meeting with the management of several stores purchased from a competitor earlier that year. In terms of the physical predicament they were in, they reflected on the moment playfully as "HR at a standstill—business out of reach". That instance became the birthplace of a new global leadership approach at OBI Group, one of the leading DIY (Do-it-Yourself) home improvement retail brands in Europe doing business in 13 European countries with 560 stores, 41.500 employees and revenues of €6.4 billion in 2010.

The expansion at OBI had been at an all-time high during the previous three years, defying the world economic crisis, and the need for managers grew drastically, even exponentially. The organization had matured from a multi-national layout to a global setup and understanding, viewing the world as one market, moving talent globally and moving from a headquarters-based to a global strategic planning.[3] The group of OBI HR managers had been on their way to introduce corporate culture to the managers of the newly acquired stores. Now they were stuck in a snow-white world where sounds were muffled and time seemed to stand still. At first, they rehearsed a bit how they intended to discuss the cultural implications of the acquisition with the new managers. After a while the question came up, "what is culture anyway?" Is it everything that is not instinctive or is it better to stick to the adage of "the way we do things around here"?

At that time, OBI definitely did not have an abundance of potential to fill its new leadership positions. OBI expanded rapidly into new international markets in the late 1990s and 2000s. As in many fast growing organizations, there was no focus on developing parallel an overall corporate understanding of leadership—a global leadership approach. And, even if such approach was available, the knowledge of the evident differentiation in the leadership approach between different countries, business functions, and, definitely, between OBI headquarters and the retail stores?

The group of OBI HR managers came to the conclusion that there was dire need to develop more—and better—leaders. The essential question for the HR group was, "Did OBI need a global leadership approach, and if, what should be different in regard to the common understanding they had at that time?" Everyone agreed to get seriously involved in the topic.

REFERENCES

1. This vignette was prepared by Thomas Belker for the sole purpose of illustrating a global HR practice for instructional objectives. Global HR in Action © 2006, Global Immersion Press, All Rights Reserved.
2. Belker, T. (2013). "Global Leadership: The Value of Local Origins for Global Success," Pp. 2-14 in Claus, L., *Global HR Practitioner Handbook*, Silverton: Global Immersion Press.
3. For the internationalization of OBI, see: Claus, L. (2007). "*Internationalization of HR at OBI*." Global HR in Action Instructional Vignettes, Silverton: Global Immersion Press.

GUIDED READING QUESTIONS

1. How does an organization ensure that they have people with potential to fill new leadership positions?
2. How do we develop more and better managers?

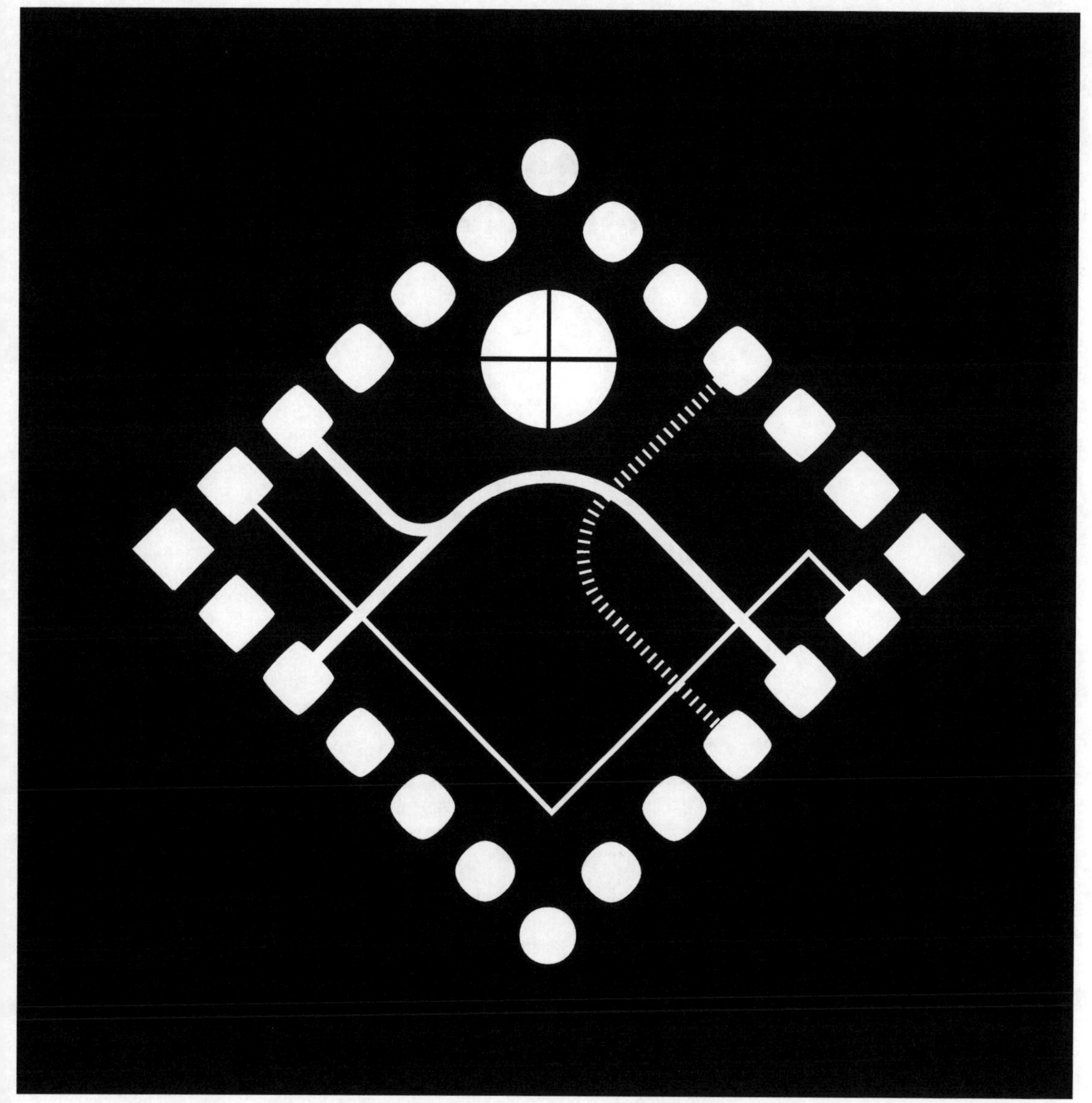

MODULE FOURTEEN

MANAGING CHANGE, INNOVATING AND EXECUTING GLOBALLY

MODULE FOURTEEN

MANAGING CHANGE, INNOVATING AND EXECUTING GLOBALLY

DESCRIPTION

This module focuses on managing change in organizations, the ability to innovate and implement successful organization-wide global change initiatives.

LEARNING OBJECTIVES

Upon completing the learning experience, you will be able to:

- Identify the underlying forces of change
- Describe and apply the change management models of Kurt Lewin and John Kotter
- Define and measure innovation
- Create and promote a culture
- Identify people and processes for successful execution and implementation

GUIDING QUESTION

Why do people and organizations resist change?

At this time, only three countries—Burma, Liberia, and the US—have not adopted the International System of Units (SI or metric system) as their official system of weights and measures. If you live in the U.S., your market prices food by the pound, shows temperature as degrees Fahrenheit in your weather reports, and the roads indicate distance in miles. Under the Carter administration, the Metric Conversion Act of 1975 was launched, but due to resounding apathy by the public, it was disbanded in 1982. Similarly, countries cannot agree on whether they will adopt daylight savings time and move their clocks back and forth in fall and bring. These are classic examples that culture eats process for lunch. While these are societal examples of resistance to change, people resist change in their organizations and in themselves as well.

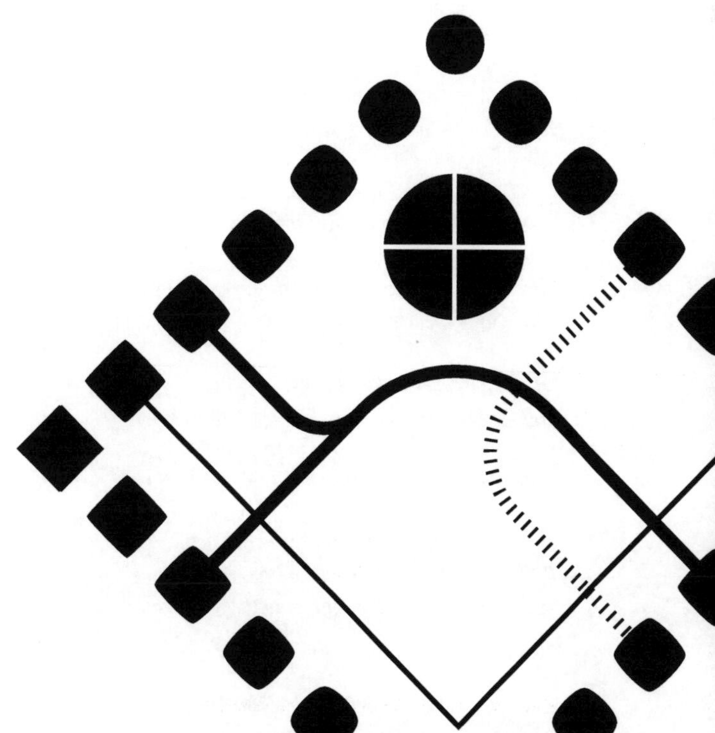

The core of change management is to understand and manage the impact of change at every level of the organization. While many people talk about change management from a conceptual point of view, it is really much harder to implement as any change has strategic, political, and cultural implications and often-unintended ripple effects. This module focuses on managing change in organizations and implementing successful organization-wide global change initiatives.

ORGANIZATIONAL CHANGE

Change is constant. People and organizations who cannot change or adapt to a changing environment cannot really survive. Change is both a leadership competency and an organizational agility. In every managerial or leadership competency model, a person's ability to manage change is always one of the critical leadership characteristics. A related managerial key competency is the ability to execute and deploy a (large) project or process—especially at a global level. The organizational agility relates to being able to implement and execute a global change.

Identifying the underlying forces, sources and drivers of change, the proverbial legend of the slowly boiling frog comes to mind. The story is often told in change management as a metaphor for people who are unable to adapt to slow gradual changes (a symbol of the frog who enjoys the tepid but slowly heating water) while crises and disruptive events are more likely to lead to change (a symbol of the frog jumping right away out if thrown in boiling water). While the legend has proven to be scientifically incorrect and real frogs behave differently, the story can still serve as a good metaphor for organizational culture.

Drivers for Organizational Change

Patrick E. Connor, Linda K, Lake, and Richard W. Stackman in their 2003 book, Managing Organizational Change, argue that change is the norm in organizational life and that "*the job of organizational leaders is not so much managing the day-to-day operations of an organization, but rather guide it through constant change.*"[1]

They identify the following underlying forces for the need for change:

- **Diversity**—the norm is that maintaining a diverse workplace is not only the right thing to do but also creates a competitive advantage if managed correctly.
- **Globalization**—working with multinational alliances and entering new markets creates 'otherness' and requires a transformation.
- **Consumers**—they are changing what they want and demand higher quality and greater value.
- **Employment practices**—the changing structure of employment sourcing, governance, and transparency.
- **Economic health**—global economic trends affecting everyone and demanding evolving relationships with state and governments (or commercial diplomacy).
- **Technology**—role of rapidly changing technology and availability of data.
- **The past**—lessons learned through crucible internal and external events and past changes affecting the organization and its people.

The sources and drivers for change can be internal or external. Internal sources for change can come from downsizing, lawsuits, leadership changes, professional associations and standards, new organizational goals, and an excess or shortage organizational resources. External sources for change are Political, Economic, Social, Technological, Legal, and Environmental factors—also known by the PESTLE acronym.

Organizational change is due to a variety of factors:

- **New structures**—restructuring, mergers, acquisitions, reorganizations, and closings;
- **New work procedures**—TQM, six sigma, reengineering, and agile management;
- **New systems**—new enterprise management systems in accounting, HR, ERP, etc.;
- **New standards**—related to performance, ethics, legal, and political environment, etc;

- **New people**—in leadership, boss, co-workers, and teams;
- **Employee changes**—such as promotions, demotions, terminations, and lay-offs;
- **Disruptions**—events threatening business continuity (natural and human-made crises, and disruptions);
- **Innovations**—leapfrogging, new tools and techniques;
- **Changing buying habits**—multiple sources of point of purchase;
- **New processes**—changes because of technology, crises, and controls;
- **Economic changes**—recession (negative) but also rapid economic development (emerging markets);
- **Global mobility**—and its impact on talent management.

Change is ultimately about uncertainty and organizational survival. The consequences of changing are usually less well known than the consequences of the status quo. One or more of the following factors usually precipitate change: a dissatisfaction with the status quo; a strong desire or need to move to a more desirable condition; the appeal of a well-thought out strategy for realizing a vision; or a crisis.

Diagnosing Change

From a practical perspective diagnosing change means communicating change with those who may not support it by asking probing questions about their concerns. When a change management initiative is deliberately introduced in an organization, the starting point is to have clarity about the project, purpose, particulars, and people of the change—referred to as the four Ps of change:[2]

- **Project**—what is the project?
- **Purpose**—why are we changing?
- **Particulars**—what are we changing?
- **People**—who will be changing?

These four Ps of a change initiative are interrelated. However, since projects are still large implemented by people the success of its execution lies in the purpose-people interaction. Hence, it is important to understand how much of the 'purpose' can be achieved if the 'people' do not adopt the change into their day-to-day work, and what percentage of the 'purpose' of a 'project' is dependent upon the 'people' doing their jobs differently? Too many large-scale project implementations in organizations do not really 'stick' because the lack of focus on the people component and how the change will affect them.

Stage Models of Organizational Change

In organizational behavior, change management is often viewed as a stage model—different stages from the before to the after.[3] Organizational change is complex and the focus of activity in a change initiative alters over time. Organizational change is bracketed by a period of preparing the organization for change and a period of ensuring the change will be embedded in the organization. One of the best-known stage modules of change is Kurt Lewin's three-step change model and force-field analysis developed in the 1940s and 1950s.[4]

The three stages of Lewin's model are:

1. **Unfreezing**—mobilization and create motivation for change—ready to change;
2. **Change**—movement toward developing new attitudes and behaviors—implementation of the change;
3. **Refreezing**—sustaining and stabilizing change—making it stick;

Social systems are highly resistant to change and organizational inertia sets in. This inertia is created by a *'force field'* in which the organization maintains a quasi-form of equilibrium—some create pressure for change; others create counterbalancing forces for stability. Lewin's force-field analysis model focuses on identifying and understanding the facilitating (forces for the change) and restraining forces (against the change). To create change, one must first disrupt the equilibrium (*unfreeze*) before the change initiative begins (*change*), and then create a new equilibrium that maintains the new conditions (*refreezing*). Change initiatives encounter strong resistance even when there is agreement on the desirability of the change. The major takeaway from Lewin's theory is that unfreezing is more successful if it is directed to reducing the forces that block the change rather than increasing the forces for change. If not managed properly, change initiatives are often short-lived with the system returning to its previous state.

Causal and Effectual Change Management Approaches

There are two different ways of thinking about change leading to two different change management approaches: causal and effectual change. Each of these change management approaches requires a different skillsets in managing the change. Causal thinkers approach change management as a waterfall project, while effectual thinkers use a more agile approach. The distinction between causal and effectual thinking originated at the turn of the 21st century in the work of Saras D. Sarvasty.[5]

1. *The Causal Change Management Approach*

There are times an organization needs to stabilize and ensure that processes already in place are working and executed efficiently and profitably. Causal change management usually starts by what 'is' and uses a step-wise improvement methodology (whether TQM, Lean Six Sigma, PROSCI, etc.) to manage and implement a change initiative that 'should' be.

This is the standard change management discipline taught in most business schools. It is very suitable to bring continuous improvement changes. Causal changes are hinged upon updating/modifying pre-existing processes. After identifying a specific process or product that is lagging in efficiency/effectiveness, the change consists of modifying and measuring the incremental improvement. Apart from that, causal change also involves upper management utilizing skills and tools to come up with changes that will be best for an organization and then rolling the initiative downward through the ranks. They will utilize methods of change management to identify change champions to help disseminate information. In doing so, they focus heavily on working through a systematic change process (as developed by Connor et al.) and trying to avoid the most common mistakes (as identified by John Kotter) to avoid failures of the change iniative. Connor and his colleagues use a causal change management approach to manage an expanded change management process with an engineering-like precision.[6] They provide a detailed stepwise process for initiating, envisioning, crafting, and conducting the change (see 14-1):

14-1. Initiating, Envisioning, Crafting, and Conducting Change

Initiating	Envisioning	Crafting	Conducting
1. Acknowledge the destabilizing forces 2. Analyze against standard model 3. Formulate problem statements 4. Suggest solutions 5. Develop ideal solutions	6. a) Describe the current organizational state b) Describe the future organizational state 7. Describe the difference between current and future states 8. Describe restraining and facilitating forces	9. a) Revise vision of future state b) Construct the transition-management profile 10. Develop strategies and tactics for the change	11. Implement strategies and tactics 12. Institutionalize the change 13. Evaluate the change

Source: Connor, P., Lake, L., Stackman, R. (2003). *Managing Organizational Change* (3rd ed.). Westport: Praeger.

Many organizations have adopted the PROSCI® ADKAR® methodology to enable and engage people in causal change initiatives:[7]

- **A** (Awareness)—pre-contemplation
- **D** (Desire)—contemplation
- **K** (Knowledge)—preparation
- **A** (Action)—action
- **R** (Reinforcement)—maintenance

Change management is no easy task. When evaluating the success of any change management initiative, organizations must evaluate whether the change really sticks. Change is complex and requires a change in the behavior of people—self (hard), others (harder), and the organization (complex).

Not surprisingly, many organizational change efforts fail!

John P. Kotter in a 1995 *Harvard Business Review* article entitled, Leading change: Why transformation efforts fail," identifies several reasons why change efforts fail and suggests corresponding ways to lead the change (see 14-2)[8]. Action steps 1 to 3 refer to mobilization (or Lewin's unfreeze); steps 4 to 6 refer to movement (change) and step 7 and 8 refer to sustaining (refreeze) the change. Note that one of the most important reasons for failure—lack of executive support—is not included in the list.

14-1. Initiating, Envisioning, Crafting, and Conducting Change

	Errors	Corresponding action steps
1.	Not establishing a great enough sense of urgency.	**Create a sense of urgency** When the urgency rate is not pumped enough, the transformation cannot succeed, and the long-term future of the organization is put in jeopardy." (75%)
2.	Not creating a powerful enough guiding coalition.	**Pull together a guiding team** Someone needs to get a guiding coalition together, help them develop a shared assessment of problems and opportunities, and create a minimum level of trust.
3.	Lacking a vision.	**Create clear, simple, uplifting visions** A sensible and sound vision communicated in five minutes or less.
4.	Under-communicating the vision by a factor of ten.	**Communicate the vision through simple heart-felt messages** Use all existing channels to communicate the essential information about the vision.
5.	Not removing obstacles to the new vision.	**Empower people** Maintain the credibility of the change effort.
6.	Not systematically planning for, and creating, short-term wins.	**Create short-term wins** Managers actively look for ways to obtain clear performance improvements, establish goals, achieve the objectives, and reward the people involved with recognition, promotion, and even money.
7.	Declaring victory too soon.	**Maintain momentum** Understand that renewal efforts may take not months, but years.
8.	Not anchoring change in the corporation's culture.	**Make change stick** Institutionalize the change in the corporate culture (conscious effort to show the people how the new approaches, behaviors, and attitudes have helped improve performance; take sufficient time to make sure the next generation of top management personifies the new approach).

Source: John P. Kotter (1995). "Leading change: Why transformation efforts fail?" *Harvard Business Review*, 73(2): 59-67.

2. The Effectual Change Management Approach
There are times an organization needs to be innovative and come up with solutions that do not exist in the marketplace. They need to create change from the ground up and rethink the assumptions underlying existing processes. Effectual change management usually doesn't start from a clearly-defined goal. Instead, the change emerges more organically out of an ideation process and they adjust the change initiative in a more agile way as they progress. This type of change management initiative uses reengineering, radical innovation, design thinking, and agile methodologies. Effectual change uses modern tools to create change from the ground up and rethinks the assumptions underlying existing processes. In this change management approach, a problem is first identified, then the team identifies the root causes of why the problem exists and how it affects other parts of the business, and finally works to correct the underlying problem. Information technology is used to support the entire process. Michael Hammer, the father of reengineering, suggests to "organize around the outcome (what is the eventual change you want to see in the organization), not the specific task."[9]

The Three Boxes
The three-box approach proposed by Vijay Govindarajan and Chris Trimble, C. (2011) is another example of an effectual change management model. It calls for people to manage the current business performance, selectively forget the past, and create the future requiring balancing resources across the three boxes:[10]

- **Box 1: manage the present**—improves the performance of your business. In box 1, all your attention is focused on the short-term needs of your stakeholders. The focus here is on exploitation, optimization, and linear innovation. The mindset is on doing it faster, smarter, and cheaper.
- **Box 2: selectively forget the past**—overcomes your dominant logic (ways of doing things). In box 2 (the past always fights back), time and space is freed up to support and create non-linear innovation. Here, barriers must be cut down.
- **Box 3: create the future**—are truly innovative and could fundamentally change your business. In box 3, all attention is on experimentation. This is where the added value is created.

The three-box model requires managers and leaders who are willing and capable of simultaneously thinking and working in these three time frames. This model requires that there are opportunities and formal processes to do so. In addition, the model is cyclical. The business models, the products, and the services created in box 3 will one day be in box 1. Depending on the context, the focus will have to be sometimes more on box 1 or on box 3. Causal change management thinking is more suited to box 1 (keep), while an effectual change management approach works better in box 3 (start).

Resistance to Change
Barriers to change tend to be people-based due to a lack of management visibility and support, employee resistance to change, and inadequate change management skills in the organizations. In his book, *The Day After Tomorrow*, Peter Hinssen suggests the following formula to gauge resistance to change:

R = f(nm)
r = internal resistance to new ideas;
n = number of employees
m = number of management levels.

Considering these factors, traditional organizations will likely have more difficulty making change stick than progressive organizations.[11]

INNOVATION
Creating an innovative culture is--together with creating a learning culture—one of the major competitive people advantages companies have. Due to globalization, innovation is an ever-present phenomenon aided by technology, communications, and changing organizational arrangements such as outsourcing, strategic alliances, joint ventures, virtual work, and organizations.[12]

Defining and Measuring Innovation

Few people will argue about the importance of innovation. What innovation means is not understood as clearly and has evolved over time. The Organisation for Economic Co-operation and Development (OECD) provides the following definition of innovation: "A technological product, innovation is the implementation/commercialization of a product with improved performance characteristics such as to deliver objectively new or improved services to the consumer. A technological process innovation is the implementation of new or significantly improved production or delivery methods. It may involve changes in equipment, human resources, working methods, or a combination of these."[13]

If defining innovation is challenging, so is its measurement. Since 2005, the Global Innovation Index (GII) uses 21 different factors grouped into seven key categories that cumulatively contribute to global innovation. Some are considered input factors (such as institutions, human capital, research, infrastructure, market sophistication) and others output factors (such as scientific outputs and creative outputs).[14] This GII is often used to rank companies and countries on innovation.

Creating and Nurturing a Culture of Innovation

Creating and nurturing a culture of innovation has been compared with parenting. "As an innovation leader, you must ground creative people in accountability for the organization's objectives, key focus areas, core capabilities, and commitments to stakeholders. Then you give them broad discretion to conduct their work in service of those parameters."[15] The following best practices are recommended for 'innovation parenting':

- **Bust hierarchy**—allow innovators to bypass barriers and hierarchies that often sap creativity;
- **Encourage the unreasonable**—support the truly impractical in some situations;
- **Don't die of indigestion**—inadequate staffing makes delivering on anything less likely. Focus on concentrating on two projects allowing immersion in a primary project and shifting gears to the other project if the first one hits a temporary roadblock;
- **Cultivate external relationships**—relationships extending beyond the boundaries of the organization are invaluable for acquiring and distributing knowledge;
- **Hire the best and fast**—select people who are willing to join multiple projects and to move from one to another as needed.

EXECUTION AND IMPLEMENTATION

"Plus ça change, plus c'est la même chose" in translation means "the more it changes, the more it's the same thing." This French proverb used by Jean-Baptiste Alphonse Karr in the January 1849 issue of his journal *Les Guêpes* ("The Wasps") implies that apparent change to something is merely superficial and does not affect its essence and expresses a resigned acknowledgment of the fundamental immutability of human nature and institutions. It also reflects a certain kind of disillusionment or resignation by people who have change imposed on them. That is what we mean when change does not stick! So, how does one get buy-in from people so they do not resist the change? In some cultures, people will nod approvingly in support of a specific change and not voice concerns but will use malicious compliance when the change is executed. Malicious compliance means local managers agree to programs from headquarters but sabotage their success, ultimately making the change initiative fail.

Strategy is about making choices and implementation is about execution. The consulting firm McKinsey coined the phrase, "a strategy is only as good as its execution," meaning that when a strategy fails it usually is because it was not well executed. Paul Evans uses a simple equation to look at the effectiveness of execution: Q x A = E, where Q is the quality of the planning, A is the acceptance of the decision, and E is the effectiveness of the execution.[16]

Most managers are good at the quality of the plan—let us give them 9/10 out. However, let us assume the implementation is botched up—let us give them 5/10—then the effectiveness of the execution is only 45%! If we can make the implementation of the plan as good as the plan itself (i.e., 9/10), then the effectiveness of the execution is 81%. Note that perfection is not achieved but with a good execution, there is greater chance the change will stick.

How can we better manage change and improve execution? A good starting point is to hire and grow teams that are open to change and are even willing to take the initiative to change. Furthermore, it is helpful to examine the change initiative from the perspective of the three lenses (strategic, political, and cultural) and simultaneously focus on processes and on people. The strategic lens focuses on having a good plan and a process to execute it. The political lens can help us with people resistance by understanding the various requirements and concerns of the stakeholders. The cultural lens focuses on the meaning and fit of the change with the organizational culture—how the way we do things around here will be different.

Evans equates whether change succeeds with fairness and describes the five E's required to make the change process successful:[17]

1. **Engagement**—people want their views to be heard; there is a right to refute; communication is sincere and genuine.
2. **Exploration**—different options are explored.
3. **Explanation**—people are informed of the decision; decisions are based on sound facts and reasoning.
4. **Expectations**—decisions are translated into clear goals, action plans, and behaviors; the meaning of a commitment is clear; there is appropriate coaching and support.
5. **Evaluation**—decisions are applied with consistency; desired behaviors and results are rewarded.

No change initiative can be successful without communication, education, and training of the people involved in and affected by the change process. The ultimate outcome of the change, its ROI, and valid analytics must show whether the change is working or not. Change is hard at each level (self, others, and the organization) but necessary to adapt to the rapidly changing and uncertain environments in which we live and work. ▮

REFERENCES

1. Connor, P., Lake, L., Stackman, R. (2003). *Managing Organizational Change* (3rd ed.). Westport: Praeger.
2. Creasey, T. Connecting Change to Business Results: The 4Ps Exercise. Prosci (Accessed: June 1. 2019). https://blog.prosci.com/connecting-change-to-business-results-4-ps-exercise.
3. Ancona, D., Kochan, T., Scully, M., Van Maanen, J., & Westney, D. E. (2005). *Managing for the Future: Organizational Behavior & Processes* (3rd Ed.). Cincinnati: South-Western College Publishing.
4. Lewin, K. (1947) "Frontiers in Group Dynamics: Concept, Method and Reality in Social Science; Equilibrium and Social Change," *Human Relations*, 1(1): 5-41; Lewin, K. (1951). *Field Theory in Social Science: Selected Theoretical Papers* (ed. Cartwright D). New York: Harper & Row.
5. Sarasvathy, S. D. (2001). "Causation and Effectuation: Towards a Theoretical Shift from Economic Inevitability to Entrepreneurial Contingency," *Academy of Management Review*, 26(2): 243-263.
6. Connor, P., Lake, L., Stackman, R. (2003). *Managing Organizational Change* (3rd ed.). Westport: Praeger.
7. What is the ADKAR Model? (Accessed: January 5, 2019). https://www.prosci.com/adkar/adkar-model
8. Kotter, J. (1995). "Leading Change: Why Transformation Efforts Fail," *Harvard Business Review*, 73(2): 59-67.
9. Hammer, M., & Champy, J. (1993) *Reengineering the Corporation: A Manifesto for Business Revolution*. New York: Harper Collins.
10. Govindarajan, V. & Trimble, C. (2011) 'The CEO's Role in Business Model Reinvention', *Harvard Business Review*, 89 (1/2): 108-114.
11. Hinssen, P. (2017). *The Day After Tomorrow: Hoe Overleven in Tijden van Radicale Innovatie*. Leuven: Van Duuren Management.
12. Wallack, H. (2013) Global Innovation. Pp. 191-209 in Claus, L. *Global HR Practitioner Handbook* (volume 1). Silverton: Global Immersion Press.
13. Oslo Manual: The Measurement of Scientific and Technological Activities," Organisation for Economic Co-operation and Development (p.9), accessed December 6, 2010. http:// www.oecd.org/science/innovationinsciencetechnologyandindustry/2367580.pdf
14. Xu,Q., Chen, J., Xie, Z., Liu,J., Zheng, G. & Wang, Y. (2006). "Total Innovation Management: A Novel Paradigm of Innovation Management in the 21st Century," *Journal of Technology Transfer*, 32, 17–19.
15. Ishak, Waguih (2017), *Creating an Innovation Culture*. (Accessed, November 15, 2019). https://www.mckinsey.com/business-functions/strategy-and-corporate-finance/our-insights/creating-an-innovation-culture
16. Evans, P. (2012). *Combining People and Organizational Development – What Really Works*. Greece: AHRMIO Annual Conference.
17. Ibid.

GUIDED READING QUESTIONS

1. What are the drivers of change?

2. What are the stages of Kurt Lewin's change model?

3. How do we define and measure innovation?

4. How can we improve the implementation of a change initiative?

FOLLOW-UP CRITICAL THINKING QUESTIONS

1. What is my major takeaway from this reading?

2. What do I already know about this subject?

3. What follow-up questions do I have about this?

4. How can I apply this in real life?

KEY TERMS

Change
Causal change
Effectual change
Engagement
Evaluation
Execution
Explanation
Exploration
Expectations
Facilitating forces
Force field
Implementation
Reengineering
Refreeze
Restraining forces
Unfreeze

LEARNING ASSESSMENT

Critically reflect on the content and the different concepts in this module and rate your own competency using the assessment scale.

Competency	I never heard of it	I heard of it but have limited knowledge of it	I can reasonably explain it to others	I have used it, done it, applied it
Field force analysis	0	1	2	3
Change management	0	1	2	3
Innovation	0	1	2	3
The three-box model	0	1	2	3
PROSCI® ADKAR® methodology	0	1	2	3
Global implementation	0	1	2	3

MODULAR-SPECIFIC ASSESSMENT

How Good Are Your Change Management Skills?
MindTools
The quiz helps you assess your change management skills.
https://www.mindtools.com/pages/article/newPPM_56.htm

VIGNETTE

HOW UNILEVER CHANGES AND REINVENTS ITSELF[1]

Progressive companies—whether established a century ago or a recent startup—must continuously change, innovate, and reinvent themselves, especially when it comes to their people management practices. Jacob Morgan, author of *The Employee Experience Advantage* (2017), argues that "*We need HR to not be HR*." With that, he means the momentum is opportune for HR to come to the foreground and evolve from a "hiring, firing, and compliance" to a "moving the organization forward" mode. Employers must pay attention to three factors (the physical environment, technology, and organizational culture) that have a positive or negative impact on how employees experience the organization.[2] This is exactly the focus Unilever, a 90-year old British-Dutch company, has taken through focusing on change and innovation.

Unilever makes some of the world's best-known household-name brands. They make and sell about 400 consumer goods in 190 countries and employ 155,000 employees in 100 countries. Here are some examples of how Unilever is changing the experience of their employees through a series of intangible benefits with regard to purpose, internal mobility, learning & development, talent acquisition, talent analytics, total rewards, and chatbots.[3]

- **Purpose**—employees are asked to build their own purpose statement and share their current (and desired) skills.
- **Internal mobility**—a voluntary program, called FLEX Experiences, connect people with opportunities to build skills or work on different projects across all the different department and geographies within the business. Using internal platforms (Gloat, Workday), Unilever employees become part of the company's talent network and the system finds great projects for them to work on.
- **Learning & Development**—uses a learning platform curating internal and external content into the form of a relevant personalized daily feed for each individual based on each person's 'purpose and passion.' The content is aligned with: 1) the needs of the job 2) the aspiration of employees and 3) the learning method the employee most prefers.
- **Talent acquisition**—to respond to its 2 million applications a year, HR uses technology (including games, quizzes, video interviews) to complete the hiring process and allow applicants to gain an understanding of whether they would fit in, their strengths, and what careers might be best suited for them in the company.
- **Talent analytics**—the company analyzes internal and external sentiment to understand how employees are feeling, especially around organizational change.
- **Total rewards**—an "open, fair, consistent, and explainable" performance-based reward structure that recognizes people who have delivered results and have the right values for the business. Employees have access to a Total Rewards Statement in real time, including being able to keep track of their progress and potential. A 'Rate-my-Reward' feature allows people to tell the company what they think of every aspect of their package.
- **Chatbots**—HR uses natural language processing (NLP) bots (Ask Una) as a first point of contact to process large number of simple HR queries at its HR service center.

As Unilever's CHRO, Leena Nair has gained rock star status beyond her company as a social media influencer, she admits that her passion and investment in promoting the employee experience is—foremost—good for the business! Unilever is a business that genuinely seems to care about making a difference putting the employee experience at the core of the employer brand and employee value proposition (EVP). As Anuradha Razdan, VP HR, Home Care, and Head of Global Talent Attraction and Employer Brand at Unilever said: "*When you join Unilever, it is not just a job; you are joining a movement to create* ***a better business, a better world, and a better you****. You are more than your job title because you create a much bigger impact in the world through the work that you do.*"[4]

REFERENCES

1. This vignette was prepared by Professor Lisbeth Claus for the sole purpose of illustrating a global HR practice for instructional objectives. Global HR in Action © 2019, Global Immersion Press, All Rights Reserved.
2. Morgan, J. (2017) *The Employee Experience Advantage: How to Win the War for Talent by Giving Employees the Workspaces they Want, the Tools they Need, and a Culture they Can Celebrate*. New York: John Wiley & Sons.
3. These Unilever examples are taken from: Claus, L. & Monaghan, D. (2019) *Dynamic Open Talent*. Global HR Consortium/IT Roundtable.
4. Sundberg, J. (2020). *How Unilever Developed a New EVP and Employer Brand*. (Accessed: February 4, 2020). https://linkhumans.com/unilever/

GUIDED READING QUESTIONS

1. How do technology and organizational culture at Unilever impact the employee experience?
2. How is improving the employee experience good for business?

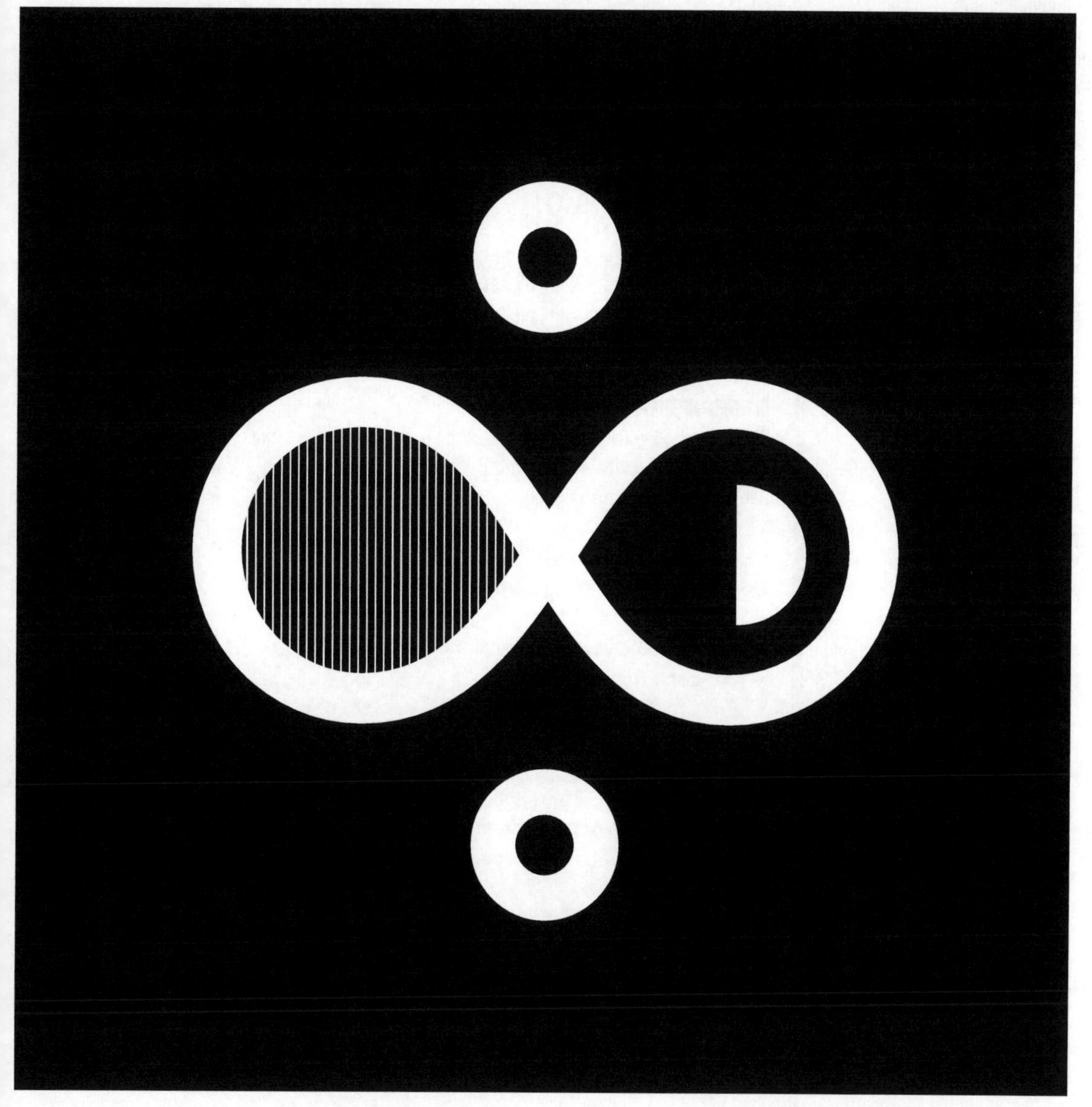

MODULE FIFTEEN

MANAGERIAL ETHICS, COMPLIANCE, CORPORATE SOCIAL RESPONSIBILITY, AND SUSTAINABILITY

MODULE FIFTEEN

MANAGERIAL ETHICS, COMPLIANCE, CORPORATE SOCIAL RESPONSIBILITY, AND SUSTAINABILITY

DESCRIPTION

This module explores ethics and compliance in decision-making and looks at corporate social responsibility and sustainability in terms of the human capital of an organization.

LEARNING OBJECTIVES

Upon completing the learning experience, you will be able to:

- Distinguish between ethics and integrity
- Describe the ethical triangle
- Provide a framework for the discussion of managerial ethics
- Identify ethical dilemmas in management situations
- Identify the steps in ethical decision-making
- Describe the requirements of the Foreign Corrupt Practices Act (FCRA)
- Identify human capital indicators of social responsibility
- Distinguish between corporate responsibility and sustainability

GUIDING QUESTIONS

Are there circumstances when a 'minor' ethical infraction is warranted? What does sustainability mean in people management?

Examples of scandals pertaining to lack of ethical behavior—too many to list—are found in business, government and non-profit environments all over the world! These offenses are often perpetrated by people throughout the organization from top to bottom. Some organizations define their values and communicate them to everyone. But, a lot of companies do not have a 'Corporate Value' for ethics and integrity because it is basically expected of any employee. Why is it so difficult for people in the workplace—from the front line to the C-suite—to have a moral compass? How do employees, managers and executives demonstrate a culture of ethics across their organization and in their relationships with stakeholders? How do people do the right thing in the face of difficult situations? How does one get a better grasp of the complexity of ethics and how it applies in day-to-day work?

MANAGERIAL ETHICS[1]

The study of ethics in the context of management has long been neglected and has struggled to compete for space in crowded management curricula. This neglect has had dire consequences. For decades, the dominant economic theories pioneered by economists such as Milton Friedman[2] of the Chicago School of Economics and Michael Jensen[3] of the Harvard Business School has pushed the idea that a corporation's sole objective should be to maximize profits for shareholders at any cost. These theories had significant impacts on the expectations and education of generations of managers. A history of rampant unethical behavior worldwide throughout in businesses, governments, and non-profit organizations has sharply eroded public trust and fostered cultures that neglect commonly shared moral beliefs. There is, however, a growing recognition this trend must be reversed.

Pressured by consumers, governments, and scandals, companies are starting to take moral issues of right and wrong seriously. Whether to avoid law suits, the possible impact on their bottom line, the expectations of the talent they use, or the desire to be a responsible corporate citizen, the ethical conduct of companies by doing the right thing can be used to improve their image and reduce liabilities with customers and regulatory agencies. The study of ethics in management and business is growing in popularity, and corporations are increasingly taking their ethical obligations to society more seriously. The reintroduction of concepts like corporate social responsibility into the public consciousness and stated goals of for-profit organizations marks a major shift in beliefs regarding the ethical obligations of those in the business world.[4] In response to these shifts, management must now establish the guidelines through which these new ethical considerations should be pursued.

Ethics and Ethical Relativism

Ethics, the set of moral values that dictate a person's behavior, is an exceedingly important yet fiercely debated subject. What constitutes ethical behavior, how the ethics of a person's behavior should be evaluated, and how unethical behavior should be handled by society is subject to controversy. While a set of core theories and principles have been developed in the literature on ethics, the ethical landscape is in constant flux. Determining appropriate responses to ethical dilemmas often requires the use of multiple principles and is heavily influenced by an individual's upbringing and personal beliefs.

The field of ethics becomes especially challenging when it is applied internationally, or when differences in cultural beliefs and practices are considered. Ethical relativism, the notion that "*because different societies have different ethical beliefs, there is no rational way of determining whether an action is morally right or wrong*," cuts to the core of this dilemma.[5] Those who support ethical relativism might argue that culture should be heavily weighed when evaluating the ethics of an action. For example, while an action that upholds individual rights over the greater social benefit might be highly ethical in an individualistic society, a more collectivist society might find that same action unethical.[6] Critics, however, hold that a set of commonly held moral standards must be adopted and agreed upon in order for societies to survive. They contend that ethical relativism, in practice, produces wildly incoherent and unacceptable consequences. If this theory is to be adopted, they argue, "it does not make sense to criticize the beliefs and practices of a society as long as the members of the society conform to their own ethical standards."[7] Regardless, ethical relativism and cultural beliefs must be carefully considered when ethical dilemmas are evaluated in global contexts.

Ethical Principles

Ethical principles have significant impacts on how the ethics of any given actions are perceived. Whether consciously or unconsciously, managerial decisions, organizational value statements, and codes of ethics are often grounded in these same principles. Having a clear understanding of the theoretical underpinnings behind these principles are critical to evaluate the ethical standing of an organization or manager.

This module will use five basic ethical principles to analyze ethical decision-making. These theories are well established in the broader literature on ethics, and they provide valuable frameworks through which ethics in management can be studied.[8] They include utilitarian theory, rights theory, distributive justice, ethics of care, and virtue ethics. A case study will be included to help apply these different ethical principles.

1. **Utilitarian theory**—the belief that ethical actions are those that maximize social benefit and minimize social harm.
2. **Rights theory**—the belief that the ethics of an action should be evaluated by balancing the rights of those impacted by that action.
3. **Distributive justice**—the belief that an ethical action is one that produces a fair balance of costs and benefits to those impacted.
4. **Ethics of care**—the belief that an ethical action is one that protects and cares for any individuals with whom a person has a "special relationship."
5. **Virtue ethics**—the belief that ethical actions display positive moral virtues.

While ethics are often studied through somewhat extreme examples or thought experiments, it is important to consider how these principles apply in day-to-day management and decision-making. If managers consistently adhere to a set of ethical beliefs and behaviors in their day-to-day decision-making, they not only model that behavior to those they manage but also develop systems through which they can evaluate the far more complex and challenging dilemmas they may encounter.

Let's illustrate these five theories with two case studies.

> *A team of five custodians and one supervisor working for a small US government agency has encountered internal problems. Four of the custodians and the supervisor are from the same ethnic background and are part of a tight community. The fifth custodian does not belong to that ethnic group and has felt ostracized from the team. He has complained extensively, causing problems over several years. This year, the supervisor retired. There were two potential candidates to replace him. One candidate, who is part of the same ethnic group as the previous supervisor, is far more qualified with an excellent interview and references. The other candidate is still qualified but not on par with the first candidate. He belongs to a third ethnic group. The department wonders if it can choose to not hire the more qualified candidate because his ethnicity might contribute to an ongoing problem and choose instead to hire the less qualified candidate because his 'neutral' ethnic background might help solve the issue? (This is referred in this module as case 1).*

> *A rural, family-owned physical therapy clinic is dealing with a sensitive personnel issue. A well-liked employee has recently developed a hearing problem, and the disability is impacting her job performance. The employee was originally a front desk employee, but her hearing loss prevents her from effectively communicating with customers over the phone and in person. Recognizing this issue, the owners re-trained the employee to assist the therapists with patient care. However, it quickly became evident that the employee's inability to hear the timers and sensors used by the clinic was putting the safety of patients at risk. At this small clinic, there are no other viable positions that match the employee's skill level without moving her to a part-time position. How should the owners respond to this dilemma? (This is referred in this module as case 2).*

1. Utilitarian Theory

Utilitarian theory posits that the "*morally correct action is the one that maximizes net social benefits, where net social benefits equals social benefits minus social costs.*"[9] There are four noteworthy assumptions made by this theory. First, the theory assumes the ethics of an action should be judged purely by its results (and never by the means it took to attain those results). Second, the theory judges ethical behavior on how it impacts society at large, rather than how it impacts the person who makes the decision. Third, the theory makes judgements based on all current and future impacts. Finally, the theory assumes the only ethical choice is the one that has the best possible balance of good and harm.[10]

There are numerous criticisms about this theory. To start, some argue the theory is largely impractical, as the concepts of 'social good' and 'social harm' are incredibly difficult to measure in accurate and non-controversial ways.[11] Making decisions in accordance with utilitarian principles essentially necessitates perfect information, which is an unrealistic expectation in real-world scenarios. Given the highly complex ethical dilemmas often faced by managers, accounting for all possible externalities of a decision can be a near-impossible task. Second, the theory can run in direct contrast to other ethical theories, particularly rights theory.[12] In cultures that highly value individualism, the sacrifice of individual rights for the social benefit is extremely controversial.

> *UTILITARIAN THEORY*
>
> ***Case 1 Analysis****—hiring the less qualified candidate could solve the years-long internal strife and benefit the team over the long term. While any hiring manager should proceed with caution when making decisions on this basis, hiring a supervisor who belongs to a third ethnic background could diffuse tensions by removing the previously existing 'in vs out' group dynamics. Although this would come at a significant cost to the more qualified candidate, it would maximize the overall net social benefit by enhancing the function of the team in the long run.*
>
> ***Case 2 Analysis****—the most ethical decision would be to help the employee find work at another business or move her to a part-time position. The negative impact on the safety of patients combined with the unavoidable frustration of the employee who is unable to perform appropriately makes this work situation untenable. A utilitarian theorist would argue that the best option for all stakeholders would be for the employee to seek a job with another business that can better accommodate her.*

2. *Rights Theory*

Rights theorists believe that the "*morally correct action is the one that the person has a moral right to do, that does not infringe on the moral rights of others, and that furthers the moral rights of others.*"[13] More simply, rights theory focuses on whether an individual has the right, or entitlement, to either perform or be protected from an action. It focuses entirely on the ethics of the method taken. The morality of any action must be determined with the balance of individual rights and interests in mind.[14]

Immanuel Kant's categorical imperative, *The Groundwork of the Metaphysics of Morals*, is defined as "*a moral law that is unconditional or absolute for all agents, the validity or claim of which does not depend on any ulterior motive or end.*"[15] The categorical imperative then provides a framework through which individual rights can be judged. There are three basic tests of Kant's categorical imperative: reversibility, universalizability, and respectability/consent. Reversibility questions whether any person performing an action would agree to have the action performed on them. Universalizability questions whether an action performed by an individual would still be acceptable if every person on earth performed that action. Respectability and consent questions whether those affected by an action have consented to the action and are impacted in ways that maintain their respect.[16] Any action that passes these tests is considered ethical under Kant's categorical imperative.

RIGHTS THEORY

***Case 1 Analysis**—not hiring the more qualified candidate on the basis of his ethnicity is a serious (and illegal) breach of that person's rights. The more qualified candidate has a clear legal and social right to be considered for any job position without their ethnicity factoring into the decision. Although the motivation to neutralize the team's internal ethnically driven strife is understandable, the hiring manager lacks the prerogative to violate the rights of the more qualified candidate on those grounds. Therefore, the decision to hire the less qualified candidate would be a seriously unethical decision.*

***Case 2 Analysis**—letting the employee go or moving her to a part-time position on the basis of her disability is a violation of that person's rights. The employer should make every attempt possible to accommodate the employee's inability to hear. However, it is also important to consider the rights of the patients to have a safe and accessible clinic. Finding a balance between the rights of the employee and patients is critical.*

3. Distributive Justice

Those who subscribe to the principle of distributive justice believe "*the morally correct action is the one that produces a fair distribution of benefits for everyone who is affected by the action.*"[17] The question of how to evaluate what constitutes a 'fair' distribution of costs and benefits is contested, but it is generally agreed that an action that distributes costs and benefits similarly to similar individuals is fair. Attempting to narrow the definition beyond that generates disagreement.

Five approaches to distributive justice can be used to assess the fairness of any outcome.[18]

1. **Egalitarianism**—regards all humans as similar and therefore deserving of a perfectly equal distribution of costs and benefits.
2. **Capitalism**—believes a person's contributions to society should be the determining factor in the balance of costs and benefits they receive.
3. **Socialism**—holds that capitalist incentives do a disservice to societal wellbeing, and that needs and abilities should instead be used to evaluate fair distributions.
4. **Libertarianism**—maintains that "whatever happens as a result of the free choices of individuals is fair."[19]
5. **Distributive Justice**—suggests the only fair approach to distributive justice is one that is blind to self-interests (Rawls' Principle).[20]

DISTRIBUTIVE JUSTICE

***Case 1 Analysis**—those who examine ethics using distributive justice would be careful to weigh the more specific circumstances of the case. The following are questions that a distributive justice theorist may consider. Are any of the ethnic groups especially disadvantaged? Is the ostracization of the minority on the team real or perceived? Are there other factors playing into their ostracization? Is the internal strife harming the team's productivity? Etc. These considerations would then be balanced and evaluated using one of the five approaches to reach a conclusion.*

***Case 2 Analysis**—evaluating this case using distributive justice again leads to complex conclusions. Depending on the perspective selected, a person might consider the following questions. Have all possible accommodations been considered? How easy is it to find alternative employment nearby? How serious is the inconvenience to patients or risk to patient safety? Etc. By evaluating these considerations alongside one or more of the approaches to distributive justice, an individual can better define what constitutes a 'fair' resolution.*

4. Ethics of Care

Ethics of care argues that "*a person's moral obligation is not to follow impartial principles, but rather to care for the good of the particular individuals with whom the person has concrete special relationships.*"[21] With foundations in late-20th century feminist literature, ethics of care rejects the objectivity and impersonality dominant in previously developed ethical principles. It argues that ignoring the relationships held between individuals, such as familial or romantic relationships, is unethical and ignores the realities of human social behavior. This is especially important when it comes to those individuals who rely on a person's support and would be vulnerable without it. The 'web of relationships' described in this theory can be defined quite broadly to include not only close relationships (friends, family, romantic partners), but also those in the communities in which a person lives. To be excluded, however, are relationships "*based on domination, oppression, hatred, violence, disrespect, injustice, or exploitation.*"[22] To those who believe in the ethics of care, actions that responsibly nurture and develop people with whom a person has a relationship are the most ethical actions.

> *ETHICS OF CARE*
>
> ***Case 1 Analysis****—ethics of care is poorly suited to examine this specific case. In general, any individual with a personal stake in a hiring decision should remove themselves from that decision-making process.*
>
> ***Case 2 Analysis****—focus on the relationship the owners of the business have with their employee. In this rural and tight-knit community, the relationships between business owners and their employees are especially close. Given the difficulty of finding alternative employment in a community this small, it could be argued that the owners have an obligation to go out of their way to accommodate their employee. Letting the employee go or moving her to a part-time position would be unethical under this standard.*

5. *Virtue Ethics*

Virtue ethics contends that the "*morally correct action is the one that displays good moral virtues and does not display bad moral vices.*"[23] This ethical principal is heavily reliant upon character traits embodied by a person's actions. If a person's actions can be described using positive traits, such as compassionate, cooperative, fair, or courageous, that person would be acting ethically. If a person's actions can be described using negative traits, such as hostile, lazy, stubborn, or inhumane, then that person would be acting unethically. One clear criticism of this principal is that it relies too heavily on vague personal attributes and ignores the impacts that a person can have through their behavior.

> *VIRTUE ETHICS*
>
> ***Case 1 Analysis****—virtue ethics is also poorly suited to examine this specific case. However, a virtue ethicist might consider whether the hiring manager's decision could be described as just or fair. Likely, any decision that rejects a candidate on the basis of their ethnicity would run contrary to these virtues and thus be unethical.*
>
> ***Case 2 Analysis****—similarly, a decision by the owners to let the employee go or move her to a part-time position on the basis of a disability would reflect negative vices (e.g. unfair or disloyal) and be unethical.*

By using a combination of the principles described above, managers can not only select the most ethical alternatives in dilemmas they personally face, but also identify and critically examine the behavior their employees through ethical lenses. How to respond to unethical conduct when it is identified, however, is an entirely different challenge.

Responding to Unethical Behavior: Dynamic Consistency and its Criticisms

The relationship between individuals' moral thought—their internal sense of morality—and ethical behavior—how they act under environmental pressures—is a complex and controversial question. It is also the key to determining how managers should react to unethical behavior when it arises.

Dynamic consistency is the "*tendency for a person who holds a particular moral standard to act according to it and to feel guilty when he does not.*"[24] Dynamic consistency has both defenders and critics. If one assumes dynamic consistency is valid, managers should focus entirely on attracting and maintaining an inherently ethical workforce. Time spent training employees to act ethically or promoting workplace environments that might minimize pressures to act unethically is time wasted. If a manager encounters unethical behavior, the logical response would be to remove the employee before they inevitably repeat their offense. If one assumes that dynamic consistency is invalid, managers should shift focus from developing an inherently ethical workforce to creating workplace conditions that remove pressures for employees to act unethically.[25] That, combined with appropriate ethical training programs, allows employees' moral thought to dictate their ethical behavior in the workplace. How is dynamic consistency affecting ethics in management? Managers should seek a cultural compromise by balancing these two tactics. This entails using hiring/firing decisions to create an optimally ethical workforce while simultaneously removing pressures that might make this ethical workforce stray from their internal moral convictions.

Ethical Conduct

At a personal level, how do people develop their ethical standards and use it a basis for their ethical conduct at work? Personal ethics are developed through many influences:

- **Individual attributes and personal values**—shaped through institutional influences such as parents, family, friends, education, religion, media, experience, and the personal clarification of these values. People come into organizations with a personal values set;
- **Societal expectations**—values and norms about what's right or wrong are socialized through culture and managed through social control;
- **Work environment**—company code of ethics, policies, and procedures, the interpretation and enforcement of these rules, whether people are leading by examples (especially executives and managers), the overall organizational culture, and the possible gaps between these elements influence how people behave;
- **Laws and institutions of a country**—the legal framework (for example the Foreign Corrupt Practices Act in the U.S. and the Bribery Act in the U.K.) and the institutions that are set up to enforce the laws and influence behavior.

Max H. Bazerman and Ann E. Tenbrunsel show how ethical breakdowns in organization are widespread due to cognitive biases and organizational systems that blind managers to unethical behavior. They describe the five barriers to an ethical organization as follows:[26]

- **Ill-conceived goals**—setting goals and incentives to promote a desired behavior, but they encourage a negative one;
- **Motivated blindness**—we overlook the ethical behavior of others when it's in our interest to remain ignorant;
- **Indirect blindness**—we hold others less accountable for unethical behavior when it's carried out through third parties;
- **The slippery slope**—we are less able to observe others' unethical behavior when it develops gradually;
- **Overvaluing outcomes**—we give a pass to unethical behavior when the outcome is good.

Ultimately, ethical behavior is about resolving dilemmas that arise from the relationships that (business) people have with stakeholders (investors, customers, other employees, creditors, competitors, unions, and the government). The basis of ethical conduct is to recognize there are ethical issues, analyze the issue in a broader framework or context, and behave according to principles and guidelines when making decisions.

Practical guidelines for ethical decision-making:

- Identify the ethical issue;
- Recognize the dilemma for the person;
- Figure out how it impacts others;
- Identify possible courses of action (behaviors) and their consequences;
- Identify the values and principles underpinning these actions;
- Decide what to do.

On a personal level, 'defining moments' can have a major impact. A defining moment is when someone is urged to make a pivotal decision that requires dilemma reconciliation and, at face value, rarely has a 'correct' response. But the moment is pivotal and changes the person forever.[27]

Ethical Issues in Technology and Artificial Intelligence

With the increased focus on the use of data, artificial intelligence and robotics in organizations, it is also imperative to talk about technology ethics. The use of data, robots, and artificial intelligence in the workplace raises a number of emerging ethical issues that have yet to be fully explored. Artificial intelligence—used extensively by tech giants such as Alphabet, Amazon, Facebook, IBM, and Microsoft—shows great promise but also raise a number of ethical issues that have not yet fully been explored. Jochanan Eynikel writing about ethics and technology in a 2017 book, *Robot aan het Stuur* (Robot at the Wheel), argues that technology is never value free. With the advent of smart (semi) autonomous technology, the ethical side of innovation becomes even more import than ever for the firm and the society.[28]

Looking at ethics and risk assessment for new technologies, Julia Bossmann reflects on the leading ethical issues brought about by the increasing use of artificial intelligence:[29]

1. **Unemployment**—what happens after the end of jobs?
2. **Inequality**—how do we distribute the wealth created by machines?
3. **Humanity**—how do machines affect our behavior and interaction
4. **Artificial stupidity**—how can we guard against mistakes?
5. **Racist robots**—how do we eliminate AI bias?
6. **Security**—how do we keep AI safe from adversaries?
7. **Evil genies**—how do we protect against unintended consequences?
8. **Singularity**—how do we stay in control of a complex intelligent system?
9. **Robot rights**—how do we define the humane treatment of AI?

In her 2019 book, *The Age of Surveillance Capitalism*, Shoshana Zuboff shows vast amounts of data are collected on individuals with limited privacy and owned and operated by what she labels 'private surveillance capitalism.' This creates huge data monopolies by a few companies (Amazon, Facebook, Google, Microsoft, etc.)—governed by their own iron laws rather than regulated by lawmakers—giving these corporations the power to predict and control our behavior. The use and exploitation of that knowledge, authority, and power has many ethical dimensions—whether they are used for good or evil purposes.[30]

COMPLIANCE

While legal compliance is different from ethics, compliance with the organizational policies and procedures as well as compliance with the laws of the countries where companies operate (domestically or globally) are paramount—even if one disagrees with these policies, procedures, and laws or they conflict with our personal values. One of the managerial responsibilities—as an agent of the organization—is ensuring that individuals and teams comply with existing with organizational policies and procedures and enforce them consistently. In addition, managers must ensure that due process and fairness is given to all people regardless of their actions. Management practices are also intricately linked to the laws and regulations of the countries in which employment is exercised. As a result, the legal framework requires its professionals to develop the know-how and resources to effectively manage legal compliance across borders. While knowledge of all applicable employment laws is the starting point, reinforcing the rule of law—everywhere and every time—is the key for ensuring compliance. Once an understanding of how the regulatory environment operates is developed, management must identify any risk or obstacles related to non-compliance with existing regulations and develop solutions for compliance.

An issue that often comes up—especially in international operations—is bribery and corruption. In many countries, giving 'bribes' or providing facilitating payments to get things done is an acceptable business cultural business practices (e.g., 'la mordida' in Mexico; 'dash' in South Africa; 'baksheesh' in the Middle East, India and Pakistan; 'pots de vin' in France; 'Schimmengelt' in Germany; 'bustarella' in Italy, etc.). In the U.S., the 1977 Foreign Corrupt Practices Act (FCPA) makes it illegal for U.S. firms to influence through bribes or to corrupt the actions of foreign officials and executives to purchase their products. Grease payments (small amounts) are permitted but publicly held companies must have accounting procedures to justify them. Countries are not equal when it comes to corruption. Transparency International publishes an annual Corruption Perception Index for 180 countries around the world and ranks countries based on different indicators of corruption.[31]

CORPORATE SOCIAL RESPONSIBILITY AND SUSTAINABILITY

Firms produce benefits versus harm by simply operating. In addition, managers make many decisions on a day-to-day basis and some of them are not always sustainable.

Corporate Social Responsibility

Corporate social responsibility (CSR) is an organization's "*commitment to improve community well-being through discretionary business practices and contributions of corporate resources.*"[32] CSR is the obligation a business assumes toward society. It is the continuing commitment by business to contribute to economic development while improving the quality of life of the workforce and their families as well as of the local community and society at large.

CSR is often expressed on a continuum from stockholders (past) to stakeholders (current). In past thinking, organizations were expected only to meet the needs of their shareholders (and to a lesser extent their customers and employees). In current thinking, organizations must be explicit about the economic and social benefits they bring. Today, many companies not only engage in social responsibility initiatives, but also devote considerable resources to reporting CSR activities to a wide array of corporate stakeholders.

CSR of a company can be viewed under an umbrella of different activities organization undertake in dialogue with their various stakeholders beyond the stockholder: business ethics, corporate structure and governance, human resource practices, labor and human rights, environmental management, community involvement and economic development.[33]

An entire lexicon has been developed around CRS including the following concepts:

- **Business Ethics**—moral issues that commonly arise in the business world;
- **Corporate Citizenship**—a set of behaviors that demonstrates CSR;
- **Corporate Governance**—the structure and relationships that determine corporate objectives and performance monitoring mechanisms (management team, Board of Directors, investors, shareholders);
- **Ecological Footprint**—the impact of one's action on the natural environment;
- **Iron Law of Responsibility**—the social responsibility of businesses and businesspeople need to commensurate with their social power (size, financial resources, visibility);

- **Stakeholder Management**—any group or individual who can affect or is affected by the actions of the firm;
- **Sustainability Management**—meeting the needs of the present without compromising the ability of future generations to meet their needs;
- **Transparency**—voluntary self-reporting of a company's objectives, policies & procedures with respect to CSR and business ethics as well as its compliance successes and failures;
- **Triple Bottom Line**—putting environmental concerns and people equity issues on an equal footing with shareholder return.

The following leading practices are proposed to support CSR initiatives in an organization:

- **High Level Support**—clearly communicate the company's ethics and CSR policy as an integral part of the overall organizational strategy and ensure executive support;
- **Create a CSR culture**—foster a culture that confronts difficult questions about ethics, the environment, and social responsibility;
- **Training**—educate employees and managers on the code of conduct;
- **Reporting and Advice Mechanisms**—encourage staff to report questionable conduct and ask for help with their own ethical dilemmas (no retaliation);
- **Performance Management**—evaluate and reward employees for integrating company values in their daily work life;
- **Ongoing Communication**—share stories and lessons learned;
- **Find the Sustainability Sweet Spot**—focus on what is good for both employer and employees.

On August 19, 2019, the Business Roundtable (BRT) issued a "*Statement on the Purpose of a Corporation*" signed by 181 CEOs, mostly of Fortune 500 companies with a commitment to lead their companies for the benefit of all stakeholders. The statement is a radical change from earlier statements that, in the past, focused primarily on shareholders. The five pillars of 'The Purpose of a Corporation' are:[34]

- Delivering value to their customers;
- Investing in their employees;
- Dealing fairly and ethically with suppliers;
- Supporting the communities they do business in;
- Generating long-term value for their shareholders.

Sustainability[35]

Earlier, we described sustainability management as meeting the needs of the present without compromising the ability of future generations to meet their needs. In sustainability, it can often be difficult to measure immediate results or the Social Return on Investment (SROI) of sustainable activities.36 When it comes to sustainability, there is a pressing need for individuals and organizations to engage in the global warming discourse and actions as the climate change is anthropogenic or caused by human activity of individuals and corporations. It causes floods, droughts, fires, and an array of ecological disasters, exacerbates social inequalities, and results in countless deaths globally and disproportionately places the burden of externalities on groups contributing least to climate change.

In the contemporary and historical sustainability management literature, three key themes emerge showing that organizational change management strategies can integrate sustainability into capitalist business practices by:

1. Motivating individuals to prioritize sustainability innovations;
2. Establishing new business models;
3. Enforcing these changes as the new industry standard.

When it comes to sustainability, many global companies have gotten into the game—some of them accused of greenwashing (Nestle, BP) while others have actively engaged in a transition to a sustainable business model (Patagonia, Unilever, Nike, Hewlett Packard, etc.). In sustainability, buy-in without follow-through and effectively undergoing organizational change can be observed in the form of greenwashing.[37] As climate activist Greta Thunberg, at the age of 16 and representing a whole new generation, said addressing world leaders at the U.N.'s Climate Action Summit in New York City on September 23. 2019: "*How dare you pretend that this can be solved with just 'business as usual' and some technical solutions?*"[38] Today, companies are facing increasing sociopolitical and ecological pressures for sustainability from both their external and internal customers.

While the management literature is replete with examples of unethical, irresponsible, and/or corrupt corporate behavior at one time or another (companies such as Dow Chemical, Enron, Monsanto, WorldCom, Fifa, Walmart, Boeing, Houston Astros, Volkswagen, USA Gymnastics, to name just a few), we can also think of companies having dealt with rights and/or wrongs situations in a more exemplary way: For example, how Johnson & Johnson dealt with the Tylenol recall in 1982 and how Starbucks dealt with a racial insensitivity crisis in 2016. These big company (un)ethical examples are only the tip of the iceberg. A company's ethical behavior is not just the result of the 'one bad person' problem. They are as important as the small decisions people (employees, managers, and executives) make on a day-to-day basis in organizations. ▌

REFERENCES

1. The ethics section of this module was prepared with the support of Graduate Research Assistant, Matt Taylor (Willamette University MBA Candidate 2021).
2. Friedman, M. (1970). "The Social Responsibility of Business is to Increase its Profits," *New York Times Magazine*, September 13.
3. Lemann, N. (2019). *Transaction Man: The Rise of the Deal and the Decline of the American Dream*. New York: Farrar, Straus and Giroux.
4. Chong, K. (2017). "Millennials and the Rising Demand for Corporate Social Responsibility," *California Management Review*, January 20 (Accessed: January 20, 2020). https://cmr.berkeley.edu/blog/2017/1/millennials-and-csr/
5. Velasquez, M. G. (1998). *Business Ethics: Concepts and Cases* (4th ed.). Upper Saddle River, NJ: Prentice-Hall.
6. Hofstede, G. (1980). *Culture's Consequences: International Differences in Work-Related Values*. Beverly Hills: Sage; Trompenaars, F. (2012). *Riding the Waves of Culture: Understanding Cultural Diversity in Business*. New York: McGraw Hill Education.
7. Schumann, P. L (2001). "A Moral Principles Framework for Human Resource Management Ethics," *Human Resources Management Review*, 11(1-2): 93-111.
8. Ibid.
9. Ibid.
10. Ibid.
11. Velasquez, M. G. (1998). *Business Ethics: Concepts and Cases* (4th ed.), Upper Saddle River, NJ: Prentice-Hall.
12. Schumann, P. L. (2001). "A Moral Principles Framework for Human Resource Management Ethics," *Human Resources Management Review*, 11(1-2): 93-111.
13. Ibid.
14. Ibid.
15. Kant, I. (1964) *Groundwork of Metaphysics of Morals*. New York. Harper & Row (H. J. Paton, trans.).
16. Ibid.
17. Schumann, P. L. (2001). "A Moral Principles Framework for Human Resource Management Ethics," *Human Resources Management Review*, 11(1-2): 93-111.
18. Ibid.
19. Rawls, J. (1971). *A Theory of Justice*. Cambridge, MA: Harvard University Press.
20. Schumann, P. L. (2001). "A Moral Principles Framework for Human Resource Management Ethics," *Human Resources Management Review*, 11(1-2): 93-111.
21. Ibid.
22. Ibid.

23. Hoffman, G. L. (1963). "Child Rearing Practices and Moral Development: Generalizations from Empirical Research," *Child Development*, 34: 295-318;
24. White, R. D. (2002). "Do Employees Act Like They Think? Exploring the Dichotomy Between Moral Judgment and Ethical Behavior," *Public Administration Quarterly*, 25(4): 391-412.
25. Max H. Bazerman and Ann E. Tenbrunsel, (2011). "Ethical breakdowns," *Harvard Business Review*, 89(4): 58-65.
26. Badaracco, J.L. (1997). *Defining Moments: When Managers Must Choose Between Right and Right*. Cambridge: Harvard Business Review Press.
27. Eynikel, J. (2017). *Robot aan het Stuur*. Tielt: Lannoo
28. Bossmann, J. (2016). *Top 9 Ethical Issues in Artificial Intelligence*. October 21 (Accessed: February 4, 2020). https://www.weforum.org/agenda/2016/10/top-10-ethical-issues-in-artificial-intelligence/.
29. Zuboff, S. (2019). *The Age of Surveillance Capitalism*, New York: Hachette Book Group.
30. Corruption Perception Index (2018). (Accessed : December 20, 2019). https://www.transparency.org/cpi2018
31. Kotler, P., & Lee, N. (2004). *Corporate Social Responsibility: Doing the Most Good for Your Company and Your Cause*. New York: John Wiley & Sons.
32. Phillips, R. and Claus, L. (2001). Corporate Social Responsibility and Global HR. *International Focus*. Alexandria, Society for Human Resource Management.
33. Business Roundtable Redefines the Purpose of a Corporation to Promote an Economy that Serves All Americans (2019). August 19 (Accessed: August 20, 2019). https://www.businessroundtable.org/business-roundtable-redefines-the-purpose-of-a-corporation-to-promote-an-economy-that-serves-all-americans
34. The sustainability section of this module was prepared with the support of Graduate Research Assistant, Shannon Lee (Willamette University MBA Candidate 2021).
35. Hörisch, J., Freeman, R. E., & Schaltegger, S. (2014). "Applying Stakeholder Theory in Sustainability Management: Links, Similarities, Dissimilarities, and a Conceptual Framework," *Organization & Environment*, 27 (4): 328-346.
36. Lee, K.-H., & Saen, R. F. (2012). "Measuring Corporate Sustainability Management: A Data Development Analysis Approach," *International Journal of Production Economics*, 140(1): 219-226; Seuring, S., & Gold, S. (2013). "Sustainability Management Beyond Corporate Boundaries: From Stakeholders to Performance," *Journal of Cleaner Production*, 56, 1-6; Sharma, A., Iyer, G. R., Mehrotra, A., & Krishnan, R. (2010). "Sustainability and Business-to-Business Marketing: A Framework and Implications," *Industrial Marketing Management*, 39 (2), 330-341; Schaltegger, S. S., & Wagner, M. (2006). *Managing the Business Case for Sustainability: The Integration of Social, Environmental and Economic Performance*. Sheffield, UK: Greenleaf.
37. Transcript: Greta Thunberg's Speech At The U.N. Climate Action Summit (2019). September 23 (Accessed: December 1, 2019) https://www.npr.org/2019/09/23/763452863/transcript-greta-thunbergs-speech-at-the-u-n-climate-action-summit.

GUIDED READING QUESTIONS

1.What are the different ethical theories/principles that can be used to justify behavior?

2. What organizational activities fall under corporate social responsibility?

3. How can organizations become more sustainable?

FOLLOW-UP CRITICAL THINKING QUESTIONS

1. What is my major takeaway from this reading?

2. What do I already know about this subject?

3. What follow-up questions do I have about this?

4. How can I apply this in real life?

KEY TERMS

Corporate citizenship
Corporate governance
Corporate social responsibility
Ecological footprint
Ethics
Greenwashing
Integrity
Iron law of responsibility
Stakeholder management
Sustainability management
Transparency
Triple bottom line

LEARNING ASSESSMENT

Critically reflect on the content and the different concepts in this module and rate your own competency using the assessment scale.

Competency	I never heard of it	I heard of it but have limited knowledge of it	I can reasonably explain it to others	I have used it, done it, applied it
CSR	0	1	2	3
Compliance	0	1	2	3
Ethics	0	1	2	3
Sustainability	0	1	2	3

MODULAR-SPECIFIC ASSESSMENT

Integrity and Work Ethics Test
Psych Tests
This test measures whether you are a person an employer can trust without fail. This validated test consists of 242 questions and takes 60 minutes to complete.
https://testyourself.psychtests.com/testid/3977

ETHICS VIGNETTE

DOING BUSINESS IN CHINA—INTERNATIONAL ETHICS IN ACTION[1]

Charles Patton's company sent him to China to oversee the building of a new manufacturing plant. The company originally considered building its plant in Guangzhou, but, due to rising labor costs, determined that investing in Sichuan province would be more cost-effective. The government officials in Chengdu were eager to see the company invest in their region and had been very helpful in providing the initial permits. The company sponsored many dinners for their Chinese hosts and Charles made every effort to establish strong ties with local businessmen and government officials. As the project progressed, however, Charles had more and more difficulty obtaining approval from the necessary government agencies. Considerable time and money had been sunk into getting the plant built and Charles was feeling pressure from headquarters to get the plant up and running.

In a meeting with Liu Jing, his contact in the municipal government, Charles expressed his concern that the bureaucratic process to obtain the requisite permits was going more slowly than anticipated. Charles was eager to speed up the process and wondered if she had any advice. A few days later, Liu Jing came to Charles' hotel. She suggested that Charles had not been generous enough with the government officials, and that a few well-placed gifts might help speed the permit process. Charles was taken aback and said that the laws in his country, not to mention company policy, prevented him from doing so.

Liu Jing smiled and handed Charles a piece of paper with the name of a local physician. She indicated that if Charles went to this doctor, the doctor would prescribe a costly medical procedure. As the cost would not be out of line with accepted international rates and the claim would be difficult to investigate, the insurance company would not likely question its validity. The insurance company would pay the fee to the doctor, who would take a small cut and turn the rest over to the appropriate government officials. For a quick doctor's visit and a few insurance forms to fill out, Charles would have his permits.

REFERENCES

1. This vignette was prepared by Professor Lisbeth Claus for the sole purpose of illustrating a global HR practice for instructional objectives. Global HR in Action © 2012, Global Immersion Press, All Rights Reserved.

GUIDED READING QUESTIONS

1. How should Charles react?
2. What are Charles' and his company's possible legal, PR, and other liabilities if Charles agrees to the doctor's visit?
3. How could Charles obtain the permits without going to the doctor?

ETHICS VIGNETTE

WAL-MART STORES INC. ALLEGED NON-COMPLIANCE WITH THE U.S. FOREIGN CORRUPT PRACTICES ACT WHEN DOING BUSINESS IN MEXICO[1]

When U.S. companies operate abroad, they are subject to the Foreign Corrupt Practices Act of 1977 (FCPA). The FCPA prohibits bribery of foreign government officials. While the law allows for modest *de minimus* grease payments to facilitate business dealings with minor officials of foreign governments, it imposes a strict code of conduct for the employees of U.S. companies operating around the world. The behaviors that constitute bribery and corruption may be in sharp contrast with generally accepted local practices of doing business. Still, U.S. companies operating abroad must comply with this extra-territorial anti-bribery legislation. In 2010, the U.K. followed suit and enacted similar legislation with the passage of the Anti-Bribery Act.

Wal-Mart, one of the world's largest companies, is currently (as of April 2012) under investigation by the U.S. Department of Justice over allegations its Mexican affiliate (Walmex) paid $24 million in bribes to accelerate its Latin American growth. Wal-Mart Stores, Inc. operates approximately 10,130 retail units under 69 different banners in 27 countries and has more than 2,200,000 employees. The company opened more than 2,100 stores and restaurants in Mexico since entering the market in 1991.[2]

On April 21, 2012, David Barstow of the New York Times published a lengthy article documenting the Wal-Mart internal response to the Mexican bribery practice since the allegations of Mexican wrongdoing became known to them at HQ in 2005. The allegations contend that Wal-Mart in Mexico bribed Mexican government officials through the use of *gestores* (i.e., local shadowy facilitators who bribe on someone's behalf and take a cut) to obtain local permits for building stores in Mexico. Supposedly, 441 such improper payments were made by the company to local government officials where they needed permits to build new stores.

U.S. Wal-Mart executives in Bentonville, Arkansas, although aware since 2005 of the rumored illegal bribery practices under the FCPA, allegedly decided to stifle an internal investigation, cover it up and remain silent to its outside stakeholders (including U.S. and Mexican government officials and their stock- and stakeholders). In the first day of trading after the news broke, Wal-Mart's stock fell five percent.

Bribery and corruption are a global problem. National and cultural differences about its acceptability differ around the world. Mexico is widely known for local corruption. Bribery even has its own colloquial term—*mordida* (or bite)—a payment required to get permission to conduct business. Transparency International, an independent organization who takes a stance against corruption, publishes an annual Corruption Perception Index. In the 2011 index, Mexico scored a 3 out of a possible 10 (with 10 being the least corrupt) and ranked 100 out of 183 countries in terms of corruption.[3]

What is likely to happen to Wal-Mart as the U.S. (and the Mexican) government is investigating the allegations depends on a number of factors:

- Which anti-bribery provisions did they violate?
- How many improper payments were made and to what extent can they be documented?
- What is the magnitude of these bribery payments?
- What ill-gained financial returns did the company derive from bribing the foreign government officials?
- Did they keep adequate records of the allowable grease payments?
- What was the behavior of senior management at U.S. headquarters when they discovered the possible bribery?
- Was there a pattern of cover up of the actions by their executives?
- Is there a pattern of corrupt behavior throughout the company and in other countries where it operates, or is this an isolated Mexican case?
- Is there a global position within the company that educates and assists executives, managers, and employees on global legal compliance with regard to bribery and corruption?
- How well is the company cooperating with the investigation by the U.S. Department of Justice?

Based on cases prosecuted by the U.S. government, Wal-Mart is likely to settle this case with the Department of Justice without an indictment through a deferred or non-prosecution agreement. This would likely require Wal-Mart to pay (possibly enormous) fines and penalties and make changes in its *modus operandus* throughout the company with regard to how its employees around the world are expected to conduct themselves when operating abroad.

REFERENCES

1. This vignette was prepared by Professor Lisbeth Claus for the sole purpose of illustrating a global HR practice for instructional objectives. It is based on the original *New York Times* article of April 22, 2012 that broke the story. http://www.nytimes.com/2012/04/22/business/at-wal-mart-in-mexico-a-bribe-inquiry-silenced.html?_r=1 (Accessed April 25, 2012).
2. http://finance.yahoo.com/q/pr?s=wmt. (Accessed April 25, 2012).
3. http://cpi.transparency.org/cpi2011/results/ (Accessed April 25, 2012).

GUIDED READING QUESTIONS

1. What are the major provisions of the Foreign Corrupt Practices Act for U.S. companies?
2. How did/should Wal-Mart executives respond to the bribery allegations?
3. What are the likely consequences for Wal-Mart if the allegations are found to be true?
4. Would the vignette be different if Wal-Mart were a British, French, Brazilian, Russian, Indian, or Chinese company?

SUSTAIN-ABILITY VIGNETTE

MOVING BEYOND AUDITING FOR MORE EFFECTIVE OVERSEAS SUPPLIER MANAGEMENT AT NIKE, INC[1]

In the late nineties, the global footwear and apparel brand Nike, Inc. suddenly found itself in crisis regarding labor practices at the outsourced factories of their overseas suppliers. Nike had historically created a cautious don't-ask, don't-tell relationship with its suppliers. At first, Nike brushed off the accusations of unacceptable "sweatshop" conditions, stating the fact that it did not own or control any of its suppliers' manufacturing facilities, and attempted to convince the public that the working conditions were acceptable for the local region. But the pressure from activists and media was relentless. CEO Philip Knight began to take it personally, realizing that his own integrity was being attacked, as well as Nike's bottom line.

Finally, Knight began to change course and view Asian outsourcing as more than just a subcontracting relationship in the legal sense by acknowledging a moral responsibility as well. In 1998, Nike announced a commitment to change with its *New Labor Initiatives* by extending their Code of Conduct and began to hold suppliers accountable. Nike also pushed the entire industry to become more transparent and responsible, engaged with activists, and even helped from the Fair Labor Association (FLA).

In 1999, Nike created their "North Star" goals based on a future vision of zero waste and toxic substances by the year 2020. Sustainability (environmental, economic, and social) was being integrated into Nike's operations driven by departments such as Sustainable Manufacturing & Sourcing and Sustainable Business & Innovation. By 2007, Nike ranked #3 among the 100 Best Corporate Citizens identified by Corporate Responsibility Magazine. It had appeared as though Nike successfully transformed itself from being the target for sweatshop accusations to a model player and innovative leader for fair labor and environmental sustainability practices.

Despite all these compliance accomplishments made by Nike and other multinational corporations (MNCs), global companies still have a long way to go as dire working conditions and harsh environmental pollution persist in overseas factories. Indeed, the challenge of seeking sustainable and socially responsible supply chains is persistent, global, and cross-sector. Within the context of aggressive globalization, many MNC's sourcing activities have expanded to further and further geographically diverse suppliers and subcontractors, exponentially increasing the complexity and risk of their supply chain networks. Though this trend of international contract manufacturing may allow MNCs to seek the lowest cost products and outsource many of non-core functions of the supply chain, industries are learning that legal and moral corporate social responsibilities (CSR) and liabilities, including labor, health and safety, and environmental standards can never be fully outsourced.

To mitigate the risk of crises like Nike experienced, MNCs have attempted to cover liabilities beyond their own corporate borders and govern the CSR standards of their contracted suppliers overseas. Most MNCs today adhere to some Code of Conduct (CoC) for labor and environmental practices. These are often based on International Labour Organization or other global standards. The most common method for MNCs to extend their CoCs to their suppliers is through supplier evaluations and feedback or audits.

MNCs often select third party auditors to conduct factory site visits, and then rely on the documentation that comes out of such to determine a supplier's level of compliance. In fact, over the last two decades, social compliance auditing itself has become quite a large industry globally. Yet, several factors hinder the effectiveness of well-intended supplier evaluations via CoCs and audits:

1. Inadequate legal regulations and enforcement in host countries

First, the weaker rule of law within developing nations to which manufacturing is typically outsourced makes the protection of workers by labor law enforcement and government action virtually non-existent. This creates a serious barrier to overcome in order to extend the CSR standards expected of suppliers in the host countries.

2. Systematic falsification of audit data

With the lack of assistance from the local government, factory managers are often pressured to falsify audit answers and documentation of their labor conditions. Cheating on the compliance requirements in order to pass buyers' audits and satisfy certification organizations is widespread. They prepare their employees with the 'right answers,' and because the employees know their paycheck is dependent on the success of the factory, they comply. Often suppliers will keep two sets of books, one internal and one for the auditors.

3. Conflicting priorities

Bottom line economics is still priority number one for most businesses and their sourcing decisions. As much as MNCs promote their Codes of Conduct and CSR standards, they pressure their suppliers to ever reduce production costs. These conflicting expectations constrain suppliers and many buyers choose not to push too hard with their suppliers. Many MNCs still view most of their potential gains for implementing ethical CSR practices within the realm of marketing.

4. Inadequate follow-up assistance

A key limitation with auditing is that its effectiveness depends on the quality of the information collected and on what buyers and suppliers do with that information. Perhaps the most frustrating for suppliers is that even when an audit does uncover violations, the buyer rarely offers substantial assistance to correct the problem. Even if a corrective action plan is suggested, it is largely expected that the supplier implements and pays for the solution.

5. Scale and complexity of global supply chain networks

Major global brands source their production through hundreds of manufacturers around the globe. Many MNCs have only a few people trying to manage their entire global supply chain network. The scale and complexity of supply chain network increases exponentially as direct 'Tier One' suppliers are expanded to include Tier Two raw material suppliers as well as the many subcontractors (authorized or not) with which the Tier One factories do business. This complexity is often managed by establishing liaison offices in each major manufacturing country or region where the MBCs operate. Even with such robust offices, it is still a challenge to allocate resources to CSR compliance issues due to the lack of Universal Standards.

As the above challenges indicate, the missing link between CSR expectations and results does indeed revolve around people, communication, relationships, and culture. MNCs must move beyond monitoring and auditing and develop an integrated supplier development for more effective CSC. Operations and human resources are intimately related at a fundamental level and a better integration of human resources into the supplier management operations of the global company are proposed to move from supplier monitoring to greater sustainability.

Three leading practices are suggested for effective overseas supplier management. The first leading practice suggests MNCs to go ahead and conduct the supplier evaluations and audits to capture baseline data, but also focus on the root causes of CSR issues, rather than just identifying a checklist of violations. The second leading practice is to invest in strengthening the supplier-buyer relationship with human interaction including employee exchange and co-location. Evaluations alone are necessary but insufficient tools when the goal is to build supplier capabilities. The exchange of buyer and supplier employees enables outsourcers to share and convey tacit and rich know-how to their suppliers. The third leading practice is to offer suppliers extensive training and development and follow-up assistance. Implementation of these steps should be customized to the unique characteristics of each MNC and their supply chain networks.

Nike's Corporate Responsibility Report for FY 2008-2009 states, "*By working with contract manufacturing management, we aim to create a sustainable framework for improving working conditions by identifying and addressing the root cause of issues as they arise. We also address manufacturing management buy in, cultivating a more skilled and competent work force and achieving a consistent approach to human resource management across all factories (...) This is a new standard of factory self-governance.*" (p. 61)

REFERENCES

1. This vignette was prepared by Professor Lisbeth Claus and Research Associate Merrilee Avila for the sole purpose of illustrating a global HR practice for instructional objectives. Global HR in Action

GUIDED READING QUESTIONS

1. Which factors hinder the effectiveness of well-intended supplier evaluations?
2. How can global HR take a leadership role in effective overseas supplier management?

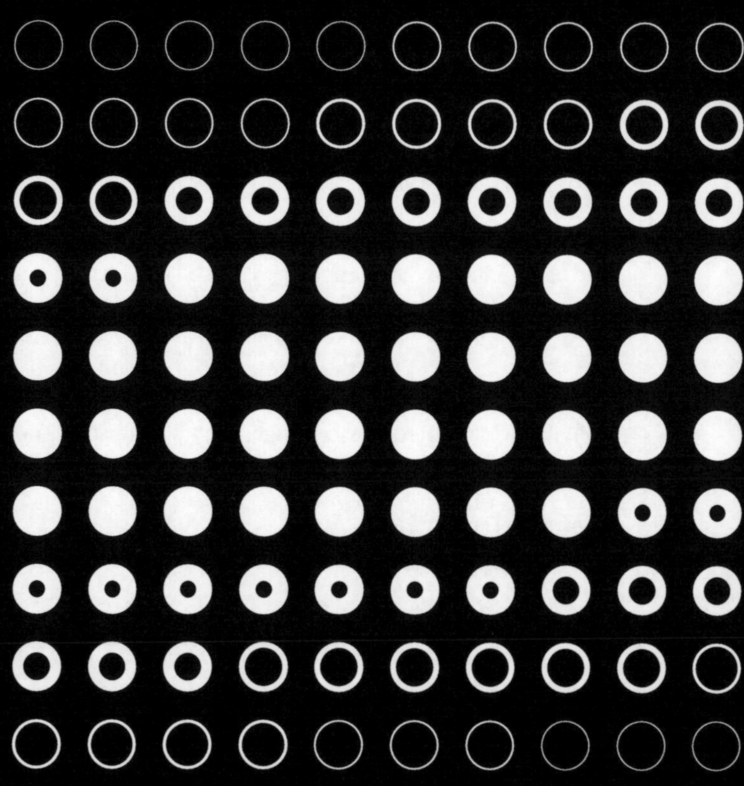

MODULE SIXTEEN

SELF MANAGEMENT, WELL-BEING, AND PREPARING FOR CAREER TRANSITIONS

MODULE SIXTEEN

SELF MANAGEMENT, WELL-BEING, AND PREPARING FOR CAREER TRANSITIONS

DESCRIPTION

The basic premise of this module is that effectively managing others and being managed requires managing oneself and identifying one's own strengths. It explores the process of self-discovery of one's strengths and reviews ways to build a personal brand around these strengths while maintaining overall well-being and stress management. In addition, this module focuses on the development of tangible and intangible assets for career transitions in light of the 100-year life.

LEARNING OBJECTIVES

Upon completing the learning experience, you will be able to:

- Describe the relationship between stress and performance
- Identify your strengths
- Build the elements of a personal brand
- Explain the impact of the population pyramid of a country on the dependency ratio
- Describe the tangible and intangible assets of a resilient career
- Calculate the future value of contributions and the present value of withdrawals of a pension plan
- Make behavioral decisions that contribute to your own wellness
- Discuss your own, employer's, and society's role in resilient career life and work transitions

GUIDING QUESTION

When is a strength a strength?
What is the probability that I will be one of the two people that lives to be 100 plus?
How prepared am I for the 100-year life and its transitions?

JOSE was the first one in his family to ever earn a college degree. Upon graduation, he was offered a job at Xerox where he interned as a student. After a series of promotions, he became a manager and was very much liked by his team and colleagues. Shortly after his 45th birthday, and 21 years with the company, he and several of his team members lost their jobs primarily due to technological unemployment. With no updated resume in hand, he found himself on the job market competing with much younger, tech-savvy, and lower-salaried people.

When KATHY was recovering from cancer, dealing with divorce, and leaving her job to become a contractor, her life was not what she wanted to it to be. "I needed someone without their own agenda to help me manage my life," Kathy recalled. I decided to hire a coach and she helped me to reinvent myself, create an action plan, look forward, and stay focused.

JOE is an HR Director at a large tech company where he manages a team of 320 HR professionals across the globe. He recently started to suffer from health issues; he is overweight, does not exercise, has poor eating habits, and shows symptoms of sleep deprivation. He plans to take a gap year as he is determined to practice self-care as his first priority. In his gap year, he wants to get in the habit of taking better care of himself by getting rest, exercising, eating right, and spending quality time with his son. He is also learning meditation to help alleviate stress down the road.

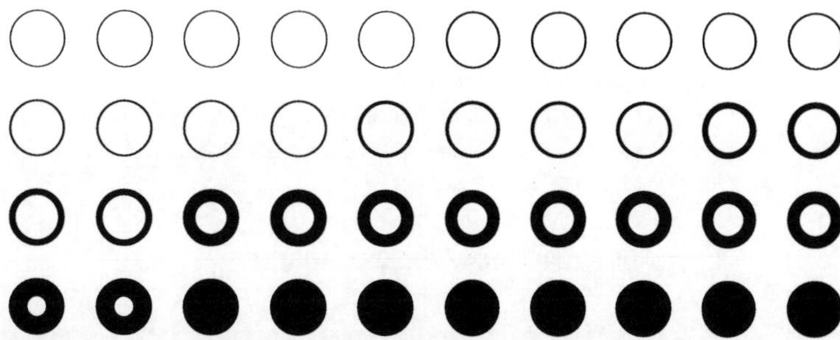

SELF MANAGEMENT

In the past, employers were driving the careers of their employees. This is generally no longer the case. Everyone has to carve their own place in the world, be agile, and know when to change course. Workers must now—wherever they are in the life cycle of their career trajectory—understand the implications of the new organization, the new world of work and the worker, and take steps to 'own and direct' their career and, foremost, manage themselves. As Peter Drucker said, "*Great achievers have always managed themselves. We have to develop ourselves and place ourselves where we can make the greatest contribution.*"

In a classic 2005 *Harvard Business Review* article entitled, "Managing Oneself," Peter Drucker identified five essential soul-searching questions to consider about oneself:[1]

1. **What are my strengths?**
   A person can only perform really well from their strengths. However, we are not really good at knowing what we are good at! The only way to discover our strengths is through feedback analysis, which brutally shows you areas where you are not particularly competent and where you have no strengths and cannot perform exceptionally.
2. **How do I perform?**
   A few common personality traits usually determine how a person performs. Strengths are a matter of personality (i.e., one's cognitive and learning styles) and how a person performs is a given, just as what a person is good (or not good) at is a given. The general rule is not to try to change one's—or for that matter other people's—personality traits as this is unlikely to succeed. Rather, we need to try to work hard to improve the way people perform from their unique base of strength.
3. **What are my values?**
   Values are reflected in the morning mirror test: "what kind of person do I want to see in the mirror when I get up?" This choice is largely based on one's personal values. Organizations have values reflected in their organizational culture (how do we do things around here?). Our personal values and the values of the organization where we work must be aligned. Working for an organization where the value system is unacceptable or incompatible with our own condemns a person to frustration. When personal strengths and personal values are in dissonance with the organization, it ultimately affects performance.
4. **Where do I belong?**
   Belonging is where strengths and value are aligned. Successful careers happen when people are prepared for opportunities because they know their strengths, their method of work, and their values. It is important for people to find a work environment that aligns with their strengths, how they perform best, and how the organizational culture matches their values. After all, work is an important part of daily life and work contributions ideally align with living a worthy life.
5. **What should I contribute?**
   This question has three distinct elements: (1) What does the situation require?; (2) Given my strengths how can I make the greatest contribution to what needs to be done?; (3) What results have to be achieved to make a difference? As we plan our work contributions—for example, for the next year—we must be clear and specific of our values, have stretch goals that are within reach. Our goals have to not only be meaningful for ourselves as well as the organization but also visible and measurable.

As Peter Drucker concluded, "*The effective executive makes strengths productive. He (sic) knows that one cannot build on weakness.*" Strengths are not just what we are good at and weaknesses are not just what we are bad at!

Strengths

We tend to believe our strengths are best judged by our successful achievements—meaning strength is equal to performance. If you are like most people, you have some activities or tasks that you do very well, but hate doing. You have the ability but it drains you. Such activities are not necessarily strengthening you. The opposite is also true. Some activities that you are currently not performing well on may not be weaknesses—but undiscovered or untrained opportunities for strength.

In his 2007 book, *Go Put Your Strengths to Work*, Marcus Buckingham further builds on Drucker's self-management framework.[2] He posits that we operate at near perfection when working from our strength. Think about how good we are at our hobbies! We are often led to believe that we must work on our weaknesses rather than our strengths. Yet, one 'util' of energy we invest in our strengths has a geometric return, while one 'util' of energy we spend on our weakness only has an arithmetic return. According to Buckingham, we must take responsibility for claiming our strengths by recognizing the signs. SIGNs of strength are:

- **S=Success**—when you do an activity, you feel effective and in control (self-efficacy);
- **I=Instinct**—before you do the activity, you look forward to doing it. You can't wait to do it;
- **G=Growth**—while you are doing the activity, you feel inquisitive and focused. You may lose track of time and two hours feel like only a few minutes have passed;
- **N=Needs**—after you have done the activity, even if you are tired, you feel fulfilled.

We discover our strengths through feedback, but most feedback accentuates the negative! Laura Roberts and her colleagues developed a powerful tool to help people understand and leverage their strengths. They called it the '*Reflective Best Self*' (RBS).[3] This exercise allows a person to develop a sense of their personal best and to increase their future potential—doing more of what they are good at!

Weaknesses

While many managers shun the term weakness, a common belief is that people should concentrate on working on their weaknesses. But spending time on weaknesses takes time and energy away from your strengths. Today, people and companies avoid using the term 'weaknesses' and rather euphemistically call them 'growth' opportunities. This does not mean that we should ignore our weaknesses. On the contrary, we must bring our weaknesses up to the bar—especially those weaknesses that stand in the way of our strengths. In today's environment, the professional bar is quite high and requires breadth as well as depth expertise. It is highly unlikely to turn a weakness into a strength, but we can stop or minimize the impact of the weakness. It is not acceptable to ignore weaknesses that result from our ability to be agile! Buckingham uses the acronym STOP when it comes to working on our weaknesses:[4]

- **Stop** doing it and see whether anyone notices. This won't work all the time, but somehow some tasks become redundant or other people find things that you do not like invigorating;
- **Team up** with someone who has your weakness as a strength and vice versa;
- **Offer** up a strength and make it valuable enough to others so that it takes up more of your time and crowds out the time spent on the weakness;
- **Perceive** the activity through the lens of a strength. If you hate confrontation, for example, but are strengthened by asking penetrating questions, approach a potential confrontation by asking a penetrating question instead.

Successfully stopping the weaknesses allows a person to focus on Buckingham's six-step strength discipline:[5]

1. Bust the myth that fixing one's strength is the path to success;
2. Get clear by labeling the strengths where you are consistently near perfection;
3. Free your strengths by volunteering your strengths to the team;
4. Stop your weaknesses by navigating away from activities that weaken your performance and standing with your colleagues;

5. Speak up by having strength and weakness conversations with your teammates and managers so that they can know how to set you up to make the greatest possible contributions;
6. Build strong habits.

In summary, Buckingham argues the strategy of freeing ones strengths requires one to:[6]

- **Focus**—identify how and where this specific strength helps you in your current role;
- **Release**—find the missed opportunities in your current role;
- **Educate**—learn new skills and techniques to build this strength;
- **Expand**—build your job around this strength.

As we have seen, it's a low value pursuit to turn true weaknesses into strengths. Ignorance is self-defeating. Know what you need to know and focus on using your strengths. Think about what new skills and experiences you can develop and adopt that you currently do not have and will become strengths for future opportunities. For example, somebody who is already fluent in two languages may decide to learn a third language to be more productive in a global role. Your manners matter too as ignored or poorly treated people are most likely to be disengaged. Self-esteem, self-confidence, having an internal and external locus of control, and building emotional stability and resilience enhances your mental toughness. But remember, it takes both self-efficacy—the belief that you can do it—and agency—the discipline to do it! Self-management and changing oneself requires us to reflect on a number of questions:

- How do I become aware of my strengths?
- How can I build on my strengths?
- How can I bring my weakness up to the bar?
- How do I learn from failure?

There is also value in enjoying what you do in your job. Thinks about a strength that you also enjoy, as not everybody enjoys doing wok that maximizes their strengths. Martin E.P. Seligman a strong promoter of the positive psychology of well-being refers to *"the good life is using your signature strengths every day to produce authentic happiness and abundant gratification."*[7] Many companies now have assessments in place for employees to find their strengths, identify their purpose, and build upon them.

Learning from Failure

Failure is inevitable in today's complex work and organizations. Yet failure is often ignored, not allowing the person and the organization to learn valuable lessons from failures. Amy C. Edmondson believes there are misguided beliefs that failure is bad and that we automatically learn from it. In a 2011 Harvard Business Review article, she shows failure is inevitable and some failures are even good as they present invaluable opportunities for learning and growth. According to Edmondson, there are three types of failures:[8]

- **Preventable failure**—usually involves predictable operations where deviations from specifications occur, shortcuts were taken, preparations were ignored, mistakes were made that could have been prevented. This is the only type of failure that really must be avoided at all costs.
- **Complex failure**—the person has good knowledge about what needs to be done (i.e., the processes and protocols) but a unique combination of internal and external factors (needs, people, and problems) came together to produce a failed outcome. This is where action and retrospective reviews are most valuable.
- **Intelligent failure**—are at the frontier where 'good' failures occur quickly and on a small scale often because the person is working in areas in unchartered areas or areas where they don't have the required expertise. This type of failure provides the most valuable information.

Successful learning from failure is not simple. It requires context-specific strategies. People often process failure internally or privately with high physical and psychological reactions rather than processing failure externally; where the failing person shares their failures with another person who can help humanize the failure. Edmondson argues that talking about failure builds relationships, makes the person who fails more approachable and likeable, turns 'malicious' into 'benign' envy, makes work more efficient, and people more resilient. But sharing failures requires a safe space or an organization with a culture of learning from failure and a person with the integrity to share their failures and not blame others. First, leaders must understand how the blame game gets in the way and must work to create an organizational culture in which employees feel safe admitting or reporting on failure. Strong leadership can build a learning culture—one in which failures large and small are consistently reported and deeply analyzed, and opportunities to experiment are proactively sought. Taking an understanding stance on failure is not the same as having an 'anything goes' work environment—preventable failures must be controlled! In many job interviews, the question is often asked, 'Tell me about a time that you failed at work and overcame the challenge.' A great way to prepare is to create a mental 'resume of failures' focusing on how you analyzed and learned from complex and intelligent failures and were able to avoid preventable failures.

THE 100-YEAR LIFE

Lynda Gratton and Andrew Scott in a 2016 book entitled, *The 100-Year Life: Living and Working in an Age of Longevity*,[9] argues that with a longer lifespan, the three-phase-model of education, work, and retirement is broken and that people will need to hone both their tangible and intangible skills to re-create themselves throughout their life.

Living Longer

Longevity and the new world of work affects us all, but especially the millennials who by now (the year 2020) fill nearly half of the workforce.[10] The good news for millennials is that they are still young and can take action early—i.e., the future value on investment contributions over more years than people in midlife! The bad news is that the challenges of millennials and generation Z are great and will require them to have considerable career resilience to balance work and life. The basic premise of Gratton and Scott's book is that a child born today (after 2016) has more than 50% chance of living over 100 years with slight variations by country. In France and Italy, a child born today has a 50/50 chance to reach age 104, in the US age 103, and in Japan age 107. Moreover, people who are 20 today have a 50% chance to be 100; if 40 today that age is 95; if 60 today the expected life span is 90 years of age. These dramatic improvements in life expectancy during the past century are due to decreased infant mortality, tackling of chronic diseases of middle and old age; better health, nutrition, medical care, education, technology, sanitation, and income.11 Increases in life expectancy are happening all over the world albeit with a delay in some markets, mainly underdeveloped ones. However, these life expectancy probabilities are not distributed equally, and the probability that you are among the 50% of living 100-plus years is heavily dependent on socio-economic status (occupation, education, and income) and the associated health and lifestyle choices.

Birth and death rates affect the population pyramids of different countries, the dependency ratio, and the societal retirement age norm. A population pyramid is a graphical representation showing the age-sex distribution of a given population. One side of the y-axis shows the distribution of the populations by sex (males on one side and females on the other), the x-axis shows the percentage of population by age or cohort grouping (usually in 5-year intervals). While contrasting the population pyramids of different countries, very different pictures emerge at the country level (see www.populationpyramid.net). The aging of the population and the workforce is a global phenomenon that started in Japan and Europe, is now in the U.S., and will soon be in the emerging and underdeveloped markets. Note that a population pyramid does not consider migration (immigration and emigration) but only takes the number of births and deaths into account. Migration can dramatically change the consequences of the age structure of a society and its available workforce. The population pyramid of a country is a powerful predictor of the future as the shape of the pyramid impacts the dependency ratio and the expected time period people are likely to live upon retirement (if retiring at age 65 remains the norm). Add other elements to that data—the low savings rates and high debt of people, the precariousness of the Social Security systems due to aging populations, the move of retirement plans from defined benefits to defined contributions, and the impact of the 4th industrial revolution on work and the worker—the important question becomes whether people will be able to deal with (in)voluntary work transitions and have enough retirement income for that predicted longer lifespan.

The dependency ratio is an age-population ratio of those who typically are not in the labor force (the dependent part ages 0 to 14 and 65+) and those typically in the labor force (the productive part of the labor force between the ages 15 to 64). The dependency ratio measures the pressure on productive population to support the non-productive people. The dependency ratio also has important ramifications for social security (i.e., how many working people support non-working people), economic growth potential (a decrease in the labor force and an increase in the elderly population could slow economic growth and may have long-run economic consequences), and the taxation of those who work.

In 1889, Bismarck introduced the first old-age social insurance program in Germany and set '65' as the norm for retirement. It is interesting to note that at the time of the founding father of social security, most people never lived that long! But today the norm of '65' as a retirement age is likely as much of a fiction as it was in Bismarck's time when it was established. With the prospect of a 100-plus-year life for half of the people born today, they will live up to 40 years in retirement if 65 remains the retirement age norm—but likely without the financial security they expected or need!

The Reality of the 100-Year Life

1So what does the 100-year life prospect really mean in terms of living and working in an age of longevity? Gratton and Scott come to the following conclusions:12

- The three-stage life (education, career, and retirement) is over and the lockstep career will end. Life will become multi-staged with transitions being the norm. These transitions may be enriching and/or painful for people.
- If you live longer you will need more money. That leaves few alternatives: you will either work longer (people will be able to work into their 70s or even 80s as many older people stay younger for longer); you will choose to live with less; or you will have to save and work more than you want to, have to, or are capable of doing.

But getting the finances right will not be everything. It will likely also not be sufficient. New uncertainties and challenges regarding work and the worker are brought about by the 4th industrial revolution. There will be new jobs and skills requirements and thousands of jobs that are predicted to disappear due to artificial intelligence. People living and working longer will also result in generational complexity of multiple generations having to work together.[13] Within the U.S., many baby boomers are staying longer in the workforce. Rather derogatory terms such as 'OK Boomers' and 'Go Boomers' are going viral and leading to some generational conflict and resentment by younger generations for 'older' workers remaining in the workforce. It should be noted that the 50-plus and baby boomers are an important part of the freelance workforce.

CAREER RESILIENCE

Building a resilient career will require balancing one's tangible and intangible assets. Gratton and Scott describe the assets people will need to develop to build a resilient career.[14] An asset is something that can provide a flow of benefits over time. While tangible assets are physical assets that can be measured and traded easily (such as financial assets and others), intangible assets cannot be traded (bought & sold) or substituted. They are not reversible. Nobody can really take away intangible assets...they are priceless! There are different types of tangible and intangible assets (discussed later). Intangible assets are not independent from tangible assets but they play a reciprocal role on the development of tangible assets and there are synergies between the two. If one wants to have a sustainable career, it is necessary to manage these assets as a portfolio. How will we prepare ourselves, the people, and our organizations for a resilient career? If work-life is going to span 50-60 years, one simply cannot burn the candle at both ends. People and organizations will have to design work and lifestyles that are more flexible and more responsive (i.e., resilient). Work and life will have to evolve at a sustainable and agile pace as part of a multi-stage life with a variety of careers, some sprints but also breaks and transitions to renew oneself.

There is quite an ongoing debate as to who is responsible for building career resilience. Whose responsibility is it to develop and balance the tangible and intangible assets of the workforce so people can build a career in a resilient and sustainable manner? Everyone seems to agree there are three major players (individual, employer, and society). But the values and beliefs as to whom carries the major responsibility are very culturally and nationally different around the world—with some societies putting the major responsibility on the individual and others focusing more on social protection and a safety net. Independent of the society's prevailing culture and structure regarding work, it is generally assumed that individual workers will bear more responsibility for their career through their choices. Employers will likely experience an upcoming battle for talent and it will behoove them to manage the employability of their worker through upskilling and reskilling—whether classified as employees or contract/freelance workers. Society will also have to change its norms to reflect the new work-life reality. The educational system as we know it will likely be disrupted and government will have to develop laws and policies to address the changes. In other words, the 100-year life requires major changes at all levels—self (micro), employers (meso), and society/government (macro). We explore each level.

Micro Level Interventions (Self) for Building a Resilient Career

What are the personal (and family) assets required for the 100-year life and how can you build them? The 100-year life requires people to take into their own hands the planning of their careers and create new and different working life scenarios. In doing so, people will need to balance the development of their financial assets (income for transitions and retirement) and non-financial assets (family and friend relationships, physical and mental health, and happiness).[15]

While the new working life scenarios will likely unfold in stages, some of these work-life changes are already with us today. As we transitioned from the 3rd to the 4th industrial revolution, many employees have already experienced involuntary disruptions and setbacks in the classic three-stage model under which we still largely operate. Manufacturing jobs have been outsourced and offshored, middle-level jobs have been eliminated as a result of reengineering, and economic downturns have led to layoffs. However, people have been affected equally with low-skilled workers, youth, and those above 50 feeling the impact the most.

The new working life scenarios (will) require a lot of economic and psychological resilience of people and integration of the rational and emotional meaning of work and life including non-work. According to Gratton and Scott, the new potential work scenarios will not be recreation (as promised by the 20th leisure society) but transitions in terms of re-creation. Reinventing oneself through re-creation will be more important than recreation.[16] There will be much more experimentation and search for authenticity, especially among the millennials. Having work-life options will become more valuable and the home and work relationships will likely be transformed.

The 2019 Global Wealth Report compared millennials to baby boomers at the same age and found that millennials earn less, have higher student debt, more difficulty buying a home, lower pension savings, and greater income disparity.[17] A 2016 McKinsey report shows that millennials have a lifestyle where they spend more and do less with the money they earn (but eat out, travel, and stay at 'hotel mama'), and are more likely to be in the gig economy as freelancers, save less as low interest rates discourage savings, and are more uncertain about the future.[18] According to a report by Bank of America, millennials are starting to save more for a rainy day. In a survey of 2,000 millennials aged 23 to 37, one in six had $100,000 or more saved up, while 47% had at least $15,000 or more in savings — a significant jump from 8% and 33% according to MarketWatch.[19] The results are a promising improvement for a group who grew up during the financial crisis and has been burdened by student debt.

In order to have a resilient career, the individual worker must pay attention to both sets of assets—tangible and intangible ones (see 16-2).

16.2: Tangible and Intangible Assets for Personal Career Resilience

Tangible Assets	Intangible Assets
Financial assets	Productivity assets
Work, home, and life balance	Vitality assets
Lifestyle	Transformational assets

Source: Gratton, L. & Scott, A. (2016). *The 100-Year Life: Living and Working in an Age of Longevity*. London: Bloomsbury Publishing.

Tangible Assets

Gratton and Scott identify three categories of tangible assets: (1) financial assets; (2) work, home, and life balance; and (3) lifestyle.[20]

1. Financial Assets

Financial assets are monies that are easily available or accessible, usually in the form of various financial instruments that can be turned into cash when needed. These financial assets are required for being able to make needed transitions (whether voluntarily or not) through life to reinvent oneself and/or provide a retirement income in the future. The typical sources of retirement income (social security, company retirement plans, and savings) all have their own disruptions and are likely to provide less protection for the worker:

- **State or government pensions**—usually Social Security and other defined benefits that ensure a certain amount for the worker upon retirement. Future social security solvency requires later retirement ages and/or less payout.
- **Employer sponsored retirement plans**—usually in the form of a defined benefit plan (a pension with a set promised payout) or a defined contribution plan (such as a 401K for corporations or 403B for non-profit organizations in the U.S.). In a defined contribution plan, the worker puts in their own pre-tax money reserves (often matched by the employers) and has the market risk of the investment over time. Defined benefit plans where the employer carries the risk have all but gone the way of the dinosaurs.
- **Self-accumulated reserves**—such as individual retirement accounts (IRAs), home, saving, and other assets. Of course, the liabilities the person owes on these assets (such as mortgage loans, student debt, etc.) must be deducted.

A typical problem in an introductory MBA finance class is, '*what percentage of my income do I need to contribute to retire at a certain age to have enough cash to withdraw for the rest of my retirement life*.' Prevailing norms used to be—that is during the 3rd industrial revolution era—that 10% of your income set aside at the start of your career would allow you to retire with 50% of your final salary. But, if you live much longer, 10% will no longer be sufficient. Let's use an exercise on the future and present value of a typical retirement plan as an illustration. Over a person's lifetime, when they start making contributions to a retirement plan—whether matched or not by an employer—the contributions accumulate interest over time. At the time of retirement, a series of withdrawals are made over the number of years one is likely to live—as determined by actuaries or personal preferences of the retiree. In both, series of contributions and withdrawals, a number of assumptions must be made:

- Contribution assumptions include start age of contribution, end age of contribution, start income, real income growth, real return, inflation, and savings rate;
- Withdrawal assumptions include start age of withdrawal (retirement); end age withdrawal; 1st withdrawal as a percent of last income;
- The future value of contribution is based on nominal income growth, nominal return, and number of contributions;
- The present value of withdrawals is based on first withdrawal, number of withdrawals, and present value.

Using 25 as the start age and 66 as the end age for contributions, a person would make 42 annual contributions. With a starting salary income of $50,000 (and assuming a real income growth of 1%), an annual contribution of 10% of that income, a real return of 3% and inflation of 2.5%, the future value of their contributions is $1,336,123.78 one year before retirement. In calculating the future value of contributions, the nominal income growth is 3.53% and the nominal return is 5.58%. At age 67, the person wants to start making annual withdrawals until they reach age 95. This will require 28 withdrawals. One year prior to retirement, the present value of withdrawals is $1,336,123.78. The first annual withdrawal is $72,986.52 or 34.07% of their last income (calculated to meet the other requirements). This example illustrates that saving 10% of their salary will not account to 50% of their last income (see 16-3). However, the person may have other assets that provide an income such as social security benefits (or the sale of a home). For anyone looking for financial retirement assets, we paraphrase a Chinese proverb, "*the best time to plan for your retirement was 20 years ago. The second best time is now.*" There are two other tradeoffs that can be made in terms of financial assets, namely balancing work, home, life, and lifestyle. Because they are tangible assets, tradeoffs can be made! We often fail to consider those as tangible assets—perhaps because they are somewhat un-American!

2. Work, Home, and Life Balance

The first tradeoff that can be made is how we integrate our work and other life roles. How do we allocate our time for work and other aspects of our lives such as personal interests, family, social, and leisure activities? The choices we make today here (rather than having them imposed on us) are not only linked to our values and beliefs, but also have long-term ramifications. A useful way to explore the challenges of discovering our identity was proposed by Robert Dilts, who developed the neurological 'logical levels' of change (see 16-4).[21]

16-4. Neuro-Logical Levels Model

Spiritual	Vision & Purpose	For whom? For what?
A. Who I **Am** - *Identity*	Permission & Motivation	Who?
B. My **Belief** system - *Values and Meanings*	Mission	Why?
C. My **Capabilities** - *Strategies and States*	Maps & Plans	How?
D. What I **Do** or have **Done** - *Specific Behaviors*	Actions & Reactions	What?
E. My **Environment** - *External Context*	Constraints & Opportunities	Where? When?

Source: Dilts, R. (2014). A Brief History of Logical Levels (Accessed: December 2010). http://www.nlpu.com/Articles/LevelsSummary.htm

16-3. Retirement Planning: Future and Present Values

Contributions	
Start age	**25**
End age	**66**
Start income	**50,000.00**
Real income growth	**1.00%**
Real return	**3.00%**
Inflation	**2.50%**
Saving rate	**10.00%**

Withdrawals	
Start age	67
End age	**94**
First withdrawal*	34.07%

**Percentage of last income*

Calculation of Future Value of Contributions	
Nominal income growth	3.53%
Nominal return	5.58%
Number of contributions	42
Future value	1,336,123.78

Calculation of Present Value of Withdrawals	
First withdrawal	72,986.52
Number of withdrawals	28
Present value	1,336,123.78
Gap	0.00

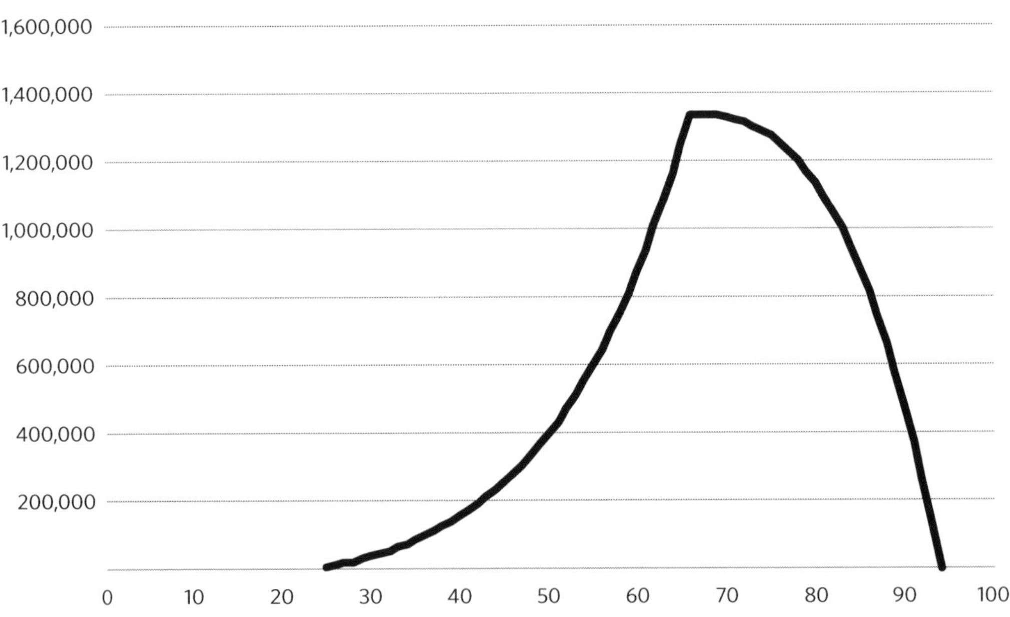

Source: Developed by Professors Michael Dothan and Lisbeth Claus (2016) as integrated materials for the MBA Finance and Organizational Behavior/HR courses at Willamette University.

Amortization Table

Age	Contribution	Return	Withdrawal	Balance
25	5,000.00		0	5,000.00
26	5,176.25	278.75	0	10,455.00
27	5,358.71	582.87	0	16,396.58
28	5,547.61	914.11	0	22,858.30
29	5,743.16	1,274.35	0	29,875.81
30	5,945.61	1,665.58	0	37,486.99
31	6,155.19	2,089.90	0	45,732.08
32	6,372.16	2,549.56	0	54,653.80
33	6,596.78	3,046.95	0	64,297.53
34	6,829.32	3,584.59	0	74,711.43
35	7,070.05	4,165.16	0	85,946.64
36	7,319.27	4,791.53	0	98,057.44
37	7,577.27	5,466.70	0	111,101.41
38	7,844.37	6,193.90	0	125,139.69
39	8,120.88	6,976.54	0	140,237.11
40	8,407.15	7,818.22	0	156,462.47
41	8,703.50	8,722.78	0	173,888.75
42	9,010.30	9,694.30	0	192,593.35
43	9,327.91	10,737.08	0	212,658.34
44	9,656.72	11,855.70	0	234,170.76
45	9,997.12	13,055.02	0	257,222.89
46	10,349.52	14,340.18	0	281,912.59
47	10,714.34	15,716.63	0	308,343.55
48	11,092.02	17,190.15	0	336,625.72
49	11,483.01	18,766.88	0	366,875.61
50	11,887.79	20,453.32	0	399,216.71
51	12,306.83	22,256.33	0	433,779.88
52	12,740.65	24,183.23	0	470,703.75
53	13,189.75	26,241.73	0	510,135.24
54	13,654.69	28,440.04	0	552,229.97
55	14,136.02	30,786.82	0	597,152.81
56	14,634.32	33,291.27	0	645,078.40
57	15,150.18	35,963.12	0	696,191.69
58	15,684.22	38,812.69	0	750,688.60
59	16,237.09	41,850.89	0	808,776.58

Age	Contribution	Return	Withdrawal	Balance
60	16,809.45	45,089.29	0	870,675.32
61	17,401.98	48,540.15	0	936,617.44
62	18,015.40	52,216.42	0	1,006,849.26
63	18,650.44	56,131.85	0	1,081,631.55
64	19,307.87	60,300.96	0	1,161,240.38
65	19,988.47	64,739.15	0	1,245,968.00
66	20,693.06	69,462.72	0	1,336,123.78
67	0	74,488.90	72,986.52	1,337,626.16
68	0	74,572.66	74,811.18	1,337,387.64
69	0	74,559.36	76,681.46	1,335,265.55
70	0	74,441.05	78,598.49	1,331,108.11
71	0	74,209.28	80,563.46	1,324,753.93
72	0	73,855.03	82,577.54	1,316,031.42
73	0	73,368.75	84,641.98	1,304,758.19
74	0	72,740.27	86,758.03	1,290,740.43
75	0	71,958.78	88,926.98	1,273,772.22
76	0	71,012.80	91,150.16	1,253,634.87
77	0	69,890.14	93,428.91	1,230,096.10
78	0	68,577.86	95,764.63	1,202,909.33
79	0	67,062.19	98,158.75	1,171,812.77
80	0	65,328.56	100,612.72	1,136,528.62
81	0	63,361.47	103,128.04	1,096,762.05
82	0	61,144.48	105,706.24	1,052,200.30
83	0	58,660.17	108,348.89	1,002,511.57
84	0	55,890.02	111,057.61	947,343.98
85	0	52,814.43	113,834.05	886,324.35
86	0	49,412.58	116,679.91	819,057.03
87	0	45,662.43	119,596.90	745,122.55
88	0	41,540.58	122,586.83	664,076.31
89	0	37,022.25	125,651.50	575,447.06
90	0	32,081.17	128,792.78	478,735.45
91	0	26,689.50	132,012.60	373,412.35
92	0	20,817.74	135,312.92	258,917.17
93	0	14,434.63	138,695.74	134,656.06
94	0	7,507.08	142,163.14	0.00

3. Lifestyle
The third tangible asset is the lifestyle that we have (consumption) or rather the choices we make regarding consumption. If we live longer, we will need to work longer, spend less, save more, and probably eventually live with less!

Intangible Assets
Gratton and Scott identify three categories of intangible assets: (1) productivity; (2) vitality assets; and (3) transformational assets.[22] Remember, these assets are intangible and cannot be traded!

1. Productivity Assets
Competencies, reputation, and professional ties are intangibles that support productivity at work and boost income and career prospects.

- **Competencies**—the knowledge (tacit and explicit) and skills acquired through education, learning, and experience. The financial benefits of knowledge and skills are significant provided the knowledge is valuable, rare, difficult to imitate or substitute; the value it creates in combination with others (team). What, when, and how we will acquire these will change significantly and be a lifelong endeavor to stay relevant.
- **Reputation**—the personal brand ensuring that you can be trusted to behave competently and ethically under a variety of circumstances.
- **Professional ties**—the strong ties (from networking theory) and professional social capital that you accumulate (or the actions and behaviors you undertake that cement your reputation).

2. Vitality Assets
Vitality assets are the antithesis of stress. They are what makes us feel happy and fulfilled, motivated and positive. In short, the essence of your physical and mental health and psychological well-being. Refer to our next section on well-being.

3. Transformational Assets
The capacity and motivation to successfully achieve change and make transitions. They include self-knowledge, the capacity to reach out to diverse networks, and openness to new experiences.

- **Self-knowledge**—accrual vs possible selves; self-efficacy (I know that I can do this) and agency (I have the discipline to do this).
- **Capacity to reach out to diverse networks**—our weak ties (from networking theory) in a variety of our communities of interest.
- **Openness to new experiences**—our ability to find creative solutions and routine-busting.

To build a resilient career we must have a self-development (coaching) conversation with ourselves.[23] This conversation includes a number of questions:[24]

1. Do I do the right thing? (in terms of organizational strategy)
2. Do I do the things right? (compared to others in the group)
3. What are my strengths? (feedback)
4. How do I continue to develop further? (70:20:10)
5. Am I in the right place?

Obviously, these questions and responses may change based on the stage of life.

The Center for Creative Leadership (2016) identified eight steps to become more resilient:[25]

1. **Accept change**—find ways to become more comfortable with change;
2. **Become a continuous learner**—learn new skills, gain new understanding, and apply them in times of change;
3. **Take charge**—take charge of your own career and your own development;
4. **Find your sense of purpose**—assess setbacks within the framework of a broader perspective;
5. **Skill shift**—reframe how you see your skills, talents, and interests;
6. **Reflect**—reflection fosters learning, new perspectives, and self-awareness;

7. **Cultivate relationships**—develop and nurture a broad network of personal and professional relationships;
8. **Pay attention to your self-identity**—for your identity apart from your job.

Most successful people would say that having a good boss supporting your career development is essential. Therefore, when seeking a new job, focus on who you will be working for and the company culture rather than the job title, company name, and compensation package.

In their 2018 book, *Imagine it Forward: Courage, Creativity and the Power of Change*," Beth Comstock & Tahl Raz suggest a number of self-management exercises such as the permission slip, bucket list, dragon slayer challenge, and job crafting.[26]

- **Permission slip**—write out a series of things you are scared of or are putting off doing, then write yourself a permission slip, choose a permission at random each day and carry out the task.
- **Bucket list**—get yourself accountable for getting out of your comfort zone by creating a monthly bucket list. 'I can do this' list for weeks 1, 2, 3, and 4.
- **Dragon slayer challenge**—whenever you feel a negative emotion related to work bubble up, take note and write a sentence or phrase in a dragon slayer log. Include entries of moments of fear and negativity voiced by your colleagues and friends about the industry and job. At the end of the week, take a look at what you have written down. Do the observations and comments add up to a larger problem or trend and what are you going to do about it?
- **Job crafting challenge**—on Monday morning, add a new task or project (that you are excited about!) to your set of responsibilities. Develop your thesis and how you will approach it, think about developing skills in new areas, and how you can begin to develop the project.

Building a resilient career also requires branding ones-self. Develop your short (monthly) and longer-term developmental (annual) goals, share them with your manager and mentors and build your personal brand around your strengths and passion. After defining your brand, you must weave the value proposition into a story or message that can be consumed by your audience. Reflect on what your story is, how this aligns with your brand, and what your value proposition is or the unique benefits you will bring to an employer that others won't? Value proposition questions are:

1. What are the most important roles you have filled for current and previous employers? In your community?
2. What transferable skills do these experiences provide you?
3. What accomplishments did you achieve and what did you do better than people in similar roles did?
4. What special projects were you assigned?
5. How did working with others affect your work assignments?
6. Did any of this work help you realize something about yourself that you didn't realize before?
7. What kind of recognition did your receive for your efforts?

Not all careers are a straight light at a 45-degree angle. Plateaus (or treading water) are needed at certain points of career development to master essential skills and experiences. In a dynamic open talent environment, the focus is on #ZigZag careers or lateral careers rather than a stepladder.[27] Too many people move to another company without understanding the pace of a normal career path. Too many people with a lot of talent burn out and nose-dive because they were promoted too fast in their career and were not fully prepared for the demands of a larger role.

Meso Level Interventions (Employer, HR, Manager) for Building a Resilient Career

The structure and sequencing of time is effectively a social construct. The implicit assumption that age and stage in life are one-and-the-same thing hard-wired into so much of the corporate HR practices, marketing, and legislation. New ecosystems are emerging, requiring fundamental changes. People want to be more flexible in terms of their skills, possible work locations (office, remote, co-sharing), timing of work (flexibility) and employment status (employees or contingent workforce). Each of these options carries advantages and disadvantages for both the employer and the talent.

In a 1994 *Harvard Business Review* article entitled, "Toward a Career-Resilient Workforce," Robert Waterman, Judith Waterman, and Betsy Collard discuss the company's obligations in building a resilient career for their workers.[28] They argue that with the erosion of the long-term covenant between employee and employer, companies will have to be much more open with their workers and maintain a continuing dialogue about the company's business, its direction, and market challenges so that employees can determine what skills they need to prepare themselves for the future. Instead of focusing on employment, both employer and worker will have to focus on employability. Employers can be helpful in enhancing the career resilience of their workforce and help people explore opportunities, promote lifelong learning, upskilling and reskilling, better support no-fault exits, not allowing managers to have the power to block a job transfer unilaterally, and making managers better learning and development coaches.

Macro Level Interventions (Society) for Building a Resilient Career

Conversations at the societal level can counterbalance the vulnerability of the individual worker against the employer's desire to optimize productivity and labor efficiencies. In his 2020 book, A World Without Work, Daniel Susskind shows income inequality—as measured by the Gini coefficient—has risen significantly in the past decade in most developed countries. Even when using a different measure of income inequality—ranking income groups from low to high and seeing how they changed over time—U.S. data show that since 1980, income has remained anemic for the people who earned the least and has soared for the one percent who earned the most. Finally, when looking at a third measure of income inequality called top (income) inequality—or the proportion of total income that goes to the top 1% who earn the most—has also increased significantly grown the U.S and the U.K. and even in countries such as Finland, Norway, and Sweden, which are regarded for their equality. According to Susskind, the reasons are that there are unequal returns both on human and traditional capital for that group as wages and salaries are being distributed in unequal ways (executives vs non-executives, men vs women).[29]

Income inequality and technological employment are interrelated. Resilient career management is being talked about a lot but very few people have come up with viable solutions beyond upskilling and reskilling. There is a lag between the social, ethical, and regulatory norms and institutions and the current management context. The legal and regulatory environment, institutions (e.g., benefits, social security, income taxation, welfare, privacy protection, education and lifelong learning, etc.) and the social norms (e.g., the value of work, career paths, work transitions, etc.) need to adapt and be reformed to close the gaps—or even perhaps be completely reinvented. A number of proposals are at the core of these societal labor economics discussions such as a robot tax, universal guaranteed income, and the development of new learning and educational models.

- **A robot tax**—to slow down the effects of robotization would require employers who replace employees with robots to pay a tax. These funds are then used to assist displaced workers and minimize the effects of job loss created by replacing humans with robots.
- **Universal guaranteed income**—is "a regular income paid in cash to every individual member of society irrespective of income

from other sources and with no strings attached."[30] It is a means to reduce the growing inequality between those who have and don't have work. It is different from social insurance and public assistance welfare schemes by providing a basic floor of support on which an individual can stand unconditionally.

- **New learning and educational models**—preparing workers with the skills that employers need are also part of the societal conversation. The current educational model (and especially higher education) is based on older labor models and lacks the agility to produce a workforce with the skill level that meets the current and (largely unpredictable) future needs of employers. Educational institutions can provide a combination of both liberal education—developing critical thinking and lifelong learning capabilities—and professional education—the specialized and agile skill set required for work productivity. Such learning will need to be lifelong over a person's life cycle.
- **Upskilling and reskilling**—employers can build into their strategic workforce, plan the need to upskill and reskill workers, and provide lifelong learning opportunities for the workforce.

Career resilience is a shared responsibility (self, employer, and society). The ability of people to balance their tangible and intangible assets will become the new definition of success![31] Succeeding in work and in life may require very different skills. The notion of well-being (and even happiness) of the workforce is gaining traction not only with workers but also employers.

WELL-BEING

Wellness, a central concept of positive psychology, is more than the absence of disease but a holistic integration of physical, emotional, social, spiritual, and intellectual health. It requires the active participation of the person to make choices for '*eudaimonia*' or Greek for 'good life'—being happy, engaged, and experience meaningfulness. Workplace health and wellness promotion is made up of a variety of benefits, policies, health promotion programs and activities, behavioral nudging, and employer support designed to promote healthy choices which keeps the worker healthy and safe. There are a variety of reasons progressive employers are paying attention to employee wellness:

- Rising healthcare costs mostly by both the employer and the employee—especially in the U.S.;
- According to the Center for Disease Control (CDC)32, four of the top 10 of the most costly health conditions for U.S. employers come from such as agina pectoris (or chest pain), high blood pressure, diabetes, and heart attacks—related heart attacks and stroke conditions;
- These chronic conditions are largely attributed to lifestyle and behavior;
- Health issues are linked to productivity, absenteeism, and overall engagement;
- The possible return on investment for corporate well-being programs;
- The sweet spot that healthier employees are good for both employers and employees/workers.

A company that pioneered the wide spread used of health promotion is the California-based retailer Safeway. Being self-insured—companies that are self-insured are more likely to focus on reducing healthcare costs by wellness programs—they understand that a wellness-focused approach not only has the potential of increasing employee health (meaning greater productivity, less absenteeism, etc.) but also reduces healthcare costs. Using a combination of incentives and nudging, 'Health Measures' pays for preventive tests, offers employee rebates in health insurance premiums for staying within certain limits regarding four common (and costly) medical risk factors—smoking, obesity, blood pressure, and cholesterol. They have revamped their cafeteria menu options, subsidize healthy food choices, have a loyalty program for their on-site gym use (including a free cafeteria lunch after eight visits) and frequently lobby

Washington for reforming the healthcare system.[33] Other companies have taken a progressive approach towards well-being. Leena Nair, CHRO at Unilever, asserts that for every $ invested in wellness, the company gets a tenfold return.[34] Starbucks introduced mental health benefits for its partners and there are many more examples of companies taking a new approach to employee overall well-being.[35]

The five elements of a comprehensive Workplace Health Program as defined by Healthy People 2010 are:[36]

1. Health education;
2. Links to related employee services;
3. Supportive physical and social environment for health improvement;
4. Integration of health promotion into the organizational culture;
5. Employee screenings with adequate treatment and follow-up.

The management of well-being in the workplace—supported by an array third-party vendors—is still in its infancy and must deal with fundamental issues such as the underutilization paradox, the measurement fallacy, behavioral health of people, and workplace stress.

- **Underutilization paradox**—despite the wide array of benefits provided by companies, work-life balance, and well-being benefits, employees and managers often fail to take advantage of them. Underutilization rates are tied to three major elements: (1) Employee characteristics—do employees need or know about the benefits offered?; (2) Managerial characteristics—do managers' 'ideal worker' archetypes inhibit use of these benefits?; and (3) Organizational culture--does the organizational culture support use well-being initiatives? Lack of alignment of these three elements in an organization contributes to the underutilization paradox.[37]
- **Measurement fallacy**—poor research designs and unsubstantiated claims plague the analytics of well-being programs. In their 2019 book, Investing in People, Wayne Cascio, John Boudreau, and Alexis A. Fink elaborate on the methodological issues in measuring health care program effects and the lack of rigorous research designs and statistical analyses to draw proper conclusions.[38] Most companies (and their vendors) use no control groups when evaluating their workplace health programs, biases due to self-selection of participants, unit of analysis issues across worksites, and the subjectivity of the choice of variables in their cost-effectiveness, cost-benefit, and return-in-investment analyses. While the authors affirm that health promotion programs can yield significant benefits for both employers and employees, these workplace initiatives need to be scrutinized in a controlled and longitudinal manner to see whether the cost benefits are realized and the employee behavior results in behavioral change over time.
- **Behavioral health**—behavioral economics tells us decision-making is 'predictably irrational,' especially when it comes to engaging in current behavior that affects the future! The adoption of psychological and analytical techniques (combined with the use of technology and artificial intelligence) to encourage and nudge the behavior of employees and managers to produce healthier and happier workplaces is fast growing. Applications, data mining, and sentiment analyses are increasingly being used by employers to nudge workers toward making better health choices.
- **Stress**—the culprit of most corporate health issues lies in coping with the stress of the work environment. The relationship between stress and performance as expressed in the 1908 Yerkes-Dodson curve—yes we have known this for over 100 years—shows there is a healthy tension between intended performance, actual performance, panic zone, breakdown, and burnout. We need a certain amount of stress to reach optimal performance, but after the tipping point of too much stress, performance declines and leads to burnout. That tipping point is likely different for different people and it is a managerial responsibility to help manage a person's tipping point.

Managing stress requires problem-based, emotion-based, and lifestyle-based coping.

- **Problem-based coping**—can we fix the problem or remove the stressor?
- **Emotion-based coping**—where can I find support, perspective, and relaxation?
- **Lifestyle-based coping**—do I have healthy diet and get exercise, rest, and sleep?

Two areas that are receiving greater attention in the workplace are mental health and mindfulness. Multitasking, the pace of daily life activities, and social isolation are pulling people in different directions and contributing factors to stress, behavior health issues, and depression. Mindfulness—or being aware of the present moment—and practicing mediation are used to improve emotional heath. Increasingly, companies are offering medication apps, on-site mindfulness sessions, yoga, and wellness centers. In their 2012 book, Super Brain, Deepak Chopra and Rudolph Tanzi use the SHIELD method to prevent stress and the resulting bodily inflammation. The acronym stands for Sleep, Handle stress (through meditation), Interact with others, Exercise, and Diet—all lifestyle-related endeavors.[39] How shiny is your shield when it comes to work and life?

Frequent periods of career transition and uncertainty require a more non-linear—also called 'boundaryless' and 'ZigZag' career. Ownership of that career has increasingly become the responsibility of the worker. Reskilling and upskilling are some of the structural solutions that employers are increasingly supporting as more and more of the tasks that make up a job become automated. People's identities are closely linked to the jobs they do. Yet, they constantly need to reinvent themselves to remain relevant.

Karoline Strauss, K. Mark A. Griffin and Sharon K. Parker coined the term 'future work self' to refer to how to people should think about their professional identity in the future. The term refers to an individual's representation of himself or herself in the future that reflects his or her hopes and aspirations in relation to work. Salient future work selves provide individuals with a motivational resource by generating a motivating discrepancy (between the actual vs future self), enabling the exploration of new possibilities, and invoking a mental simulation of the future—all leading to proactive career behaviors.[40]

We hope to nudge you with this module to take stock of the assets you need to pursue a resilient career path while meaningfully integrating your work and life, maintain your well-being and those around you. May you have the blessing of always enjoying your work! ▮

16-6. Yerkes-Dodson Stress Curve

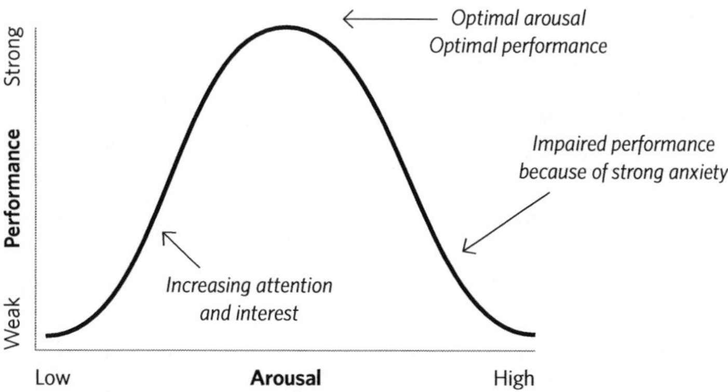

Source: Yerkes-Dodson law. (Accessed: January 5, 2020). https://en.wikipedia.org/wiki/Yerkes%E2%80%93Dodson_law

REFERENCES

1. Peter F. Drucker (2005). "Managing Oneself." *Harvard Business Review*, 83(1): 100-109.
2. Buckingham, M. (2007). *Go Put your Strengths to Work: 6 Powerful Steps To Achieve Outstanding Performance*. New York: Free Press.
3. Roberts, L., Spreitzer, G., Dutton, J., Quinn, R. Heaphy, E., & Barker, B. (2005). "How to Play to Your Strengths," *Harvard Business Review*, 83(1): 74-80.
4. Buckingham, M. (2007). *Go Put your Strengths to Work: 6 Powerful Steps To Achieve Outstanding Performance*. New York: Free Press.
5. Ibid.
6. Ibid.
7. Seligman, M. (2011). *Authentic Happiness*. Nicholas Brealey Publishing.
8. Edmondson, A. (2011). "Strategies for Learning from Failure," *Harvard Business Review*, 89(4): 48-55.
9. Gratton, L. & Scott, A. (2016). *The 100-Year Life: Living and Working in an Age of Longevity*. London: Bloomsbury Publishing.
10. Lynch, A. (2008). *ROI on Generation Y Employees*. Kennewick: Bottom Line Conversations, LLC.
11. Gratton, L. & Scott, A. (2016). *The 100-Year Life: Living and Working in an Age of Longevity*. London: Bloomsbury Publishing.
12. Ibid.
13. Grubb, V. (2017). *Clash of the Generations: Managing the New Workplace Reality*. Hoboken: John Wiley & Sons.
14. Gratton, L. & Scott, A. (2016). *The 100-Year Life: Living and Working in an Age of Longevity*. London: Bloomsbury Publishing.
15. Ibid.
16. Ibid.
17. *Global Wealth Report Credit 2019* (2019). Credit Suisse (Accessed: January 31, 2020). https://www.credit-suisse.com/about-us/en/reports-research/global-wealth-report.html
18. Dobbs, R. et al. (2016). "Poorer than their parents? Flat or Failing Incomes in Advanced Economies." *McKinsey Report*, July 16 (Accessed: July 30, 2019). https://www.mckinsey.com/~/media/McKinsey/Featured%20Insights/Employment%20and%20Growth/Poorer%20than%20their%20parents%20A%20new%20perspective%20on%20income%20inequality/MGI-Poorer-than-their-parents-Flat-or-falling-incomes-in-advanced-economies-Full-report.ashx.
19. Fottrell, Q. (2018). There's Been a Spike in the Number of Millennials with $100,000 Saved. MarketWatch, February 4 (Accessed: July19, 2019). https://www.marketwatch.com/story/finally-some-good-news-about-millennials-a-growing-number-save-100000-2018-01-23
20. Gratton, L. & Scott, A. (2016). *The 100-Year Life: Living and Working in an Age of Longevity*. London: Bloomsbury Publishing.
21. Dilts, R. (2014). *A Brief History of Logical Levels*. (Accessed: June 30, 2019). http://www.nlpu.com/Articles/LevelsSummary.htm
22. Gratton, L. & Scott, A. (2016). *The 100-Year Life: Living and Working in an Age of Longevity*. London: Bloomsbury Publishing.
23. Staats, B.R. (2018). *Never Stop Learning: Stay Relevant, Reinvent Yourself and Thrive*. Harvard Business Review Press.
24. Brooks, A.W. &John, L.K. (2018.) "The Surprising Power of Questions," *Harvard Business Review*, 96(3): 60-67.
25. The Center for Creative Leadership (2016). 8 Steps to Become More Resilient. November 6 (Accessed: January 10, 2019). https://www.ccl.org/blog/8-steps-help-become-resilient/.
26. Comstock, B., & Raz, T. (2018) *Imagine it Forward: Courage, Creativity and the Power of Change*. New York: Currency.
27. Claus, L. & Arens, L. (2019). *#ZigZagHR: Why the Best HR is no Longer HR*. Silverton: Global Immersion Press; Claus, L. & Monaghan, D. (2019) Dynamic Open Talent. Woodinville: Global HR Consortium/HR Roundtable
28. Robert H. Waterman, Judith A. Waterman and Besty A. Collard (1994). "Toward a Career-Resilient Workforce," *Harvard Business Review*, 72(4): 87-95.
29. Susskind, D. (2020). *A World Without Work: Technology, Automation, and How We Should Respond*. New York: Metropolitan Books.
30. Van Parijs and Vanderborght (2017). *Basic income: A radical proposal for a free society and a sane economy*. Harvard University Press, Cambridge.
31. Gratton, L. & Scott, A. (2016). *The 100-Year Life: Living and Working in an Age of Longevity*. London: Bloomsbury Publishing.

32. *Workplace Health Promotion*. Center for Disease Control. (Accessed: January 20, 2010). https://www.cdc.gov/chronicdisease/resources/publications/factsheets/workplace-health.htm
33. Strassel, K.A. (2009). "Mr. Burd Goes to Washington," *The Wall Street Journal*, June 19, (Accessed: January 20, 2019). https://www.wsj.com/articles/SB124536722522229323
34. Unilever. *Improving Employee Health, Nutrition & Well-Being*. (Accessed January 20, 2020). https://www.unilever.com/sustainable-living/enhancing-livelihoods/fairness-in-the-workplace/improving-employee-health-nutrition-and-well-being/.
35. Gurchiek, K. (2020). Starbucks Unveils Mental Health Initiatives for Employees. January 14 (Accessed: January 16, 2020). https://www.shrm.org/resourcesandtools/hr-topics/benefits/pages/starbucks-unveils-mental-health-initiatives-for-employees.aspx
36. Healthy People 2020. Center for Disease Control. (Accessed: January 20, 2010). https://www.cdc.gov/nchs/healthy_people/hp2010.htm
37. Nixon, A. and Claus, L. (2014). Global Work Life Balance and Stress Management. Pp. 175-196 in: Claus. L. (ed.), *Global HR Practitioner Handbook*, volume 2. Silverton: Global Immersion Press.
38. Cascio, W., Boudreau J.W. & Fink, A. (2019). Investing in People: Financial Impact of Human Resource Initiatives. Alexandria: Society for Human Resource Management.
39. Chopra, D. & Tanzi, R. E. (2012). *Super Brain: Unleashing the Explosive Power if Your Mind to Maximize Health, Happiness, and Spiritual Well Being*. New York: Harmony Books.
40. Strauss, K., Griffin, M.A. & Parker, S.K. (2012). "Future Work Selves: How Salient Hoped-For Identities Motivate Proactive Career Behaviors," *Journal of Applied Psychology*, 97(3): 580 -598.

GUIDED READING QUESTIONS

1. What are strengths and weaknesses?
2. How do I work from my strengths?
3. What are the implications of the 100-year life?
4. What is the difference between tangible and intangible assets?
5. What are examples of types of tangible assets for a resilient career?
6. What are examples of types of intangible assets for a resilient career?
7. What can I do to build a more resilient career?
8. What can employers do to make my career more resilient?
9. What can society do to make my career more resilient?

FOLLOW-UP CRITICAL THINKING QUESTIONS

1. What is my major takeaway from this reading?

2. What do I already know about this subject?

3. What follow-up questions do I have about this?

4. How can I apply this in real life?

KEY TERMS

Agency
'Anything goes' work environment
Bucket list
Buckingham's six-step strength discipline
Career resilience
Cognitive style
Competencies
Complex failure
Contract worker
Dependency ratio
Dragon slayer challenge
Emotion-based coping
Employability
Freelancer
Guaranteed income
Job crafting
Knowledge, Skills, Abilities, and Other person-related factors (KSAOs)
Individual Retirement Accounts (IRAs)
Intelligent failure
Leisure society
Learning style
Lifestyle-based coping
Liberal education
Lockstep career
Mindfulness
Neurological 'logical levels' of change
Non-productive population
Organizational scholarship
Permission slip
Personal brand
Population pyramid
Positive organizational scholarship
Problem-based coping
Productive population
Productivity assets
Professional education
Reflective Best Self (RBS) exercise
Reinventing oneself
Reputation
Robot tax
Robotization
Self-knowledge
Self-management
SIGNs of strength (Success, Instinct, Growth, Need)
STOP (stop, team up, offer, perceive)
Three-phase-model (education, work, and retirement)
Transferable skills
Transformational assets
Vitality assets
'Util'
Yerkes-Dodson curve
3rd & 4th industrial revolutions

LEARNING ASSESSMENT

Critically reflect on the content and the different concepts in this module and rate your own competency using the assessment scale.

Competency	I never heard of it	I heard of it but have limited knowledge of it	I can reasonably explain it to others	I have used it, done it, applied it
Strength management	0	1	2	3
Learning from failure	0	1	2	3
The 100-year life	0	1	2	3
Tangible and intangible assets	0	1	2	3
Career resilience	0	1	2	3
Well-being	0	1	2	3
Underutilization paradox	0	1	2	3
Stress management	0	1	2	3
Mindfulness	0	1	2	3

MODULAR-SPECIFIC ASSESSMENT

Reflective Best Self

In the RBS exercise, the person sends an email to 10 people they know and trust their reply to the sentence, '*one of the greatest ways that you add value is that you...*' The responses allow a person to recognize patterns and find common themes (strength table) by looking for a positive interpretation in the quotes that others provide. These themes allow one to compose a self-portrait of strengths.

Source: Roberts, L., Spreitzer, G., Dutton, J., Heaphy, R., & Barker, B. (2005). "How to Play to Your Strengths," *Harvard Business Review*, 83(1):45-80.

Psychological Safety

A seven-question instrument that measures the psychological safety in an organization.

Source: Edmonson, A.C. (1999). Psychological safety and learning behavior in work teams. *Administrative Science Quarterly*, 44(2):350-383

VIGNETTE

THE NEW CRISIS OF MENTAL HEALTH IN THE WORKPLACE[1]

'*It is what it is*' is a saying I often hear when people are dealing with a mental health crisis. According to the World Health Organization, one in five adults experiences some form of mental illness. Mental illness includes a broad spectrum of conditions from mild depression to severe mental illness, many of these conditions have a genetic component exacerbated by environmental life and work stresses. With the proper care, many can lead a good and productive life, even if stabilizing a crisis and getting the appropriate care often takes several months.

Unfortunately, the current workplace is not set up to deal with the mental health fragility of its workers and society has stigmatized and criminalized mental illness. So what can companies, and especially HR, do to assist its workers who experience mental health issues? The 'wellness' discussion that is gaining traction in the workplace is, of course, a step in the right direction but barely scratches the surface mainly because mental health intervention has to be coordinated and comprehensive.

Here are a few leading practices surfacing in the scant HR literature on the topic:

- Destigmatize mental illness;
- Talk openly about mental health;
- Educate yourself and others;
- Train managers to recognize common behavioral symptoms;
- Refrain from using language that further stigmatizes mental illness;
- Encourage people to seek the help they need and refer employees to appropriate care;
- Encourage the use of Employee Assistance Programs (EAP) early to deal with less severe issues;
- Expand mental health benefits for continued and longer-term coverage including medical care, hospitalization, medication, and psychotherapy;
- Identify key positions, work activities, and occupations known to have high prevalence of behavioral health issues due to stress and burnout;
- Establish Employee Resource Groups (ERG) focusing on specific conditions (such as bipolar disease, substance abuse, autism, etc.); life events (divorce, child custody, death of a family member, financial problems, etc.); and employee affinity groups (professionals, people working with vulnerable people, etc.);
- Expand wellness programs focusing on stress reduction, meditation, yoga, wellness walks, weight control, coping mechanisms, resilience, meditation, etc.;
- Provide apps that nudge employees to engage in healthy behaviors;
- Ensure legal compliance with local employment laws and don't discriminate against people with mental illness;
- Include behavioral health as part of the company's duty of care responsibility;
- Introduce modified work and flexibility to give employees purpose through partial work contributions (and earnings);
- Encourage leaders to acknowledge their own mental health fragility and be transparent about it;
- Create an overall culture of wellness that values taking care of oneself and others.

While several companies in Europe and the United States have taken a lead in supporting the behavioral health of their employees, very few have a comprehensive approach to deal with the mental health fragility of its workers. Often a mental health crisis of a worker—especially in countries with limited social protection—results in the loss of a job and income, the use alcohol and drugs to sooth the pain, social isolation and, in the worst scenario, may lead to homelessness.

Progressive *#ZigZagHR* employers are not satisfied with the status quo when it comes the mental health and well-being of their workers. They understand their duty of care or the legal and moral responsibility for the health, safety, security, and well-being of their workers! The expanded definition of duty of care includes the right to a workplace that is not only free of harassment, bullying, and stigma but promotes the inclusion and belonging of different people each with their own authenticity. While nobody wants to be the poster child for mental illness, the obstacles the workplace puts in their way should not leave the most fragile and vulnerable people with the feeling that *'it is what it is.'*

REFERENCES

1. 1This vignette is an updated version of a column by Lisbeth Claus in *#ZigZagHR Journal*, Issue #4, January 2020, p.41.

GUIDED READING QUESTIONS

1. Which stressors at work impact your mental well-being?
2. What can you, your manager and company do to alleviate the negative impact of these stressors?

EPILOGUE WHAT? SO WHAT? NOW WHAT?

In *Innovation at Amazon Through Culture and HR Technology*—a vignette at the end of Module 9 on HR Digitization and People Analytics—Peter Vermeulen described the culture of innovation at Amazon, the hypothetical PRFAQ (Press Release & Frequently Asked Questions) managers are required to write before their DOC is approved. Throughout the writing of this book, Peter kept us on our toes by constantly asking in typical Amazonian fashion, *What? So What? Now What?'* We end our book, *Be(Come) an Awesome Manager: The Essential Toolkit for Impact Leadership*, in a similar way and with a manifesto-like set of management takeaways.

WHAT? SO WHAT? NOW WHAT?

Here is how Lisbeth, Scott and Peter see it:

- **What?**—in this book, we look at managerial capabilities, how to evaluate them, and build the ones needed to create value for the customer, the employees and the organization. Through user stories, vignettes, examples, guided reading questions, interactive exercises, and assessments we explain how to reflect on your own capabilities and determine areas for self- improvement and growth.
- **So What?**—most organizations neglect the role of managers, undervalue it and, therefore, suffer from a lack of strong management capability. Employees want managers who will provide goals as well as direction, feedback and coaching—and who recognize and reward them for good performance. Yet not all managers are delivering on these expectations and this has ripple effects for the organization in terms of engagement, productivity and retention risks. Today's workforce has options, and people are clear about the fact that they want to work for companies that will invest in their ongoing development. Employees want managers to help grow their careers and support them along the way—and if their bosses don't step up, they will leave and take their talent elsewhere!
- **Now What?**—if you've ever managed or been managed, you'll understand the critical role that managers play in engaging, motivating and retaining critical employees and talent. But, while good intentions count, managers cannot make a real impact when they do not have the necessary knowledge and skills to back them up. This book is an opportunity to assess your own skills, create your own development plan, and gain new insights. The important part is that you reflect on what worked well and, especially, what did not work well in your past experiences and learn how to improve your skills in the next situations.

PRFAQ

At Amazon, a Press Release (PR) is written from the perspective of the hypothetical future after the proposed product has been released. We wrote this press release after sharing a copy of the book with different potential users to indicate how we dream big!

> *FOR IMMEDIATE RELEASE*
> *Contact: Lisbeth Claus*
> *Company Name: Global Immersion Press*
> *lclaus@willamette.edu*

> ***GLOBAL IMMERSION PRESS RELEASES ESSENTIAL TOOLKIT FOR IMPACT LEADERSHIP***
>
> *Silverton, Oregon, March 29, 2020*
>
> *This book was slated to be released on March 27, 2020 at the 5th Annual Global HR Conference held at the Mercer Island Event Center, WA. Due to duty of care*

measures taken by employers in light of the Coronavirus, this annual gathering was postponed. As a result, the ***Global Immersion Press*** *released its new book virtually using LinkedIn.* ***BE(Come)an AWESOME Manager*** *is written by* ***Lisbeth Claus*** *(a Professor of Management and Global HR at the* ***Willamette University MBA****) together with two seasoned HR executives,* ***Scott Baker*** *(VP People at* ***Command Alkon****) and* ***Peter Vermeulen*** *(Managing Partner at* ***Terra Humana****, previously at Amazon).*

The book focuses on managerial capabilities to operate in the new world of work. Following a modular approach, it takes the learner through 16 topics essential for leadership of progressive companies. Readers who previewed an advanced copy indicated how the book adds value to them and their organizations.

According to ***Carol Olsby****, Managing Director of* ***Carol Olsby & Associates, Inc.****, Founder and Chair of the* ***HR Roundtable*** *and Co-Founder and Chair of the* ***Global Human Resources Consortium****, the book is a collection of top research and thought-leader recommendations on what is required of early career managers to executives to be successful today and in the future.*

Alex Dass*, Diversity & Inclusion Program Administrator for* ***Salem Hospital****, is eager to develop her skills and contribute to the team in a meaningful way. Her company values self-directed learning of its employees. She knows that she "owns her career." Having received her MBA five years ago, she loves the fact that she can self-study the modules at her own pace and reflect on the guided reading questions.*

Abbie Samson*, VP of HR at* ***Inrix****, knows that her co-workers have superb technical skills but may lack some of the soft skills. She organizes monthly "Lunch and Learn" sessions for anyone interested in developing managerial skills. Using the learning-in-a-box tools the book provides, she recommends that different team members prepare a module and take the lead in facilitating the session.*

Cheryl Berger*, HR Director for* ***Hood River County****, mainly relies on self-directed learning opportunities for her ongoing development. While she is quite familiar with the more traditional management body of knowledge, she is eager to learn and keep up with what progressive companies are doing and how she can experiment with these new ideas in the workplace.*

Sutapa Bhattacharjee*, Associate Professor at the* ***University of Dhaka*** *in Bangladesh, teaches organizational behavior, leadership and management at the Institute of Business Administration. She assigned the book as a textbook for her students—to their delight as the cost of the (paperback or electronic) book is much lower than the price of an average business textbook in her country. She also can take advantage of the learning-in-a-box tools (PowerPoints, quizzes and interactive exercises) to teach her class.*

Nicole Mauri Tanis *is Director of Leadership Development for a $3B privately held company with over 15,000 employees. While her company has an extensive leadership development program, her trainers use the book and the learning-in-a-box tools to supplement their training offerings in a hybrid manner (self-study, discussion groups, classes, and workshops). The only cost the company incurs is the purchase of the book (paperback or e-book) for each trainee.*

Danreb Oira*, HR Leader at* ***Amazon*** *Customer Service in the Philippines, provides each member of his team with an e-version of the book so that he can help his team develop a growth mindset.*

BE(Come)an AWESOME Manager *is available from Amazon in paperback ($29.95) and as an e-book ($19.95)*

FREQUENTLY ASKED QUESTIONS (FAQs)

Prospective readers of this book are likely to have the following questions:

Is this another management academic book?

This is not an academic book but a toolkit for emerging leaders. While this book is largely based on evidence-based academic knowledge developed by various organizational behavior and management academics, it is augmented by the practical professional experience of the authors.

Who is the intended audience of this book?

This book is geared at a professional audience whether an emerging, continuous learning or 'I didn't really want to be a manager' manager!

- **The Emerging Manager**—is a person who aspires to be a future manager and is seeking opportunities to practice leading and managing within their current role.
- **The Continuous Learning Manager**—is the person who actively seeks to learn new managerial skills and abilities or strengthen their current ones. There is a strong likelihood that you are in this category by reading this book. This person also relishes the positive impact he/she can make in developing, stretching, and encouraging their employees.
- **The 'I didn't really want to be a manager'**—this person really does not like being a manager and/or may be burnt out. Perhaps they were promoted into the position because they had good technical skills and knowledge.

How do I use this book?

This is not the kind of book that you will read cover to cover in one sitting as you would a novel or other non-fiction book! To the contrary, bite-size learning, module by module, is key to your understanding of the depth and breadth of the various topics. In addition, the learning-in-a-box toolkit provides different ways to digest and apply what you are learning.

What materials are available in the learning-in-a box?

For each module, there is a set of multiple-choice questions (with answer key and the page numbers where the answers are in the book), a PowerPoint® slide presentation, and set of interactive exercises (with instructions, template and debrief).

How do I obtain the learning-in-a-box materials?

Simply connect with Lisbeth Claus through LinkedIn and send her a message to receive a complimentary pdf of the learning-in-a-box materials.

Why did you publish through Amazon KDP instead of a traditional publisher?

Having published books with both traditional publishers as well as Amazon KDP, the advantages of reduced cost, increased flexibility, and enhanced speed provided by a print-on-demand model is a better fit for our purposes—provide high value at low cost to the reader.

Where can I order this book?

You can order this book from Amazon. Just type the book's title into the search engine.

Can I get volume discounts for my company?

If you wish to order (paper) copies in bulk for distribution at a conference, workshop, or class, contact Lisbeth Claus, Scott Baker or Peter Vermeulen on LinkedIn for bulk rates and shipping.

Are the authors available for keynotes?

Lisbeth, Scott and Peter are frequent keynote and conference speakers. Contact them personally through LinkedIn to check their availability and rates.

Can the authors help with the HR development of people in my company?

Lisbeth and Peter are available to provide custom management development workshops around the world. In addition to English, they can also conduct these in Dutch and French! Contact them through LinkedIn.

THE AWESOME MANAGER MANIFESTO

In conclusion, we extract the following takeaways from our experience and each one of the modules we covered. We present them as a manifesto for AWESOME managers—whether you are or want to become one!

Introduction: **Lifelong Learning is Key to Employability**	Never stop learning.
Module 1: **Managing in the New World of Work and the Worker**	Embrace a new way of working and own your career.
Module 2: **The Strategic Lens and Organization Design**	Structure still matters!
Module 3: **The Political Lens**	Stakeholders have different interests that must be reconciled.
Module 4: **The Cultural Lens**	Respect people of dissimilar worldviews, faiths, genders, races, and abilities. Culture matters.
Module 5: **Equity and Equity through DIBs**	Celebrate both our differences and what we have in common. Allow people to bring their authentic self to work!
Module 6: **Individuals, Teams, and Teamwork**	For knowledge to be valuable, share it with others on the team.
Module 7: **Motivation, Engagement, and the Employee Experience**	You cannot really motivate others but you can create a (de)motivating environment. Innate motivation still requires effort.
Module 8: **Decision-Making and Behavioral Economics**	Be aware of and don't act on your unconscious biases. Avoid common decision-making traps!
Module 9: **People Analytics and HR Digitization**	Rely on data rather than opinions. Track and measure what you do.
Module 10: **Managing People, Projects, and Processes**	Master and utilize proven professional tools. Focus on what you can control.
Module 11: **Talent Management Reinvented**	Experiment, experiment, experiment. Focus on the employee as an internal customer who serves your customers.
Module 12: **Performance Management**	Create a culture where regular performance feedback and coaching are the norm.
Module 13: **Day-to-Day People Management**	Give your co-workers the benefit of the doubt before you judge. Observe, listen, ask questions and be kind to others.
Module 14: **Managing Change, Innovating, and Executing Globally**	Change is the new normal.
Module 15: **Ethics, Compliance, Corporate Social Responsibility, and Sustainability**	Focus on doing the right thing. Your reputation and integrity matter most.
Module 16: **Self Management, Well-Being, and Preparing for Career Transitions**	As Stephen Covey suggested, "*Sharpen Your Saw.*" Enjoy your work but also find meaning outside of your work.
Epilogue: **What, So What, Now What!**	There's no time like the present. Time to act is now.

You picked up this book because you want to learn and grow your managerial capabilities. You are the type of person who wants to invest in your own development and growth. Congratulations! There is a lot of information in this book and it may seem overwhelming. Some sections in this book may inspire you, others be challenge you. Challenge yourself to a five or 10-degree shift in your managerial skills and knowledge. The interactive format of the book provides you with an opportunity to challenge your own pre-conceived ideas and beliefs about management. Take notes, journal and set goals for yourself. Decide on what you will try out and experiment, experiment, experiment.

The book is about developing your own managerial skills. Remember that is an area totally within your control. Avoid being frustrated and distracted by top-down strategic plans, organizational design, organizational culture or other possible dysfunctionalities in your organization. It is easy to look across the organization and see everything that 'needs' to be fixed. Don't! Focus on what you can control, namely how to manage and lead the team of precious individuals who work with you and/or report to you. Onward!

You are never finished learning and stretching as a manager. The role you are in will change as your responsibilities do and no two teams will be the same in your career journey. A manager's role demands that you frequently re-invent yourself by trying new techniques and honing your managerial strengths. You will need to adapt your managerial style based on your boss, your team and organizational objectives, and the individuals—likely coming from multiple generations, personalities and cultures—on your team.

Although being a manager can be challenging and stressful at times, it is also extremely rewarding. The opportunity to lead and develop a team of individuals to perform at their highest level is one of life's greatest rewards. Ask anybody the name of their best teacher or manager that grew and developed them and there won't even be a pause in the person's response. The legacy of a good boss lives long after people move on to different jobs or retire. What is your legacy going to be?

We send you off with the words of Professor Clayton M. Christensen (1952-2020):

> *"Management is the most noble of professions if it's practiced well. No other occupation offers as many ways to help others learn and grow, take responsibility and be recognized for achievement, and contribute to the success of a team." (2010).*

ADVANCE PRAISE FOR
BE(COME) AN AWESOME MANAGER

The global experience of the authors really comes through in this book. Lisbeth and Peter are career globetrotters (and polyglots) who understand first-hand the importance of culture and its local nuances.

ALAIN VERSTANDIG
President, Net Expat, USA.

Many times, managers wish they had a methodical guide using all three lenses of work life (strategic, political and cultural) on how to put into practice organizational and people management disciplines—and, as a result, better themselves and others every day. This is the one! In a modular format for bite-size learning, whenever time allows!

ANNA MAMALAKI
Organizational Development Consulting Director, Business: The Human Aspect LLC, USA.

Professor Claus has a unique talent for capturing the most relevant issues of work and then translating them into real-time, real-life learning interventions. This highly practical, timely guide is no exception. In my ongoing quest to be an AWESOME manager, I never miss an opportunity to benefit from her insights and foresight.

BRAD BOYSON
Former Executive Director, SHRM Dubai, UAE.

Awesome Manager is a collection of top research and thought-leader recommendations providing early career managers to executives with a roadmap to be successful today and in the future. This book and the "Learning Tool Box" resource ensures readers have all the necessary tools to achieve their ongoing goal of being an Awesome Manager!

CAROL OLSBY
Managing Director, Carol Olsby & Associates, Inc., Founder and Chair of the Seattle HR Roundtable and Co-Founder and Chair of the Global Human Resources Consortium, USA.

A breakthrough and exciting approach to becoming a great manager! This book reflects the passion the authors have for developing awesome managers based on 25 years of experience in business and HR. It covers tried-and-true management practices, but also introduces progressive practices. If you want to learn more about your management style to become a better manager without intrinsically changing who you are, this book shows you how to optimize your leadership for your organization.

DANIELLE MONAGHAN
VP Talent Acquisition, Uber, USA.

Awesome is the right word. What a great opportunity to learn from such thought leaders as Lisbeth, Scott and Peter. They do a wonderful job creating a powerful, yet flexible, program based on decades of research and actionable tools. Their 16 "bite-sized" modules explore, with the rigor of an MBA, every aspect of being a great manager. I particularly like their global, societal, ethical and business perspectives. A great resource and contribution for all of us.

DAVID C. FORMAN
President, Sage Learning Systems, Author of Fearless HR and Fearless Talent Choices—that will make or break your business, USA.

Be(come) an AWESOME Manager does not miss a beat in helping managers become life-long learners and understanding what it takes to manage in today's new world of work. This is one of the best books I've seen in a long time with a unique and hands-on approach.

DEB COHEN, Ph.D.
Author Developing Managerial Proficiency: A Self-Directed Learning Approach, USA.

In an era when CEOs are having sleepless nights due to disruptive technology, companies are scrambling to promote a High-Performance Work System (HPWS) by developing awesome managers. This indeed is the book for you to show the way. Built on the rich academic and corporate experience of the authors, this book very lucidly translates the rigorous conceptual knowledge into action-orientation and workable HRM propositions.

DEBI SAINI

Emeritus Professor HRM, Indian Institute of Management, Ranchi, India.

What a resource! This is a book that you must have on your shelf if you are in a management role. It will serve as immediate consultation from both a theoretical perspective and a practical perspective. These two combined make for an incredibly strong place to manage from.

DEBORAH BUTLER

Clinical Associate Professor Managerial Sciences, Georgia State University, USA.

All of us are facing the effects of the technological impact and we have to reinvent ourselves and our ability to keep on learning. By giving very structured and effective solutions to these challenges, this new book will become a genuine reference for HR experts, managers and executives.

FLORIN LUCA

Strategist, Transformer, Board Member, Romania.

A brilliant approach to the age-old question of belonging, this book will help people see the reflection of their greatness while in the same mirror recognizing their commonality with their peers. It will give us all the permission to be our wonderfully and fearfully made whole selves.

GRANT DOSTER

SVP, Global Inclusive Leadership, Lee Hecht Harrison, USA.

Throughout my career, I have first-hand witnessed how intellectual curiosity and the pursuit of lifelong learning are two critically important keys to personal and corporate growth. I believe this book serves as a great reminder of their importance and offers an actionable set of tools for every individual wanting to grow.

HANS MELOTTE

Executive Vice President, Chief Supply Chain Officer, Starbucks, USA.

This book is fueled by expertise every individual can learn from. Happy it became a 'glocal' book where the topics are global but the approaches can be used locally.

HASSAN AL HILOU

Strategic advisor, keynote speaker, author, Ik ben Hassan, Belgium.

Be(come) an AWESOME Manager is a comprehensive guide to help leaders develop their competencies in the most critical areas of management and leadership. This richly packed volume covers sixteen key areas that are essential for all leaders to manage well. The book is written in a format where the reader can digest the whole volume to gain a complete understanding of what it takes to develop one's potential, or the reader can simply select the topic they are most interested in, such as building teams, engaging employees, decision making, day-to-day people management, or many more practical topics. This book is immensely valuable for managers, HR leaders and executive coaches!

JEFFREY E. AUERBACH, Ph.D.

MCC, President, College of Executive Coaching, USA.

The hardest thing to manage is the soft side of management including human behaviour, culture, and values. The more we integrate technology in work, the greater the importance of soft skills to cope with the human factor of HR. The blend of insights in this book set you up for future-proof management.

JOCHANAN EYNIKEL

Business philosopher, ETION, author Robot aan het Stuur, Belgium.

Peter, Lisbeth and Scott have combined their 100+ years of deeply relevant leadership and organization development experience in a wonderfully insightful and practical book. Whether you are an MBA student, early career leader or seasoned executive, you will discover new learnings that will surely help you lead yourself, your teams and your organization to thrive during these times of unprecedented global and technological change.
LISA ALVAREZ-CALDERON, CHRO
Bill and Melinda Gates Foundation, USA.

Be(come) an AWESOME Manager is a valuable resource for leaders of all levels- aspiring, new and experienced. Through an engaging combination of theory, case studies, reflective questions, and interactive exercises, the book covers both the fundamentals of management and the competencies needed to lead global, multicultural organizations through dynamic change. If one book will improve your management effectiveness and enjoyment, this is it!
LIZ DUFFY
President, International Schools Services, USA.

The authors bring to bear their knowledge, experience, learnings and insights to help other leaders bring their best to work every day. Leadership matters! In the end, our greatest legacy is the impact we have on people. I have no doubt this book will be a great aid to so many leaders who strive to have a meaningful impact in all they do.
LUANI ALVARADO
Global Head of Human Resources, Consumer Health Johnson & Johnson, USA.

Our new world of work requires a reinvented management approach! *Be(come) an AWESOME Manager* conducts an orchestra of managers to a symphony of contemporary management practices, showing us how to fiddle with all these new instruments to eventually play a masterpiece ourselves. The book uses a flexible modular learning format, teaching us about each instrument one at a time so we can all become a maestro of management.
LUC DE DECKER
Chief Editor, #ZigZagHR, Belgium.

The authors of *Be(come) an AWESOME Manager* get it! The key to success in a knowledge-based economy is lifelong learning. This is a 'must' read for any leader looking to make an impact in the lives of others.
MATT BURNS
Founder & Chief Innovation Officer, BentoHR, Canada.

This book will challenge your thinking! The modular approach allows for learning, absorbing and practicing the concepts quickly. Aside from the content, you get the chance to learn from the best. Lisbeth Claus is a highly sought after global expert on management who genuinely relates to multiple generations and across geographies. Peter Vermeulen and Scott Baker are forward thinking leaders connected to real workplace challenges.
MELANIE YOUNG
Vice President, Global HR, Diagnostics Division, Thermo Fisher Scientific, USA.

Having consulted and collaborated with Professor Claus for over 20 years on numerous global HR research projects, Lisbeth's uncanny ability to apply valid and reliable research into practical work and management skills is her gift to the thousands of global managers she had molded professionally.
MICHAEL MCCALLUM
VP Global, WorldatWork, USA.

As Henry Ford once said, "The only thing worse than training your employees and having them leave is not training them and having them stay." His words are probably more relevant now than ever. Lifelong learning in the cognitive era is not an option. It is a must! One of the keys in becoming an awesome manager is not only to have very solid soft/life skills but also a growth mindset balanced with grit. This brilliant, no-nonsense book written by Professor Claus together with two executive leaders offers a practical set of ideas, tools and clear roadmap to become an awesome manager who inspires and engages people to build lasting customer value.

MIHALY NAGY

Founder of The HR Congress & Digital HR Innovation Summit, Hungary.

A refreshing update and new insights to manage people and teams. In an ever faster-changing global environment, continuous learning is a fundamental capability to impact and shape the future of your business and organization and stay agile. Technology evolves faster than organizations. Data and analytics bring the next transformational challenges to people and their organization. You cannot afford to miss it! As a people leader, it's your task to drive this essential but impactful change.

STEF VERMEIREN

VP Supply Chain Planning, Johnson & Johnson, USA.

There is no such thing as a natural-born leader. Every one of us is forever works in progress and never stops learning. That's why we're on a grand journey to unboss Novartis: to develop leaders that serve their teams, and not the other way around. *Be(come) an AWESOME Manager!*

STEVEN BAERT

Chief People & Organization Officer, Novartis AG, Switzerland.

Becoming an awesome leader is a quest well worth pursuing. Lisbeth, Scott and Peter collaborated in order to share their eclectic insights in a valuable guide and reference where the synergy between theories, methods and tools truly supports the building of management skills and mastership.

SOFIA VAN OVERMEIRE

General Manager, HRbuilders, HR Talents, PAYROLLbuilders, Belgium.

This book makes a difference for every manager, novice or grandmaster. It is a path-breaking approach to lifelong learning combining the finest of two worlds: classic management thinking and progressive practices. A fresh look at human behavior and the many dualities management has to deal with daily. Outstanding!

THOMAS BELKER, CEO

PRECIRE Technologies, Germany.

Read this book if you are mentoring new leaders or entering your first leadership role. The authors are master storytellers weaving contemporary business concepts with real-world examples that inspire curious minds to consider alternative strategies and motivate even the most seasoned leaders to shift mindsets.

TINA ALEXANDER

Sr. Engagement Manager, Workday, USA.

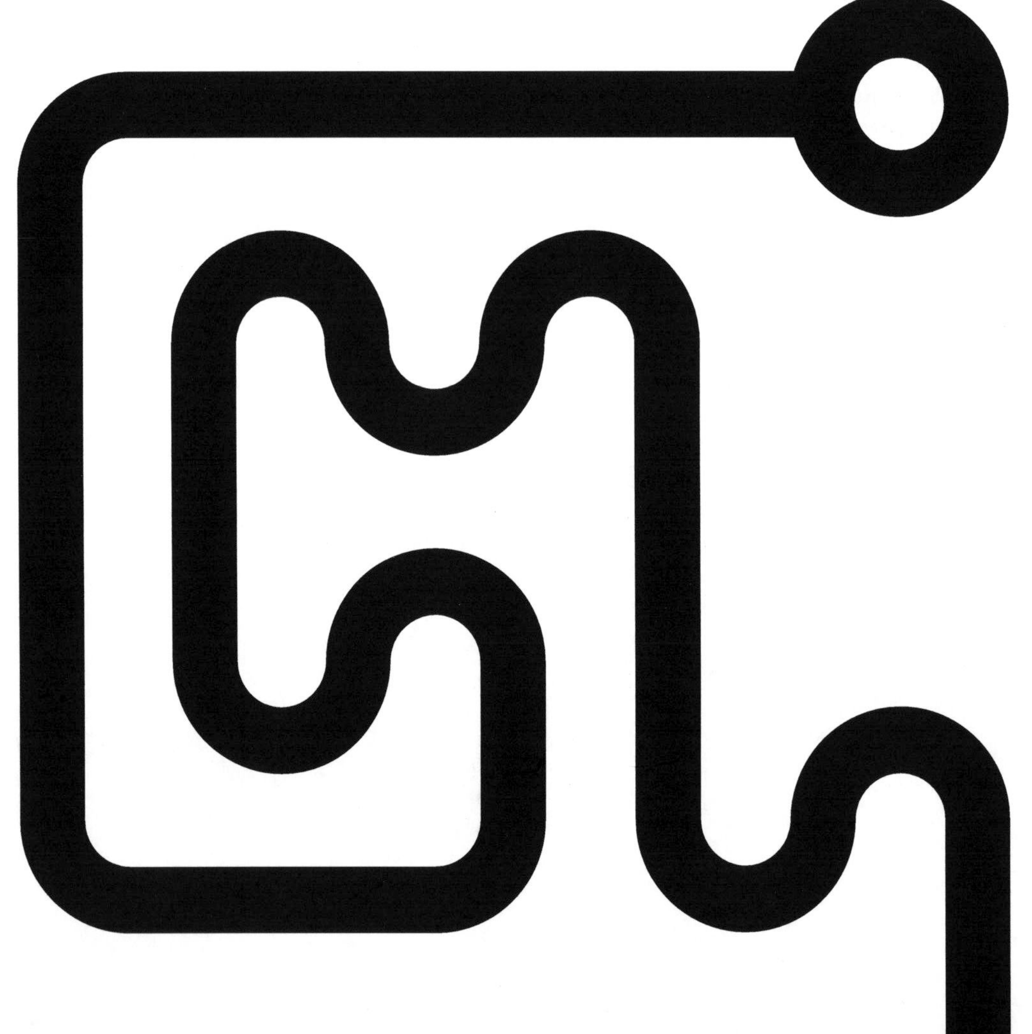